Muslim

Muslim Kingship

Power and the Sacred in Muslim, Christian, and Pagan Polities

Aziz Al-Azmeh

I.B.Tauris Publishers
LONDON · NEW YORK

L'Homme n'est qu'un effet commun, le monstre qu'un effet rare; toux les deux également naturels, également nécessaires, également dans l'ordre universel et général.

Diderot

To the Memory of Albert Hourani

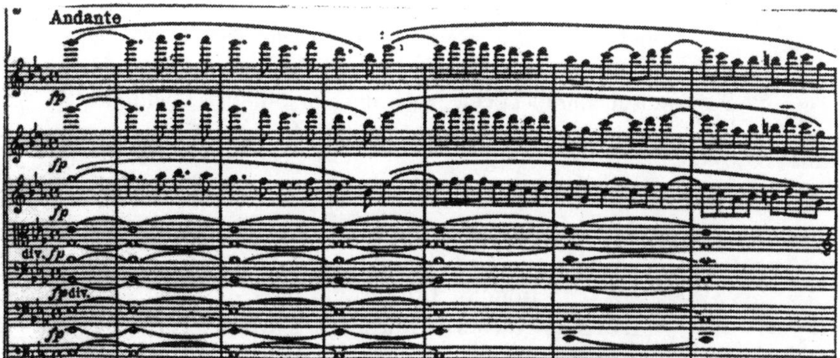

Richard Strauss, Im Abendrot

Paperback edition published in 2001 by I.B.Tauris & Co. Ltd.
6 Salem Road, London W2 4BU
175 Fifth Avenue, New York, NY 10010
www.ibtauris.com

In the United States of America and in Canada distributed by
St Martin's Press, 175 Fifth Avenue, New York, NY 10010

ISBN 1 86064 609 3

A full CIP record for this book is available
from the British Library
A full CIP record for this book is available
from the Library of Congress

Set in Monotype Baskerville by Philip Armstrong, Sheffield
Printed and bound in Great Britain by MPG Books Ltd, Bodmin

Contents

Preface

This book is a study of the enunciation and representation of royal power, mainly but by no means exclusively of power sacralised or allied to the sacred, and most specifically of royal power of imperial spread and œcumenical ambition. Such enunciations are regarded here as falling into two broad categories.

The first is discursive. It is made up of theoretical statements on royal power found in theological, legal, historical, literary, ethical, social-theoretical, and other forms of formal deliberative writing, similar statements contained in formulaic and poetical verbal enunciations, and in visual and spatial representations which together constitute ceremonial and sometimes directly political enunciation. Discursive enunciations also include metaphorical statements, whether found in the forms of writing and enunciation just mentioned or in forms of enunciation of smaller scale but greater ubiquity, such as nomenclature and regal epithets. In addition to discursive forms of enunciation, power declares itself aesthetically by means of non-propositional enunciations which include iconography and ceremonial. These can and often do have propositional interpretations and glosses in various settings, and can sometimes be seen as propositions in a non-linguistic medium, although the relationship between these modes of enunciation is very complex, and the latter share with ritual uses of language a diminution of propositional force in favour of illocutionary energy. Such visual and auditory enunciations – ceremonial, emblems of royal distinctiveness, special forms of musical performance and so on – are of extraordinary longevity, inviting different propositional glosses, and in certain periods they predominate over linguistic representations.[1]

Both categories of enunciation, the propositional and the non-propositional, contribute to a variety of construals and functions of kingship, such as the magical, the ritual, and the legal. This study does not, therefore, confine itself to the formal bodies of consistent ideas on power which have been central to the concerns of many traditional academics, but which may be at variance with what the histories they deal with posit as actually central.

The book deals centrally and in considerable detail with material derived from the history of Muslim polities, most particularly the Abbasid centuries. But it also takes up salient themes from other historical experiences which are directly related to the caliphate and other Muslim institutions, or have other types of relationship to them, or which can be compared in various modalities with them. Of special relevance here is the Late Antique Mediterranean–West Asian (or Near Eastern) civilisation belt which had a particular coherence in terms both of spatial and temporal continuity. This belt was constituted by Hellenistic and Romano-Byzantine representations and institutes, which were themselves fully complicit with so-called oriental notions of royalty and divinity that circulated in the ancient Near East of the Persians and the Babylonians and, somewhat more remotely, the Egyptians. Among other theses I argue that early Muslim polities were specific inflections of Late Antique discursive and visual forms and modes of enunciating royal and imperial power, and that the classical forms associated with Islamic history were specific and highly elaborate reworkings, over a period of many centuries, of earlier œcumenical, imperial, and politico-soteriological traditions.

For purposes of comparison, medieval Buddhist polities have also been brought into the perspective. Although some of the parallels and continuities through diffusion and borrowing are vicarious, the inclusion of these polities suggests interesting levels of generality, and possibly universality, of certain tropes for the representation of imperial power and of its relations to divinity. Their further exploration would, however, require a general anthropological study which cannot be attempted here. Equally plausible comparisons with the Inca could have been made, but these, and smaller-scale polities with interesting comparable institutions, such as those of certain African civilisations, have been omitted. Similarly, ancient Judaic kingship, though geographically and historically proximate, has been excluded because it was a local and tribal phenomenon which, unlike other traditions discussed here, had no aspirations to religio-imperial universalism.[2] It is clear from recent scholarship that ancient Israelite history is a field for which extravagant claims have been made and whose scholarship is overloaded with theological and political purposes as well as an unfounded imputation of coherence to Biblical chronology and narrative, often in clear contradiction to archaeological evidence.[3] In addition, post-Exilic constructions of the past, which were influenced by Assyrian and Persian materials,[4] tend to re-insert the topic into the broader bearings of the political and theologico-political culture of an area in which parts of Palestine did not play a central, still less a foundational, role.

It must nevertheless be stressed that the book does not present a systematic comparative study of the representations of imperial power in relation to the sacred in Muslim, Christian, and pagan polities. From its beginnings in the eighteenth and elaborations in the nineteenth century, comparatism was generally but not exclusively used for purposes of conceiving commonality in an evolutionist perspective, initially in linguistics with the construction of Indo-European in the eighteenth century (a sort of taxonomy with time as its organising structural feature) and collaterally in comparative anatomy under the influence of Linnaeus. This approach might broadly be characterised as Hegelian, but it also incorporated Comtean, Spencerian, and other moments premised ultimately on the supposition that humanity was, in various times and places, essentially endowed with similar capacities, all of which might evolve to higher forms, although different stages of this evolution might translate progress from one nation to another. It was, however, accompanied by what we might call the Herderian mode which eventually led to historism. Championed classically by Wilhelm von Humboldt, this approach, in which lines of generic filiation were intransitive, and the histories of different historical masses, cultures, or civilisations generically closed and distinct, lay at the heart of 'cultural sciences' in Germany. Today, at a time some describe as 'post-modern', comparatism, frequently impoverished by a tendency to reduce all to a tabulation of abiding tokens of exoticism and of what is taken for boundless difference, is in the full throws of a revival under the guise of celebrating 'difference'.

The general approach adopted here belongs to neither the evolutionist nor the organismic models, and is more exploratory than systematic, its purpose more suggestive than exhaustive. It indicates parallels, analogues and continuities, conceived not as effects of abiding and continuing origins, but as ever renewed redactions and forms of traditions which change signature and ostensible genealogy when transferred from one historical sense of continuity to another, for instance from the Byzantine to the Muslim. In this way, the habitual faithlessness of history is fully incorporated into the study of traditions, which are here regarded as neither elements of generic and nominal unities of genealogy, nor stable historical bundles of unique characteristics, but rather as successions of elements in a repertoire, not always well-articulated, but in distinctive configurations. It is not necessarily paradoxical that this approach allows us to indicate vast levels of generality in the enunciation of sacral kingship.

The first part of the book, which deals with various periods of Near Eastern and other histories, is necessarily less systematic than the second where the subject of medieval Muslim polities is addressed. It provides the elements of the repertoire of traditions and seemingly general notions of sacral kingship which, in Muslim traditions, were connected in historically specific configurations and across specific temporal continuities. The relative disjunction between the book's two sections is inevitable and I have not, therefore, made any attempt to contribute to comparative history except peripherally. Nevertheless the material I discuss affirms continuities in the very long term across civilisations: a *très longue durée* in the medium of enunciation – symbol, emblem, motif and analogy – in terms of which historical masses conceive themselves as civilisations, cultures and histories. These decisively and relentlessly cross putatively integral boundaries and genealogies, specifically those announced by the signatures 'Islamic' and 'Western'. I have traced specific lines of filiation, and identified common repertoires of floating symbols and tropes and their incidence across vast distances of space and time. But I have not done this in the spirit of historical typology or taxonomy. A variety of additional reasons have precluded more detailed comparisons, not least my own uneven knowledge of the material at hand. Proper comparison would have required a knowledge of Greek, Latin, Akkadian and Pahlavi sources, and to a much lesser extent of Pali and Sanskrit sources, and a knowledge of modern scholarship on these and the wider bearings of their histories on a par with the detailed and direct acquaintance with medieval Arabic sources I have deployed.

In addition, the level of monographic and analytical scholarship available in these fields is itself very uneven. While there is excellent scholarship on Byzantium for instance, there is much less material available on Pahlavi Persia, and the general methodological and conceptual level of work on medieval Muslim polities is almost uniformly poor. It is particularly wanting in the field of political theory, in the historical anthropology of power and its symbols and in allied topics which are explored with very little reliable monographic assistance. The specialist reader will find certain obscure areas of history and new fields of scholarship investigated, periodised, and reflected upon, such as the parallel histories of Sunnism and Shi'ism. Monographic deficiency has, however, meant that the Persian material is perhaps unfairly treated, which may convey a certain sense of unevenness, but may well also raise the question of precisely what may or may not have been specifically Persian about the Achamaenids and the Sasanians.

Comparison, apart from filiation, and over and above the comparison of specific cases, has thus been displaced in favour of a more open-ended investigation into such elements of concordance and generality as might indicate certain orientations for historical, anthropological, and philosophical investigation. Given that comparisons presuppose closure and hard boundaries, this orientation has been especially fruitful, enabling me to explore vast commonalities of power representation within a vast civilisation area. I hope that it will help to open up Muslim materials to historical reason and make them accessible to experts working in contiguous conceptual areas but using different historical materials. Muslim materials are rarely used in the literature on sacral kingship, in the history of religions or of political thought, or in historical anthropology broadly conceived. This is a pity since they are very rich and can contribute greatly to the sweep and remit of these disciplines.

The stress on hard differences and specificities, on purity of line and difference from the Barbarian, is of course a standard manner of self-representation and of the representation of others by all historical masses. Yet it is at variance with the actual processes of history, which are radically impure. The emphasis on pristine historical virtue represents the intervention of history – of warfare, of institutions and the interests vested in them, of the stakes embodied in postures of internal purity and historical continuity – in the realm of conception and representation, and tends to harden representations that are carried by traditions of rule. Traditions are, after all, constantly repeated motifs and formulaic enunciations of a discursive, symbolic, or ritual nature, invariably of heterogeneous origin, yet invariably cast in terms of very specific and exclusive genealogies, constructed histories, confirmed by names – Roman, Muslim and so on.

Equally germane to my argument is that the hard form of traditions not only overcomes, in its relentless imaginary genealogies, the actual history of origins, but also manages the vicissitudes of politics on behalf of royalty as an institution in continuity. The hallucinatory narcissism of royal iconography and other forms of enunciation, including theories of authority and the sacralisation of power, often coexists with the humbler realities of a very much diminished royalty, which tends to take on ever more sublime forms and prerogatives in periods of decline, as in some periods of Byzantine history or some periods of the history of the caliphate. This is not merely a reflection of the slow tempo of cultural change and the very ample rhythms of collective memory and tradition. The abstract and solemn stylisation of the sovereign in iconography and ceremonial, including the panegyric poetry so very salient for the study of Muslim kingship, and the impeccable integrity of rulership described in discourses on power, are related to historical reality in a highly complex manner. Of Byzantium, characterised by one scholar as a case that conjoins Orthodoxy with Greek humour, it may be said that the public appearance of the emperor involved 'le froncement de sourcil compensé par un coup d'oeil complice.'[5] Just as pictorial depictions of Byzantine emperors were not portraits of the sovereign but icons of sovereignty, so also treatises on kingship and ceremonial do not constitute reportage, although they are not entirely devoid of empirical elements duly sublimated. Royal ceremonial could also be regarded as a sort of *Fürstenspiegel* in condensed and representative form.[6]

The particular rhythms of change and transformation affecting the symbols and enunciations of power, and local innovations pertaining to these, are the subject for particular historical and social studies and for reflections concerning the specific mode of insertion of such enunciations into the social and political conflicts of the day: the interests of courtly parties, the durability and variation of emblematic enunciation of historical and œcumenical systems, the social action of such enunciations which might act as loci of stability, real as well as symbolic, in times of vulnerability and rapid change.

It is my hope that through the perspective adopted in this book, some progress will be made towards removing Muslim polities in the Middle Ages from the exotic and incommensurable individuality attributed to them both by their own advocates and standard scholarship, by writers and scholars both expert and inexpert. It is often implicitly supposed that Muslims engendered, at a very early point in time, *sui generis* institutions and set them out on a virtual *tabula rasa*. In the same way, it is implicitly assumed that the material out of which these institutions and ideas were constructed resides in the Muslim canon and in the institutes established at the very beginning of the history of Islam. The implication is that classical Muslim forms were born somewhat complete, and then stumbled upon the necessity of various forms of accommodation with the ambient world; their histories are consequently often construed as nothing but decline and degeneration.

If the assumptions of integrity at birth and ideal correspondence to original models were to be made of other civilisations and religions, humanistic and social science scholarship would reject them as out of keeping with the realities of all histories and of all societies. They do indeed correspond to certain Muslim traditions, for the idea of impeccability and integrity of beginnings is central to the genealogies of all traditions; but they do not correspond to historical reality and they are at variance with historical plausibility. In this book I try to bring to bear upon Muslim material the ordinary procedures and rationality of the social and human sciences and thereby to stem the tendency to over-Islamise Muslims, to infirm them into an ethereal non-historicity which places them outside the remit of all but the most specialised and antiquarian scholarship, to impute to them an exoticism and exceptionalism which places them beyond the remit of the historical understanding. My aim is to replace claims for individuality with claims for specificity, in other words, specific redactions and inflections of a generality, that of sacral kingship and oecumenical imperialism.

The book shows that the genesis of a diverse body of specifically Muslim forms of the enunciation of power required a number of centuries, that these forms were by no means *sui generis*, and that Muslim enunciations of power, even affirmations of its sacrality, were not necessarily the work of a specifically religious discourse, or confined to the Sunni or Shiʿi clerical establishments. Muslim political discourse and the aesthetics of power historically experienced in Muslim polities are here conceived as diverse, differentiated, and highly mutable. Correlatively, it is shown that Muslim enunciations of power have a far wider field of production and circulation than the priestly class of the ʿulama to whom they are normally attributed in standard scholarship, and that consequently the opinions of these elements were neither always central nor always normative. The book also looks into the concrete historical and textual conditions of Muslim discourses and other enunciations of power, and is partly the result of a profound unease with the current state of knowledge and analysis of Muslim political conceptions, and the state of knowledge of the historical, theoretical, and rhetorical conditions of these conceptions.

Part one examines salient issues from Antiquity and Late Antiquity in the Near East which provided the repertoire of conceptions and regal forms systematised and made Muslim by later Muslim polities. In addition, relevant Buddhist material is brought in to illustrate certain areas of vast generality. It ends with a brief examination of the obscure early Muslim period, which is seen here as a period of passage during which late antique forms were experimented with. Specifically Muslim forms of the representation of imperial power in relation to divinity were the work of the Abbasid period discussed in part two. Chapter five examines the discursive locations in which power was written, as to their form and to certain elements relating to their philology. The same bundle of themes is examined in its conceptual and rhetorical aspects in the subsequent chapters.

The title of the book indicates a concentration on the sacral aspects of power and its enunciation. There were of course other, secular, means of enunciating power, not the least being the dynastic and genealogical. These are not treated very deliberately here. Although there is rich material that permits such an account,[7] its analysis is the task for another book.

Acknowledgements

A book on this scale could never have been written without considerable help and support from both institutions and individuals. I had the privilege of holding a Nuffield Foundation Fellowship during the academic year 1993–94, and a Fellowship at the Institute for Advanced Study, Berlin, during the academic year 1994–95. I am grateful to these two institutions for their generosity and encouragement, and for making it possible for me to devote my time and energy exclusively to research and writing. I should also like to thank St Antony's College, Oxford, for providing me with an office and other facilities during 1993–94. In the period preceding tenure of these fellowships, I received invaluable assistance from Heather Eva and Paul Auchterlonie, both of the University of Exeter library, and I am grateful for their unfailing good will, expertise, and for ingenuity sometimes bordering on the uncanny. I am also grateful to Sebastian Brock, Susanna Elm, Carlo Ginzburg, Richard Gombrich, Renate Lachmann, Pauline Schmitt-Pantel, and Heinrich von Stietenkron, for advice and wise counsel.

A number of friends and colleagues took the trouble of reading some draft chapters and of offering advice, and I am happy to be able to acknowledge my gratitude to them: Hans Belting, Chris Gregory, Ruba Kanaan, Homa Katouzian, Panayotis Kondylis, Hans Medick, Janet Nelson, Frank Reynolds. Julie Meissami, Martha Mundy, Jean-Claude Schmitt and Fawaz Traboulsi commented on the entire draft. It is difficult to overstress the weight of their advice, although I must stop short of making any of them, or indeed any of my friends and colleagues, complicit in anything that the reader might or might not find in this book.

PART ONE

Sublime Analogies, Pagan and Monotheistic

CHAPTER ONE

Introduction

Power is by nature enunciative. No matter how routinised, the energy deployed to exercise it is never mute. It is always accompanied, further energised, and in some instances overdetermined, by declarations, displays, drones, whispers, and a myriad of other forms of enunciation. These reflect the energy of power, indicate it, display it, parody it, name it, explicate it, justify it, legislate for it. The fascination exercised by the luxuriant aesthetic of power has even led to the implausible suggestion that, in some cases such as Balinese kingship in the nineteenth century, the dramaturgy of state is in some senses *sui generis*, and the ceremonial display needs no explanation beyond itself:

> The stupendous cremations, tooth filings, temple dedications, pilgrimages, and blood sacrifices, mobilising hundreds and even thousands of people and great quantities of wealth, were not means to political ends: they were ends in themselves, they were what the state was for. Court ceremonialism was the driving force of court politics; and mass ritual was not the device to shore up the state, but rather the state, even in its final gasp, was a device for the enactment of mass ritual. Power served pomp, not pomp power.[1]

Power may indeed appear to be a hallucinatory aesthetic of solipsism, and may look as if it were speaking of and for itself, with reference to nothing but its own exercise and to no energies except its own. For it always deploys words, colours, ceremonies, objects, sounds, silences, space, gesture, movement, and a variety of propositional enunciations of a descriptive and performative nature which make it manifest in its intricate harmonies.

The languages of power are various. Some are tactile, involving direct action upon the bodies of kings and subjects alike. They take the form of special dress, of ordered ritual movement and accoutrement, decoration, and the spatial and temporal disposition of bodies and other objects in a space specially circumscribed. These together constitute ceremonial. Others are linguistic and conceptual. They comprise, among other things, the conceptual explication of the workings of power and its metaphorical or propositional extension into fields outside that of sheer force. Thus arises a problematic of order, intimately allied to notions of public and private rectitude. The problematic of order is most often, until the advent of modernity, situated in terms of the connection between terrestrial and extra-terrestrial orders, and takes the form, most notably, of the metaphorisation of power in terms of the sacred.

Such metaphorisation appears primarily to involve the casting of worldly power in terms of powers divine, and the ascription to the former prerogatives and properties of the latter, chief among them the power to create and maintain order, and power over life and death. Representations of the sacred are, after all, the site most thoroughly permeated by the opposition or counter-position of power and powerlessness, the site where the absolute power differential is most evident, indeed axiomatic and constitutive. Running metaphors of terrestrial power in terms of the sacred, and of the sacred in terms of terrestrial power can be observed in all complex societies. They betoken a primitive equivalence, expressed in a play of mirror-images, in a traffic of projections and analogies, and in the displacement of propositions and imperatives concerning the one or the other. Worldly power often makes present the subliminal ubiquity of unseen powers and transmits, by conduction, the divine writ, intent and presence that are meant to regulate the affairs of the world.

It will become abundantly clear in this book that discursive and visual forms of the representation of the sacred are constitutive prototypes of all other enunciations of power. The propositional, as distinct from the plastic, iconographic, representation of power involves legal and didactic discourses, as in works of *Fürstenspiegel*, historico-genealogical, and theological writing. Like ritual and royal panegyrics, these discourses routinise the exercise of power and naturalise its energy, by crystallising it in formal and formulaic moulds. It is one fundamental contention of this book that there is no historical or anthropological ground to the privileged position generally given by scholarship to discursive enunciations of power over other forms of enunciation. Equally salient is the reluctance to introduce anthropological thinking into the treatment of historical and of textual material – a reluctance premised on two implicit assumptions. The first is that there is a radical distinction between primitive and civilised histories, between simple and complex societies, between acephalic communities and communities organised under the auspices of a state. The second assumption is that textual material obeys certain elementary formal rules of a logical nature, to which paralogical – or generally rhetorical – argumentation is in principle foreign.

Propositional and iconographic forms for the enunciation of worldly power, and its sliding intersections with the power of the sacred, are universal. They are manifest in different forms and with varying degrees of sophistication throughout the forms of human sociality. They constitute correlative presences of power; their forms constitute a set of norms and modules of visual representation, metaphorisation and conceptual elaboration which demonstrate astonishing tenacity over time and considerable commonality across the boundaries of civilisations, cultures and empires. Within the boundaries of each, they also show a tendency to replicate the centre in the provinces and extremities after the manner of what been described as a 'galactic polity', [2] and travel from thence to strike root as the beginnings of newer, or newly named, traditions, cultures, civilisations, states, and empires.

In all such forms of enunciating power – and this book is particularly interested in large-scale, long-term power structures of œcumenical ambition – various permutations of, and variations on, the themes of a number of elementary conceptual and visual elements that display a remarkably protean nature can be witnessed, despite the very great diversity of histories, societies, and cultures.

It will not be the task of this book to elucidate the texture of the connection between representation and reality, for which a great many separate historical studies are required. What needs to be signalled at the outset as fundamentally important is that the repertoire of conceptions and representations through which power makes its enunciations is sufficiently ubiquitous to allow a treatment at a high level of generality. A particular sense of symbolic and conceptual commonality is evident, as we shall presently see, in the vast area covering the erstwhile lands of the ancient Near Eastern cultures – Semitic and Iranian – of Hellenistic Romanity, of the Indian Sub-Continent and of Southeast Asia, described by one author with a certain measure of historical injustice as 'Farther India'. Southeast Asia is rather like a Levant, connected by 'a veritable Mediterranean' formed by the China Sea, the Gulf of Siam, and the Java Sea, a vast confluence of waters which, like the Mediterranean, unified rather than separated littoral traditions.[3] The lands of northern Europe were admitted into this Euroasian system late, starting with the second half of the first millennium of the present era, more or less at the same time as the polities of Southeast Asia. But the ancient polities of China and other east Asian lands connected with the civilisation of China (Japan and Korea) seem to have remained quite distinctive until the advent of modernity, although they do share certain tropes of the representation of power.

Current representations of these histories tend to postulate cultural and civilisational boundaries that are rigid, although this classificatory rigidity, dependent on the twin notions of origin and internal continuity, is not called for by the state of historical knowledge and the possibilities such knowledge opens for sober periodisations. Yet despite the lack of historico-theoretical consensus, it is possible to work in terms of approximate criteria, such as languages, scripts, eras and empires. There is, in the first instance, the culture areas of languages written in Cuneiform, most particularly Akkadian. In this we must include the products of Iranian empires, what has been with justice termed 'Irano-Semitic' civilisation.'[4] Iranian empires were crucial, although it is difficult to judge whether there was anything consequentially novel, particularly Iranian, or *sui generis*, about them or their exercise of power. They were, first of all, the bearers by inheritance of the vast repertoire of political concepts common in the Semitic polities of the Near East, in which civilisation they continued to participate through their use of Akkadian. Secondly, because in their influence upon Graecophone polities, Hellenistic and Byzantine, no less than on the caliphate, they gave their name to the vast heritage of political notions and iconographies of the Near East, which they claimed to represent. Thirdly, they were the intermediary which reciprocally connected Indic polities and those to the west of the Iranian plateau. And, finally, they added doctrinal elements, derived from Zoroastrianism, which were to influence greatly the elaboration of monotheism, but which were incorporated into the monotheism of the Muslims without reference to their point of origin.

Iranian empires had always entered into relations of vigorous exchange, not the least important of which was with the Sanskritic culture area in certain parts of which Pali was later developed as the vehicle for the dissemination and elaboration of Buddhism – a religion which, it must be remembered, was particularly strongly represented in eastern Iranian lands at the time of the Muslim conquests. One token of this exchange, in the reverse direction, is the pillared royal hall at the Mauryan capital Pāṭaliputra, which mirrored the Hall of a Thousand Columns at Persepolis.[5] Seleucid relations with India also conducted a traffic in tokens and conceptions of royalty in both directions. Indian cultural traffic with lands east of India was far more explicit. In Southeast Asia a very far-reaching process of Indianisation effected formally-constituted official culture as a result of the importation of Brahminical Hinduism – later, of Buddhism – under the particular aspect of the royal cult, which brought in its train not only Brahmins, but the lasting legacies of a system of writing, cosmogonic myths, epic themes, certain artistic formulae, and administrative and legal conventions.[6]

Iranian-led polities also entered into vigorous relations with the realms of Hellenism and Romanity and of their primary literary and epigraphic vehicle in the Near East, Greek. If one might speak of Sanskritisation with respect to Southeast Asia, one would be able to speak similarly of Graeco-Roman classicisation in the Middle East in the centuries immediately preceding the Muslim conquests, and of the Orientalism of later Greek and Roman kingship, both in conception and in other modes of enunciation. But one must be particularly wary of imputing oriental and occidental essentialist contrasts between lands lying on either side of the Aegean which, until the rise of the Barbarian kingdoms in the European Middle Ages, were well-integrated into a Mediterranean culture area which entertained very strong relations with western Asia and its vigorous hinterland.

Indeed, one could meaningfully propose the thesis that the wars between the Achaemenid Persians (559–330 BC) and Greeks, including Alexander, like those between Sasanian Persians (AD 224–651) and Byzantines, were a token of a large-scale and long-term historical trend towards unity between the Mediterranean and west and central Asia, a unity achieved briefly under Alexander and, more definitively, in the early centuries of the caliphate. This was noted by Toynbee, but his account was inflected by the exigencies of his theory of history, so that the

Greek and Persian conquests were regarded as the 'antistrophic' implusions of two intransitive and essentially distinct civilisations, and the caliphate was then regarded as the resumption of the Achaemenid empire.[7] One Orientalist also shared this view in essence, not least in order to deny the originality of the Muslim empire.[8] Only recently has the logic of these conquests and counter-conquests been systematically developed, and viewed as an integrative and universalising movement, in which Islam consummates Antiquity, having been implicit in it due to its combination of the geopolitical scheme initiated by Cyrus and the monotheistic universalism of Constantine.[9] In this perspective, Alexander appears not so much as a Greek conquering the Persian empire as the last Achaemenid, succeeding legally to the throne and adding Greece to Iran.[10] It is hoped that the consequences of such a view of history will become evident in the chapters that follow.

Of Hellenistic classicisation in western Asia up to the borders of the Iranian plateau, it might be said that post-Alexandrian Hellenism was expressed in the implantation of Greek institutions and the adoption of the Greek alphabet (itself of Phoenician origin) for the writing of languages as diverse as Hebrew in Mesopotamia and Coptic in Egypt, much as Persian and Turkish were later to be written in the Arabic alphabet. This Hellenism equally subtended cults of royalty cultivated by the Seleucids and Ptolemies and reinforced by Roman cults of emperors and members of their families, which were of ostensible 'oriental' origin. The classicisation of the Middle East was expressed in terms of certain norms of polity and civility (including the cultivation of Roman law), although it did not involve the cultivation of Greek and Latin letters except in restricted circles, some of which were spectacularly productive (Alexandria, for instance), and some of which were the work of Syrians and Egyptians resident in Rome. It may be worth reminding the reader of some leading lights in the culture of the Hellenistic–Roman age in Syria and Egypt, or originating from thence: Porphyry (ca 232–303), Iamblichus (ca 250–330), Plotinus (ca 205–270), Numenius in the second century, and the jurists Ulpianus (d 223) of Tyre and Pappianus of Emesa (Ḥimṣ), who died in 212, not to speak of Stoic thinkers and later of Church fathers.

The diffusion by conquest and imperial relations of power and authority set up, as a central component of life in the Hellenistic era in the Middle East, the assumption of political œcumenism. This was an assumption shared alike by Roman, Persian, and Indian and Indianised imperialism, and was later to be adopted by the caliphate. Thus with the expansion, from Tadmur (Palmyra), of Arab power and influence from 269/270 and with the extension of Palmyrene military presence to Egypt, Antioch and Anatolia, the king Wahb Allāt (Vaballathus) began to claim not special local rank but imperial rank set after Roman models. He claimed to be co-emperor with Aurelian, proclaiming himself Augustus and his mother, Zenobia, the power behind the throne, as Augusta. Shortly thereafter, when war had become inevitable, Aurelian's name disappeared altogether from Palmyrene coins struck at Antioch, which were henceforth inscribed with the legend 'Imp[erator] C[aesar] Vhabalathus Aug[ustus]'.[11] Wahb Allāt's father 'Udhainat (Odenathus) in his time had used another prevalent imperial idiom, derived from the Persian imperial repertoire, and called himself King of Kings.[12] The classicising, Hellenising, and politically Romanising movement that characterised Palmyrene architecture and institutions[13] seems also to have characterised the institutions presided over by other Arab dynasties of the epoch, like the Iturean of `Anjar, and the dynasties of Ḥimṣ (Emesa) and Ruhā (Edessa) .[14] Herod the Great in Jerusalem built temples to Augustus, and worshipped him along with Yahweh.[15] For indeed it had become customary in the Hellenised Middle East by the second century BC to pay divine honours to Romans, following the custom, since Alexander, 'to worship anything that represented political power', according to a somewhat overstated formulation.[16]

Yet such œcumenism could not have been sustained nor would it have struck root had it run counter to local traditions, and by local I do not mean those traditions confined to a small locality. It is said, with much perceptiveness, that Alexander was 'In Egypt, a god and an autocrat; in Persia, an autocrat but not a god; among the Greeks, a god but not a despot, and in Macedonia neither a god nor a despot but a quasi-constitutional king.'[17] It is precisely in this way that norms of kingship and modalities and modules of culture are diffused, by superimposition, adaptation and renaming, much as, in Indo-China, imported Brahmins recognised in local fetishes the disguised avatars of their own divinities.[18] Similarly, an act of adoption is exemplified by the conduct of Aurelian who, having defeated the Palmyrene armies at Ḥimṣ and caused their flight to Tadmur, gave thanks to his victory at the shrine of the Emesan god whom the Romans called Elagabalus – a god regarded in the West as a god of the sun and worshipped as such in Rome, but whose local name, according to inscriptions, was 'LH'GBL, possibly 'god of the mountain' whose cult image was in the form of a black stone,[19] reminiscent of that of the Meccan Kaʿba. When Ramses II invaded Syria, he called his sword 'the sword of Anat', after the consort of the Canaanite god Baʿal, who helped him subdue the primeval waters of chaos and fashion order in the world.[20] Similarly, in earlier times, the invasions of Babylon in the fifth century BC by Cyrus, and by Alexander two centuries later, re-enacted the actions of their Assyrian and Babylonian predecessors and promptly performed the ritual duties of Babylonian kings, including commemorating royal temple rituals on clay cylinders.[21] Alexander's supposed Orientalism in his manner of dress and other symbols of power is well-known, but he was certainly not the first 'European' to adopt Persian royal manners, and was preceded by, among others, some Greek kings of Syracuse[22] and should rather be viewed in the light of remarks made above about his relation to the Persian polity. Persian kings were commonly regarded as exemplary rulers in Greece, despite the romanticism with which Athenian democracy came to be regarded in the nineteenth century. Persian kings were especially lavishly praised at the Macedonian court. Xenophon regarded Cyrus as the ideal monarch and the prototype of Alexander, and this universalist royal genealogy seems to have been a source of inspiration to later statesmen, including Julius Caesar.[23]

In all, Muslim polities had available a floating repertoire of immensely ancient and awesomely persistent institutions, metaphors, iconographies, and propositions concerning power, and most particularly concerning power in relation to the sacred, which they welded into distinctive forms that will be the subject of the chapters that follow. Humble beginnings in the Arabian Peninsula rapidly led to assuming the seats of power previously assumed by a long line of other polities, all of which participated in the Asiatico-Mediterranean traffic in tokens of royalty, and to elaborating these tokens – and the religious notions that accompanied them – into a set of forms which came to be identified as Islamic.

CHAPTER TWO

Kings and Gods

A symbolic and discursive currency, of obscure origins but wide incidence, is traded in the transactions of empire, divinity, and culture. Scholars have, in vain I think, attempted to derive from this currency definitely identifiable and nameable ultimate sources, some anachronistically described as Oriental, others as Western. This trade has necessarily involved the casting of an iconographic classicism, variously borne by priests, texts, and aristocracies: royal bearing, insignia, epithets, attributes, privileges and ascribed prerogatives, potencies and functions that may or may not correspond to reality. A case in point of conventions affirmed contrary to social realities is the adoption in Hinduised Burma of the caste system as a literary convention although this did not correspond to actual practice.[1] This was helped along by the didactic character of Sanskrit texts, and their propensity to reduce various aspects of the world to the form of treatises.[2] In many senses, the classicisation of conventions is evident in didactic summaries, in ceremonial, in epithets, official designations, sententious *topoi*, and much else that can be regarded as a form of ritual: such enunciations consist of punctilious and scrupulous repetition, at set times and in set locations. This is in many senses very much akin to iconographic and other visual representations which repeat set images. One famous study of Byzantine imperial art compared the imperial image to a chancery document, in which subtlety and realism give way to clarity of essential and repeated outline.[3]

Ubiquitous Regalia

Appellation, declamation, and especially the bearing of regalia, worn, touched, or otherwise proximate, were all modes of enunciating power whose specific manners constituted a set of remarkably constant iconographic conventions with a fairly limited albeit ubiquitous core. Just as pictorial modes of presentation and grandiloquent modes of address are rituals that need not measure representation against reality and are unflinchingly negligent of their actual measure in the world of power relations, so also is the abstraction of power and its reduction to various sets of visible tokens of royalty, in its way, an adequate manner of affirming, performing, or evoking the presence of royal power. This holds irrespective of the traditions, cultures, and histories in which it is inscribed.

Thus the ubiquity of the crown and the diadem, though striking, is not surprising. The Pharaoh Amenophis III (r. 1390–1352 BC) is already represented as wearing a diadem,[4] which constituted an abstract index of royalty irrespective of its 'original' association with solar cults, an association which was not always lost in the mists of time; it was revived in the Roman imperial cult from the time of Augustus.[5] But the crown always kept its common association with victory, long after it was first made of myrtle or bays and used to commemorate victory,[6] and long after its royal association was routinised in coronation ceremonies. Some of the crown's martial as distinct from royal association was preserved here and there. Such was the case, for instance, under the Abbasid Caliphate, when military commanders and conquerors were repeatedly crowned, but where the crown was generally deemed inappropriate for the caliph, as we shall see. The perfunctory bearing of the crown by some Umayyads can, moreover, be signalled, as was their use of the Sasanian idea of a magnified hanging crown or other headgear, attested by archaeological evidence.[7] As is often the case in situations where the origin of a widely-diffused and ancient symbol is sought, the idea of a hanging crown cannot be categorically said to have been derived by the Umayyads from Sasanian royal practice. Although early Umayyad coins place stylised Sasanian crowns upon the heads of caliphs and provincial governors, Arabic sources attest the use of the crown in Byzantium as well, though these late testimonies could well be confusing about the route through which Byzantium itself acquired this, or the time at which it was acquired.[8]

Although crowns were condemned by Tertullian and other early Church fathers as pagan,[9] they were later made by Christian polities, especially in the West, into objects very much their own. As is normally the case in these matters, there is evidently a remarkable degree of ritual and symbolic continuity. European kings and emperors from the Middle Ages down to the twentieth century were crowned according to rituals whose main features were directly transmitted from the Carolingian period, and whose continuity in detail was such that the coronation prayer pronounced in 1825 over the last Bourbon, Charles X, was essentially the same as that used at the coronation of Charles the Bald in 869.[10]

Other ubiquitous objects – again under the caliphate, relegated to commanders and conquerors, and regarded as the gift of the caliph, whose dignity was beyond them and could only be expressed in objects of a unique nature – were necklaces, bracelets, belts, brooches and other power accessories. Such objects and others were worn by Germanic chieftains and kings[11] no less than by Alexander the Great and by an Arab military dignitary present at the funeral of Artaxerxes III in the fourth century BC.[12] Of objects that adorn royal presence and, in some instances, stand for iconic representations of the king's formal appearance, sceptres and, from Babylonia eastwards, parasols and fly-whisks can be mentioned. The parasol is first attested on a stele erected by Sargon of Akkad. It became a standard feature on Sasanian royal sculptures, and is still an equally standard accessory of Southeast Asian kingship.[13] It was later adopted, by an uncertain route, as regalia by the Fatimid Caliphs, first in Ifrīqiya and later in Cairo, whence it passed to the Mamluks and to the Normans of Sicily.[14] The Fleur-de-lis appears on an Egyptian seal cylinder of Ramses III, on a wall decoration of Sāmarra, and on fragments of pottery from al-Fusṭāṭ. It was used as a blazon in twelfth-century Syria and appears on coins minted by the Ayyubids and the Mamluks, who also used it for heraldic purposes.[15] However, this symbol, apparently with solar associations from the beginning, achieved its most intense use in European kingship, symbolising the *roi-soleil* from the time of St Louis.[16] It is clearly the case that it was, like many other objects, regarded as an abstract token of power. These objects, as well as thrones, which are thought to be of Persian origin, were also associated with kingship in ancient India and appear to have been passed on to the Indianised territories of central Java, Siam, Japan, and China, where the posture of a sovereign seated on a throne was incorporated into Buddhist iconography towards the sixth or seventh centuries of the present era.[17]

These processes of diffusion and adoption do not constitute much of a mystery. Royal conventions, spoken or seen, can be adopted from predecessors, or simply borrowed from distant if attractive models, without this borrowing implying any similarity in the conceptions of power held by those who used them. One example is the borrowing by the Norman court in Sicily of architectural and other features of Fatimid royalty from Cairo at the expense of both Norman and indigenous Sicilian Muslim convention.[18] Another case in point would be the figure of the winged horse, which appeared in the Medieval Muslim world as an abstract form with royal connotations, but with no more than the merest hint of the mythology of Pegasus. It came later to influence European art, though there were additional lines of transmission for this symbol, which reached Byzantium from Alexandria and was later directly derived from Greek sources in the Italian Renaissance.[19] The Hellenistic *vellum*, a screen which shielded the sovereign from the public eye during ceremonies, and which seems to have originated with the Sasanians,[20] became an integral symbol of the caliphate from the time of the Umayyads through to the Abbasids and Fatimids. But this *ḥijāb* does not appear to have been adopted by non-caliphal Muslim monarchs. Similarly, the prerogative of dining in seclusion practised by Persian kings passed on to the papal court in Rome.[21] Both the habit of dining alone, and variations on the theme of the *vellum* also occurred in western Europe, most particularly at the Ottonian court.[22]

Finally, mention must be made of the somatic marks of kingship and holiness. Thus the mark that Muḥammad had between his shoulders affirmed his prophecy in line with a tradition which prevailed in Gnostic and Manichaean circles.[23] Julius Caesar had physiognomic signs which distinguished him at birth,[24] and 32 bodily marks distinguish a *Mahāpurisa*, the Great Man who, in Buddhist traditions, is destined to choose the vocations of either a Buddha or a *Çakkavatti*,[25] a world-conquering king who turns the wheel of the world (*çakka*). This assumption of a physically manifest role for destiny in the election of kings, and thus a cosmic aspect in the formation of kingship, is quite common. Two millennia later and continents away, Russians in the eighteenth century took certain somatic marks for the distinctive traits of Tsars, whose divine preordination was inscribed on their bodies and which thus made possible the identification of pretenders.[26]

Somewhat analogous supernatural favours were bestowed upon the medieval kings of France and England for their coronation; these royal bodies were famously capable, among other things, of curing scrofula by their touch.[27] From the fourteenth century, English kings were anointed with oil sent from heaven, following the lead of Edward II (r. 1307–27) who, at his coronation, followed the French royal practice of anointment with heavenly oil, which for this purpose had been entrusted in France to Thomas à Becket by the Virgin Mary herself. Centuries earlier this rite was started by Clovis (r. 481–511), who after his conversion was baptised with oil from a holy phial brought to earth by a dove thought to represent or be the messenger of the Holy Spirit . Personally entrusted to Remigius (Rémi), Bishop of Reims, this miraculous oil in its sacred phial was traditionally preserved by the abbot of the monastery at Reims cathedral.[28]

None of these matters is a very far cry from other signs of divine election that double up as part of royal iconography, most interestingly the possession of particular objects or of esoteric knowledge which assure the continuation of order and the possession of kingship. To this order belongs the esoteric knowledge of divine intent and of the future possessed by the imams of Shi'ism, or of the Greatest Name of God possessed by great thaumaturgic Sufi mystics. So too do the tablets of wisdom which, according to the Mesopotamian creation myth *Enuma Elish*, were given to the kings of Babylon by the gods. Similarly, Tablets of Destiny were bestowed by Ti'āmat, the goddess representing the primordial waters of Chaos, upon Kingu her second consort. Kingu was destroyed by Marduk who took the tablets, equipped himself with royal insignia and went on to establish order.[29] Ancient Mesopotamians thought terrestrial kingship commenced with the bestowal of royal insignia to humans by the sun god Anu, and among the regalia of Mesopotamian kings was the Register of Destinies, possession of which assured the continuance of rule.[30] In culturally and historically distant Japan, the sun goddess Amaterasu Omikami bestowed upon her grandson, who was the first to rule over the Japan, three sacred objects symbolising spiritual and temporal authority – a mirror, a jewel, and a sword. These objects remained in the possession of succeeding generations of emperors.[31] Similarly, in China, the royal lore of the T'ang dynasty (618–907) had it that the possession of certain documents of great antiquity guaranteed their holder's possession of a heavenly mandate to rule.[32] We shall see later that comparable objects assuring continuance of rule were kept by the Umayyad and Abbasid caliphs.

There does not appear to be a definite rule of transmission for the emblematic or iconographic enunciations of royalty, although it is possible for historical research to establish pathways by which it took place, and to specify the conjunctures that governed it. One instance of this indeterminacy is the adoption by some popes contemporary with the Umayyads of the long bonnet (*qulunsawa ṭawīla*) favoured by Umayyad grandees, which itself had Achaemenean and Palmyrene antecedents.[33] Much of this interplay is purely semiotic and emblematic, as we shall see.

Matters are more complicated, albeit better ordered and less subject to conjunctural shifts, when it comes to symbols with an iconic indication which might have some propositional correlate, or to declarations and other motifs that refer to statements about the relational aspects of kingship, most specifically its relation to divinity and the general conditions of worldly and cosmic order. In other words, when the iconographic enunciation of power is propositional in some pictorial or discursive manner, rather than being purely emblematic and indexical, as is the case with the fly-whisk. The narrative or propositional translation of a symbolic or plastic enunciation of kingship stands clearly in a direct conceptual relation to the formal beliefs associated with the receiving and sending parties. Yet this need not imply necessarily that the importation of verbal formulae is always constrained by the sense of these formulae, which might themselves be treated as purely emblematic. The Norman court in Palermo borrowed from Cairo calligraphic motifs carrying Koranic statements; yet these were taken over as purely decorative motifs, associated with the royal magnificence of the Fatimid palaces, that is, purely as affirmations of royal exclusivity and universality.[34]

Yet again, not all verbal enunciations concerning kings need a serious effort of semantic or conceptual translation across the spaces of history and of tradition. Like the crown or the fly-whisk, certain epithets and metaphors of power are almost universally utilised, although they are not necessarily linked with specific interpretations. In this sense, certain epithets and metaphors are applied formulaically, in a manner not dissimilar to abstract visual elements, as markers and prerogatives of kingship. Comparing the relation of king and subjects to that of father and children is almost universal. It is found in Buddhist writings no less than in the literatures of the Greeks. It was made into an official motif by Julius Caesar who construed himself as, among other things, *parens patriae*, requiring filial piety of Romans.[35] The metaphors of the physician healing a body, of a general commanding an army, of a soul animating and directing a body, of a pilot navigating a ship, are equally ubiquitous. The assertion that a king stood to his subjects as a shepherd to his flock was made by ancient Egyptians and Mesopotamians, by Greeks and Romans, by Christian and Muslim courtiers and authors on kingship and statecraft, and was taken over by the Church on Biblical authority. The metaphor of shadows – the king as the shadow of God on earth, so constant in Muslim kingship – is well-attested in Assyrian times from a saying contemporary with Asarhaddon (680–669 BC).[36] The correlative metaphor of vicarage of a God, which in Muslim dominions came to be called the caliphate (*khilāfa),* was also ascribed by Seneca to Nero.[37]

The comparison of royalty to the sun, and to the broader symbolism of light, as an abstract index, or as a metaphor for splendour, or again in association with notions of theophany, was also quite widespread, common in Iranian, Mesopotamian, Hellenistic and later Roman kingship. In ancient Iranian kingship, the king's charisma was sometimes physically apparent to his subjects as light.[38] This was sometimes associated, as previously mentioned, with the concept of a crown. With the definitive grounding of royalist and imperialist Christianism for Constantine by Eusebius (fl. fourth century, from Caesarea in Palestine),[39] which was an ideological transformation of world-historical significance, a complex interplay of allegorisation and metaphorisation, entailing the use of pagan symbols in a new context, led to the Christianisation of solar symbolism. Constantine, pagan and Christian at once, used the legend *sol invictus* on his coinage. Christ himself came to be compared to the sun, and solar imagery was freely used in speculation about God and the world. Byzantine emperors came to represent the sun ceremonially for a whole millennium,[40] in a manner not dissimilar to the astral significance taken by Nero and many later Pagan emperors.[41] Muslim polities were not, as we shall see, entirely innocent of this either.

Figures of the Sacred

The attributes and prerogatives through which power is enunciated are woven together by similes, symbols, and allegories of sacredness. Just as icons of kingship announce and confirm at a glance the possession of kingship, these figures of divinity work to elevate the royal office and its prerogatives to the status of icon of divinity. They simultaneously announce and confirm royalty by means of icons that imply a propositional rather than a conventional or indexical character. Indeed, the correlation of sacredness and of terrestrial power, both mysterious and awesome phenomena, takes place through a shared mystique, made all the more potent in a universally enchanted world in which the reality of subtle phenomena was indistinguishable from that of the more tangible. In this world the sacred is all that is related to the beyond, by analogy, emanation, descent, figure, functional parity, or apostolate, many of which relations are often brought to stand one for the other, as we shall see.

Various tropes have been used to describe this sacred mystique of power. Some societies simply divinised monarchs. Others placed them in a relationship of physical or virtual filiation with divinity. Yet others made them representatives of a god or of the gods, or set them up as agents or vicars of divinity, or at the very least recipients of divine favour and succour, and later, of the grace of God – a formula established in Western Europe as classical and canonical by the Carolingians, but attested earlier in Frankish and Anglo-Saxon usage from the seventh century. In all these, the king was a lord associated with divinity. The (brief) Athenian situation, often held as the measure of political classicism, as well as certain scruples of Roman republicanism, were historical anomalies for which extravagent claims are made.

Be that as it may, there appears to exist a limited set of archetypal forms of representation for the construal of royalty in terms of sacredness which show remarkable constancy over time and space. This is clearly the most potent way of enunciating the primacy of kingship over social life in general, so much so that it would be legitimate in this and other considerations of kingship to regard the institution as one of culture regulating, subduing and ordering the chaos and anomie of nature, both of men and, in some cases, of the inanimate elements, and fashioning them into a cultural system of order. This set depends for its constitution on a number of primitive – i.e., elementary and constitutive – notions regarding the relationship between divinity and kingship. Some of these notions were elaborated in discourses on doctrine and political theology, using a variety of philosophical and rhetorical means of argumentation. But it is imperative that these elementary constitutive notions be kept in view and scepticism maintained of the idea that elaborately discursive theological and philosophical formulations of kingship take precedence over the merely formulaic or metaphorical.

This caution is all the more imperative given the comprehensive enchantment of the worlds under consideration here: the reality within these worlds of dreams and portents, the constant intermingling between subtle and tangible beings, and the existence of gods in a divine world which, though distinct from that of men, is yet equally present as an anthropomorphic atopia that exists elsewhere, sometimes in places identifiable and visible to mortals. Among such places was Mt Meru, the centre of the world and the dwelling of the deities of Indic civilisations. If Mt Meru was atopian, Mt Olympus was clearly visible though it fulfilled a similar mythological function, as did Jabal al-Aqraʿ overlooking Ugarit on the northern Syrian coast, where Baʿal had his dwelling and from whence he sent forth storms and thunderbolts. The difference between men and gods is one of potency and of mortality, not necessarily of the order of existence or the subtlety of its substance, since these visible and invisible worlds did not have the radically different ontological status they acquired with modernity.

It was thus possible to deify mortals, most remarkably Roman emperors, and most spectacularly Egyptian pharaohs, this being a phenomenon that is 'collateral'[42] with the divinity of kings. It is asserted of the entirely different but not dissimilar context of nineteenth-century Nepal, that the divinity of kings was not a singular phenomenon, as the king acted in a universe populated by many gods in which what mattered were not questions of ontology or theology, but the relation of the king to other gods and to men.[43] Kings of Mesopotamia may have been 'mortals endowed with a divine burden',[44] but they and other kings are rather more than this. They subsist in a condition of liminality between the sacred and the profane, being both mortal and yet in possession of some of the normative and potent attributes of divinity. This liminality is expressed in the allegories and metaphors of kingship, discursive and visual, as well as in discourses on the origins, functions, and prerogatives of kingship. This conceptual repertoire is perhaps best summed up in what may well be its crudest and most literal expression as the designation of a king as a god.

The genealogy, physical and spiritual, of Egyptian pharaohs was not in doubt. At least from the time of the New Kingdom (1540–1070 BC), they were explicitly thought to have been begotten by the sun god Amun-Ra', in the form of the ruling pharaoh, upon the queen-mother. Thus a mortal being is born of divine seed. Pharaohs were also considered to be perpetual reincarnations of Horus, the son of Isis and Osiris, to whom the dead pharaoh returned in due course, becoming one with Osiris. It was in his capacity as the epiphany of Horus that the pharaoh was owed the divine honours and rites offered to him. It was, furthermore, in his capacity as carrier of Horus' *ka* that he commanded the good order of the world and guaranteed *ma'at*, a matter which will be taken up later in this chapter.

The pharaoh was therefore a being with a multitude of attributes and identities who conjoined the divine designation of royal authority with divine substance which existed terrestrially in many aspects and locations: as seed containing divine substance; as function assuring the maintenance of the world; as object of veneration, even of worship; but also as mortal and worshipper of gods. It is very difficult indeed to disengage the god from the man or the man from the god, and care must be taken not to allow the notion of the divinity of mortals to be over or under-interpreted. Scholarship on divine kingship is generally cavalier and rather negligent with regard to the conceptual aspects of divinity and mortality, to their differential values, intensions and extensions in different historical circumstances. Divinity cannot be reduced to a singular and invariant conception.

Be that as it may, the worldly function of a pharaoh is similar in its main conceptual features to that of Jesus Christ, albeit not in its precise narrative. Conception from divine seed need not always be literally construed, and its rhetorical status does not render it any less effective or significant, for such metaphors subtend intimations of contagion, of displacement. In ancient China, to take a distant example, the monarch was only metaphorically called *t'ien-tzu*, son of Heaven, in that he was thought to have been chosen on merit and given a mandate (*ming*) to rule which he transmited to his lineal descendants as long they ruled meritoriously. Otherwise the mandate would be revoked. By Han times there arose the belief that heaven supervised the details of rule by providing portents and omens which alerted the individual ruler to his relationship to the heavenly source of his mandate.[45]

Southeast Asia in the Middle Ages presents a situation which is conceptually not dissimilar from that found in ancient Egypt. Beginning with the fourth century AD, kings of Cambodia offered annual human sacrifices to their tutelary deities at the top of a mountain – Lingaparvata – at which there was a natural stone in the phallic form of a *liṅgam;* the location remained sacred throughout Cambodian history. This royal *liṅgam* had been a manifestation of the cult of Śiva incarnated in a particular king, until the introduction in AD 802 by Jayavarman II of the cult of the *devarāja* as an official religion of the kingdom. The apotheosis of Cambodian kings was thus decreed, and the king was individually identified with Śiva. The king's 'moi subtil' (*sūkṣmān-tarātman*) resided in the *liṅga* which was placed at the centre of the capital. The king thus came to partake of the same essence as the divinity, so much so that the golden *liṅgam,* which later came to embody the royal essence and to contain the king's mortal remains, was located in the centre of the capital, which was also the centre of the world, and the visible location of Mt Meru. The proliferation of pyramidal temples at Angkor embodies the apotheosis and worship of successive kings.[46]

But the divinity of kings varied according to the prevailing religion and variant beliefs about divinity and the relation of divinity to humanity associated with it. In nineteenth-century Bali, for instance, the essence of royal power, the primeval force of *śaktī* was seen to have been embodied in the *liṅga* obtained by a Brahmin from Śiva himself and handed over to the dynastic founder,[47] much like the sacred oil with which medieval European kings were anointed. A Cham inscription of the ninth century described Uroja, the dynastic founder, as a son of Śiva. We have seen kings of Cambodia allocated the status of *devarāja*, God-King, the visible form of Śiva. King Airllanga of eleventh-century Java was the incarnation of Viṣṇu, not of Śiva, as was Sūryavarman II of Cambodia who erected the famous gigantic temple of Angkor Vat in the twelfth century, and replaced the title *devarāja* with that of *viṣṇurāja.* The idea of plural incarnations was also available and in use. Angrok, the thirteenth-century ancestor of the kings of Majapahit in Java, was the incarnation of Viṣṇu; he was also a son of Śiva, and simultaneously begotten by Brahma from a mortal woman.[48] Each of these filiations fitted into a particular context of enunciation.

When, in the twelfth century, the shift to Buddhism began in

Southeast Asia, the idea of avatarship was not jettisoned but adapted to the new doctrinal environment. Jayavarman VII of Cambodia (1181–1219) changed his own designation from *devarāja* to *buddharāja*.[49] The idea that kings are incipient Buddhas, acquiring kingship because of merit and fortune (*karma*) accumulated in previous lives, was amalgamated in Burma with the possibilities afforded by the concept of an avatar. This allowed kings to regard themselves as manifestations of Śakka, the Burmese–Buddhist equivalent of the ferocious Vedic god Indra.[50] This is an altogether more complex conception. But it was successful in combining two traditions and further strengthening the repertoire of divine attribution by widening its range of displacements and condensations, or of metaphorisation and metonymisation, so that wider circles of local and learned traditions could be interpellated by a dynastic centre in process of expansion and consolidation. In Japan, during the Nara period (710–784), the emperor came, in a not dissimilar manner, to combine the attributes of the Son of Heaven and the attributes of the Bhodisattva or incipient Buddha; the Sun goddess Amaterasu Omikami was simultaneously identified with the Buddha.[51]

The multivocal character of royal apotheosis, entire or partial, assures its aesthetic of political, cultural, and social reception. The discursive elaboration of this aesthetic is textured by two complementary processes: the personification of metaphysical categories, and the metaphysical sublimation of mythological categories. Some of the most spectacular cases in point are perhaps those found in Sanskrit philosophical writings which, in the eleventh century, were denounced by al-Bīrūnī (d. 1048) for their excessive figurativeness and insufficient formalism. This was attributable, he thought, to the acceptance by the Pundits of the demands of the feeble-minded multitude for the idolatrous and sensuous figuration of divinity.[52]

Moving to another time and place, to the Hellenistic era in the Irano–Mediterranean world, we find a not too dissimilar phenomenon: the divinisation of Alexander and the Seleucid and other Hellenistic rulers in the post-Alexandrian period, and the apotheosis of Roman emperors. Both were conceptually somewhat cruder than some of the parallels described here. They seem, above all else, to have been local and imperial cults bereft of theology, but fully equipped with the institutional requirements of cults, such as temples, priests, and (in Rome at least) circus games. Being imperial, the Roman imperial cult in the provinces was catholic, localised in a manner that incorporated existing religious institutions and amalgamated Roman domination with the domination of Hellenistic–Roman cities over other cities and over the countryside.[53]

This was also the case with Alexandrian apotheosis. We have already seen that Alexander's divinity or his relation to divinity took different forms according to local conditions. Among other things, Alexander was proclaimed in Egypt to be the son of Ra', and was enthroned as such in Memphis. In Babylon he sacrificed to Marduk. The first proclamations of his divinity came from the cities of Asia Minor, following the Greek tradition of deifying heroes, real or legendary (such as Heracles), and the real or legendary founders of cities. It was also in this capacity that he was deified in Athens. Though there is some doubt as to whether or not Philip of Macedon set up a cult for himself, [54] Alexander's mother belonged to the Molossi family which had definite associations with divinity and claimed descent from Poseidon as well as a more ancient origin in the very beginning of the time of the gods, from Chronos himself.

Ideas of association between kings and gods, and between both and heroes, were very much in currency in Greece, and did not depend for their incidence on the peculiar claims of aristocratic families or on the predilections of local citizens. Isocrates, who served Philip, spoke of divine honours due to great kings, and Alexander's tutor Aristotle spoke of the likeness of great kings to gods, and followed his mentor, Plato, in the theory that if the best man should become king, he should be divinised.[55] It is noteworthy that philosophers spoke of the divinity of kings, as of divinity in general, either in demotic tones or else metaphorically, allusively, and allegorically. This discourse on royal divinity betokens an important development which inflected both Greek philosophical discourse and subsequent theological speculation: the concept of reason had been disassociated from other tropes of discourse, and the potential allegorism and symbolism of myth, and its transcription into a semantic interpretative mode, was to a large degree realised.[56] It must be stressed, however, that the intermingling of myth, reason, and allegory was to reassert itself after the Parmenides–Plato–Aristotle interregnum and was to mark the Hellenistic period under the omnivorous title of Chaldeanism.

Beyond philosophy, and following on from Alexander's well-known devotion to Dionysus and his punctilious performance of priestly functions, his successors followed suit. Ptolemy I Soter (r. 323–283 BC) erected a state cult to Alexander, whose worship was made obligatory to all subjects. Ptolemy IV Philopator (r. 221–204 BC) added to the official cult the names of Ptolemy I and his wife Berenice, and it became characteristic of Ptolemaic cults that they incorporated the worship of queens and princesses. Inscribing themselves into ancient Egyptian moulds and notions of polity, the Ptolemys (323–30 BC) came to be regarded as the divine sons of Horus. They were called the sons of Zeus-Amun and compared to Raʿ. Just as pharaos had previously sacrificed to their own *ka*, so did the Ptolemys officiate as priests of their own cults.[57]

The Seleucids (312–64 BC) similarly continued the religious policies and roles of their predecessors, including Alexander, but made the transition to divinity more gradually than in Egypt. Ahura Mazda continued to rule in Fars and Marduk in Babylon. The Seleucids performed their duties to them as well as to the Olympian deities. Antiochus I Soter (r. 281–261 BC) took the first step to the rulers' cult by deifying his father Seleucus I Nicator (r. 312–281 BC), and he was in turn deified after his own death. A further step was taken by Antiochus III (223–187 BC), who deified himself and became the priest of his own cult, clearly following Greek and Ptolemaic precedents and introducing a novelty in Semitico–Iranian lands. Later Seleucids amalgamated gods, identifying Zeus with Ahura Mazda, for instance, and took on various aspects of kingship as it was locally conceived. They claimed they were, after the manner of ancient Iranian kingship, infused with *hvarna*, a charisma bestowed upon kings by Ahura Mazda. But it is probably the case that many of these developments, most particularly the apotheosis of mortal men, was at least initially confined to narrow circles.[58]

Clearly we have here a constellation of possible conceptions regarding the divinity of kings, or their relations to divinity, which constituted a repertoire on which successive generations could draw. These conceptual and ritual elements of kingship were formalised in Hellenistic political thought which treated of matters such as the Light of Royalty, of the king as a Supreme Artificer, of kings being substantially distinct from humanity, of the royal *logos* fashioning the better qualities of subjects, of the necessity for men to imitate kings as kings imitate gods, and allied conceptions.[59] All told, mythology had made a philosophical detour and was discursively formalised. Both the mythological-ritual and the discursive enunciations of Graeco–Middle Eastern kingship were to be woven together, under conditions of imperial centralisation, in the cult of Roman emperors and its further, magnificently luxuriant, elaboration in the Byzantine notion of the Basileus which was later to contribute to the conceptual and institutional constitution of Muslim kingship. It is important at this stage to stress the radical distinctiveness of the Eastern and Western Christian conceptions that later developed, a matter which will be discussed in some detail later: in medieval Western Europe, the momentum of the conceptions under consideration here was to be dented by conditions prevailing under Barbarian rule, where Ambrosian and Augustinian thinking was to be interpreted along lines that diverged very significantly from those that constituted first Byzantium and, later, Islam.

The divinisation of Julius Caesar (100–44 BC), methodically pursued by him in his own lifetime, has been meticulously and exhaustively documented in recent scholarship,[60] and only the most salient features need be brought out. Like earlier Roman statesmen, Julius Caesar modelled himself on Alexander, as Alexander had modelled himself on Homeric archetypes.[61] Like his model, Julius Caesar meticulously performed the religious duties incumbent upon him as a patrician and a citizen. He held both the position of *pontifex maximus* and the Augurate, setting in all this an example to Augustus and subsequent emperors. He was also, like other kings ready for divinisation, of extremely ancient, indeed of archetypal lineage, belonging to the Iulii family which had its own legends of origin and its private shrines and public temples, as was usual among Roman patricians. The Iulii traced their descent to Romulus, son of Mars and founder of Rome. Romulus had come to be identified with Quirinus who, along with Mars and Jupiter, formed the prime divine triumvirate of the Romans in a structure that runs parallel to Vedic, Celtic, Nordic, early Iranian and other 'Indo–European' panthea.[62]

Just as Alexander built many Alexandrias, of which one was to become particularly famous, Caesar built at least two Caesareas. First in Greece and later beyond, he was proclaimed divine, dubbed Divus Iulius, and statues to him were erected where sacrifices were made. This was later to develop into a comprehensive cult manned by local priests. The first such *flamen Divi Iulii* was Caesar's friend and ally Marcus Antonius, who was succeeded in time by Sextus Apuleius, the brother-in-law of Augustus. There is evidence that the cult was maintained at least until the time of Hadrian, but it is supposed that it lasted longer. Some African coins bore the inscription 'Divos Iulius', pointing to local cults. When Octavian, later to be known as Augustus (r. 37 BC–AD 14), fought in the Perusine war, the missiles of his eleventh legion bore the inscription 'Divum Iulium', indicating he was fighting with the aid of a god. Defeated enemies were slaughtered at the altar of Divus Iulius.

In Ephesus, Caesar became *theos epiphanes*, much in keeping with the sense of emergent neo-Platonism. In Rome, more symbolically and rather more crudely, he was identified with Jupiter, being of divine descent and fulfilling the demand of Greek letters that he should be the most excellent of men. His statue was adorned with Jupiter's triumphal garb, mounted on a *tensa* – a special carriage reserved for the Capitoline deities – and placed alongside these deities in the Circus. The *ludi Romani* games held in honour of Jupiter received an additional day in honour of Caesar. The night before his murder, Caesar dreamt that he had been raised above the clouds and grasped the hand of Jupiter. After his death, the populace wanted him to be cremated and buried at the temple of Jupiter, but this was not to be.

Augustus gave the cult of divine emperors a far more catholic turn and from the time of his death in AD 14 until the burial in AD 337 of the first Christian emperor Constantine, 36 out of 60 emperors and 27 members of their families were apotheosised and received the title *divus*.[63] The cult of Caesar served as a model for later institutions of imperial apotheosis. Though there was some opposition in Rome to the apotheosis of emperors, refusal by the Senate to decree the divinity of an emperor became well-nigh impossible by the end of the first century,[64] although in many instances the sacrifices offered to emperors were distinct from those offered to gods, or rather to other, immortal, gods [65].

Both Augustus and Jupiter were called *pater* and *rector* (ruler), the one *hominum pater* and the other *pater orbis*. Augustus was a visible and evident god.[66] But the matter was rather more restrained than under Caesar, at least in Rome itself. Elsewhere, the imperial cult was integrated with local religious structures. It was thus subject to a process of indigenisation and domestication which constituted a component in the complementary process of further enracinating Hellenistic norms in the Asian provinces, norms now at least partly Roman in form and carrying Roman names. Augustus was identified with Zeus and took on the usual form of local or specialised cults that specify the personality of Zeus: Zeus Eleutherios in Egypt, Zeus Patroos in Asia, Zeus Olympios in Athens and in Asia, and so forth. In Rome, Ovid (43 BC– AD 17) identified Augustus with Jupiter, referred to his palace as Jupiter's house, and declared his marriage to Livia to be identical with that of Jupiter and Iuno. The comprehensive range of evidence points beyond mere flattery.[67]

Caligula (r. 37–41) accentuated this, enjoying the comparison with Alexander and identifying himself with Jupiter Capitolinus. Claudius (r. 41–54) reverted to the sobriety of Augustus and forbade (in Rome only) sacrifices to himself and prostration before him. But the process was unstoppable, continuing to gather momentum until it was instituted ever more profoundly under Diocletian (r. 284–305), who styled himself *Dominus et Deus*. Earlier, Marcus Aurelius (r. 161–180) had styled his wife *Diva et Pia*, and the Severan dynasty of Caracalla (r. 211–217) continued this trend. Pliny thought that Trajan (r. 98–117) was Jupiter's choice and deputy, and that his earthly dominion (*basileia*) replicated Jupiter's heavenly kingdom.[68] Philip the Arab (r. 244–249) entitled his wife and infant son respectively Augusta and Augustus. Not surprisingly, this was accompanied by a growing formality of court ceremonial, requiring visible signs of obeisance and an ever-increasing distance between the emperor and the patrician class. By the third century, prostration before the emperor – apparently of Persian origin[69] – became standard, and Diocletian introduced the ceremonial of kissing the purple, the hem of the imperial gown.[70]

The transition from a Roman empire to a Christian œcumenical state based in Constantinople, whose population was known as Roman (*Romaioi* – preserved in contemporary Arabic writings who referred to the Byzantines as Rūm and clearly distinguished them from the Greeks) did not present any serious conceptual difficulties. Even the rigorous asceticism of Tertullian by the end of the second century shows that Christians were beginning to appreciate Hellenistic political ideals, and conceded to the Roman version of these ideals everything short of the divinity of emperors.[71] Philo (ca 20 BC–AD 50) had fully recognised divine honours paid to emperors, and accepted, like everyone else, the epithets applied to kings. The Christian counterpart to his assimilation into monotheism of the imperial cult was Clement of

Alexandria (ca 150–215)[72] who came from the city where the fusion of political Hellenism and monotheistic faiths was theorised and discursively elaborated.

The transition from pagan to Christian empire was completed 'without any outward distortion of the concept of imperial authority': sovereign power preserved its divine character and thus 'the Roman–Hellenistic cult of the sovereign lived in the Christian Byzantine empire in all its ancient glory.'[73] The emperor Julian 'the Apostate' (r. 361–363), in his brief attempt to reverse the spread of Christianisation, had already tried to restructure polytheism along universalist lines, using Mithraism as his medium. But the universalism of Manicheanism and of Christianity proved stronger,[74] and having removed from the imperial cult its idolatrous aspects, Constantine retained all other courtly ceremonial.[75] This was not only because there was a continuity in describing gods in royal terms and their powers in terms of absolute rule, and in adapting this to describing Christ as *kyrios* and *imperator*, and depicting him iconographically as *pantocrator*. It was also eminently feasible in view of the fact, already pointed out more than once, that the vocabularies universally used in enunciations about gods and kings are, to a very great extent, interchangeable. As we shall see in detail in connection with Muslim kingship, this interchangeability is limited only by doctrinal scruples, and these were only relevant to certain contexts of enunciation of various amplitudes. Yet these enunciations themselves could, by standard rhetorical techniques and by virtue of the ambiguity of their formulation, be construed as imperial participation in the divine substance in a manner not altogether different than that of Christ himself. The virtuous emperor is the analogue of God, even when this statement is accompanied by the qualifier 'in so far as this is possible'. Though he be guided by God, the Byzantine emperor, according to this political theology, is elected by the Trinity and, indeed, emanates from it. This divine kingship (*entheos basileia*) is kingship in Christ and, indeed, in God himself.[76]

It is entirely natural, moreover, that Byzantine art should represent the emperor, the *Basileus*, as relating to God according to gestures of submission, and as making to God, both as Father and as Son, offerings made to victors, of receiving investiture from God, and other iconographic formulae which otherwise define the relation of subject to emperor.[77] This is reminiscent of the aspect of Mesopotamian and Persian kings when depicted together with Marduk or Ahura Mazda. And just as it was customary in the pagan Near East to call their own and invading kings gods,[78] Eusebius used the term *Basileus* to describe both God and Constantine.[79] Similarly, Russians from the fifteenth century at least used the term Tsar to refer both to king and to God, and indeed referred to the Tsar as an earthly god (*zemnoyj bog*), although they sometimes distinguished the heavenly Tsar and the earthly (*nebesnyj tsar, zemnoyj tsar*).[80] Christian discourse from patristic times freely adopted imperial epithets to describe God's majesty.[81]

Many ways of associating the Byzantine emperor with God and with Christ were conceived, derived from the copious patrimony of such tropes. These spanned the range of possibilities from entire separation of essence, which relates the two by the representation of the One by one entirely unlike Him, to a sort of participation in essence, which was never to be fully theorised, but was nevertheless to be enunciated by means of a rhetorical participation in common qualities such as majesty. The prime medium for the expression of this magical contiguity was the floating metaphor, the epithet, and the iconogram. Both art and ceremony employed the same vocabulary to portray imperial power and majesty without this implying that ceremony and art copied one another, for they were complementary.[82] Matters concerning the divine attributes of the emperor, which Christian doctrine rendered impossible to articulate explicitly, were now enunciated visually and ceremonially.

It has indeed been plausibly argued that the very purpose of imperial Byzantine art was to magnify the emperor and simultaneously to transpose him into ceremonial style.[83] It can be added to this that, despite the allergy of St Paul and of Tertullian to the state cults of Rome, the image was regarded in early Christianity as the seat of the divine being, possessing properties as the divine model.[84] By analogy, the imperial image conveyed the presence of the emperor as well as the holiness that resided in him, and this magic property of the image or the icon is common to all cultures. In Byzantium it was a formidable consequence of the iconoclastic controversy that the attendant sensualisation of the spiritual domain opened the visible world to the sacred, into which it could be recuperated.[85] There was a set repertoire of images obeying a set of rigorous iconographic rules, from which choices were made according to circumstances, as there was also a set of ceremonies from which choices were made which varied procedure from performance to performance according to the social and political requirements of the moment. This might dictate the exclusion of this or that symbol, or emphasis on this or that aspect of ceremonial, in order to reimpose order, redefine relations at court or in the position of the emperor, and so forth.[86]

Imperial images were designated with the epithets 'divine' and 'sacred'. These *basiliki eikones* were sent out to the provinces, where they were received as the emperor himself would have been received. New emperors were recognised by the reception of their images. And whereas previously the erection of an imperial portrait was left to private citizens, Diocletian introduced the practice of 'publication' of the imperial image, whereby this was sent to the provinces by the emperor himself, in order for it to receive homage,[87] in its capacity as his representative. The imperial name and images were fixed to military standards, sometimes embossed on officers' buckles, as they were on weights and on coins[88] – a manifestation of authority, an assurance of authenticity, and doubtless also a talisman. The qualifier *theos* (sacred) was applied in Byzantium to all matters that concerned the person of the emperor.[89] Imperial images were also, in the mid-fourth century, introduced into churches where they were venerated, and the old Roman honours paid to imperial statues were even improved upon.[90]

This participation by the emperor in the divine substance of majesty and holiness had other manifestations. The act of prostration before the emperor, the *proskynesis*, was the duty and privilege of a few,[91] much as it had been under the Sasanians and as it was to be in Muslim polities. So also was the kissing of the emperor's foot, his hand or his cheek[92] by his subjects who were all, technically, his slaves (*douloi*).[93] Muslims routinely referred to themselves as *mawlā* of the king or caliph, conveying the same idea. Manifestations of the emperor's uniqueness and lofty distance can be found everywhere and are a far cry from the soldierly acclamations by which Eastern Roman emperors had earlier acceded to power. Traces of the practice of crowning by raising the emperor on shields continued but became more than the acclamation of a commander by his soldiers and took place alongside a more elaborate and liturgified ritual.[94] It acquired a cosmic and more particularly solar significance, like the elevation of Persian kings, seated on their thrones, upon the necks of their subjects: the circular shield with a border around the middle disc became an *aspis*, symbolising the revolving spheres.[95]

The emperor alone was privileged to wear purple, which had previously been the mark of senatorial rank in Rome. In public appearances his loftiness demanded that his feet never touch the ground and emperors were consequently always elevated on a stool upholstered in crimson. On such occasions the sublime person would touch nothing that was not of crimson or porphyry. Silence had to be observed in this presence, or in the presence of objects representing the emperor, such as his image or a letter from him.[96]

Ceremonial – like iconography – was the occasion on which the worldly and the political were transposed into the mystical and religious, during which the Byzantine emperor, as previously in late Rome, became the object of a cult.[97] The emperor greeted people with the sign of the cross, and he received similar greetings. The ancient *vellum* which protected him from view itself became a cult object. The throne was to the imperial reception hall what an altar is to a church: surrounded by priests and others dressed in ecclesiastical colours, accompanied by chants in liturgical form, conveying as do other details of protocol a hieratic sense and providing a reminder, if this were required, that the imperial Roman residence was itself regarded as a temple. Indeed, in a letter from the sixth century, the imperial palace was referred to as *theon palation*, and in a tenth-century document it was qualified as *hieros*.[98]

The Byzantine emperor was, moreover, closely associated with the Trinity. He was also an extension and carrier of divine might into the world, participating in divinity according to formulae inspired by neo-Platonic ideas of emanation.[99] He was associated with the divine logos or with Jesus Christ, an idea which Christianised the Hellenistic notion of the king being the incarnation of reason in the form of the law, an idea to which we shall return. Participation in divinity by the emperor appeared so tangible that Eusebius was able to announce the possibility of personal contact and direct communication between Constantine and God.[100]

This charter for imperial autocracy received its philosophical and theological grounding in the idea which was to be the mark of monotheistic kingship, including in very strong measure Muslim kingship, that the existence of one Caesar on earth corresponded to the dominion in heaven of only one Lord, an idea which had been repeatedly stressed from southern Syria by both Origen (d. 253–54) and Eusebius.[101] This idea had been present in Hellenistic thought, and was based on the distinction between a demotic-mythological multitude of invisible forces and the neo-Platonic sublimation of the idea of a demiurgical *basileus*. But its theological lineaments were complicated. The fundamental impulse to this great transformation came from the political reading of Plato's *Timaeus* by Philo: the transition from chaos to order, from formlessness to formation, became a political act for the imposition of order, *taxis*, which was interpreted as *politeia*. This was a reading parallel to certain heathen arguments regarding Zeus, and parallel assertions were made in altogether different situations, for instance in T'ang China where political centralisation and the reinforcement of imperial power was paralleled by a reorganisation of the heavenly hierarchy according to the principle that 'there is only one Heaven (*ti'en-shang wu erh*)'.[102]

In this way, Philo influential among Christians rather than among Jews, transformed Jewish monotheism into a cosmic monarchism, with the Jews as the priests of mankind, and God as the King of Kings (*basileus basileou*), in what constituted a political solution to the metaphysical question of the One and the many.[103] It is important to note here that the Persian monarchical tradition also had the supreme ruler entitled King of Kings who, as God's representative, was entitled to assume the title of *bāgh*, God.[104] Monarchy denotes the primacy of one principle of order and causation, *mia archē*, and this was counterposed by Eusebius, Origen, and others to the multiplicity of divine principles implied by polytheism, a multiplicity which was seen as the counterpart of political fragmentation which the Christian empire of Constantine transcended in its monarchical idea.[105] The Christian analogy and adaptation of this was straightforward, in that divine Election was transferred from one restricted tribal collectivity to an œcumenical one summed up and fully represented by three correlative *basiloi*: the emperor, Jesus, and God.

The uniqueness of the king[106] and his transcendence of his subjects, as gods transcend humanity, was an idea very much in currency. Continuous reference was made by Hellenistic writers to Persian kings as exemplary. That the king was the best man was a constant motif of these writings, as was the idea that he was a preserver, a saviour in some senses (*sotēr*), of the orderly course of social existence. In Rome, this idea was naturalised by Cicero under the title *conservator patriae*, with a characteristic dose of ambivalence deriving from ideals of patrician republicanism.

This quality of uniqueness was most particularly articulated in the notion that the king was 'the law animate' (*nomos empsychos*, *lex animata*) embodying in his actions, as the best man, the *logos* of harmony which may in origin be divine, but which assures the maintenance of order and justice. This was an idea with Pythagorean resonance, which occupied a central position in Aristotelian as well as Hellenistic ethics, both of which were later to play an extremely important role in Muslim notions of kingship in relation to the *sharīʿa*. At the hands of Eusebius, *nomos empsychos* became *nomos basilikos*;[107] at the hands of others the emperor remained quite straightforwardly the law animate, *nomos empsychôs*, a notion which was made to translate his capacity as an extension of God's power.[108] In these terms, the emperor embodies the law, an idea equivalent to the contention of the pagan Themistius (ca 317–388), Eusebius' near contemporary and political theorist to the emperors Constantius II (r. 324–361) and Theodosius I (r. 379–395), that the emperor himself was the law,[109] and was therefore beyond it. This idea, of ancient lineage, was occasionally contested, as in the reign of Julian the Apostate when the conception was revived of an objective law independent of God but arising from the people who surrendered their prerogatives to the king.[110] Yet this anti-Eusebian, quasi-republicanist interregnum, was short lived. The notion of the law animate was also to circulate in Western Europe in the twelfth century in order to express the legislative role of the Pope: thus the great canonist Gratian (d. before 1159) declared that the pope was not bound by laws because he makes them.[111]

The relationship between this notion of the king as embodying divine *logos* and the idea of providence, current in Stoic writings, was of capital importance. The idea of providence itself (*pronoia*, identified in Stoic writings with fate, *heimarmēnē*) was of course semantically multivalent, open to anthropomorphic and mythological interpretations involving unmediated divine agency as well as to interpretations in terms of an impersonal regularity. Whatever the interpretation, it seems to have been conducive to the notion that kings had been elected by providence, personal or impersonal, as the best man embodying justice and paternally solicitous on behalf of his subjects to whom he is related by love (*philanthrôpos*).[112] This constellation of philosophical, metaphorical, rhetorical, ethical and Platonic and theological motifs is summed up in Eusebius' reference to Constantine:

> And in this God's friend henceforth shall participate, having been furnished by God with the natural virtues and having received in his soul the emanations from that place. His ability to reason has come from the Universal Logos, his wisdom from communion with Wisdom, goodness from contact with the Good, and justness from his association with Justice. He is prudent in the ideal of Prudence, and from sharing in the Highest Power he has courage. For he who would bear the title of sovereign with true reason has patterned regal virtues in his soul after the model of that distant kingdom … Let the friend of the All-Ruling God be proclaimed our sole sovereign with truth as witness, the only one who is truly free, or rather truly a lord. Above care for money, stronger than the passion for women, victor of physical pleasures and demands, the conqueror, not the captive, of ill-temper and wrath, this man truly is the Autokrator, bearing the title that conforms to his moral conduct. Really a Victor is he who has triumphed over the passions which have overcome mankind, who has modelled himself after the archetypal form of the Supreme sovereign, whose thoughts mirror its virtuous rays, by which he has been made perfectly wise, good, just, pious, courageous, and God-loving. Truly, therefore, is only this man a philosopher-king, who knows himself and understands the showers of every blessing which descend on him from outside, or rather, from heaven. He makes manifest the august title of monarchical authority in the remarkable fabric of his robes, since he alone deserves to wear the royal purple which so becomes him. This is a sovereign who calls on the Heavenly Father night and day, who petitions Him in his prayers, who years for the highest kingdom.[113]

The very same notions and motifs were embodied in the Code of Justinian (r. 527–565), which

> … marks the end of a long evolution. The notion of the law animate, born of the old Oriental [sic!] monarchism, nursed by the Greek rhetors and philosophers in the Hellenistic age, long resisted by the survivors of Roman republicanism, was finally adopted by the New Rome, Constantinople, and sanctioned by the Church. Its enshrinement in the Code of Justinian destined it to play its part in Byzantium, in the evolution of the medieval Papacy, and in the new era of political thought of the Western Renaissance.[114]

CHAPTER THREE

Kings in the World

We have seen kings partaking of divine substance, prerogatives, privileges and attributes, by filiation, participation, emanation, analogy and mimesis. Kings are specifically selected among mankind, or emerge to fulfil a soteriological role, sometimes, as in Buddhism, on the strength of merit accumulated in previous lives. But kings rule subjects, and the itinerary of kingship and of lines of kings is inscribed in the larger – or parallel – itinerary of both human and cosmic history in which kingship has a pivotal role. They relate to the beginning and proper order of life in society, as well as to its end.

In their worldly capacity, good and virtuous kings perform the work of the gods among people. More often than not kings were declared to be good and to have acted in conformity with the divine will, pleasure, or purpose. They did this by acting as vicars of the divinity, or as an image of divinity which could be beheld and imitated, or both. Divine imagery in the definition and constitution of kingship has already been discussed, and we turn now to the vicariate.

Representing divinity is an act in two capacities. The first is immanent, extending divine presence into the world by carrying divinity across time in salvation history, by the conceptual means of typology. The second maintains order in the world in such a manner that subjects implement the will, pleasure, or purpose of divinity. Such order is only attainable under the auspices of a state, the name given to that form of organised habitation signalled by the presence of kingship. Thus it is not only the person of the king which is related to divinity. He becomes the agency for the sanctification, in so far as this is possible, of others: a quality that comes about through the sacralisation of time and of the space of society.

Religions, like other ideational systems sustained by historical masses, are almost without exception animated by a vision of a perfect beginning maintained by repeated recapitulation. None are more systematically and relentlessly so than monotheistic religions.[1] The rhythms of this recapitulation constitute the tempo of sacred time into which sacralised kingship is inscribed. Sacralised kingship has as its task the maintenance of mundane affairs in a manner that ensures their course is constantly corrected so that it is not diverted into an independent rhythm but inscribed within the rhythm of sacred time. In the monotheistic faiths and under Zoroastrian influence the circle of time is completed by a definitive and unrepeatable End, which recapitulates the Beginning. It is not coincidental that, in all instances, this final eschatological delivery comes at the hands of a redeemer-king, or is at least construed as a royal function.

Royal Cosmography

The cosmos is one of the most salient contexts for regarding kingship as, in a broad sense, a theophanic announcement. According to fairly widely found ideas – in Buddhism, in the ancient Near East, in Shiʿi Islam, for instance – kings are allocated positions of decisive cosmic centrality. Although divine creators are the prototypes for kings, the relation of type to figure is not one of correspondence and does not involve a transference of demiurgical capacities; the cosmic centrality of kings is therefore that of preservers and maintainers of both social and natural order.

Systemic integrations of kingship within the cosmic order were staple ideas in the ancient Near East. The annual celebrations of spring, involving Anu or Baʿal, assured the regeneration of nature and the continuing cycle of the seasons. These were connected to the rhythms of agriculture, and in their primitive form most plausibly to rites of propitiation and fertility. The annual cycle in the Babylonian temple of Marduk of reciting the *Enuma Elish* epic of creation made it possible for Marduk to rise once again and re-enact and renew the control of Chaos. The gods conferred their combined powers upon him, and when Marduk rose annually the king himself was invested anew with the insignia of kingship which were placed before the gods in the temple.

There were analogous ceremonies throughout ancient Mesopotamia and Syria, and in all these the king re-enacted the primeval battle between Marduk and Ti'amat, the elemental monster and the representative of Chaos. In this way, the order of things was reconfirmed annually, and its smooth running, including the cycle of the seasons, was assured.[2] The visible forces of chaos – wild beasts, enemy attacks, disease, destructive meteorological phenomena – were kept at bay.[3] In all these ceremonies, the king performed priestly functions common to kings throughout the area, including Israelite kings. They also stood in a relation of metaphorical filiation to the gods, but unlike Egyptian kings, they did not partake of divine substance.[4]

In Egypt, the equivalent conception of kings as ultimate nodes of order in the social and natural worlds was more thoroughgoing, or perhaps more explicitly articulated. Whereas Semitic kings stood in a mimetic relationship to the gods, which they expressed iconically in ceremonies of annual renewal, the Pharaoh, divinised by Ra's *ka*, participated in the power of his heavenly father, a power *per se* generative of order. As such he became not only the manager of natural fertility, law, justice, and of cosmic order in general (*ma'at*), but their contemporary author and guarantor, who ensured that the order of society ran parallel to the order of nature.[5]

The philanthropic and terrestrially soteriological role of kings characteristic of many forms of kingship runs parallel to notions current in Theravada Buddhist polities.[6] Though formally atheistic – to the extent that a priest in modern Sri Lanka could declare that gods have nothing to do with Buddhism[7] – Theravada Buddhists have nevertheless traditionally invested kingship with a mystical quality and associated kings with attributes of holiness, even with deities. In this, Theravada Buddhism joined Sanskritic notions of kingship with the Mahayana idea of the *bodhisattva* and merged them into two overlapping though distinct notions of sovereignty: the one over human association, and the other over the cosmos.[8] The king's powers, albeit not divine, are represented as part of 'a divinely composed order of events'.[9] This, *mutatis mutandis*, bears comparison with Byzantine emperors, whose proper sacredness was expressed through the non-doctrinal media of iconography, movement, spatial disposition, and other enunciations which, though non-discursive or non-propositional in nature, were yet allegorically suggestive, even assertive. The holiness of Buddhist kings was indicated by signs, not endowed by gods, except in so far as these kings brought non-Buddhist, Brahminical or local deities, to bear upon their office.

According to works on kingship in Theravada Buddhist polities written by monks – in distinction to what may emerge quasi-propositionally from art and ceremonial – that which constitutes royal charisma is not so much participation in some divine substance, but rather a function of a mimetic *dhamma*. The king's charisma additionally derives from the confirmation of this mimesis bestowed by coronation, and symbolised by the possession of specific elements of regalia (umbrella, fly-whisk, sword, crown) which endow him with a quasi-divine quality. Like a *Bodhisatta* (Pali; Sanskrit: *Bodhisattva*), this Great Man is endowed with the 32 marks of Great Men (*mahāpurisa-lakhaṇāni*). His funeral proceeds as that of the Buddha; after cremation, a stupa is raised over the relics of his body, pilgrimage to which is a meritorious (karmic) act.[10]

But it was not only the possession by the king of the mystical quality of *anubhava*, associated with possessing magical objects, that assured the preservation and maintenance of the body social.[11] The crucial force from the doctrinal point of view was the impersonal *dhamma*. This could become a form of charisma possessed by a king, as a sort of cosmic force obeying its own inexorable laws to which he is nevertheless subject regardless of his possession of it, for the *dhamma* also rewards kings and punishes them,[12] much like providence. A king born in auspicious circumstances, having also accumulated *karma* in previous lives, might command this *dhamma*, not in a sense of possession, but in the sense of incorporation and correspondence, in much the same way as the *logos* of a Hellenistic king was the embodiment of the law at the same time as being a source of it. This is an ambivalent notion, open to different interpretations under different circumstances, certainly, but one whose ambivalence is the very source of its constancy as a universal motif, marrying royal prerogatives and natural regularity, will and norm, culture and nature, in a general rhetoric of kingship.

Inscribed within nature itself, the great king becomes a universal king and world-conqueror, *ćakkavatti*, modelled in the course of time after the image, real or legendary, of Aśoka (r. ca 270–232 BC) – who did not himself make any soteriological claims. The king as cosmic liberator was an idea which developed later in the Sinhalese, Burmese, and Thai contexts, represented in architecture, inscriptions, ceremonies, as well as the literary output, most particularly historical or quasi-historical works, of the *Sangha*, the monastic institution.[13] The wheel, which is associated as much with the solar disc as with the *dhamma*, and which normally resides in the depths of the ocean, appears to the *ćakkavatti* in the sky and enters his palace. After his death, it returns to the depths. He is distinguished from ordinary kings by the possession of seven mystic treasures, chief among which is the wheel; the others are far more mundane. He is all the more spiritual in that he is the realisation of one of the two possibilities of a *Bodhisatta:* to become either a *cakkavatti* or a Buddha.[14] His conquests, as related in canonical texts, are epic conquests, related in clearly cosmological terms, although he is depicted to be such that he conquers without force, by the sheer force of *dhamma.*[15] *Ćakkavatti* and *dhammarāja*, conquering by force of righteousness, both refer to the same universe of concepts. They are sometimes used simultaneously, but sometimes differentially, denoting rule in periods of conquest or periods of consolidation.[16] In some instances, a *ćakkavatti* is merely a prelude to Buddhahood, constituting the king as an embryo Buddha, who would come back with universal love, *mettayā*,[17] and rule with the subtle breath of the *dhamma.*

World Conqueror and World Renouncer are therefore complementary: related in a manner that has been described as a sort of 'parabolic movement', with liturgical ramifications, from king to *Bodhisatta* king back to *ćakkavatti* king again.[18] As in some other cases reviewed above, the Buddha's doctrine, influence and relics are often characterised by royal metaphors, and his relics are held to be repositories of world-conquering power.[19]

Ultimately, this sort of conception leads to notions of microcosm and macrocosm which were later to be well-articulated in strands of Muslim philosophy of the state and Muslim eschatological thinking. This later development was the result of conceptual evolution that intervened in Hellenistic times, in which were sublimated magical and propitiatory formulae, duly conceptualised and formulated in philosophical terms, although some of the earlier numerology reminiscent of Pythagoreanism persisted. An example of this would be the allusive use made by Eusebius of the numbers 1 and 3 to endow Constantine's tricennial celebrations with an universal, cosmic significance.[20] The precise magical and cosmological extensions of such allusions are not altogether clear, but there exists a rich body of Hermetism and of numerological and talismanic science – which was to be developed intensively and rigorously in Muslim lands in the contexts of the exact mathematical disciplines of alchemy, astrology, and allied pursuits – to which the Middle East was home.[21]

But Indic and Indianised territories are also replete with particularly well-elaborated and articulated numerological signatures corresponding to those in the cosmos in the context of a politico-mystical cosmography. It must be emphasised at the outset, however, that the cosmic significance of states and kingship within these structures, and the correspondence of cosmic order and the order of society and polity, does not seem to have been deliberately formulated or theorised, as it had been in China for instance. Yet there is overwhelming evidence provided by literature, inscriptions, titulature, and the cosmic numbers of queens, ministers and other office bearers, provinces, and other aspects of power in medieval Southeast Asia.[22] The more consequential and systematic medium through which nature and culture are related by analogy and correspondence, however, is iconic, and uses as its medium what we might call a geometrical numerology. This is the representation of the state, as of royalty and its immediate spatial extension, as a *maṇḍala*.

The *maṇḍala* is a pentadic or quincunical construct, composed of a centre surrounded by four cardinal points (a construct of points isomorphically expandable to 9, 17, or 33), and is of course found on textiles and in architectural arrangement, no less than in the spatial conception of the state surrounding the royal abode at the centre which, as has been mentioned, is the analogue of Mt Meru. The central organisation of capital cities in medieval Southeast Asia, with the royal abode surrounded by three ramparts and the cardinal points prescribing the location of main gates, is one that is repeated across the kingdom, constituting 'a galactic constellation' with 'a nesting pattern whereby lower-order centres and entities are progressively contained and encompassed by higher-order centres or entities,'[23] so that the centre represents the totality and embodies its unity.

The *maṇḍala* stood for many things: the structure of a divine pantheon, the spatial deployment of a state and its administration, pathways for the devolution of power. The capital was an absolute centre. Its circumambulation formed, and in Cambodia and in Burma (until not long ago) still formed, one of the most important parts of the coronation ritual. Throughout Southeast Asia, the capital contained a replica of Mt Meru, topped by a *liṅga* as we have seen.[24] Needless to say, this radial transmission of the centre and its successive duplications is not in real terms a static structure, but is characterised over time by pulsations which modify its geographical extent, and is repeatedly ordered and reordered according to the fortunes of politics and warfare.[25] It coexisted, of course, with Buddhism which, unlike Brahminism, formally regarded gods as well as kings as representing rather than embodying *dhamma* and which, also unlike Brahminism, did not regard cosmogony as creative simultaneously of culture as well as of nature. Brahminical cosmogony represented the *varṇas* (castes – lit. 'colours') of the caste system as divine creations.[26] The genesis of social order was construed differently by Buddhists.

Monotheistic Types

We have already encountered a number of conceptions of the divine foundations of kingship. To these we could add notions held by the Israelites, which were to develop in the Muslim element through the notion of prophethood as a prophetic mission, *risāla*, of a nomothetic and therefore decidedly mundane character and function. Such a mission, unlike purely spiritual and salutary prophethood (*nubuwwa*), aims at restoring to the world a form of order consonant with the nomothetic designs of divinity. The motif of divine missions is ancient, and the Old Testamental and Muslim use of it is in keeping with the old Babylonian notion of kings being sent out by the gods on apostolic missions,[27] an idea which has almost universal rough equivalences.

Thus, in this sense, righteous kingship, of which prophetic missions could be seen to form a particular type, is an agency of restoration after a period of degeneration, the two moments constituting the rhythm of salvation history. The restoration of order might indeed have a cosmic context and function that have been encountered above. But monotheistic religions, under the decisive influence of Zoroastrianism[28] and the no less decisive but still poorly appreciated influence of Manicheanism, recast this in a manner that enclosed time by postulating an end to it.[29] In this model, the alternance of righteousness and wickedness, the succession of virtuous and evil kings and times, will end and yield to the undisturbed and perpetual reign of order as decreed by divinity. The Zoroastrian messiah, Saoshyant, will signal the definitive triumph of Ahura Mazda over Angra Mainyu, will gather together the debris of time by resurrecting the dead, and usher in an eternity of incorruptibility. He will also recapitulate the beginning, being the posthumous son of Zoroaster, born of his seed, hitherto preserved in a particular lake.

In a perspective such as this, matters at the beginning were always thought to have been perfectly crafted. A Sasanian text states that men, at the beginning of time, enjoyed a perfect understanding and knowledge of religion,[30] which was diluted by the great corrupter, time, and which must therefore be eliminated at the end. This is the element that stayed on in monotheistic religions which did not adopt Avestan cosmographic and cosmogonic histories with their first men, their ages of heroes, monsters and other matters that were eventually transformed into the classical Persian epics and which survive fragmentarily in Arabic historical works.[31]

In the context of monotheism, the repetition of the beginning in history, and the re-enactments of acts of apostolic foundation, including attributes of kingship, take place at various intervals in the fullness of history, albeit in a separate register that organises the rhythm of the divinity or of divine association as distinct from the regularity of the chronometer.[32] In religious and other texts, the register of eternity within time is performed by typology, a mode of interpretation in which a specific historical or quasi-historical precedent, be it an act or a person, prefigures a later one. More visibly and in a more plastic fashion, typology was represented by ceremonial and visual arts. Thus Julius Caesar construed his victories as a re-foundation of Rome, a construction suggested already by his family link with Romulus and, through the latter, with Aeneas.[33] Similarly, acts of foundation or of innovation or vitalisation were regarded as acts of re-foundation and of restoration, usually related to a particular genealogy through which typology operates, a genealogy which was sometimes – but with the monotheistic religions, at a certain stage in their evolution, invariably – marked by the beginning of a calendar. Persian kings were not only the successors of epic heroes and recollections of *Urmenschen*, but also the initiators of new epochs which signalled the regeneration of their countries.[34] Sasanian regnal translations were signalled by alterations in the design of the crown ultimately and cumulatively leading to great complexity.[35] There are parallels and contrasts to this within the same conceptual parameters. Chinese emperors before the T'ang dynasty, under the Chou,

Shang and Hsia, for instance, marked their accession to power with modifications of the calendar signalling a new heavenly mandate to rule,[36] and hence the renovation of time with the accession of a new king.

Within the ambit of a single genealogy, most particularly one expressed in terms of a singular and constant body of canonical text with its figures and icons, which thus constitute a tradition, the play of typologies could offer limitless possibilities. In Byzantine and other Christianities, this play took two fundamental forms, both of which were used to enunciate kingship: the intertextual, which produced correspondences and equivalences between textual fragments, and that which produced equivalences between textual and contemporary personalities and institutions, and thus sacralised portions of history and of public life by incorporating them into the register of the divine rhythms.

Of the first variety examples could be multiplied indefinitely, indicating a certain suppleness and attention to the unfolding of concrete history which is open to interpretation in terms of cultural and historical conjunctures. The suppleness and effectiveness of rhetoric is no longer much appreciated, and has led one modern historian to reproach Eusebius, for instance, with the want of exegetical discretion.[37] The entire text of the Old Testament was regarded in patristic literature as a series of figures for Christ and the redemption. Moses and Jesus were thought to be related as figure and fulfilment, and Noah's Ark was regarded as a prefiguration of the church. In all cases, concrete events are removed from time and transposed to the perspective of eternity by the use of allegory, in the widest sense, to interpret Biblical figures.[38] Russian clerics in the fifteenth century interpreted Mehmet II's siege of Constantinople in 1453 as a re-enactment of Nebuchednezar's siege of Jerusalem, and this was allied to an interpretation of the date 1492 as indicating the end of the world and betokening associations with the Antichrist.[39]

The medieval West followed the Byzantine usage of the language of Christological exemplarism by designating the king as *typus christi*, at once the image and the vicar of Christ.[40] Byzantines illustrated Biblical analogies iconographically, with David, Moses, and others standing for the emperor,[41] as his prototypes. Byzantine court ceremonial re-enacted passages from the Bible, with the emperor washing the feet of twelve poor men, or inviting twelve guests to a meal on Christmas day. Byzantine coronation ceremonies were also mystically connected with the delivery to Moses of tablets on Mt Sinai.[42]

The most systematic and thoroughgoing connections between matters relating to mortal emperors and their mystical analogues were, however, forged initially in the Eusebian periodisation of history. This is not restricted to Eusebius' use of Biblical typology for his Christian emperor in his *Ecclesiastical History* [43] in a manner that synchronised profane and ecclesiastical histories. At issue was not merely the re-enactment and recapitulation of discrete acts and personalities by singular events of history, but the structuration of history in such a way that the present and the historical unfolding of which it forms part, marked specifically by Christian kingship, was seen to reflect a systematic unfolding of the moment of divinity. Thus not only was God to be found in the reflection of an earthly monarchy, but the emperor was also to be found in the reflection of the divine monarchy. This was historicised by Eusebius' synchronisation of imperial and religious beginnings in the profound metaphysical sense of acts of archetypal foundation. Subsequent moments in the same historical and temporal context became only re-enactments and recapitulations of inaugural archetypes, thus establishing a momentous archetypal synthesis that was liberally used later, in the context both of Christian and Muslim polities.

For Eusebius, revelling at the imperial peace of Augustus, combined this temporal peace with the idea of divine monarchy, and synchronised the appearance of Jesus with the full glory of Rome under the Pax Augusti. He saw this to be less a coincidence than the result of heavenly design: imperial monarchy and Christianity were born as one and together; they eradicated principles of provincialism and nationalism in favour of empire, and in a parallel movement suppressed polytheism which was inextricably connected to locality. Thus whatever eschatological expectations may have been involved with early Christianity were transposed by Eusebius to the register of his own time as a political order of utopian measure.[44] In this light, the transition from Augustus to Constantine was one between imperial foundation and its equally momentous accomplishment and closure upon the essence of its beginning through a re-enactment of this beginning which involved the elevation of the imperial office to a divine monarchy.[45] Constantine was the unspoken agent of a victory for Christianity, a victory which properly belongs to the Saviour.[46]

Eusebius' thoughts on this matter were a systematisation of Philonic polemics against polytheism and of certain patristic elaborations of Augustus and Christ.[47] These systematic Christologies of history were most particularly formulated by Origen, and were to have a profound consequence and influence, through St John Chrysostom (d. 407) and St Ambrose (d. 397) and most systematically Orosius (d. ca 418) in Spain, who developed a veritable theology of Augustus. Orosius construed the reign of Augustus as a mysterious indicator, typologically, of the coming of Jesus: his closing of the temple of Janus was taken as foreshadowing the Epiphany of Christ who was indeed, from birth, included in the census, and was thus *ab initio* a Roman citizen.[48]

Thus both Augustus and Christ were types manifested in the person of the emperor. The Byzantine empire was the Roman empire, and the Basileus was the figure of Augustus Caesar. Correlatively, the emperor and the state he governed, by definition universal and œcumenical, constituted a manifestation of order divinely sanctioned. This was to lead, as we shall see, to much rivalry over the title to Romanity, and correlatively to true Christianity, between the Byzantines and the Latin and Germanic powers in Western Europe. Constantinople was designated *Nea Romē*, New Rome, a name that remained, like the designation of the emperors as the emperors of the Romans, in constant use throughout Byzantine history. Byzantines were merely the inhabitants of Constantinople, which had been founded where ancient Byzantion once stood. As an ecclesiastical title, Romanity still today forms part of the title of the patriarch of Constantinople.[49]

In its œcumenical Roman capacity, Constantinople was to be the defender of Christendom until the end of time. Its citizens were the new Chosen People and Byzantium the New Israel, associations that were ingeniously crafted by Byzantine clerics out of Biblical references, complemented over time with Constantinian and other imperial references.[50] The condition of citizenship in this New Israel was naturally Christianity of the correct, Orthodox, creed. Theodosius' and Justinian's suppression and eventual eradication of pagan Hellenism and Romanity, which involved the silencing of the Delphic oracle, banning the Olympic games and the Eleusian mysteries, ransacking temples, closure of the school of Athens, and much else, are well known and need not be repeated here.

This process was doctrinally consecrated by precisely specifying the definition of citizenship as adherence to the right creed as agreed in the Councils of Nicaea (325) and Constantinople (381). It was further accentuated and crystallised in the context of Byzantine–Muslim wars. This also involved the elaboration of the idea of holy war which was deployed in the context of these wars, defensive in the seventh and eighth centuries and offensive in the tenth and eleventh. It was also used in wars to recover territories lost to Charlemagne's claims to Romanity, and in a ceaseless series of offensive and defensive wars in eastern Europe and the Caucasus, some of which had the ostensible aim of Christianising the Slavic peoples.[51] There emerged in this context a sort of official religious ethnology which construed the history of specific races as the anti-history of heresy: Arians first, then Armenians (curiously at a time that saw the Armenianisation of the Byzantine imperial house) and finally Latins.[52]

This œcumenism was to be conveyed to other components and analogues of the Orthodox Byzantine polity, particularly to the Slavic polities of Bulgaria, Serbia, and Russia. The Byzantine emperor was, in Eusebius' phrase, 'the Universal Sovereign',[53] and the Byzantine emperors thought of themselves as the Caesars of every Christian in the world. Constantine's letter to the Sasanian King of Persia – who equally cherished ideas of a universal monarchy which would encompass the whole inhabited world[54] – in defence of Persian Christians indicated the thrust of the monarchical idea that sustained it: that the one emperor of Christians corresponding to the one God in Heaven is a universal sovereign of all Christians everywhere. The expansion of the kingdom of God and of empire were coterminous.[55] In the same spirit, Patriarchs of Constantinople affirmed imperial authority over Russia and, derivatively, their own authority over the Russian clergy who, until the middle of the thirteenth century, were headed by a Greek Metropolitan sent from Constantinople.[56]

The suggestiveness of this idea of universality centred in Constantinople around the person of the emperor was such that the rulers of even strong independent states following the Romano–Christian Byzantine model not only recognised the title to universality, but sought ratification for their rule from the Basileus. We shall see that this model paralleled in the relation between the Caliphate and independent provinces and overlords. Universality was a title all the more ostentatiously used after the crowning of Charlemagne in AD 800.[57] Even the most burdensome and humiliating Byzantine agreements with other, stronger states were drawn up in the form of privileges granted by the emperor, much as he granted privileges to his subjects.[58] This was the sole political language of sovereignty available in the domains of Orthodoxy. Thus, when the powerful Simeon of Bulgaria (893–927) felt able to practice ritual and official independence, he wished not to eradicate Byzantium, but to substitute his own state for the universal state based in Constantinople in the terms of the latter. He settled for less, as did other Balkan potentates of equivalent power, such as the Serb Stepan Dušan (1331–55).[59] When Mehmet II conquered Constantinople, he inherited the œcumenical role of his defeated foe and adopted the title of Kayser-i Rūm, Caesar of the Romans.[60]

Thus the Byzantine motifs that were carried to Moscow by its patriarchate, which was subordinate to that of Constantinople, came locally into their own with the Ottoman conquest of Constantinople in 1453. With this event, the idea of Holy Russia was born, signalling 'the entry of Russia into the Middle Ages', according to one scholar.[61] Lore based on Biblical typological interpretation, of a blonde people destined to rule and, later, to restore the Roman empire based in Constantinople, was fused with Byzantine motifs to generate the idea that Muscovy became the land of the Elect, the epiphany of Israel, centred around a capital, Moscow, which with the fall of Constantinople had become the Third Rome ruled by the inheritors at once of the Byzantine and Roman emperors. Ivan III (r. 1462–1505) was dubbed the New Constantine of Moscow.[62] Thus the transformation of this motif into the motif of Moscow as the New Jerusalem was effortless, and entailed its own visible enunciation. Until 1453 Hagia Sophia had embodied the Church for the Russians; afterwards the Church of the Resurrection in Jerusalem acquired this status and an exact replica of it was built near Moscow.[63] Correlatively, Russian sovereigns in the sixteenth century, including Ivan IV Grozny (the Stern – usually rendered as Ivan the Terrible), who reigned during the period 1533–1584, claimed not only a typological continuity with Augustus, but a consanguinity between the Russian Tsars and emperors of Rome[64] that was over and above their relationship through Ivan's grandmother, who had belonged to the Palaeologi imperial family of Byzantium and was the niece of the last Byzantine emperor.

It is, in this context, hardly surprising that Byzantine political commentary was hostile to the very idea of a Roman Pope declaring a Crusade which it regarded as an usurpation of imperial prerogatives. The Crusade involved, among other things, the sacrilegious notion of warring monks, in addition to soteriological and eschatological elements not shared by Byzantines, including the idea of a papal army.[65] This was all over and above the entirely justified perception of a Latin menace to Byzantium. With the sacking of Constantinople by Crusaders in 1204, indeed, the infidel was no longer so much the Turk, with whom a *modus vivendi* had long been established, including princely matrimonial alliances, as the Latin.[66]

Hence it was difficult for Byzantines to swallow the decree of the union of churches agreed at the Council of Florence in 1439, and vigorous resistance was shown to it until the very end of Byzantium by those who had more trust in God's help against the Turks than in that of the Latins.[67] Subsequent events were to prove them right. The union had caused such disarray that the last Byzantine emperor remained uncrowned because of questions about the legitimacy of the pro-union Patriarch, and of the Emperor's failure to add his voice to this opposition.[68] It says a lot, incidentally, about Byzantine imperial iconography that the seals and coins issued by the last emperor nevertheless represented him with a crown.[69]

Ultimately, Byzantium and papal Rome were both literally and metaphorically, at once a Rome and an anti-Rome. The city of Rome not only had associations with the Augustan empire but also a positive eschatological value which replaced the earlier layer of negative eschatology associated with the Book of Daniel.[70] Much the same body of political ideas that constituted the Byzantine empire floated amongst Barbarians in Western Europe for whom Constantinople, the New Rome, was far less handy than the original. This body of ideas was complicated by the disunity that prevailed in territories under Barbarian rule. It is attested, for instance, that the throne, the purple, and the diadem were in use amongst Arian Vandal kings from the 530s at the latest; kings habitually acted according to *imitatio imperii*.[71] Barbarian kings, in fact independent, conceived of their rule as by imperial sanction. The Byzantine emperor in 508 conferred upon Clovis an honorary consulate, patriciate, and regalia, implying that the Frank's victories over the Visigoths were victories for the empire.[72] Despite the patent state of imperial disaggregation and the calamitous reverses suffered in the East and all around the Mediterranean at the hands of the Arabs, and despite scepticism in Western Europe of ideas of a Christian œcumene, most particularly in Spain as theorised in Isidore of Seville's denial of political universalism, there is much to suggest that it was not only ceremonial and other paradigms that were devolved and used, but also the idea of a Christian *res publica* surviving until the end of time, as suggested in the prophecies of Daniel.[73]

Thus matters went further than the construal of Merovingian kings as Solomons and Davids, or the designation of Frankish kings as *minister dei.* More was involved than the designation by Pope Paul I (757–767) of the Frankish aristocracy as the chosen race, or the conception of the Franks generally, through the anointing of their kings, as a New Israel.[74] This did not exclude the view, prevalent among the Franks, that Byzantine royal aesthetics were excessive or that kings should be more humble in their statements concerning their relations with God.[75] Romanity was in general regarded as coterminous with civilised order, whatever the facts of contemporary reality which might have rendered this notion incongruous. Romanity was, moreover, identified as the fourth world-monarchy which was to last until the Second Coming. Yet conditions changed, and the idea became to some extent congruent with reality with the emergence in the eighth century of the Frankish *Grossreich* and the inclusion within it of Rome.[76] Roman power and authority in the West thus devolved to the Carolingians, which historical writing construed as *translatio imperii*, a concept designating the transfer of custody over the Roman empire from one people to another.[77]

But for present purposes the crucial point is that the cleavage which emerged over the centuries culminating in the great schism between Orthodox and Catholic Christianity in 1054, or between the Orthodox and the Latins, was far more profound in its political complexion than a dispute over the custody of Romanity. It was a cleavage written into the very distinctive conceptions of kingship, Byzantine and Latin. These sustained divergent notions of the relative position of kings with respect to God on the one hand, and subjects on the other, a position adulterated and disaggregated by the presence in western Europe of the papacy. From the eleventh century in particular the papacy was an institution of anti-kings, as it were, to which kings counterposed postures of themselves as virtual anti-popes. The 'infinite cross-relations between Church and state, active in every century of the Middle Ages, produced hybrids in either camp,' in which the mutual borrowing of insignia, prerogatives, titulature, and much else affected 'in the early Middle Ages, chiefly the ruling individuals, both spiritual and secular, until finally the *sacerdotium* held an imperial appearance and the *regnum* a clerical touch.'[78] Even the martial vocabulary of kings entered into ecclesiastical usage: *gladius* was often used by Patristic authors to refer to the coercive and punitive power of the state, and it was indeed so used in Roman law. Among Carolingian authors, the term began to be applied to spiritual power.[79] And, in 1150, Bernard of Clairvaux gave the notion a practical turn by formulating the idea of the Crusade under Papal direction.[80]

In Byzantium, religious and political conceptions and vocabularies were fully entwined in the context of a state that was a *corpus politicum mysticum*,[81] a mystical body politic. Indeed, it appears meaningless to speak of the distinctiveness of the one or the other; both belong to the register of mystical majesty. The Latin West produced a decidedly different line of evolution. This involved, in theory at least, church and state as distinct entities which did not produce, and could not develop into, a theocracy, although they interpenetrated conceptually and socially, and cast themselves in the image each other. The isomorphy between church and state, pope and king, divine and terrestrial order, for all its force, remained ever emergent, and never seems to have developed into a complete correspondence of the one with the other. This Western distinctiveness, as was suggested, was already implicit in the Augustinian and other Latin positions. Its imputation to Byzantium, often made in works of scholarship, appears to be 'a historical and philological error'.[82] It is a projection eastwards of certain Latino-Catholic clerical theories, though certainly not of all trends contained within Latin theories of kingship which did not necessarily subordinate royal power to episcopal authority, nor did they always involve the primacy of hierocratic notions.[83]

Yet this does not in any way imply a simplistic suggestion of the familiar cliché about Church and State, the one indicating a clergy in control of higher ends and the other referring to lay rulers overseeing more mundane matters and acting merely as the secular arm of the church. This stereotype is common in modern scholarship no less than with medieval ecclesiastical authors. For the Latin West had also available the corpus of Eusebian ideas regarding state and faith, king and Christ. These ideas, most particularly of the divine election of kings and their quasi-sacerdotal character, were indeed very widely used, most particularly by Barbarian and later Carolignian kings followed by other kings in conflict with popes.[84] In the context of this conflict of papacy and empire, the distinction between temporal and spiritual, a distinction emphasised by Augustine, was also widely deployed, in what amounted to 'a political Averroeism'. This was complemented by imperial practical encroachment into the domain of the Church, although such encroachment was not expressed theoretically, as this possibility had been foreclosed by centuries of theorising ecclesiastical prerogatives. It was instead 'diffused'[85] and took the form of piecemeal liturgical and ritual attributions and roles.[86]

But Eusebian ideas, at the hands of clerical authors, seem to have been transposed in distinctive ways, and to have come into their own from the eleventh century in tandem with the invigorated imperial papacy which managed to strip from the emperor the authority to appoint the pope, investing it instead in the College of Cardinals. These ideas were, under the influence of Ambrose and Augustine, spiritualised to a great extent. Ambrose held as agnostic a view of Romanity as he did of empire.[87] Yet in terms of this Augustinianism, deployed against empire, the state could and was regarded to a certain degree as the executive and secular instrument of salvation whose key lay with the Pope. Kingship may indeed be granted by grace of God, but it was the Church that mediated this grace, and as such *regnum* and *sacerdotium* could both be contained in the concept of the Church.[88] Simultaneously, the hierocracy construed itself along monarchical lines. Priesthood imitated kingship, and the papacy imitated empire, just as empire had imitated priesthood. The Roman papacy used the example of Rome under Constantine to the extent of construing, in the eleventh century, the *pontifex Romanus* as Caesar and the College of Cardinals as the Senate. Papal coronations developed fast. Pope Gregory VII in 1075 asserted his exclusive right to imperial insignia, and a Lateran inscription of 1125 proclaimed the Pope to be a royal priest and an imperial bishop (*regalis sacerdos, imperialis episcopus*).[89]

These notions were built upon ideas of monarchical humility and papal primacy reflecting, first, the situation in the Patristic age in the West when Pope Gelasius (492–496) insisted on the distinction between pontifical and regal domains and argued that emperors (of Byzantium) should abjure the sacral character of their office. He was, in effect, arguing against the notion of a priest-king. This trend was reinforced by the forged *Constitutio Constantini* (The Donation of Constantine) of the eighth century, in which Constantine is claimed to have granted to the Roman Papacy the power and privileges of empire in the West, although it does seem that the early as distinct from the late medieval importance of this forgery is somewhat exaggerated.[90]

The fundamental flaw in the papal theory of relations between papacy and empire, of course, was that 'no pope could ever find an emperor who would accept the subordinate role devised for him.'[91] Both empire and papacy were acts of divine grace, and both Eusebian and Augustinian–Gelasian motifs were deployed by both parties to this struggle over the period of many centuries. When an emperor like Charlemagne did succeed in asserting an authority over the Church which paralleled that of Byzantine emperors, his claim to authority was made not on the basis of a Christian Hellenism, but on a distinctively Western European conception of the state's function within the Church.[92] This conception made it possible to produce, in the twelfth century, the notion that the emperor should ideally be the vassal of St Peter and of his vicar, the Pope.[93] Western kings were never able to develop an autonomous sacrality, but were always part of an hierarchical system in which sacrality was formally, symbolically, and ritually monopolised by the Church.[94] This also led to the development by the popes of a notion of royal competence and incompetence, and an aggressively profane conception of kingship yielding the idea of impeachment of a *rex inutilis*[95].

Such a notion would have been inconceivable in Byzantium. This was not only because of the direct exercise of imperial authority over the church, which had intermittent and occasionally had vigorous parallels in Western European history. Justinian understood imperial power as placing the spiritual sphere in imperial custody for the proper functioning of the sacerdotal order.[96] After all, the political order headed by the emperor and the kingdom of God were coterminous. Indeed, although a clerical hierarchy did very much exist in Byzantium, it produced no hierocratic theory and claimed no monopoly of active participation in the church which, after all, comprised all Christians.

Byzantine ecclesiastics, moreover, did not claim to be the unique mouthpiece of God.[97] The parallels with later and contemporary Muslim polities of the *umma* are manifest.

The fact that the patriarch crowned the Byzantine emperor from about AD 450[98] – a long evolution from military acclamation to liturgification which did not exclude secular elements in ceremonial, paralleling certain features of later Carolingian coronations[99] – did not indicate that the investiture with the crown was essentially a clerical act, although it was eminently religious.[100] Crowning by the Patriarch of Constantinople was not the only visible manifestation of divine election of the emperor; his choice and acclamation by the army, representing the *vox populi*, was an act divinely inspired, and behind which the *vox dei* was omnipresent.[101] Divine choice is polyphonic and multivalent, though it converges in the person of the emperor.

The entire corpus of rule was, as we have seen, mystical in many senses, and depended for this on the office of the emperor. The existence of the Byzantine Church was inconceivable without that of empire, or at least of a state that would confer ecclesiastical office upon the Patriarch. After the conquest of Constantinople by the Ottomans it was the Sultan who enthroned the monk Gennadius, a vocal anti-unionist, as patriarch, and gave him the insignia of office: the robes, staff, and pectoral cross.[102] This could not have been possible had the head of state also held the papal attributes claimed by the notion of Caesaro-Papism. Such a notion is inappropriate for describing the office of Basileus, not least because it is anachronistic, projects an alien Western historical development onto Byzantium, implies the parity of offices, and is historically very much an oversimplification.[103]

The 'vague imperial priesthood' of the Byzantine emperor[104] was decidedly consequential. Byzantine emperors were holy persons, to whom the epithet *hiereus* was always applied according to the decisions of the Council of Chalcedon in 451 and the Synod of Constantinople in 499.[105] The one occasion of papal refusal to acknowledge this title was by Gregory II (pope 715–731), who was not so much expressing objection to the principle as resisting the iconoclasm of Leo the Isaurian (675–741).[106] The privileges endowed on the church by the emperor emanate from him[107] as a supralegal and supracanonical authority. Being *nomos empsychos*, as we have seen, the emperor was a nomothete. Constantine was not only a New David and a new Solomon, but the 13th Apostle, and the imperial personality had mystical – indeed mystagogic – extension.[108]

The Eusebian programme was worked out in endowing the emperor with priestly attributes,[109] which if not hierocratic were at least spiritual, both theorised and enunciated in terms of ritual. Such, for instance, were the ritual privileges allowed to the emperor from which all were debarred except the patriarch; or the emperor's receipt from the Patriarch of the Eucharist, which was not received by the laity; or a number of legal privileges enjoyed by the emperor, along with members of his family, and shared with clerics [110]. But the Emperor was not quite a cleric: he stood above clergy and laity alike as God's representative, a matter that detracted from neither his sacred – not sacerdotal[111] – character, nor from the exclusiveness of the priestly class into which, by rhetorical inversion, he was initiated as a *depotatos*, the lowest rank in the ecclesiastical hierarchy.[112] Although the Byzantines did not make as much of anointment as did Latin Christians, the emperor was nevertheless the Lord's anointed, the patriarch being simply anointed 'in the spirit'.[113] The paradigm of despotism is here complete.

Hierarchy (*taxiarchia*) is a general description of all order, and this order is maintained by autocracy, of which the clergy form a part. Having soteriological significance, any breach of imperial order became sacrilege. For *taxis*, the economy of the world in general, is but a manifestation of the divine economy contained in the design of the world. The executor and enforcer of the worldly economy is the emperor, who also rules over space and time themselves as *Kosmokrator* and *Chronokrator*, only a shade more specific in his approach, asymptotic as it is, to the omnipotence of Christ, the *Pantocrator*.[114]

Virtue and Order

There were parallels to these notions of imperial œcumenism and transhistorical relevance in other, faraway politico-religious traditions. Buddhist monarchs were equally acclaimed as universal sovereigns who stemmed from a real or metaphorical lineage so ancient as to be coterminous with the instauration of order at the very beginning of civilised sociality.

According to an early Buddhist text, the *Aggañña Sutta*, humanity in each cosmic cycle (without inaugural beginnings, in accordance with Buddhist principles) arose out of the increasing materiality of primal, exalted, and formless Brahma-beings: giving in to desire, they ate increasingly substantial food and thus descended to a lower condition, a process repeated at successive stages until humanity was thus begotten.[115] Thus humanity itself was born of divine degeneration. It does not appear that the emergence of kingship to arrest the process of degeneration, as we shall see later, implies partaking of divinity by this particular avenue. The 'parabolic movement ... from king to Bodhisatta King (Buddha) back to king again' that we have encountered already appears a separate process by which kings acquire divinity or quasi-divinity by association with a deified and crowned Buddha and members of the Buddhist and related Panthea. When anthropomorphic images of the Buddha began to appear – these are generally though not universally dated from the beginning of the Common Era – the tradition we have already encountered concerning the 32 somatic marks of kingship played an important role in iconography. The historiography of the Buddha came increasingly to represent him in royalist terms, as a *Ćakkavatti*, through the symbols of which he came to be represented and venerated in rituals intimately connected with sacral kingship. Later, from the middle centuries of the first millennium of the Common Era, certain circles, Mahayanist in all probability, carried the royal symbolism of Buddhahood to such an extent that the very images of the Buddha came to be crowned.[116]

This and much else bespeaks a profound and seemingly rapid transformation of early Buddhist motifs and their rapid constitution by means of Brahminical notions of kingship, which is made the carrier of *dhamma*. Impersonal, the *dhamma* is embodied in a king who also embodies the essence of various Vedic and post-Vedic Brahminical divinities. The king embodies divinity, and he also wields the *dhamma* and maintains it as a custodian or a vicar of this impersonal force which rules nature, and might with a righteous king rule society. Thus the righteous king in his embodiment of the *dhamma*, the *dhammarāja*, moves on from the Brahminical idea of *rājadharma* by which Brahmins sanctified kingship by ascribing a dharmic character to royal action. Indeed, in Burmese royal ritual of the Pagan period (849–1287), Brahmin and *bhikkhu* (Buddhist monk) complemented one another.[117] The whole evolution of Buddhist kingship in Ceylon, whose beginning is conventionally identified with the rule of Dutthagāmaṇī (r. ca

161–137 BC), like that in Southeast Asia, is marked by a certain Sanskritisation, and by confirmations and reconfirmations involving the receipt of sacred relics from India which confirmed the Buddha's authority.[118]

This indicates that since the person of the king was thought to embody the *dhamma*, he became in a sense *dhamma* incarnate and personalised, and was therefore doubly sacralised: in his connection with Brahminical gods, and in his dhammic vocation, for the *dhamma*, albeit impersonal and atheistic, nevertheless possesses all the attributes of the sacred. The *dhamma* is endowed with a charisma which, in invigilating the state, transforms the latter into a mystical entity, and causes its 'apotheosis'.[119] The *dhamma* is, moreover, construed according to images of sovereignty and royal transcendence.[120] An entire body of *dhammasattha* literature arose in medieval South-east Asia outlining virtuous and wise conduct incumbent upon social collectivities, and in these texts royal actions and functions are not set forth separately from those emanating from other sources or incumbent upon others. A comprehensive scheme of conduct is set out, to be invigilated by the *dhammarāja*.[121]

It might be recalled here that this literature incorporated worldly, pragmatic, non-ethical matters which had provided the substance of the Brahminical literature on *arthaśāstra*. Both constitute works of what later came to provide the substance for *Fürstenspiegel*, though less dependent on *exempla* than the latter. Among other developments, the Burmese kings of the Pagan period prompted the composition a literature of *dhammaśāstras*, Pali equivalents of Sanskritik *dhammaśāstras*, which were to develop into the Thai *Thammasat*. In this body of writing, Hindu traditional and religious material was left out, and the result was a secular code of royal action which used the name of Manu as an authority, although Manu was here represented in a Buddhist aspect as the servant of the *Māhasammata*, the first ruler of the world.[122]

The wheels deployed by the king are represented as a wheel of the *dhamma* (*dhammaćakka*) and the wheel of command (*āṇāćakka*). These run parallel, like the wheels of a chariot; yet each has its own particular register. The distinction between these notions, very profound and articulated in terms of an elaborate vocabulary,[123] is smothered by the rhetorical and discursive assertiveness of the notion of *dhammarāja*. This notion seems to have increasingly incorporated arthaśastric elements – comprising the elements of instrumental political and social action by kings

– with the spread and crystallisation of Buddhist polities, many of which had replaced, by royal decree, Brahminism by Buddhism, and, as we have seen throughout, retained multifarious elements from the former. If the Buddhist kings of Thailand or of Burma were described as *dhammarāja*, therefore, they brought to the impersonal charisma of the *dhamma* a charisma of their own, deriving not only from the inherent mystique of royalty and of all power, but also from the associations of individual sovereigns with members of the Vedic and post-Vedic pantheon. At ground level, the authentication of royal connections with divinity in medieval Southeast Asian Buddhist polities enlisted the tutelary spirits and *genii* of the local folk.[124]

This charisma was treated and distributed much as Byzantine emperors distributed their icons and other regalia in the provinces. Aśoka is reported to have sent out visible tokens of himself, having distributed relics around his empire and housed them in the innumerable stupas he built, thus establishing his 'ritual hegemony'.[125] Like all pre-modern polities, centralisation was technically very difficult to achieve,[126] and hegemony was always relative and exercised by many means, including ritual and mystical, so that 'the raja of rajas was more a presiding apical ordinator than a totalitarian authority.'[127] Indeed, the cosmological idiom that we have encountered earlier, imbricated with the sacredness of royal space, 'if read correctly, can be shown to be a realistic reflection of the political pulls and pushes of the centre-oriented but centrifugally fragmenting polities. In this instance myth and reality are closer than we think.'[128]

Just as by rendering dhammic the social order by means of representing polity as a sacred space presided over by a representative – and also the incarnation – of divinity, so also were royal genealogies means for sacralising royal time, or the time of society under a dynasty, in a manner that is roughly parallel to the enterprise of Eusebius, and later with the caliphate. The *Ćakkavatti* ideal was associated with a mythic cycle concerning the acquisition by the righteous king of the wheel and its return to the ocean. It was also associated with a mundane, if great, time – that of ancient 'Aryan' kings who ruled in exceptionally propitious times. Like them, *Ćakkavatti*s are to appear in the future to restore just order.[129]

Kings of Southeast Asia habitually drew up worldly genealogies for themselves which ran alongside these symbolic genealogies. In these genealogies, they stood metonymically for great *Ćakkavatti*s of the past, paradigmatic among whom was of course Aśoka. These genealogies also often involved miraculous geneses establishing continuity of statehood personalised in a succession of kings culminating in present sovereigns.[130] King Kyansittha of Pagan in Burma (1084–1112) associated his own spiritual genealogy – that is, his previous lives – with kingship in the Indian holy cities of Benares and Patna, and with the classical kingdom of Pyus in Burma. His royal–spiritual itinerary was to be continued in the future, when he was to be reborn on a still higher plane as a Buddha and saviour of the world.[131] In a very comprehensive way, a sixteenth century genealogy of the Thai kingdom of Chiangmai, like many others, portrayed the state as a primordial order, in which kingship and Buddhism were coterminous. Much like other representations of this genre – in Buddhist as well as monotheistic polities, like the Muhammadan beginning or the Immaculate Conception – miraculous genesis sets the beginning of relevant time, and subsequent history is constant repetition. Throughout, the peoples over whom kings preside are wholly subsumed in the king, and have no independent existence.[132]

It does not seem that in these situations the *sangha* had a role which in any way paralleled or directly continued the actions of the kings, on behalf of things sacred and sublime, on their subjects. The monastic order supplied the intellectuals who wrote histories and genealogies, mediated magically between subjects and gods and between kings and gods, and supplied the local forms of an overweening Buddhist royalism. Periodic 'purifications' of the *sangha* by kings throughout the histories of Ceylon and of South-east Asia, involving the drawing up of institutes for its internal workings and its material wealth, constantly reasserted royal authority, and it appears that strong ecclesiastical hierarchies materialised under strong kings and became shadowy under weak ones.[133] At the limit, as in nineteenth century Bali, it appears that priests were emblems of the king's sanctity, parts of his regalia.[134]

Yet the *sangha* keeps the conscience of the *dhamma*, most particularly when the actions of kings according to the *āṇā*, reason of state, contravene precepts of action according to the *dhamma*,[135] at least in theory. But it is by reason of a state within a state instituted as a moral entity that kings rule, for the genealogy of the state is decidedly worldly. It has already been indicated that Buddhist political literature had taken over and adapted Brahminical political writing, the paradigm of which was Kauṭliya's *Arthaśāstra*, a text probably written for the Mauryan King Chandragupta, who came to the throne in 321 BC,[136] and very widely used for the instruction of princes over many centuries in Ceylon and South-east Asia.[137] This last was centrally structured around the notion of politics as the art of *daṇḍanīti*, the wielding of *daṇḍa*, the rod of kingship. This and the sceptre of kingship were, in Buddhist writings, replaced by the wheel, which bespoke the incorporation of affairs of worldly command into modes of expression that bestowed upon them an association with the *dhamma*, an association which rhetorically delivered the idea of subsumption. Thus came about Aśoka's 'linguistic innovation':[138] *dhamma-vijaya* (conquest by *dhamma*), *dhamma-sambandha* (kingship based on the *dhamma*), *dhamma-rati* (pleasure in *dhamma*), and many other terms similarly suffixed, which transposed conventional Brahminical notions into another moral and doctrinal key, without necessarily changing their sense. This sense is merely set alongside a moral and religious ideal of *dhamma* which, as if by contagion and contiguity, suffuses and structures its meaning – much in the same way that the sharʿist epithet is applied to a variety of acts and notions in Muslim discourses, as we shall see.

Indeed, the notion of good and just order incorporated in the notion of *dhamma* was certainly not absent from Brahminical traditions. It appears in Vedic literature under the highly complex term *ṛta*.[139] The same term, along with *asha*, was used in ancient Iranian writings to denote the same complex of ideas. What *dharmaśāstra* works do is to transfer the share of *karma* from the Brahmin to the king, from whence it flows down to his subjects, and this flow is controlled by the king's just use of *daṇḍa*.

Kings emulate the energetic action of the gods. In this way, after the Asokan paradigm which permeates Buddhist political thinking and action, the king's creative and corrective role in human affairs is maintained, and 'the multiplier effect' of kingship on the conduct of human society is eloquently expressed.[140] As a complement to this, Brahminical literature from the *Mahābhārata* onwards tended to subordinate arthaśastric notions to *dharma*, and then proceeded to include both under the ambit of *rājadharma*:[141] So arose a situation in which moral and pragmatic matters were expressed in terms of each other, in which the one was seen, by mere declaration, to stand for the other. Muslim and Christian polities provide equally interesting instances of this rhetoric.

In all cases, kings were regarded as makers of their epochs, being the guarantors, in the fickle order of humanity, of order both pragmatic and moral, as indeed of order in general of which *dhamma* in the social world formed only part. The world, as we saw with reference to the ancient Near East, is characterised by the succession of order and disorder, which is the sole rhythm of a human history without a discernible worldly direction. The very foundation of kingship and of dhammic order is an answer to this vexed and chronic threat of disorder:

> The centuries of Sinhalese history, like that of each people, are written in blood. Intrigue follows intrigue. Parricides appear *seriatim*. Subversion, treason, infamy, and unrest unfold in ritualistic regularity. The threat of disorder is constant, stayed only by strong monarchs who contain their adversaries. Whether viewed on the level of society or in the realm of man's spirit, the confrontation with disorder looms as a permanent vocation.[142]

Though there is a higher purpose in life, ultimate release (*mukti*) through the *nibbāna* (Sanskrit: *nirvāṇa*) for those who can achieve it, the precondition for this is economic sufficiency which can only be guaranteed by a stable order. The affinity of this to Sasanian and Muslim discourses on the Circle of Justice and on the twinning of religion and kingship will be evident later.

Hence the formation of kingship. There are a number of pre-histories of the state circulating in Buddhist works, all involving forms of degeneration of subtle beings, but they all concur that, with the differentiation of human functions, the need for a king arises out of lawlessness, violence, and avarice, and the king imposes order on human collectivities by applying to them the prerogatives of the rod.[143] We thus have a contractual notion of the state and of order which is at variance with the classical Brahminical view of the castes as original divine creations. The principles of order are thus timeless, and indeed, culture is fully nature. In the coming to be of kingship by contract is involved general assent (*mahājanasammata*), for the aim and function of kingship is the protection of family and property by the *dhamma*.[144] All this fits well with the Kauṭilyan Circle that was later to become central to thinking about the state in Muslim polities. Under the name of the Circle of Justice, this conception was attributed by Muslims to Persian royal wisdom. According to it, the ability of the king to rule is dependent on the treasury and the army, which in turn are dependent upon wealth and labour, which flow from agriculture and trade, which in turn, to flourish, depend on royal control[145].

The *dhamma* may be the lynchpin of this chain of interdependence, but it is only operative with the sanction of the rod, whose use, given the pessimistic view of human nature upon which this line of thinking is based, was seldom questioned. This sanction is embodied in the king whose attributes are variations on the theme of absolutism.[146] The correlation of absolute rule and justice, and between justice and the perpetuation of order is almost universal. In Zoroastrian Iran, the social organism, defined as caste hierarchy, is maintained by the maintenance of the distinctions within it and of the visible marks – ritual, vestimentary, and so forth – that signal these distinctions. The maintenance of this order is the median just order, an order without inflection or distortion, thus conforming both to truth and to righteousness – to *aśa/ṛta.*[147]

CHAPTER FOUR

An Interregnum: The Early Muslim Polity

The Arab imperial polities that emerged from the conquests of the seventh and eighth centuries brought to fruition the trends of Late Antiquity and their œcumenical thrust. First under the Umayyads (661–750) and later under the Abbasids (749–1258, 1261–1517) and their successor states, these new polities inherited and institutionalised the Achaemenean–Alexandrian project of bringing the lands of the Near East and Central Asia under the aegis of a unitary polity joined to the Mediterranean littoral. The eastward drift of Romanity was accentuated, but its thrust was detached from the Roman heartland at a time when the Roman provinces in Europe, including Gaul and Britain, had turned inwards and commenced an historical evolution very much of their own. Simultaneously, the westward drift of the Sasanians was consummated objectively in the world-empire formed by their erstwhile Arab vassals. Arab interest in the Dark Continent was confined to perfunctory forays into and colonisation of the southern Italian and, later, of Gallic littorals. Spain and Sicily, whose conquest was completed in 827, had always been lands of Romanity, and the defeat of the Arab army by the Franks at Poitiers in 751, seen generally in Western historiography as a decisive turning-point, was really no more than the repulsion of a raiding party, not of the forward army of occupation.

Muslim polities in constitution were thus the legatees of political languages and forms of enunciation of power, and of the relation of power to the sacred, that had grown out of various histories, 'Oriental' and Roman, and had interpenetrated and spread in many directions across what is often construed as the fault-line between Iranian and Hellenistic domains. Enunciative modes of power were thus homogenised to a certain extent, or rather reduced in time to a stable and fairly constant repertoire throughout the territories that were to be welded by Arab–Muslim imperialism into one vast economic zone, whose transactions stood in the Golden Age on pillars of relatively stable gold dinars and silver dirhams. Allied to an emergent political culture and to Muslim representations of the sacred, these territories, following endemic warfare and economic decline from the latter part of the ninth century, were able to preserve a very pronounced sense of urban cultural and institutional uniformity. In other words, this late antique world crystallised a repertoire of politico-cultural norms, called traditions, after a paradigm that was institutionalised by the Abbasids. This paradigm was discursively, aesthetically, and socially reproduced at provincial courts, later at the capitals of independent polities, all of which partook of it, adapted it, and regarded it as the natural œcumenical order of things.[1]

It is now anachronistic to presume that the Rightly-Guided caliphate (632–661), the primitive proto-Muslim polity at Medina and later briefly at Kūfa, had produced statutes and forms of state and of kingship of any determinative or definitive character that informed the later crystallisation of Muslim polities. The Muslim religion and the texts and exemplary genealogies that are ascribed to the formative period of Islam were later elaborations created over many generations in the light of conditions prevailing in polities the Arabs set up from Iraq and Syria. Elements derived from the slight Arab tradition of kingship, heavily impregnated by Byzantine and Iranian paradigms, were combined with the enduring heritage of Semitic religion, priesthood, and kingship. Muslim forms did not arise *ex nihilo*, nor quite simply from the writ of a Book; to propose otherwise is absurd in the light of historical reason.

The incipient, experimental forms that kingship took in Damascus and Ḥarrān, under the Umayyad caliphal signature, were selections of materials from a repertoire that was available. The same could be said of the later, more decided and definitive forms produced in Baghdad and Sāmarrā'. These were far more tightly articulated and connected to an internal monarchical dynamic which had established itself firmly and which, by the reign of al-Ma'mūn (r. 813–833), had freed itself of the last vestiges of the Arab tribal polity by the abolition of the *dīwān*. These forms crystallised and were propagated throughout the Muslim œcumene. Various innovations were added to the Baghdadian norms by the Fatimids (909–1171), first at Mahdiyya and later in

Cairo, and these were to enter the standard repertoire of the Syro–Egyptian Ayyubid (1169–ca. 1260) and Mamluk (1250–1517) polities.

Emphasis must be placed on the length of this process of crystallisation, which took place under the effect of factors both exogenous and endogenous to the constitutive Arab elements of this polity. It might be compared with the equally long process by which 'Islamic art' was generated – even the arabesque, or what was later to be called the arabesque, did not acquire the distinctive form associated with Muslim domains before the tenth century.[2] Centuries were to elapse before 'classical Muslim' forms were generated. It must also be added that Arabic sources themselves do not warrant the assumption that definite forms or ideas of government existed at Medina, or that they could be deduced from deeds and statements of the Prophet of Islam, Abu'l-Qāsim Muḥammad b. ʿAbd Allāh of the Hāshimid clan among the Meccan tribe of Quraysh.[3] This is so not only because the history of the first years of the Muslim polity is particularly obscure, in spite of the richly detailed, but not wholly convincing, picture of it produced by classical Muslim sources and reproduced in modern textbooks; the consummateness ascribed to this early period runs contrary to the normal course of historical events, even altogether extraordinary ones like the Muslim conquests.

What did exist throughout the Arabian Peninsula on the eve of Islam were various paradigms and usages of kingship which accompanied the staggered formation of relatively large-scale but intermittent dominions centred around courts located on the edges of the desert. To these one must of course add the ancient tradition of south Arabian kingship, made possible and sustained by agricultural and trade surpluses. These polities, especially those of northern Arabia, appropriated, indeed conspicuously consumed, royal goods and prerogatives without these enunciations of power becoming in their turn generalised as political cultures. Some of these dynasties were Christian, as with both dynasties at the northern fringes of Arabia, the one (the Lakhmids in the East) allied to Persia and the other (the Ghassanids in the West) to Byzantium. It might be assumed that the former had no specifically religious notions of polity over and above what was prevalent in Sasanian domains regarding the divine associations and charisma of the king; there is no evidence whatsoever that Syriac literature, produced under Sasanian patronage, took an interest in political matters or in any matter that was not ecclesiastical,[4] in sharp contrast to Græcophone Christianity, as we have seen. East and Southeast Arabia were in any case heavily influenced by Zoroastrian royal norms.

Nor would it be legitimate to claim, in any consequential way, that Muslim polities were formed according to Koranic paradigms of rule. Sacred canon is of course never univocal. It is, rather, a quarry of discrete textual units which are forever being valorised in very diverse historical contexts. In this sense, the meaning of canonical texts is inexhaustible, not because of some mystery that inheres in them and is ever removed from mortal comprehension by an asymptotic distance, but because the very canonicity attributed to them is ever constituted and reconstituted by a hermeneutic appropriate to specific conditions of interpretation and of valorisation. This applies irrespective of the vexed question concerning the historicity of early Muslim narratives and the related question of the early history of canonical composition, a matter which has been hardly broached for the Koran or for the *ḥadīth* (prophetic traditions).[5]

In the same vein, one can hardly overstress the salience of anachronism in both the traditional Muslim narratives and modern scholarship based upon them. Of special pertinence in the present context is the projection into the first century of Islam of formal theological disputes and debates over the nature of political authority by medieval heresiographers and theologians by modern scholars who paraphrase, to a great degree uncritically, the narratives that occur in these medieval sources. There were indeed social conflicts and political disputes of politico-doctrinal implication in the first century of Islam, but these were localised and episodic, and do not constitute so much the actual origins of later formal and concerted formulations, as much as symbolic origins cast as justificatory genealogies, as pre-figurations in a mode of historical construal in which typology plays a very substantial role. These conflicts – the paradigm for them was that between the Umayyads and ʿAlids – were over genealogical legitimism, running parallel to a religious register, that of religio-genealogical or priestly legitimism. They are best studied as part of an historical anthropology of early Muslim kingship, not a study of the classical Muslim forms which are the subject of this book. There is no reason, for example, to assume, as is generally done, that the Kharijites implied a doctrinal as distinct from sociopolitical practical notion of appurtenance to or exclusion from Islam, or to ascribe to early ʿAlids later notions of the imamate that needed a very long genesis.[6]

All political traditions, conceptions, and institutions that arose in the course of Muslim histories gradually came to be enunciated with discrete, *ad hoc*, references to the Koran and to the prophetic archetype. Others were related to events that occurred ostensibly in the course of the Umayyad–ʿAlid conflict. Yet any perusal of the various medieval Arabic works of Koranic exegesis would reveal that scholars definitely did not pursue political readings of the holy text but interpreted discrete verses from it politically only in other discursive contexts. The political exegesis of the Koran is a thoroughly modern literary form. Indeed, if one were to read the Koran and the *ḥadīth*, one would not be left with the impression of a definite conception of rulership, except for a general charter of sublime absolutism not far removed from previous monotheistic conceptions that were classically expressed by Eusebius, tempered here and there with appeal to the tribal spirit of consensus or to an episodic anti-hubristic ethic of fraternity, common mortality, and equality before God

In all, there is the image of a God beyond limitation, including moral limitation, whose omnipotence is truly beyond good and evil. In a manner analogous to the Byzantine polity, Muslim polities construed a formal theology of kingship which was complemented by a distinctive practical theology of kingship, evident in actions and iconographies from which it can be read and inferred. In its elevation of the king-caliph to sublime heights by analogies and typologies, this practical theology of power was out of tune with the limitations required by formal theology, which stresses the indivisible sovereignty of God. It was not long before the image of divine omnipotence was copied by kings as an attribute of their sublime status and of their election, and concretised this by the floating paradigms of royal enunciation and sublime analogies and correspondences that Late Antiquity had made available.

The particular stamp which made Muslim forms evolve a certain distinctiveness was not generic, but one of reference to a specific historico-prophetic genealogy. The caliph was a king who presided over an order divinely desired, what later came generically to be known as the *sharīʿa*, the Arabic equivalent to *nomos*, *dhamma* and *maʿāt*. His expertise lay in 'the craft of kingship'[7] which is the craft of politics (*siyāsa*): the king's appropriate knowledge is of political skill, his equipment consists of soldiery and aides and governors and servitors, his material is his subjects, the result is his salvation.[8] The analytical distinction in formal discourse between the regal and religio-legal aspects is imperative. It was specifically noted by many medieval Muslim authors and will be taken up in detail in what follows.[9]

Relatively new to the world of œcumenism and empire, early Umayyad caliphs sought to inscribe themselves into a universal history of world-empire. This was displayed, for example, in a painting at the Umayyad castle of Quṣayr ʿAmra, which portrayed the six kings of the world (including those of Byzantium, Abyssinia, and Persia) paying homage to the new Arab master of the world. It can also be found in the claim by Yazīd III (r. 744) that he was the rightful descendant not only of his grandfather and founder of his royal line, Marwān b. al-Ḥakam (r. 684–5), but also of Chosroes and of Caesar – this last term referring to the Byzantine monarchy.[10] Emblematic objects of universal sovereignty, real or imaginary, were rapidly and actively acquired by the caliphs[11] as emblematic means of inscription within a history of universal sovereignty. At once wondrous and unique, these objects were replete with the indivisible uniqueness of sovereignty, and simultaneously fulfilled in a wonderful manner functions required by kingship and by its craft of ruling over an essentially unruly humanity. One such object was reputedly a mirror brought from the Sindh to Muʿāwiya b. Abī Sufyān, the first Umayyad caliph (r. 661–680), or, according to another report, given to Marwān b. Muḥammad, the last Umayyad (r. 744–750), by an unnamed Rabbi. This mirror, which the Abbasids were said to have taken over until it disappeared, enabled its user to see the reflection of things happening at a distance. It was said to have been originally given by God to Adam to facilitate communication amongst his progeny, from whom it passed to Solomon and his successors.[12] Another such wonderful object seized by the Abbasids from their predecessor dynasty was a banquet-table of Indian royal origin which prevented whoever ate from it from satiety; yet another was a certain stone from which knife-handles were carved, which sweated if food served to the sovereign were laced with poison.[13] The history of such objects is sometimes related in detail, as are the erratic appearances of a certain precious stone, taken over from the Sasanians, which assured the death of its owner if inscribed – with what is not indicated.[14]

Many less wondrous objects were taken over for particular purposes, or at least experimented with. The necklace and throne as insignia of royalty are reported for pre-Islamic Arabs at least once, with reference to the Arab leper king of Ḥīra, Jadhīma al-Abrash, the contemporary and ally of Ardashīr, the founder of the Sasanian dynasty in the third century.[15] It is also clear that it was the Umayyad governors of Iraq, veritable viceroys of the East, and others in the milieu of Kūfa which descended in many important ways from traditions of the Nestorianised but ceremonially Persianised Lakhmid dynasty at Hīra, who introduced the use of Sasanian royal norms of dress and audience. Indeed Ziyād b. Abīhi (d 673) was compared to Anūshirvān by contemporary Persians.[16] It is also well-known that the Medinan caliph 'Umar b. al-Khaṭṭāb (r. 634–644) reproved Mu'āwiya, who was later to become the first Umayyad caliph, for adopting Sasanian usages, although the saying, whose reference is obscure, might well be apocryphal. The moon crescent with an inner star, to this day the emblem of Islam, was a distinguishing mark of late Sasanian throne buildings [17] and was adopted very early on.

The Umayyads accumulated indices of royalty indefatigably. Some were taken over from the vast repertoire available to them, while others were designed according to the personal disposition and taste of individual caliphs and subsequently retained as indices of royalty. Surprisingly, crowns were used only perfunctorily by at least one Umayyad crown prince, but never, it seems by any Umayyad or Abbasid caliph. The apparent exception was al-Mu'taṣim (r. 833–842), who is reported on one occasion to have worn a crown set with the famous gem possessed by the Abbasids called The Unique (*yatīma*).[18] But this may have had to do with his relations to his military entourage, as the ceremony took place in a restricted context. The *tāj*, a word of Syriac origin, initially designated a tiara, a word used for all regal head-dress incorporating gold and precious stones.[19] It was conferred by caliphs, starting with al-Mu'taṣim, upon their victorious commanders throughout the Abbasid period,[20] and by commanders upon victorious lower commanders[21] although, as we shall see, crowning took on a special significance in the Buyid period (932–1062). The *tāj* was also worn, in the form of an elaborate turban, by the Fatimids in Cairo. The perfunctory and episodic use of royal indices persisted well into Abbasid times. Under al-Muʿtaṣim, when the seditious Pāpak was defeated and lured into captivity, he was dressed in royal robes and paraded before he was taken into the caliph's presence, where he was stripped naked and executed horribly.[22] This inversion is of course somewhat similar to the Roman Saturnalia, and to Babylonian and old Persian rituals, whose affinity was first noted nearly a century ago.[23]

Be that as it may, it was Umayyad governors in Iraq who introduced into Arab courts regal traditions such as processions, formal audience arrangements, and the receipt of gifts during the Persian festivals of Nawrūz and Mihrajān.[24] Muʿāwiya famously introduced the private caliphal compartment in the mosque (*al-maqṣūra*). It was destined to have a very interesting and significant aesthetic history, and to be cultivated with much intensity throughout the periods of Muslim religious architecture, perhaps most spectacularly at the Great Mosque of Cordoba.[25] Muʿāwiya is also credited with the introduction of caliphal seating prerogatives – the *ḥijāb* or curtain that separated the caliph from his audience – and the *ṭirāz*, textiles especially woven for the caliph's personal use or gift with his name woven on the edges which, from an uncertain date, required the establishment of specialised workshops. Later Umayyad caliphs further refined vestimentary distinctions by reserving yellow and red garments for the caliphal family. Sulaymān b. ʿAbd al-Malik (r. 715–717) is credited with particularly elaborate dress.[26] Many Umayyad and Abbasid caliphs, following the Lakhmids and Sasanians, set aside, albeit erratically, particular days of the week for drinking in public;[27] but caliphal drinking, even with intimate courtiers, seems to have died out with time. It seems also that the increasing formality of courtly life was reflected in the time of ʿAbd al-Malik b. Marwān (r. 685–705), who forbade his company from conversing in his presence,[28] a not surprising fact given the centrality of his rule in the formation of the state system.

Not unnaturally, the formality of courtly life under the Umayyads, though constantly elaborated, does not seem to have crystallised into ceremonial institutes and regular procedures, but was forever shifting and everywhere intermixed with aspects of informality – of seating, of conversation, of reference to caliphs and their address by their names – with which the sources are replete. In the words of one scholar, it is possible to speak only of an 'ambiance cérémonielle' with reference to the Umayyads, whose ceremonial had not yet crystallised into ritual forms.[29] Indeed the construction by Hishām b. ʿAbd al-Malik (r. 724–743) of a hippodrome at Damascus and the introduction of various games, further elaborated under the Abbasids with polo and other activities and accompanied by the playing of chess and of dice games under Hārūn al-Rashīd (r. 786–809), [30] can be regarded as a space of relative informality and fairly open participation for the caliphal entourage.

There seems indeed to have been a reversion to more open familiarity of address and of access under the first Abbasids, most particularly al-Saffāḥ (749–754) and al-Manṣūr (754–775).[31] Some Umayyads and early Abbasids – in contrast to the Prophet and earlier caliphs – are reported to have prevented people from kissing their hands,[32] although this seems to me to betoken less humility than a posture of archaising and exclusivist Arabism, built upon a false memory of simpler times, amidst the sea of non-Arabs, some of them sophisticated, incorporated into the state. It seems, moreover, that the earliest Abbasids had been reared in the idiom of Arab tribalism rather than that of royalty, and in a context where they and the Umayyads mutually referred to each other as cousins. The first Abbasid caliph was in fact a stepson of ʿAbd al-Malik b. Marwān.[33] Caliphs continued personally to preside over public prayers and over the pilgrimage to Mecca until al-Rashīd, after whom this practice died out except for the one time when al-Mutawakkil (847–861) led the pilgrimage convoy in person.[34]

Yet within this mixture of formality and informality, the uniqueness of the caliph, sustained by the absolute power he wielded whenever he could, was the principal element in the accumulation of indices of kingship. Al-Jāḥiẓ (d 868), with his customary wit, later stated with reference both to Muslim and Sasanian monarchs that the prerogative of royal uniqueness was such that if a king were capable of monopolising air and water, he should do so, for it is in such display of sheer capacity that royal splendour resides.[35] The caliph had the exclusive use of certain insignia, colours of dress, and other indices of his distinctiveness. His lofty – and as will become apparent, sublime – status was expressed, with equal force, in verbal enunciation, no less than in the verbal-iconographic enunciations one witnesses on Umayyad and Abbasid coins. These still bore Sasanian and Byzantine insignia, such as crowns and robes, in addition to the name of the caliph or his viceroy in the East, well into the

Marwānid period and slightly beyond it, until the end of the seventh century and the beginning of the eighth.

Exclusive attributes of kingship were also enunciated in pictorial motifs, although these were not of great significance after the Muslims adopted a thoroughgoing iconoclasm, apparently in tandem with that of Byzantium, and derogated the importance of the pictorial enunciation of power. Pictorial representations thus became decorative motifs associated with kingship but disassociated from the function of conceptual or allegorical representation or of propositional statement that they may have had at their point of origin; this is a phenomenon altogether common in the history of art.

One such image is of Pegasus which appears as an abstract form with royal connotations in the Muslim world.[36] Another, more important, is the image and symbolism of the rayed nimbus, evoking associations between the sun and its rays and the caliphal person of al-Walīd b. Yazīd (r.743–744) at the Khirbat al-Mafjar pleasure palace, much as similar images were associated, in Byzantium, with the personalities of Christ and of the Basileus. On present evidence, however, it must be said that the association of the caliphal person with light was discursively used only at a late date, as, for instance, in tenth-century Cordoba or a little later in Baghdad with reference to the caliph al-Mustaḍī' Billāh (r. 1170–1180), whose very title makes him the recipient of divine luminosity.[37] Of immense antiquity, with a history stretching from Bactria to Rome where it was associated with Sol and Jupiter, this image was also used in Palmyra and elsewhere in the area in association with gods. In Sasanian Iran it was used to convey the divine charisma of kings, royal splendour and good-fortune (*hvarna*, *farrah*, and other possible transcriptions) represented as a nimbus of fire surrounding the head of the monarch.

In Muslim domains this was to have a long and complex career: from Umayyad Syria through to Abbasid Iraq, Aghlabid Ifrīqiyā, Umayyad Spain, Fatimid Egypt, and Ilkhanid Iran, it was represented in architecture, mosaics, metalwork, and painting.[38] It is imperative, however, to guard against over-interpretation, attractive as this might be, especially of its occurrence in periods other than the early Umayyad, Fatimid, and later Iranian periods. Correlatively, its occurrence, for instance, in Mamluk metalwork surrounding the representations of individual sultans, ought to be regarded as a royal decorative motif without conceptual correlates.[39] Political authority may thus indeed be 'expressed in hubristic visual terms',[40] and the hubris goes very much beyond visual representation; but it is not an abstract play of signs of power entirely without enunciative expression or propositional intention.

Another royal emblem was the round city which radiated out towards world dominion, an architectural idea prevalent in cities of the Near East for one and a half millennia before the Arab conquest. This was first used in a somewhat basic form in the construction of Kūfa by Saʿd b. Abī Waqqāṣ , beginning in 638, where it was later centred around a green cupola with celestial associations which seems to have been used by Muʿāwiya and al-Ḥajjāj (d. 714), viceroy of the East.[41] Another feature was the association of a palace with a mosque of smaller dimensions, running along an axis which traversed the central reception hall (*'īwān*) occupying the very centre of the city.[42] All these ideas came together in the original design of Baghdad.[43]

But yet again, emphatically to interpret Baghdad as an Islamic *mandala* conceived on Buddhist principles, though this may not have been absent from the minds of some who worked on its design,[44] is to confuse the intention of the designer with the possibilities of consequential interpretation by the receiver. The sense of centrality conveyed by kingship, which draws in the world, is very much present and was, as we shall see, to develop very substantively. Yet it does not bear conceptual comparison with the idea of a *mandala*, and it does not account for other features of the original design of Baghdad, most particularly the function of seclusion and exclusion betokened by the fast centrality of the caliphal residence with respect to the round design of the city. If pre-Islamic conceptual associations for the idea of the round city are to be sought, they should refer rather to the astral associations of the cosmic throne halls and of the king himself in Sasanian capitals, associations that were very ancient and went back to Achaemenean Babylon.[45] Similarly, the quartenary division of the world,[46] an idea of Sasanian provenance, was retained and governed the conception of royal urbanism in the original design of Baghdad. However, it never corresponded to actual administrative divisions, nor did it acquire anything but a marginal position in Arab–Muslim geographical conceptions, which adopted the septenary division of Ptolemaic zonal geography. Nevertheless it retained a certain rhetorical currency, where the world was referred to as 'all quarters of the earth' (*arbāʿ al-arḍ*). Whatever interpretation of the design of Baghdad one may adopt, caliphs were clearly addressing their subjects in a visual language of power that they could understand.

Over and above these and other visual announcements of royalty were verbal enunciations. These did not, for the Umayyads, include regnal titles, although it is reported that Muʿāwiya held the title an-Nāṣir li Ḥaqq Allāh,[47] which is most likely to have been simply an epithet for occasional use in the context of the war with ʿAlī b. Abī Ṭālib (r. 656–661). But as for the Sasanians, Byzantines and others, crucial to the kingship of the Umayyads, and later of the Abbasids, were the similes exclusively used for the conveyance of the royal idea and metaphorically representing the royal person. Many of these were to have a long and rich career in Muslim discourses on power.

Kings were likened to herdsmen and helmsmen. A king, according to a saying attributed to the Prophet, is God's shadow on earth. He is to his subjects as a soul is to a body. A king is the best of men, and stands to his subjects as the head – or, alternatively, the heart – stands to other parts of the body. All these statements are ubiquitous. Although they had all been current in the area for many long centuries, their immediate source in the Umayyad period seems to have been Sasanian. Their wide currency in Arab Muslim circles came towards the end of the Umayyad period. Moreover, like divinity, kingship is indivisible. Here reference is always made to the Koranic statement (21:22) to the effect that matters cosmic would be disaggregated had there been more than one god. From this analogy with indivisibility and unicity were drawn, in parallel, the indivisibility and unicity of both divine and mundane kingship drawn earlier and most consequentially by Eusebius. It was this Koranic verse which was apparently used to justify, in the early Abbasid period, the fate of Abū Muslim (d. 754), who had been veritable master of the East.[48] To the unicity of God corresponds the unicity of the king who, like the Prophet, is elected by God (*muṣṭafā*), and entrusted by Him with the affairs of the world, as his trustee (*amīn*) and vicar (*khalīfa*): the caliph is God's caliph, his treasury God's wealth, his army God's army, his enemies the enemies of God.[49] A tributary relationship is posited between the caliph and his subjects modelled on the paradigm of the one between him – as a mortal – and God, with the one a calque of the other. Thus, just as the caliph shepherds humanity, so is he in turn shepherded by God.[50]

It is manifest that the caliphate was regarded as the direct and immediate legacy of God. Modern scholarship has shown the title *khalīfat Allāh*, God's caliph, to have been in constant and ubiquitous use. The results of this line of research have not been entirely satisfactory beyond the provision of copious citations, not least because scholars have generally sought, in standard Orientalist fashion, a simple and invariant sense to the term God's caliph, and also because of an excess of zealous antipathy to the subject,[51] or of analytical insufficiency.[52] Another flaw in such scholarship is the unwillingness to take the title seriously and give it the consequence it merits in historical reality. It is instead viewed as 'unofficial' and 'tentative' on the grounds that it is at variance with 'official doctrine'. There is a pronounced preference for regarding as representative of 'official doctrine' the priestly view of what was later to become the *'ulamā'* that the caliphate is the vicarage of prophethood, not of God directly,[53] and to relegate the sacral notion of the caliphate exclusively to the domain of 'popular' conceptions.[54] It is true that the term 'God's caliph' occurs frequently in popular writing like the *Arabian Nights*.[55] But the official priestly view of the title was introduced slowly under the Abbasids, with the process of crystallisation of the *'ulamā'* institutions, and ran alongside the standard, central, and equally official designation of caliphs as God's caliphs, even by the hand of the same authors.[56] The document issued by al-Ma'mūn appointing 'Alī al-Riḍā as his successor, written in the caliph's own hand, refers to the office as the caliphate of God, while the heir-apparent, in his letter of acceptance, refers to his future caliphate as an office mandated by God, as did the witnesses to both documents.[57] Standard documents of Abbasid caliphal appointment refer to the office as God's caliphate.[58]

Earlier use of the term caliph designated quite simply the fact of succession to the position of command occupied by the Prophet,[59] but this conception was very rapidly supplemented – or perhaps superseded – by more sublime associations. The National Museum in Damascus holds a coin minted in erstwhile Sasanian territories during the reign of the second caliph,'Umar b. al-Khaṭṭāb, which carries the legend 'Khalīfat Allāh'.[60] This is all the more salient as coins minted under early Arab dominion in former Byzantine and Sasanian territories retained most of their original features, including crosses, Pahlavi writing, the crowned heads of former Sasanian kings, fire altars, representations purporting to be of the caliph, and much else, before being superseded first by dīnārs featuring the figure of ʿAbd al-Malik himself and dated 76/695[61] and later, from 77/696–7, with purely Arabic epigraphic coins.[62]

The caliphate is a highly polyvalent concept, as titular and other general designations of long standing that obtain in human societies invariably are. In all, the epithet God's caliph *per se* contains little that is specifically Muslim, and virtually nothing that is generically Muslim, most particularly as it was generally – though by no means universally – repudiated in priestly legal and pietistic discourse. Its terms are Arabic, its conceptual senses are those of Late Antiquity which Islamic histories in the Middle Ages gathered together, inventorised definitively, pruned and re-named. Specifically, even generically Muslim inflections and conceptual trajectories for the legacy of Late Antiquity came later, from about the latter part of the second Muslim century. The specific lineaments of the caliphate of God will, in this light, be familiar against the background of earlier chapters of this book, it being the repository of sublime charisma, directing the affairs of the world in accordance with the wishes of God, with all the wealth of associations, metaphors, theologies, and other manners of profiling the connection between a god, or assembly of gods, and the king who runs the world in their or in His behalf. As for the salutary archetypes of mankind, these were to be the caliphs themselves, until their example was displaced much later by the archetypal man Muḥammad, represented as canonical *sunna*, and speaking with the priestly tongue of the *ʿulamāʾ*. It is precisely here that the Muslim inflection of the Late Antique notions of power in relation to divinity is located. Also significant in this respect is the royal or caliphal duty of leadership in prayer, which seems an echo of priestly and cultic functions performed by the Meccan aristocracy before Islam, whose holy family had been the Umayyads, and taken over by Muḥammad himself.

The notion of God's caliphate in the Umayyad period was intially, like much else at the time, circulated orally: in panegyric poetry, delivered in the course of political orations, or reported in conversations by the caliphs themselves and others. Its presentation and enunciation had not yet been formalised in prose, although many of its fundamental elements were nevertheless definitively established and used, dispersed through all manner of political and social practices. It also occurred in early Arabic epistolary, including the earliest works of *Fürstenspiegel*, like the famous epistle to the heir apparent by ʿAbd al-Ḥamīd b. Yaḥyā al-Kātib (d 750), supreme stylist and secretary to the last Umayyad caliph.[63] It occurs in royal ceremonial as well as on Umayyad coins. In all, it occurs in combination with motifs of tribal primacy and military prowess, and of the particular honour of the Umayyad clan.[64] As we shall see, the notion of God's caliphate is congruous with the Shiʿi notion of the imamate officially adopted at a later date. This doctrine of political authority was never absent from the theory and practice of the Sunni caliphate, although it was never formalised in legal and religious doctrines of public authority. The conflict between ʿAlī and Muʿāwiya was one between equivalent claims to power by divine mandate, both buttressed with differently inflected notions of tribal filiation.

The notion of God's caliphate also occurs in combination with an entirely secular title, that of *amīr al-muʾminīn*, which was to be a standard appellation of all caliphs and their common manner of address. This title indicated overall command of the exclusive political community composed of Muslims which in the early period consisted largely of Arabs. These other contexts should not be unduly marginalised in an overall picture of notions of rule.

God's caliph is God's legatee. He accedes to his position, like Moses, by divine election, even by a measure of predestination.[65] He is blessed by God, guided by Him, personifies his authority, and intercedes between Him and mankind. God's caliph is in charge of the Kaʿba – indeed, inherits the Kaʿba from God [66] – and is granted the caliphate just as the Prophet is granted prophethood.[67] There is in this conception a direct relationship between God and the caliph unmediated by the Prophet, and indeed a 'virtual parity' between caliphs and the Prophet is implied.[68] All these and many other attributes of the caliph of God were later to be transferred to the person of Prophet, when he was transformed into the human paradigm textually set and classicised in the *sunna*. By the Ayyubid era, the Prophet was, along with his sacralisation, 'royalised' and his tomb in Medina was guarded by a corps of eunuchs. Under the Mamluks, this institution (whose remains still exist today) was much enhanced, leading to the increasing segregation of the tomb itself, which became, after the royal fashion, a *maqṣūra*.[69] Correlatively, the caliph came increasingly to be formally conceived as the successor of the Prophet, although the Caliph's simultaneous and direct identification with sacrality did not abate as long as the Abbasids remained in Baghdad.

In other words, the divine presence in the world is so personified by the caliph that the prerogatives of the two are in complete correspondence, irrespective of theological and juristic definitions and elaborations of the caliphal office. Indeed, this charter for royal absolutism partakes fully of the notions of omnipotent absolutism that permeate Judaeo–Muslim traditions of divinity. The God of the Koran and of the Muslim history of prophecy is an absolute agent, narcissistically active and reactive in turn, creating or elevating nations, peoples, and empires with a view to obtaining obedience and adoration, and annihilating them when obedience and adoration were not forthcoming. The amorality of divine action in history, divine action being quite literally beyond good and evil, is presented also as a caliphal prerogative. Sayings are attributed to Muʿāwiya and al-Ḥajjāj to the effect that right and wrong are equal before the caliph. In a certain way, the caliph creates the dispositions of right and wrong, being God's trustee and thus presumably having His prerogatives in full measure. The caliph is here fully the heir to the notion of the supra-legal king. Muʿawiya is said to have quoted the last Lakhmid king, an-Nuʿmān b. al-Mundhir (d. ca 602), in saying that acts of punishment or of mercy by kings are performed purely as manifestations of power and capacity, a sort of transcendental narcissism acting on the world in an abstract manner that merely affirms this very primacy. Thus also, conquered lands are God's, and consequently the caliph's, who can thus dispose of wealth without restriction under the signature of divine prerogative.

Correlative with these charters for absolutism were secular arguments for caliphal prerogatives, mostly in the form of wisdom literature often attributed to sagely Persian kings. ʿUmar b. ʿAbd al-ʿAzīz (r. 717–20), among others, is credited with the saying that the corruption of rulers causes the corruption of the multitude, but that the opposite is not true.[70] This statement is based on an assumption, constant throughout Muslim histories, that it is kings and the character of kings which constitute polities, for men are by nature evil and fractious and can be curbed only by overweening, omnipotent authority. Evil disposition, according to the eloquent statement of this pessimistic view of human nature by ʿAbd al-Ḥamīd al-Kātib, 'inheres in people as fire inheres in a [flint-] stone.'[71] Such an innate disposition can be checked only by absolute kingship sustained by justice – the even distribution of subjection and of lawfulness among subjects – which commences the famous 'circle of justice' variously ascribed to Ardashīr, Anūshirvān, and ʿAmr b. al-ʿĀṣ, but which we have seen above to occur in Kauṭliya as well: that power can only be sustained by men, men by wealth, wealth by prosperity, and prosperity by justice.[72] Yet for all this, as for the various notes of pious humility struck by Umayyad monarchs – ʿUmar b. ʿAbd al-ʿAzīz was later to be cast by sharʿist Islam as almost archetypal in this respect – Umayyad discourses on power remained relentlessly hubristic in their consideration of the this-worldly station of the caliphal office, and correlatively sublime in their notion of divine prerogatives and election.

Not unnaturally, the charisma of caliphs carries with it magical or quasi-magical attributes. Certain rain-making capacities were attributed to Umayyad caliphs, or at the very least the implication is made that their rightly-guided actions are at once the analogues of rain, and the cause for actual precipitation.[73] This was also in keeping with the pre-Islamic Arab procedure of *istisqāʾ*, supplication for rain, which made this rite a matter for the Lord of a shrine (*bayt*),[74] and for which there was later to be a definite place in Muslim devotions. The belief is reported in the Umayyad period that caliphs were immune from the plague.[75] A certain caliphal invincibility is implied by the saying of the second Abbasid, al-Manṣūr, that duplicitous and hypocritical courtiers will be revealed by God to the caliph through a number of signs, mostly slips of the tongue, and that God will afflict the bodies of such individuals with strokes and other misfortunes.[76]

Yet there does not seem to have been deliberate and systematic statement and elaboration of these and allied primitive concepts circulating in Umayyad times, as the requisite discursive formation had not yet come into a self-sustaining existence. Nor does there seem to have been institutional and definite ceremonial ways in which such conceptions of the caliphal office were enunciated, except in the medium of panegyric poetry which had fully formed structural and conceptual features and whose delivery was ritualised, as part of courtly ceremonial, from at the very least the earliest days of the Abbasids.[77] The poetic tropes of kingship spread right through the Umayyad and Abbasid periods and constitute the most consistent and continuous late antique presence in Muslim polities.

It seems, though, that the Umayyad period was one of unrestrained, even playful, experimentation with the prerogatives, privileges, and enunciations of kingship, which were quite directly and personally exercised. It was towards the end of the Umayyad period and during the first few decades of Abbasid rule that political material collateral with royal absolutism and general conceptions of charisma was textually inventorised, thus providing a repertoire of types, motifs, narratives, and conceptions, which were to be variously quarried throughout the centuries and territories of Muslim histories. It is to the constitution of this political canon and other canons of relevance, indeed to the very constitution of the political field, that we now turn.

PART TWO

Muslim Polities

CHAPTER FIVE

Writing Power

The first century of Islam was an interregnum, a period of transition from Hellenistic and Sasanian regimes to an œcumenical polity which built upon the debris of both. This heritage was collated by new configurations of power, most saliently central, imperial power which constituted itself under the signature of Islam. The interregnum was a period in which elements of older order and form were experimented with. A massive repertoire of imperial norms, concepts, and practices was made visible to the Arab newcomers and this was inventoried, organised and intermixed with new elements that emerged, in the course of history, under the Muslim signature. To these elements were added, albeit in smaller proportions, ingredients from pre-Islamic Arabian norms and concepts of kingship and of the priesthood (themselves heavily permeated, indeed almost constituted, by the ambient imperial ethos and vast repertoire of Semitic histories and religions).

Of the sheer mass of the late antique heritage were constituted, under Muslim imperial aegis, forms of politcal order and representations of these forms that aggregated elements of this heritage into the new traditions of the Muslim polity. These forms have reached us chiefly through the medium of script. There is, as we saw in the previous chapter, a certain body of ceremonial and other political action through which the exercise of power and its underlying conceptions can be read. But these too have come down to us in textual form, in chronicles and other histories, and in various discursive locations in which power and its conception and exercise was treated. Visually communicated enunciations of power, numismatic, architectural and otherwise, also exist. Their interpretation, however, raises a number of methodological and epistemological questions which cannot be taken up here[1] and are, in any case, almost invariably allied to textually-based knowledge.

The textual enunciations of power that concern us are constituted in the form of traditions. As always in the case of traditions, a mass of concepts and practices is organised in the form of topoi, motifs and genealogies. Their deployment is in turn organised on a larger scale of enunciative modality in genres of high and low-brow writing by and for different bodies of authors, readers, and listeners. The traditions of a literate society preserve a certain coherence across vast times and spaces in the form of real or virtual memory textually stored and telescoped into moulds and structures suitable for transmission and retrieval. It is in the form of traditions standing in for actual memory that genealogies are constituted.

A Corpus of Universal Wisdom

Muslim political genealogies have been ascribed – both in medieval Muslim sources and the modern Orientalist transcription of these sources in the form of scholarship – largely to a Persian legacy sprinkled with Greek political notions, admixed with the Muslim canon. In so far as it indicates the inchoate quarry, the enunciative mass, out of which Muslim political traditions were constituted and organised formally, this is incontrovertible. But it marginalises the axial question: that of the manner in which this material was composed. The obsession with chasing after individual instances of textual origin and influence, so fundamental to the Orientalist vocation, obscures the far more consequential matter of coherence within the Muslim material itself.

It is well known that Arabic translations of Sasanian and Greek texts on politics were available early on, and that this material, along with Arab tribal and, later, Muslim religious and military lore was widely read at court. Political wisdom literature – an inventory of political skill and instances of misfortune which were thought to instruct and advert – was widely cultivated at the Umayyad court. Muʿāwiya, like Marwān b. Muḥammad, held regular sessions where such literature was read aloud.[2] The latter's secretary, ʿAbd al-Ḥamīd al-Kātib, as we have seen, was the author of what seems to have been the first Arabic epistle of this kind in which the crown prince was offered advice on royal conduct: on self-restraint, secretiveness, fairness to one's generals, and so forth. Political wisdom literature existed alongside Arab testamentary literature – epistolary advice to heirs or appointees. There is evidence of such literature from the Medinan period and it was still composed well into Abbasid times, buttressed by what seem to be early Arabic Umayyad adaptations of Hellenistic opuscules and epistolary literature attributed to Aristotle.[3] These were combined with themes from writing of apparently Sasanian origin to form the earliest Arabic body of writing on politics, [4] a genre that with time became highly conventionalised in both form and content.[5]

The earliest texts of political wisdom are well-known and were to be paradigmatic for the entire tradition of Arabic political writing. The work of Ibn al-Muqaffaʿ (d. 756), the so-called *Testament of Ardashīr*, and somewhat later the *Tāj* of al-Jāḥiẓ (d. 868) were of paramount importance in this respect. Persian kings were thought to have been exemplary in their wisdom and political savoir-faire, and stories sustaining this view are legion throughout Arabic writing.[6] So much so, indeed, that one author, writing in Egypt in the third Muslim century, protested that other peoples, particularly the Greeks, were not being properly appreciated because the Persian reputation had appropriated almost entirely the tropes of political wisdom.[7] He then proceeded to produce three testaments ascribed to Greek sages which were congruent in content with the staple fare of Arabic wisdom literature.

Yet it seems that direct, unmediated and unilineal borrowing, in writing as in administration,[8] is exaggerated. We must accustom ourselves to think of inter-textual cross-referencing as a space containing a thicket of mirrors in which a uniform body of enunciations is plausibly claimed as their own by many traditions. This is not unnatural in a situation where a repertoire of concepts and topoi was contained within an ambient Late Antiquity. The pursuit of origins, and the collation of sets of origins by naming them in an exclusive manner, is the standard procedure for building a typological genealogy for a preconceived present. After all, ʿAbd al-Ḥamīd al-Kātib used Greek material in his epistles,[9] and the famous bibliography of 987 by the Baghdadian bookseller an-Nadīm reported translations of Aristotle's epistles to Alexander made early, by a client of Hishām b. ʿAbd al-Malik, which the translators thought were congruent in spirit with available Persian material.[10] These spurious epistles, known in the Latin West in translations from the Arabic (into Latin, French, English, German, Italian, Catalan, Castillian, Dutch) as the *Secretum Secretorum*, do indeed contain much that indicates Persian interpolation or provenance: a conversation between a Magian and a Jew, the quartenary division of the earth, praise for Bactrian camels,[11] exhortation to use Turkic soldiery, numerology reminiscent of Chaldean lore, elaborate talismanic notions with Semitic sounds.[12] The Romance of Alexander itself, in its Arab versions, is heavily impregnated with notions of ideal rulers ascribed to the Persians.[13]

Yet the question of what was generically 'Persian', rather than linguistically, dynastically, and geographically Persian as distinct from late Hellenistic Near Eastern – apart from Zoroastrianism – constantly surfaces, not least in connection with books of entirely Persian ascription. One such work is *Jāvīdān Khirad*, the *Perennial Wisdom* composed in Arabic by Miskawayh (d. 1030), whose textual history begs the question of whether the origin was actually Persian, or a Middle Persian rendition of an Arabic text ascribed to Persian authorship.[14] There is ample evidence in the medieval Arabic texts of the transference of attribution for particular sayings and acts, indeed of the interchangeability of authorities according to discursive need or other leaning.[15] A measure of plausibility is often evident in terminology. Witness the use in the so-called Greek Testaments of the term 'city' where 'state' might be used in a text attributed to Persians or others, in a text which is otherwise no different in content from what might be attributed to Persian or Arab authors or sages.[16] There are also some doubts about the actual provenance of the famous *Letter of Tansar*, where the probability is of a late Sasanian text attributed to the time of Ardashīr but duly edited in the manner of its time.[17] Yet the extant Persian text is itself a translation from the Arabic text of Ibn al-Muqaffa', whose history is unknown and in which the relation between authorship and translation is entirely unrecoverable. The same applies to other Persian texts of putative Sasanian provenance.[18] The textual history of the celebrated *Kalīla wa Dimna*, itself based ultimately on the Sanskrit *Pānchatantra*, involves much more than the standard Arabic text of Ibn al-Muqaffa', with a complex web of relations between Arabic, Syriac, and Pahlavi versions.[19]

It is thus difficult and probably otiose to make up general classes of textual influences which could then be referred to Persians and Greeks. This procedure betrays an unjustifiable privileging of the correct printed text over other manners for the transmission of knowledge, and too much of nineteenth-century philological assumptions ascribed to the eighth and earlier centuries. Many of the texts in question have extremely complex histories of composition and redaction, and only the history of the Arabic original of the *Secretum Secretorum* has been studied in detail.[20] If, for instance, one were to examine the provenance of the idea of the just middle (*iqtiṣād, iʿtidāl, tawassuṭ*), which is so crucial in political wisdom literature, as a principle of moral and sagely behaviour, one would naturally think of Greek moral theory contained in the notion of *mesotēs*. But equally it is necessary to be aware that this idea, regardless of its Aristotelian canonisation, had been current among Zoroastrians who raised it to the rank of a cosmological principle.[21] We cannot say that wisdom came from the Persians and, in an auxiliary manner, from the Greeks, and that philosophical notions came from the classical Greeks almost exclusively, at a time when the influence of classical Greek texts was late and came upon grounds prepared – in writing, verbal discourse, and in the interstices of discourse, by the Near Eastern Hellenistic synthesis which presents itself under the suitably vague name of Stoicism.[22] Indeed it is quite well-known that Greek sententious literature was available during the Umayyad period as well as some longer texts.[23]

Analysis of extant wisdom and political literature confirms this indeterminacy of attribution. The illustrious *al-Adab al-kabīr* of Ibn al-Muqaffaʿ amply demonstrates the concordance of Persian and Greek wisdom, as does *Kalīla wa Dimna*.[24] The ubiquity and indeterminacy of this body of sentences is reflected in the fact that much sagely reflection related in the writings of Ibn al-Muqaffaʿ is unattributed. We witness in both works, as in others, parallels with Semitic proverbial literature – some of it attributed to the legendary Arab Luqmān – intertwined with Mandean literature, prophetic sentences, pre-Islamic Arab sayings, the Babylonian wisdom of the sage Aḥīqār, transcribed onto the tongues of animals as in the *Pānchatantra*, *Kalīla wa Dimna*, and the fables of Aesop, all of which inhabit the same sagely and wily universe.[25] Such was the concatenated universe of mirrors we call Late Antiquity which Muslim imperialism tidied up, rendered recoverable after a more orderly manner, and made its own.

With his customary perspicacity, Miskawayh stated that his aim in composing the *Perennial Wisdom* was to bring forth a primeval wisdom shared by Persians, Indians, Greeks, and Arabs.[26] Indeed, this procedure is standard in the constitution of all absorbent, developing historical masses, where diversity, while acknowledged, is taken to obscure a unity of perennial wisdom variously expressed. The recognition of diversity within the universal register of perennity is the means whereby groups in the process of incorporation within a centrally conceived cultural and political pattern construe their genealogical parity or filiation with dominant groups. This occurred during the process of Islamisation under Muslim political dominance, as it had previously occurred under the cultural dominance of historical masses, otherwise defined as Persian or Greek, which were now being incorporated into the Muslim register. Thus, for instance, philosophy within the bounds of Muslim polities conceived itself as a perennial philosophy running alongside and intertwined with the history of prophecy, which itself incorporated Arabian prophecies and sages.[27] Sabeans adopted the same genealogical strategy to incorporate themselves within the vast concept of Islam.[28]

This orderliness of form, made possible by the centripetal conditions afforded by the Muslim œcumene, is premised on amnesia over origins, and on the attribution of specific qualities to particular personalities or nations. Hence the political sagacity of the Persians as a topos, the philosophical wisdom of the Greeks, the poeticalness of the Arabs, or indeed the personalities of Alexander, Homer, Socrates, Imru' al-Qays and others, are titular contexts and textual spaces within which are gathered and organised for purposes of codification, traditionalisation, and archival identification, narratives about various types of behaviour – wise, amorous, or valorous – each correlative with a topos identified with a name.[29] The topos of Alexander was even invoked to sustain theses of Muʿtazilīte theology and to lend them perennial sagely authority.[30] The same procedure underlies the formation of the notion of prophetic *sunna*, which attributed to the Prophet authoritative statements of social practice and belief as well as contestations of these: the Prophet is a topos wherein are mingled historical and ahistorical – indeed, anachronistic – attributes as the fount of social, dogmatic and intellectual authority, and consequently as the modality of archival inscription in a self-constituting Muslim culture. The formation of a written corpus of *ḥadīth* is subject to the same historical rules of formation as are literary topoi; its incorporation into political writings will be considered later in this chapter.[31]

The enunciative form of this order, with respect to political material, is topical and aggregative, narrative and non-theoretical.

It sought the proper and salutary formation, by individual example, of political skills derived from the wisdom of universal epigones. This wisdom is displayed in narratives of individual actions which are personalised in topoi such as, most famously, that of Ardashīr construed as the archetypically wise ruler.[32] Political material throughout the body of Arabic writing is thus a repertoire of examples relating to the craft of politics the aim of which is to promote correct action learned as a skill acquired by the repetition of exemplary acts in the past. The emphasis on exemplary behaviour, *ʿibra* (*uswa* or *qudwa* in the realms of morality and piety), is everywhere central to works of political craft. It is explicitly highlighted in works of history which are also meant to instruct by example;[33] for repetition of these acts is thought to produce a skill, a *habitus*, translatable into salutary practical action. The wisdom of the epigones is sometimes attributed to a veritable mythology of the past, with Koranic, Biblical, Pahlavi, and Sanskritic analogues: namely that men were then superior in all respects, including their emblematic endowment with larger bodies and longer lives.[34] These exemplary acts are narrated topically in *Fürstenspiegel* or chronologically in works of history; the only work to combine the two, with a topical preface followed by a historical narrative, was the *Fakhrī* of Ibn Ṭabāṭabā, also known as Ibn al-Ṭiqṭaqā, composed under the Mongols in 1301-2.

The crucial point here is that nowhere is a theory of kingship or of the state attempted: political material is composed of narratives of political behaviour, salutary or otherwise. The state is not the topic of political study, but is constituted as a topic in historical narrative where it acts as an unreflected mode of textual organisation.[35] It will become apparent later that kingship is taken up and constituted as a topic with respect to technical efficacy on the one hand, and to narrative pseudo-historical genesis on the other. It was not taken up in itself and constituted as a topic of scientific investigation, that is as a topic defined in itself. By science (*ʿilm*) is here understood the general sense conveyed by *Wissenschaft*,[36] an orderly procedure for the investigation and exposition of political material in terms of a broader methodological context.[37] This was explicit and clear to the practitioners of this genre,[38] and was one premise for the development by Ibn Khaldūn (d. 1406) of his *ʿilm al-ʿumrān*.[39]

It has already been stated that collections of political narratives and sentences, some ascribed to specific bygone rulers and sages and others without such attribution, existed from the Umayyad period. The classical texts of this genre comprise those of ʿAbd al-Ḥamīd al-Kātib, Ibn al-Muqaffaʿ, Arabic testamentary texts, *Kitāb al-Tāj*, the *Testament of Ardashīr*, the *Secretum Secretorum*, and, later, the Greek Testaments, as well as various elements brought together in collections of wisdom literature, the fullest – and latest – of which was the *Mukhtār al-ḥikam* (Choice Wisdom) of al-Mubashshir b. Fātik (d. ca 1087).[40] Direct allegory is of course best represented by *Kalīla wa Dimna*, which is attributed to the Indian sage Bidpai who, at the command of his king, sought to put positively and negatively exemplary behaviour by rulers or subjects in the form of animal stories. In such a way, it was thought, commoners would be instructed through entertainment, while kings would receive advice allegorically and thus without impertinent audacity on the part of the adviser.[41] It was a golden rule of courtiers not to proffer advice directly as this could be construed as *lèse-majesté*, and could have dire consequences.[42]

This mode of politico-allegorical story-telling was well recognised. It was most lucidly explicated by Ibn Rushd in his discussions on Aristotle's *Rhetoric* and *Poetics*, where he drew clear parallels between *Kalīla wa Dimna*, historical works, *ḥadīth* collections, and the Homeric epics,[43] which all constituted narrative arguments transferring the effect of one particular onto another. Such allegorisation also made its way into the Arabian Nights[44] and, when fully conventionalised, came to be used in some *Fürstenspiegel* as well.[45]

Kalīla wa Dimna was the most extensively read, quoted, versified, translated and emulated repertory of example and allegories.[46] In the fifth century of Islam a similar work was composed, with the same pedagogic intent,[47] but of decidedly inferior quality. Similarly, *Kitāb al-Tāj* was interminably quoted throughout the body of Arabic literature,[48] as was the *Testament of Ardashīr* and other sayings attributed to him. The *Testament of Ardashīr* was reproduced in full by many authors, including Miskawayh, and also versified.[49] Wisdom literature attributed to Greek sages and philosophers, and the *Secretum Secretorum*, were literarised through versification and through expression in rhymed prose (*sajʿ*). 'Greek' wisdom was composed as *maqāmāt*, and compared with that of the Arab poet al-Mutanabbī (d. 965). Indeed an entire treatise was composed on this subject by Abū ʿAlī Muḥammad b. al-Ḥasan al-Ḥātimī (d. 998), entitled *al-Risāla al-Ḥātimiyya fī mā wāfaqa al-*

Mutanabbī fi shiʿrihi min kalām Arisṭū ('A work on the concordance between the [sagely] sentences of Aristotle and the poetic [wisdom] of al-Mutanabbī'). This treatise was, in turn, extensively quoted by later authors. It expressed the mutual incorporation of sentences attributed to the Greeks and Arab–Muslim sententious literature, including pronouncements on politics.[50] It is noteworthy that from the twelfth century Latin literature in medieval Europe – building also on an antique tradition – witnessed the commencement of its own body of organised *exempla*, of which the *Disciplina Clericalis* of the Spaniard Petrus Alfonsi was the first.[51] Composed of narratives of Arabic provenance, this work was to be highly influential and very widely disseminated.[52]

We find that these works attributed to Persians and Greeks provide the main topical and narrative material for all subsequent works on politics in the specific sense, and in the political chapters of literary anthologies which were of such great importance in constituting the repertoire of common learning and literacy of courtly and other circles of the Muslim œcumene. In all, the circulation and recycling of this textual material obeys the conditions of literarisation in two senses. First, it is constituted of quotation in sundry contexts, often with much redundancy as citations from different sources of statements to the same effect are piled up one upon the other, amounting in effect to the open multiplication of authorities for identical or similar statements and narratives. Second, each of these sayings and each of these authorities is regarded as merely an instance of a perennial and ubiquitous political wisdom on this or that topic: clemency, strictness when necessary, secretiveness, justice, and so on. A correlative of this is the almost total lack – except in writings by Ibn Khaldūn and Ibn Rushd and, occasionally, others – of reference to contemporary politics. Limiting cases for this are perhaps best illustrated by writing of Naṣrid courtiers in Granada in the fourteenth and fifteenth centuries, such as Ibn al-Khaṭīb (d. 1375), who, living in mortal pressure from northern foes, wrote on politics using the form of rococo topoi, discoursing on the art of government in the form of dialogues between Persian sages and Hārūn al-Rashīd.[53]

More representative was, for instance, Abu'l Ḥasan al-ʿĀmirī (d. 922) who quotes Ibn al-Muqaffaʿ freely, despite his criticism of the latter for taking over too eagerly what al-ʿAmirī regarded as Avestan as distinct from Muslim principles of public order and morality.[54] The fourth/tenth century author Abū Ya'lā b. al-Farrā' composed a work on royal embassy in which he quoted maxims attributed to Alexander, no less than narratives ascribed to sundry Persians, various caliphs and military commanders.[55] The famous Abu'l-Ḥasan al-Māwardī (d. 1058) quotes on equal footing the Koran, *ḥadīth*, Ardashīr and other Persian kings and sages, as well as the *Secretum Secretorum*, which he took to be an Aristotelian text.[56] The *Fürstenspiegel* of Ghazālī (d. 1111), not long after, written in Persian and in 1199 translated into Arabic, quotes narratives of the Arabs and Persians, no less than Greek sagely and royal wisdom, with an extremely bare authorial voice which spells out clearly the compilatory, aggregative character of discourses on government based on a topical organisation of its essentially historical or pseudo-historical narrative and sententious material.[57] When, under the Almoravids in the Maghrib, al-Murādī (d. 1096) was entrusted with provincial legal and courtly functions and sought to compose a *Fürstenspiegel* to instruct the rough young princes of the upstart dynasty, his work contained seventy-four citations from Ibn al-Muqaffa', twenty-three from *Kalīla wa Dimna*, and thirteen from the *Secretum Secretorum* and the Greek Testaments. Many of these citations could, as suggested, simultaneously be attributed to more than one of these sources. This work became the standard Maghribi text on the subject and was often quoted, sometimes at very great length, in subsequent Maghribi works on politics (but not by Ibn Khaldūn).[58]

All these are but examples drawn particularly from works that were widely circulated century after century. That observations made about them apply equally to the entire corpus of political writing, be it in the form of works specifically devoted to the craft of politics or to political offices such as the vizirate,[59] or to the political sections of the literary compilations of *adab*. Of these, the work of Ṭurṭūshī (d. 1126) was crucial, not for introducing a new form of organising materials, or a novel way of thinking about politics, but for assembling, after the aggregative manner of *adab*, the repertoire of material pertaining to politics. Ṭurṭushī's *Sirāj al-Mulūk* thus constitutes a compendium which was extensively quarried by subsequent works, including works on government in Persian and Turkish which circulated in Ottoman, Mughal, Safavid and other Persophone polities.[60] The work of Ṭurṭūshī, Ghazālī, and others after the end of the eleventh century also contained another element which was to accrue in importance: namely, the homiletic tone which was to incorporate much specifically Muslim or Islamised material, by way of example and precept, under the impact of works of shar'ist politics. The writings of al-Māwardī here were paradigmatic.

Before this subject is taken up it is necessary to look more closely at the mode of composition of the discourses on politics in the Muslim œcumene, for in this lies one of the instances of power enunciated. Power in these works is enunciated episodically and ideally, as ideal episodes, as *exempla* of particular salience or even impeccability which, by being tirelessly repeated, take on some of the characteristics of the ritual enactment and re-enactment of power which is displayed in ceremonial.

Topics of Power

What, then, are the topics of power? Central is the active energy of power (*sulṭān*) itself which was as central to anecdotal literature as its was held to be axial to the body politic. The literary compendium of Ibn Qutayba (d. 889),[61] which is the example for all subsequent work of this kind and a principal source of courtly and general literacy over hundreds of years opens with a section on power (*sulṭān*), followed by a book on war, books on human nature and dispositions, on knowledge, asceticism, friendship, cuisine and, finally, on women. As usual in this kind of work, the text lacks an authorial voice altogether and consists of a string of narratives of various sources. The *Book of Power* rehearses the standard repertoire of topics that occur in Ibn al-Muqaffa' as in the works ascribed to Greek authors: the axial position of a king in the organisation of social order, the cautionary etiquette required of courtiers, the giving and taking of advice, the hazards of passion, on betrayal, clemency, injustice, and offices granted by a ruler – governor, chamberlain, judge, secretary.

Though most of the narratives quoted as illustrations of such topics are of Arab provenance, they are almost exclusively of a secular nature, and are indeed intermixed with examples drawn from Persian, Indian, and Greek epigones. Similarly, the equally important – indeed, quasi-canonical – compilation of Ibn 'Abd Rabbih (d. 940)[62] organised the material of its various Books, each named after a precious stone, around congruent topics. The first is entitled, not unnaturally, 'The Pearl of Power': it treats, in order, the axial position of the ruler, the necessity for obedience to him, the etiquette of his companionship, his choice of subordinates, justice, and the direct impact of his virtues and vices upon the moral tenor of his subjects. It then takes up the topic of ministers, the notion of a just imam, leniency, humility, firmness, advice, the legal system, and allied topics. The 'Pearl' is followed by other sections of allied topical relevance: war, generosity, addressing rulers, followed by knowledge and allied topics. In all we again witness the complete lack of an authorial voice. The anecdotes here are almost exclusively of Arab provenance, which is not unnatural given that the author was a linguist. The section on the just imam deploys as a topos 'Umar b. 'Abd al-'Azīz, the ideal ruler, receiving an epistle from the sagely ascetic al-Ḥasan al-Baṣrī (642–728). The sage advises him according to standard formulae: to be wary of hubris, to be to his subjects as a shepherd, a father, a mother, and as a heart amongst the bodily organs. The ruler will thereby interpose himself between God and his creation, 'hearing God's discourse and conveying it to them, regarding God and showing them.'[63] Other works of the genre are similarly constituted. It must also be emphasised that these works were read and quoted by authors of very differing orientations, and find a certain continuity in later, philologically-minded works of ethics such as that of the great Ibn Ḥazm, in which Ibn Qutayba's topical divisions are replicated, as is his general manner of presenting his material.[64]

Works specifically devoted to political topics, the *Fürstenspiegel* and the genres that emerged from them, are similarly structured. Here, however, the authorial voice is stronger, although it is not yet quite truly distinct from the sagely example that inspires it. It joins the voice of the example narrated as a confirmatory authority when quoted in later works of the same genre or of other genres. The topical organisation of material is wedded to an essayistic mode of exposition, as distinct from the aphoristic and aggregatively narrative mode which predominates in works of general literary compilation where direct authorial intervention is entirely precluded. The essayistic approach is strongest in the early, foundational works – in Ibn al-Muqaffa', in Arabic epistolary writings, and in the *Kitāb at-Tāj*. It grows weaker over the years, becoming very sparse from the time of Ṭurṭūshī, although it persists in works of a strong philosophico-ethical inspiration like the philosophical treatise on ethics and politics by Naṣīr ad-Dīn al-Ṭūsī (d. 1274),[65] and in other works composed in Persian, most notably that of the vizier Niẓām al-Mulk (1018–1092).[66] But, in the non-philosophical works at least, the authorial voice, essayistic as it may be, is equally aggregative, piling paraphrase upon historical reference in such a manner as to enhance a pre-existing topical repertoire without conceptual addition.

Philosophical or quasi-philosophical discussions of politics were normally prefaced with psycho-epistemological prolegomena as a prelude to a discussion of ethics because ethical perfection and justice were believed, in this genre, to be achievable after the classical fashion, by striking a balance between the appetititive, the irascible or animal and the rational faculties of the soul. The prolegomena were normally followed by a sketch of practical philosophy, of which politics forms a part consequent upon ethics and ethical behaviour by individuals and collectivities.[67] Ibn Rushd thought of ethics as constituting the general part of politics, and government the particular.[68] However, barring the works of Ibn Rushd and Ibn Khaldūn, there is little reference to historical reality in works with a philosophical flavour, and with the exception of these two, in addition to works of Ṭūsī and Ibn Sīnā (d. 1037) and Miskawayh to a lesser extent, there is little relevance to contemporary political or politico-religious notions.

Thus the formidably-wrought *Nasirean Ethics* is, in its own way, captive to the conventional topics of the genre. The Third Discourse of the work, dealing with politics, is conceptually premised on the two previous sections dealing with the soul, the faculties, ethical ends, followed by government of self and household in the light of these Aristotelian precepts. Apart and in distinction from the philosophical developments which structure the order in which the topics are treated and the manner in which they are profiled, the work is still topically divided into the elements of the normal repertoire of *Fürstenspiegel*: human association, the necessity of order imposed by a ruler, the manners of kings, retainers, friendship, order and hierarchy. There can be no doubt that the *Nasirean Ethics* is as deliberately structured around a philosophical profile as any, and that it constitutes one of the most outstanding philosophical treatments of politics and of political theology written in Arabic or Persian. Yet, unlike Ibn Khaldūn's *Muqaddima*, its topical political repertoire remains largely governed by the genre of *Fürstenspiegel*. In this it resembles somewhat the work of Ibn al-Azraq (d. 1491) which was designed along lines of propositional consequence in imitation of Ibn

Khaldūn, but which, despite its formal schematism, follows the aggregative rules of the *Fürstenspiegel* genre.[69]

Bereft of a philosophical outlook, other works that preceded this in the genre were of lesser quality, and far more firmly captive to its aggregative structure. Their normal topics are derived from Arab epistolary works, Ibn al-Muqaffaʿ, al-Jāḥiẓ and works attributed to the Greeks. Their constant repertoire consists of the necessity of kingship, the benefit (and occasionally inherent worth) of justice, temperance, reason, clemency, generosity, and auxiliary matters such as subordinates, ambassadors, political and military ruses, etiquette, and sundry anti-hubristic advice and advertence, by example, against falling captive to one's passions. Also treated are correlative subjects, such as the political necessity of forbearance, and the inadvisability of partiality to particular members of the court.

In all, disquisitions on kingship and its necessity – later incorporated within the discourse on the caliphate – are divided into two principal and broad topical categories. The one concerns affairs of state and the conduct of the ruler in his official capacity, which includes the need to exercise rational control over oneself and one's actions, desires, and proclivities. Relations between kings and courtiers are also taken up, as are questions of etiquette and ceremony, elements of governmental rationality such as the imperative of justice, the necessity of secrecy, and systems of reward and punishment. External relations are infrequently dealt with but war, and especially the deployment of spies and of ruses, is a very commonly-treated subject.

The other topic concerns the ethical principles of self-mastery as pre-requisites for the proper exercise of power. *Fürstenspiegel* written with this orientation include the two extant works in the genre by Māwardī,[70] and tend to lay out the ethical preconditions of just rulership before taking up its centrality and prerogatives, but always premise the primacy of the former on the axial position of the ruler within the body social. This is, in a way, a metaphor for the primacy of king over society which is the principal purport of the latter.

These detailed emphases on the ethics of the royal person are, however, altogether less common within the genre of *Fürstenspiegel* than works that treat royal ethics as a matter of state and in terms of reason of state. They are peppered here and there with sundry general moral exhortations which have no consequential effect on the structure of the text or on the order in which material is arranged within it. They include the famous *Fürstenspiegel* of Ghazālī and Ṭurṭūshī as well as the *Kitāb at-Tāj* and the *Secretum Secretorum*. In all, there is little conceptual difference between the two manners of approaching the subject, save the relative weighting of different aspects of kingship in their order of exposition. It must also be said that exposition of this topical material is sometimes quite cavalier in its inattention to any specific order, and is sometimes given to the predominance of what approaches sheer anecdotalism, as in a work by Ibn Ẓafar, originally a Sicilian who later lived in Mahdiyya and Ḥamā where he died in 1169.[71]

Different circumstances of composition often dictate slight variations in the expository disposition of the material and, occasionally, in its content. Thus, for instance, the work of Murādī to which reference has been made, written as it was for the instruction of the uncouth and unlettered princes of a new dynasty which had recently emerged from the trans-Saharan trade routes, opens with an exhortatory section in praise of literacy, reading, and instruction, and includes much elementary matter on etiquette and hygiene, such as the need to refrain from coughing, spitting, or picking one's nose in public, this advice being treated not as admonition, but as an extension of royal decorum and gravitas. To this is added the staple fare of the craft of rule.[72] In contrast, the contribution to this genre by al-Qalʿī (d. 1232–3), a Syrian resident in a remote part of South Arabia, paid no heed to local circumstances but was composed in the conventional manner, citing sententious sayings and praiseworthy acts of a lofty nature.[73] Another work contains an extensive treatment of equestrianism and the hunt.[74] In its treatment of the king's person, the *Secretum Secretorum* includes an extensive disquisition on the human body, on diet, hygiene, *materia medica*, physiognomy and other gnomic and 'subphilosophical'[75] materials. The *Fürstenspiegel* of Abū Ḥammū in its turn concludes with a chapter on physiognomy, regarded here as central to the efficient exercise of kingship. It is surprising that Arabic *Fürstenspiegel* do not generally incorporate much physiognomic material, which was, after all, widely disseminated in works of anecdotal literature and was a subject of deliberate concern and writing.

In line with the spirit of the more ethically-inclined *Fürstenspiegel*, works written by members of the *ʿulamāʾ* corps tend to cite much material about kings humbled by religious personalities, and narratives relating to kings who revere the pious. They tend to make much of sermons of exhortation to do good and of anti-hubristic reminders of the Great Leveller, of the rewards of paradise and the torments of hell; they also tend to conjugate ethical qualities with religious piety.[76] There is even an entire book devoted to the standing of *'ulamā'* with caliphs and kings which is attributed to Ghazālī, probably without justification.[77] These writers thus interpolate into books for kings homiletic Muslim material to which had often been assimilated material deriving from Greek and other wisdom. At the limit, the genre turns into exhortation and preaching. Thus a manual of preaching material by Ibn al-Jawzī (d. 1201) of Baghdad contains quotations ascribed to Plato and Aristotle on the management of one's own person [78] along with worldly and other-worldly wisdom derived from the Koran and *ḥadīth*. Ibn al-Jawzī's compendium, dedicated to the caliph he served, is itself organised around topics congenial to the world of the *Fürstenspiegel*, with disquisitions on justice and related matters. Manuals of preaching are collections of preacherly material, not only pietistic and homiletic, but historical, lexical, *mirabilia*, prophetic narratives, general knowledge, in addition to Koranic material classified by subject[79] and therefore readily recoverable in the light of the required context. Medieval Latin Christianity also produced a considerable body of similarly authoritative *exempla* for sermonising purposes.[80] Thus royal preaching is inflected by the requirements of its setting and aim; but at the same time it brings to bear exemplary material which is only secondarily profane, and which consists largely of precedents and examples which are specifically Muslim, and quite often particularly Muḥammadan. It is this inflection that will be examined now.

It has been noted that the *'ulamā'*, some of whom were particularly illustrious, like Ghazālī and Māwardī, often wrote works of advice for kings. In some instances these works are indistinct from those written by courtiers – for example, the *Tashīl an-naẓar* of Māwardī or the *Mustaẓhirī* of Ghazālī, a book composed for the caliph al-Mustaẓhir which displays its author as a courtier, not as the moralist who appears in other works.[81] The *Tashīl* of Māwardī commences quite explicitly with Aristotelian ethics and material of Greek origin takes precedence over material of Arabic and Muslim provenance. This makes the opening section of the book closer in structure and spirit to philosophico-moral works on politics, such as the writings of Miskawayh (who is not quoted by Māwardī, but who quoted directly from Arabic translations of Greek works). The *Tashīl* then moves on to a detailed, though topically and discursively conventional, discussion of kingship and its functions and prerogatives.

In all, the composition and thrust of these works conform to the genre, with its aggregative organisation, its repertoire of topics, its conception of power and justice, its sense of hierarchy at the apex of which the king (or caliph) stands, its craftsman-like aims for political skill that was meant to be recoverable from the *exempla* they narrate. What *Fürstenspiegel* from such priestly hands add, however, is material yielded by the intersection of religious and more narrowly sharʿist formulations of political wisdom, and the sectional interests at court and in society at large of the *ʿulamāʾ*. The discursive means by which these matters are integrated in *Fürstenspiegel* is the reformulation of certain common themes and sentences of political wisdom in terms of Koranic and prophetic textual paradigms and genealogies.

Thus perennial political wisdom, attributed to Persians, Greeks or others is renamed and recast as prophetic or Koranic and inserted in a distinctive genealogy that is specifically Muslim. Persians and Greeks, and indeed Arabs, are displaced by Muslim authorities or, at the very least, Muslim authorities are adjoined to the standard repertoire of Persian and Greek wisdom, sometimes in the same sense. One example of such a mixture can be found in Ghazālī's famous *Book of Counsel for Kings*.[82] The concordances between sayings attributed to Muḥammad and those attributed to Greek and Persian sages in this book would repay a close study.

This is how the Muslim character of public institutions was brought about. The corollary of this development is the genre of sharʿist politics, *siyāsa sharʿiyya*. The earliest formulation of this genre was by Māwardī and his Ḥanbalī contemporary and fellow-courtier, Abū Yaʿlā b. al-Farrāʾ (d. 1066), who was *qāḍī* of the caliphal harem in Baghdad and who composed a work very similar to the more famous *al-Aḥkām as-sulṭāniyya* of Māwardī. The latter rapidly became the standard treatment of what came to be regarded as the standard and classical treatment of the caliphate in its legal aspect. It was widely quoted and deferred to, and treated as a foundational text to be glossed, summarised, and commented on.[83] This and other books on the legal arrangements of government lie at the intersection of legal writing (*fiqh*) and writings on politics. They are simultaneously *Fürstenspiegel*, preserving the basic absolutist, pedagogic, aggregative, exemplary, and consultative character of their paradigms, and works of jurisprudence which are prescriptive on the basis of analogies and direct examples stated in narrative form like the *exempla* of the *Fürstenspiegel*. But in them, naturally, the example that is put forward for the guidance of the caliph consists exclusively of Muslim precedent. It is this which makes them specifically Muslim works on politics and books of Muslim jurisprudence. Such jurisprudence is in fact but a repertoire of exemplary precedents with legal force.

Yet the actual literary genealogy of *aḥkām* works is not the *Fürstenspiegel* but compilations of legal precedent such as collections of traditions and sayings on agrarian taxation exemplified by the *Kitāb al-kharāj* of Abū Yūsuf (d. 797) or indeed the classical collections of *ḥadīth*. This would have been the genealogy perceived by the authors concerned, although it should not prevent us from associating these *aḥkām* works with the social, political, and cultural contexts from which they arose, namely, caliphal and sultanic courts. Very much like *Fürstenspiegel*, then, *aḥkām* works are instruments of absolutist government which specify the pragmatic and ethical content of the *Fürstenspiegel* as sharʿist. The topics of justice, equity, and the rational ethics of the political craft are displaced as to their origin from perennial examples provided by Greeks, Persians, and Arabs, to a perennity exclusively recoverable within Muslim textual and exemplary paradigms. These topics are intermixed with the standard topical repertoire of *fiqh* concerning public affairs, duplicated in part in general legal compendia: the imamate and caliphate, its powers and prerogatives, its public duties, primarily cultic and legal organisation, taxation, warfare, and the maintenance of internal stability, and finally, the delegation of authority and its modalities and offices. In all, the topical repertoire is narrower and more firmly fixed, having been definitively set by Māwardī.

Like *Fürstenspiegel* and works of jurisprudence, books of *aḥkām* consist of a topical aggregate of exemplary precedents. But the exemplary precedents of *aḥkām* works are regarded in the guise of legal judgements, or lead to legal consequences derived from them by a variety of jurists. They have inherent in them a charisma, a certain obligation and a burdensome spirit of command whose bases transcend those of sheer political instrumentalism. In addition to exemplary material derived from the vast repertoire of narratives concerning the Prophet, these works also contain direct performative statements of command or prohibition attributed to the Prophet or emanating from the Koranic text. And yet works of *aḥkām* do not seriously restrict the options of the persons to whom they are presented: they are not codes of law which, after all, are a modern phenomenon unknown and inconceivable to Muslim jurisprudence, but rather a body of general prescriptions, precedents, and equally legitimately grounded variant rulings within the bounds of which the caliph can exercise his judgement. Indeed, scholars of officious adherence to a particular school of Sunni law and of more pronounced theological taste, like Juwaynī (d. 1085) who combined a great intellect with a narrow mind, sharply criticised the latitudinarianism characteristic of the genre.[84]

Power Islamised

The overall context in which this development took place and consolidated itself was the emergence of the *ʿulamāʾ* as a corporate group, with the incipient institutional crystallisation, in the tenth century, of the schools of Muslim jurisprudence including the beginnings of Ḥanbalī and specifically Shīʿi imamist jurisprudence. This was followed by the progressive professionalisation and institutionalisation of the *ʿulamaʾ*, from the time of the Saljuqs and with the emergence of the *madāris* colleges which energetically provided the necessary economic and social context, especially under the Mamluk sultans.[85] These developments constituted Sunnism as we know it, at a time when Twelver Shīʿism was also crystallising.

Sunnism, of course, implies the adoption of the prophetic *sunna* as the definitive repertoire of salutary precedent, for belief as for action, and the correlative displacement, with varying degrees of severity, of other genealogical charters for the present. This tendency towards the adoption of an omnivorous totalising central discourse did not always match official state religious policy. Ibn al-Muqaffaʿ early exhorted the caliph, without success, to supersede the individual judgements of jurists and their use of spurious prophetic *sunna* with a definitive code of laws.[86] The persecutionist efforts of al-Ma'mūn and al-Mu'taṣim are commonly thought of as an attempt to impose a state dogma, a view far too simple to account for these religious policies in which the role of Mu'tazilism is in any case exaggerated.[87] It was only in the Buyid era that an effort was made by the caliphate, especially under al-Qādir (r. 991–1031) and his son and successor al-Qā'im (r. 1031–1075), to pronounce an official state catechism with caliphal sanction along crypto-Ḥanbalī lines which came to constitute the basis of subsequent Sunni dogma.[88]

The Muslim priestly class was closely allied with these developments. Abū Ya'lā was personally instrumental in formulating the creed of al-Qādir,[89] and his contemporary Māwardī was very much the theorist of caliphal absolutism in an age of a crystallised Sunnism emergent around the figure of the caliphate.[90] The formation and canonisation of the corpus of *ḥadīth*[91] was lent particular force by the legal synthesis of Shāfi'ī (767–820) and built on the pietistic image of Aḥmad b. Ḥanbal (d. 855). It was this textual corpus which replaced other genealogical charters for thoughts, beliefs, and deeds. The *'ulamā'* were, after all, the agency of Islamisation, not in the sense of conversion to Islam, but in the sacralisation of the world and its reading, under the Islamic signature, in terms of conformity or non-conformity with the prophetic type. They were the agency which could identify with Islamism things of this world, constitute them as Islam, name them, form them into a tradition of scholarship and learning, and into an ethos. Islamisation was contained most copiously within the corpus of writings of juristic theory, *uṣūl al-fiqh*, which was coeval with the emergence of the *'ulamā'* as a corporate group. *Uṣūl al-fiqh* treated the affairs of the world as if they were recoverable and comprehended entirely within the bounds of an Islam which the *'ulamā'* were defining within the textual boundaries of the Koran interpreted, the *ḥadīth* vastly expanded, the genealogical charters of this corporate group organised under the title of consensus, and analogies drawn from these three sources by its members.[92]

There is a considerable body of historical narratives ascribing to Sunnī divines, most particularly Ibn Ḥanbal and his followers, a variety of miraculous deeds.[93] This popular charisma was accompanied by and crowned with the theoretical case for the primacy of priestly opinion and the correlative primacy of Sunnī textualism in matters of public life, a doctrine which crystallised into set forms with the institutional crystallisation of the *ʿulamāʾ* as a priestly sodality. Juwaynī declared, without any reference to the caliphate which he did not estimate very highly, that kings should stand to the *ʿulamā* as they would to the Prophet since the *ʿulamāʾ* have inherited the mantle of prophecy.[94] His pupil al-Ghazāli, while in the usual way exhorting sovereigns to heed the advice of the *ʿulamāʾ*, sets the *ʿulamāʾ*, in his description of the hierarchy of paradise, immediately below the prophets.[95]

Ultimately, all this crystallised into the famous doctrine that the *ʿulamāʾ* were the Prophet's successors, more or less at the same time as the caliphate was going into eclipse. Ibn Jamāʿa (d. 1333) declared taking counsel from the *ʿulamāʾ* to be an obligation of the sovereign, be he king or caliph.[96] In the same vein, Ibn Taymiyya (d. 1327), the most rigorous exponent of Sunnism, regarded kingship as a form of piety and of the propriation of God,[97] thus delegating to the *ʿulamāʾ* ultimate authority over matters of legitimacy. The parallels with and direct influences upon this line of thinking of Shiʿi notions are evident, and run in tandem with the transference to the Prophet of Sunnism some characteristics of the Shiʿi imam, including infallibility.[98] The representation of the *ʿulamāʾ* as an autonomous group capable of standing in for political power in the regulation of public affairs in the absence of a convincing king or without necessary reference to him or, in the case of the Shiʿa, an *imam*, follows explicitly from this priestly autonomism,[99] and was correlative with legal doctrines about such matters as the legitimacy of prayer without explicit license from the sovereign.[100]

This doctrine of priestly primacy in the public sphere, and the premise of clerical purity, was amply sustained by the literary topoi that had circulated for centuries in works of anecdotal literature, in *Fürstenspiegel* and in homiletic and pietistic works. One such topos was the tragedy of a state secretary, later of a cleric, afflicted with the service of an unjust king; there was even blanket condemnation of all dealings with the state on the grounds that these were inevitably compromising and corrupting. Legal consequences were attendant upon serving an unjust ruler, which was often deemed illicit, though licit if undertaken under duress and by royal command. Such service was often associated with the golden rule that one day of disorder is worse than a year of injustice, or that sixty years of injustice are preferable to a single night without a ruler,[101] and consequently to the proposition, set out in standard Sunni creeds, that obedience to the power in place is imperative.[102] Other topoi regarded religion and the state as correlative and attempted to derive from this a doctrine of the dependence of the state on a religion prior to it and constituting its means of regulation.[103]

It is therefore not the case, as is often maintained, that Muslim rulers had increasing recourse to secular politics and that this provoked a religious commentary by the *ʿulamāʾ*.[104] It is rather that a properly religious field available for the members of the clerical *ʿulamāʾ* sodality was in the process of social constitution and intellectual elaboration. *Siyāsa* as the distinctive form of action by the ruler had always been available and constituted the public domain. But *siyāsa* as a relative form of action by the sovereign is premised on the identification and availability of *dīn* as a distinctive field in its own right and independent of sovereign will and action. This was the novel development under description here. There is no evidence whatsoever that Muslim rulers prior to the development of the corporatist Islam of the *ʿulamāʾ* were any more consummately sharʿist than those who followed, that they had deteriorated, or that the *sharīʿa* had once flourished but had now atrophied: this is a trope of salvation-historical historism which does not derive its force from the study of historical reality. It rests on an unreflected assumption on the part of both the *ʿulamāʾ* and orientalist scholars, in each case equally defiant of the logic of history, that Islam was integrally and definitively constituted at an early stage in its existence, after which it could do none other than deteriorate.

The crystallisation of *ʿulamāʾ* corporatism, institutional and intellectual, and with it a tradition grounded in textualist traditionalism, was the decisive factor in this process. It is indeed the case that the notion of the Prophet's *sunna* came to replace the charismatic notion of the caliphate.[105] Though there is no room here for tracing this process in detail, it should be emphasised that the corporatism of the *ʿulamāʾ* went in tandem with traditionalism, which took the form of generating the body of *hadīth* in which the Prophet was made the topos for all manner of prophetic and extra-prophetic matters. This process of textualist traditionalisation started early in the Abbasid period but matured very slowly, as such matters do in real history. One can indicate beginnings in a famous Abbasid epistolary testament dated ca 820–22 which, along with the staple topics found in testaments or *Fürstenspiegel* of the time, contained much pietistic material, exhorting the prince to adhere to the traditions of the Prophet, a conception of primacy that was only just emerging at the time. It also exhorted its recipient to be punctilious in observing devotions, and to keep the company of *ʿulamāʾ*.[106] The contrast with the epistle of ʿAbd al-Ḥamīd al-Kātib, written seven decades earlier, is very striking, although both texts share the same repertoire of political wisdom material, topically as well as conceptually.

Be that as it may, the development had a certain impact on the topical content of *Fürstenspiegel*, though not on their structure or conceptual content. *Fürstenspiegel* were the location where the development first made itself felt, before developing into the fully-fledged genre of *siyāsa sharʿiyya*. The citation of specifically Muslim authorities, including the Koran and the actions and words ascribed to the prophet has already been mentioned. Ibn Taymiyya presents his famous book of *siyāsa sharʿiyya* as a mere commentary on a certain Koranic verse which he regarded as constituting the entirety of just politics.[107]

Germane here is the correlative feature of the almost entire displacement of non-Muslim authorities by the example of Arab and Muslim sayings and actions which convey very much the same conceptual and topical apparatus and are often of the same order as those attributed to Greek or Persian sages. This is a feature of a *Fürstenspiegel* of mid-thirteenth century Mosul,[108] or indeed of the *Baḥr al-fawāʾid* which contains only three references to Persian pre-Islamic material, while its references to Alexander are again derived exclusively from Muslim traditions[109] or the Islamised form of other traditions. In another thirteenth-century text of the genre mention of Aristotle occurs only once and other non-Muslim authorities, with the exception of a small number of Persians, recede into anonymity and are referred to as 'sages'.[110] What must be added is the accretion of devotional, pietistic, and homiletic elements within these works and the eventual emergence among Sunnis of the equivalent topic of the caliphate and the imamate within it, eventually leading to the emergence of a new genre.

Ṭurṭūshī (d. 1126) for one added to his famous works various specifically sharʿist chapters. Of these, a salutary royal character that assures the order of states, or the standing of kings in the Koran, and interpretations of Koranic statements regarding the relationship between rulers and ruled may be specifically mentioned.[111] But these matters do not contain topical or conceptual elements that add to the rest of the work or have any consequential effect on its constitution, or to the treatment of these same subjects without reference to their Muslim character. Indeed, the quotations from the Koran and prophetic tradition throughout this and other similar works do not in their turn structure the discourses on kingship conceptually or topically, but are rather assimilated to the conceptual and topical requirements of the genre, acting as authorities for assertions anterior to quotation or reference.

Māwardī for his part not only stressed the need for kings to receive advice and sermons from the priestly elements in their entourage, as we have seen, but also gave a central role to religious institutes, concepts and the acquisition of religious knowledge in the training of royal character.[112] The *Sirāj al-mulūk* of Ṭurṭūshī, which was to become standard, opens in the form of a priestly sermon with a discourse on the necessity of preaching before kings. Ghazālī, in his turn, commences his famous *Fürstenspiegel*, *al-Tibr al-masbūk*, with pietistic material that he famously standardised in his celebrated *Revification of the Religious Sciences* (*Iḥyāʾ ʿulūm ad-dīn*) and its shorter version, *The Alchemy of Felicity* (*Kīmiyāʾ as-saʿāda*), and opens it with a chapter on faith. This then proceeds to the statement that was to become standard in writings of this type, that just kingship, under which Muslim jurisprudence becomes the 'law of politics',[113] is a divine benediction upon its incumbent, assuring the most consummate felicity in this world and in the hereafter.[114]

Ibn Taymiyya added the further refinement that rulership is the greatest of all religious duties, on which the maintenance of religion depends.[115] The homiletic tone of Ghazālī and his pietistic orientation were to become almost constitutive of much later writing both as an ethos and a source for reverent quotation. Finally, a work composed at the time of the Crusades specifies the impurity of faith as an impediment to the stability of kingship, on a par with cowardice, heedlessness, and other deleterious traits of human character.[116]

But the topic of the imamate or the caliphate, as distinct from kingship, was only tangentially an element of concern to books of political wisdom, except for a work by the Andalusian Ibn Riḍwān (d. 1381), who opened his *Fürstenspiegel*, written for the Granadan Naṣrids, to whom the institution of the caliphate was very remote, with a chapter on the caliphate, which refers particularly to Māwardī, treating of its necessity and of the obligation to obedience incumbent upon subjects written with specific reference to Māwardī.[117] But the distinctiveness of the caliphate here is topical, not conceptual. It is treated as a distinctive form of government only nominally, while its conceptual constitution conforms to that of kingship generally, and is indistinguishable from its topics. The topic of the caliphate in this work is, however, distinctive in so far as it contains a chapter on what had, since Māwardī's *aḥkām*, become defined as the legal obligations of the caliphate, such as the conservation of religious traditionalism, enforcement of penal statutes, maintenance of frontier fortifications, collection of taxes, and other matters.[118] Indeed the rest of the book treats, quite consistently and clearly, of kings after the manner current in the genre including the near-absence of an authorial voice. In all cases it is assumed, in the discourse on power, that the institutes and structures of the caliphate correspond in practice and conception to those of kingship in Muslim domains, although they are legally distinct,[119] a question that will be taken up in detail in chapter 7.

It is clear that Ibn Riḍwān's concern with the caliphate, and indeed the very constitution of the caliphate as a topic for writing on politics, was made possible by its formal topical availability which emerged with Māwardī and crystallised in his work, taking on the canonical form in which it came down the ages. Indeed, we see in Ibn Riḍwān (parallel developments in the East will be taken up presently) a certain tendency towards the prescriptive sharʿification of royal action and an attempt to subject it to a number of functions which were defined in legal works on the caliphate and were thus endowed with a sharʿist ethos and charisma. All these were in fact functions of rulership in general, like taxation and military organisation, which had been sharʿified by their insertion within a specific textual genealogy referring to the Koran, the *ḥadīth* and consensus – a reference that allowed them to be the voice of the *ʿulamāʾ* sodality. With Ibn Riḍwān, this sharʿification was episodic and partial, one topic among many addressed within the ambit of kingship, with the caliphate as an elevated form of kingship.

In *aḥkām* works the topic of the caliphate was multivalent: it was treated as a form of kingship, fulfilling the functions naturally performed by kingship in human society and claiming the prerogatives of kingship among which obedience was paramount. It was simultaneously regarded as in some way prior to kingship, conveying a sense of order that is normatively prior to kingship in the sense of being more primeval, deriving from the history of prophecy which is coeval with the history of the world.

The caliphate also uses the functions and prerogatives of kingship to fulfil meta-political ends. The imbrication of the political or natural aspects of kingship and its meta-political functions goes further. The constitution of the caliphate in terms of jurisprudential norms of charismatic origin – Koranic and Prophetic – achieves a correspondence between the sacrality of the caliphal office 'naturally' constituted by pre-existing historico-political traditions and its sacralisation by means of jurisprudential norms which, according to their construction by *ʿulamā*, are normatively prior to this particular office. If, at the limit, a caliph does not comport himself in accordance with a form of legality which is constitutive of his office, the caliphal charisma comes to override that of the legal system: it is the opinion of the vast majority of jurists that sedition, whatever its cause and even when directed against a miscreant or maleficent ruler, is illegitimate.

The political, at the limit, thus overrides the meta-political. A clear conceptual congruence can be perceived between the *Fürstenspiegel* and *aḥkām* works, and this continues later, and far more clearly, in works of *siyāsa sharʿiyya*. The first of these genres of writing on politics adopted the notion of justice as the crucial element in the assurance of stable rule and in the maintenance of the human interest served by the formation of political collectivities. The latter two genres specify this element of justice with the maintenance of a particular form of legal order indicated by charismatic origin and termed the *sharīʿa*, which is simultaneously conducive to human interest in this world and to salvation in the next. There is therefore a double congruence between the sharʿist and the natural orders of politics, between the caliphal and the royal: a conceptual congruence relating to the maintenance of order by means of justice, and a natural congruence involving the maintenance of order by the maintenance of polity irrespective of whether sharʿist justice is in place. As Ghazālī, among others, observed, order is maintained by justice irrespective of whether the royal guardian of justice be a Muslim or otherwise.[120] This was in keeping with the ubiquitous topos of dividing kingship into three types: a self-destructive one based on caprice and passion, a workable one built upon reason and force, and finally, kingship based on religion. The last is the most perfect and most conducive to consent of subjects, but rational kingship is no less workable a system, being based on calculations of human interest. [121] This classification of governments is correlative with the philosophical classification of cities, built upon Platonic models, that abound in Muslim philosophical discourse.[122]

Thus works of *aḥkām* typically commence by stipulating the necessity of the caliphal office as derived from traditionalist textual sources, usually but not always accompanied by its derivation from the natural fractiousness of men who contrive to contract one among themselves to keep order with the application of force.[123] It is often the case that the latter, naturalist, argument is the subject for a refutation, not on account of its lack of a naturalistic explanatory force, but for its irrelevance to the legal argument for the necessity of the imamate which, being a legal argument based on the principle of consensus, must derive its force and sense from the argumentative repertoire of jurisprudence which regards consensus as one of its bases. Hypothetical history or sociology with naturalistic notions of human interest, irrespective of the force of these arguments, are not salient to the legal foundations of the Caliphate.[124]

The arguments here are congruent with those one finds in systematic works of dogmatic theology (*kalām*), which normally end with a chapter on the imamate. The inclusion of this topic in the ambit of theology was not the result of a specific theological history of writing on the theory of politics, but of a topical aggregation specific to the constitution of the thematic conformation of *kalām* in the course of the specifically political history of its emergence. A scholastic compendium on theology indicates this historical point quite explicitly. Its author, al-Taftāzāni (d. 1390) clearly states that whereas the question of the imamate and of public authority is really one that belongs to jurisprudence, being a question of practice and not an article of belief, the dialectical needs dictated by the emergence and crystallisation of the faith made it necessary that it be addressed.[125] Earlier and in a similar vein, the theologian and jurist al-Āmidī (d. 1233) regretted the inclusion of this topic among the concerns of theology because it was one of controversy laden with irrational passions and malevolent conjectures concerning the Companions of the Prophet, and was not a matter essential to doctrine. Nevertheless, in keeping with convention, he presented a standard treatment of it in his theological compendium.[126]

Clearly, the matter involved arguments against the Shiʿi notion of the imamate as a fundamental article of dogma. Taftāzānī's account contains a detailed sketch of all available notions of the imamate, Sunni as well as Shiʿi.[127] Thus chapters on this subject in works of dogmatic theology came to include refutations of the main Shiʿi doctrines concerning the impeccability, omnipotence, miraculousness, and heritability of the imamate.[128] They also comprised reflections on the legitimacy of public authority which derived from debates concerning the legitimacy of the Medinan caliphate, most particularly Shiʿi arguments concerning the priority of ʿAlī and the illegitimacy of the other caliphs at that period, and the assertion that the Prophet explicitly designated ʿAlī as heir to his authority. Some Sunnīs had responded to this latter assertion by a counter-argument from authority, on the basis of certain *ḥadīth* narratives that the Prophet designated not ʿAlī, but Abū Bakr as his successor. The ʿAbbasids meanwhile affirmed throughout the designation by the Prophet of al-ʿAbbās and of his progeny; theological works written under the ʿAbbasids were silent on this latter assertion.[129] Sunnism and Shiʿism claimed different genealogies for legitimacy, the one continuing from the Prophet through to the Umayyads and the ʿAbbasids, and the other denying legitimacy altogether to this line of caliphal transmission, and consequently denying also its role in the register of Heilsgeschichte.[130]

Abū Yaʿlā b. al-Farrāʾ deals with these matters explicitly. He distinguishes his two contributions to the subject of the imamate, the one contained in a theological treatise, and the other in a legal work of *aḥkām*, by stating that the former dealt with controversial and dialectical matters pertaining to the necessity of the office, the arguments for its necessity, and aspects of its practical constitution and institution. The latter, however, assumed the right – Sunni – interpretation to be pre-given, and proceeded to detail the legal prerogatives, offices, and functions entailed by it.[131] Indeed, this inclusion of political topics in works of theology indicates the force of the process of appropriating the world in which the *ʿulamāʾ* were engaged; these treatments are not conceptually distinct from treatments in works of *aḥkām*. That philosophical treatments of politics are actually distinct in form and provenance led Ghazālī to classify them as serving the merely secular political interests of kings.[132]

Be that as it may, one of the important offices that derive from the caliphate according to its legal formulation is that of natural kingship, the sultanate, which is legislated as an executive arm of the overarching authority of the *sharīʿa* represented – indeed embodied – by the caliphal office. To the sultanate devolve the functions of the caliphate by legal delegation, and it is herein that we can clearly see, in the works of *aḥkām*, the genesis of the genre of *siyāsa sharʿiyya* which legislates for the legal order to be maintained in the absence of the caliphate, whose meta-political goal is overseen by the corporation of the *ʿulamāʾ*, reflecting the symbiotic relationship between this corporation and political authority.[133]

The distance between *aḥkām* and *siyāsa sharʿiyya* works is minimal. The works on sharʿist politics incorporate the contents of works of public jurisprudence relating to the tasks of political authority, such as taxation, appointments, punishments, warfare, the guardianship over public morals and the upkeep of public religiosity and of the legal system in general. We have here a *Fürstenspiegel* with an omnipresent sharʿist inflection that is perhaps more visible than the secular matters so inflected, and which attempts asymptotically to subordinate the political to the meta-political under the title of the *sharʿ* and of confining politics to that which conforms with the meta-political.

Ibn Taymiyya states of his famous work within this genre that it is a precis of 'divine politics' (*siyāsa ilāhiyya*) and 'prophetic delegation' (*ināba nabawiyya*), assuring the institution and continuity of 'just politics',[134] justice here being defined with reference to its sharʿist bearings as determined by traditionalists whose references are entirely textual. The transformation of public into religious institutes takes the form of ascription to Muslim canonical authorities. The attack mounted in these works on extra-sharʿist punishments and other prerogatives of kingship, including taxation, reveals the conception of an impersonal lawfulness as the guardian and regulator of the public sphere, but nevertheless a lawfulness whose impersonality is ratified by the *ʿulamāʾ*.

This and similar positions resulted in general statements to the effect that the *sharīʿa* is itself the very substance of politics.[135] It results that any accreditation of politics as a sphere distinct from the *sharīʿa* is a presumption upon the *sharīʿa*, with the impious implication of merely human law-giving.[136] Alternatively and correlatively it could be stated by Ibn Qayyim al-Jawziyya (d. 1350), one of Ibn Taymiyya's most important pupils, that just politics is itself no more than a branch of the *sharīʿa*, not in the restrictive sense of textual literalism, but including human interest implicit in spirit of the *sharīʿa* and accessible to the human mind. Thus from this perspective, just politics is distinctive only in the terminological sense, for in fact it is nothing but the justice of the Prophet. The distinction is not one between politics and *sharʿ*, but between *sharīʿa* and non-*sharīʿa*.[137] That Prophecy is but one means of assuring human interest by means of particularly just politics was a notion that had already been rejected by Ibn Taymiyya, who held prophecy to be an unmediated act of divinity which is absolutely incommensurable.[138]

It should be noted that the notion of human interest within the ambit of *sharʿ* was a matter that had been taken up in Muʿtazilism, then generalised by Ghazālī and Ibn Rushd (d. 1198), and finally brought to a prodigious formalisation and crystallisation by Shāṭibī (d. 1388), although in the mainstream theological works of the Ashʿarites it was thought to derogate from divine omnipotence. Yet it was an attempt at a much larger and far more rigorous scale to cast the world into the mould of the sharʿist reading than that attempted for politics in the manner just suggested.[139] Altogether, both devolve to building actions of the present on paradigmatic actions, commands, and prohibitions contained in the canon. Thus works by Ibn Taymiyya, Ibn Qayyim al-Jawziyya, or Ibn Jamāʿa (d. 1333) – all three Syrians of the Mamluk period – are books of institutes, prescriptions, and precedents concerning the mass of matters that arise in the public domain, from taxation to criminality to war and cultic organisation, compiled by *ʿulamāʾ* for rulers. In this they are, like the work of Māwardī, works of *aḥkām sulṭāniyya* quite literally. Ibn Jamāʿa explicitly states that his work was a compilation of just such *aḥkām sulṭāniyya*,[140] with the distinction in Mamluk times having become one between such *aḥkām*, and the deliberate treatment of the topic of the caliphate.[141]

In all, we get in works both of *aḥkām* and of *siyāsa sharʿiyya* what has been termed a 'mixed theory' of the imamate, which, exemplified by Ghazālī, incorporated the sultanate within the legal institutes of the caliphate.[142] In the case of the latter genre, which contains no material on the proper legal means of accession to power which forms part of the juristic formulation of the caliphate, the sultanate is incorporated within the sharʿism which forms the material of the caliphate. The caliphate appears therein as an institution which may be an optimal form of government, but by no means exclusive in its pertinence to the life of human society. If religious authority assuring the maintenance of order lacks a caliphal apex, this same charisma can be seen to reside with the corporation of the *'ulamā'* as the repositories of the *sharī'a*, a corporation which fulfils the same function of overseeing the rectitude of order and its conformity with the requirements attendant upon 'divine politics' and 'prophetic delegation'.

Thus the latitudinarianism of the *aḥkām* works, as legal works for and by practical jurists, and of *Fürstenspiegel*, is implicitly declared by the more rigid quasi-codified works of *siyāsa shar'iyya* to be inadequate because such latitudinarianism allows far too much room for imperfection and for considering matters of this world to possess a flow of their own, not all of which can or should be invigilated by the *shar'*. The corporatist priestly project of self-empowerment and of sociopolitical omnipresence could not tolerate this.

It will be clear from the foregoing that Arabic, and more generally Muslim, writing on politics in the Middle Ages does not contain or constitute a theory of the state. Nor does it regard kingship as more than the sum total of royal activities, which are described and tabulated but not theorised. It is true that there are, in general, indications about the types of government, be they based on religion, on reason, or on caprice. But this is a typology of royal motivation, not a theory of the state. There were also available many redactions of the idea, not exclusive to Ibn Khaldūn, that states commence with vigour, later tempered by confidence, and terminate in effeminacy and injustice, and that each of these stages has correlative royal characters and propensities.[143] This view is variously attributed to Platonic and other origins, was very frequently expressed in moralising and censorious terms,[144] and was very long lived, finding expression in various Ottoman writings on politics where it took on an elaborately theoretical turn in the form of a vitalist and organismic metaphor.[145]

But this is again not a theory of the state, not even in the work of Ibn Khaldūn, where these topics find their most eloquent and detailed statement, and where some elements of the organismic metaphor just mentioned were also present.[146] The state is here abstract activity personified in the detailed actions of the king, while history is not the history of a state, but the history of a particular royal line. In this Ibn Khaldūn was in agreement with the historiographical tradition to which he was a faithful heir in his historical practice, regardless of his intention to subvert certain elements of this tradition. Writing on the state, moreover, even when restricted to the person of the king and certain classes of acts taking place during his reign, was formally not part of writing on politics, but of historical literature, in which the state is no more than the temporal extension of power – manifested in its detail – continuously performed by an historical actor.[147] Writing politics, in short, is not theoretical discourse, but disquisition on praxis and its skills. Politics is an art, learnt like all other arts by practice, imitation, and the creation of a *habitus*. Thus it consists of maxims and examples, not of general statements concerning a particular object of study for it is, according to well-known Greek vocabulary, *techné* and therefore beneath the dignity of *teoría*.

CHAPTER SIX

The Absolutist Imperative

Power Enunciated

All Muslim discourse on political association is premised on a pessimistic anthropology. With the exception of the Muʿtazilī theologian Abū Bakr al-Aṣamm (d 816 or 817) who postulated the hypothetical condition of a collectivity internally driven by justice to the extent of not requiring perpetual correction from above,[1] it was the universal consensus of medieval Muslim authors of all persuasions, writing in all genres, that the nature of humankind is such that its orderly collective existence can only be guaranteed by unrelenting maintenance on the part of a vigilant ruler. This custodian of the body-social coerces the members of the human collectivity into a form of order which goes against the anarchic, violent, rapacious, and unjust nature of individual human beings in their state of nature.

From this anthropology was derived the imperative of absolutism. In the form of a state order, absolutism constitutes a culture that overrides the impulses of mere nature to which human beings, congenitally recidivist, can so easily abandon themselves. The worldly consequence of prophethood, as distinct from its purely salvational function in the divine scheme of things, was construed after the same functional aspect deriving from the same pessimistic anthropology. But the theoretical statement of this matter was in some dispute as the standard position put forward by theologians asserted that the imperative of prophethood was dictated by the sheer command of God and could not be evaluated in terms of human interest. Prophethood in this sense cannot be reduced to rational-pragmatic considerations of utility. Mere utility does not necessarily yield prophecy, but it does yield political collectivities, comprising the vast majority of humankind, no less efficient in their collective life for being entirely worldly and unconnected to prophetic missions.[2] This matter was much in evidence in theological and legal-theoretical discussions, and yielded in some authors, most notably and persuasively Ibn Rushd, a certain notion of natural law.[3]

The anthropology of prophecy outlined here – ubiquitous despite its unpopularity among many theologians, and its explanation in terms of worldly utility and theodicy[4] – was based on the same arguments as those on which the consensus over the imperative of absolutism was grounded. Beginning from an argument from the need for human beings to form collectivities, this imperative was grounded in a profound and elementary structural and metaphysical principle of medieval Muslim thought which regarded all composite entities as unnatural and therefore in need of coercion in order for the state of composition to be maintained. This applied to somatic composites constituted by the primacy within them of a particular element, humour, or temper no less than to human collectivities which, in their composition, transpose individuals from a state of nature to a cultural condition which endows the chaos of natural existence with the unnatural form of a cultural order, constituted and guaranteed by political power.[5]

The coming about of this composite order of humanity, invigilated by the absolutism of kingship, was described in various ways corresponding to the genres, traditions, or conceptual apparatus by means of which the transition from nature to culture was recorded. Ultimately, descriptions of the transition from the state of nature to the culture of political collectivity, ubiquitous albeit not very extended in the body of medieval Arabic writing,[6] take up the theme of sociality as a corollary to the necessity of the division of labour. Humans are not separately capable of satisfying their need for clothing, food, shelter, and protection against attacks by wild beasts. The need for sociality was also seen to lie at the root of humanity's capacity for speech.[7]

The fuller statements of this human itinerary from individual to collective existence[8] postulate its beginning in collaboration for the pursuit of food, which brings in its train the need for storage, entailing the erection of permanent structures which in their turn require protection and organisation; hence a rudimentary form of social order expressed in the hierarchy of owner and guard. The rudiments of a public sphere thus emerge, parallel to the emergence of a private sphere imposed upon men by the need for the preservation of the species, which induces them to seek wives both for purposes of breeding and managing the household. Increasing complexity brings about the interdependence of individuals who provide each other with their respective products: food, clothing, dwelling, crafts, weapons, and so forth. This sociality is, in a certain interpretation, what constitutes humanity, or civility in the Aristotelian sense,[9] and the condition for the attainment of perfection and felicity as understood by the Platonising tradition in Muslim philosophy.[10]

With sociality comes the necessity of inequality,[11] along with unevenness and conflict. The concomitance of these conditions and their necessary correlation was so axiomatic in Muslim political culture of the Middle Ages that they constituted part of some caliphal *bayʿa* documents, topoi of popular literature, or the occasion for analogies drawn with the animal kingdom.[12] Order has no other cause than diversity, and can only be maintained by constantly managing diversity, inequality, unevenness, and conflict which – given the naturally fractious, base and unruly character of humanity – can only be managed by force. This thesis is the *locus classicus* of all Muslim discussion of the necessity of kingship, be it attributed to the Koran and the Prophet, to Plato or to others.[13]

In this context the king is the holder of ultimate custodial authority, famously referred to by Ibn Khaldūn as *wāziʿ* but also referred to as *wazʿa*, *shawka*, *ghalaba*, and more generally *mulk* and *sulṭān*. The idea that the establishment of an overwhelming authority reflects a specific empirical historical itinerary marking a specific beginning for the suppression of the state of nature is not always explicitly stated, although the quasi-evolutionist implication is almost always drawn. It can be corroborated by the view of barbarism prevalent in medieval Arab and Muslim letters as a condition defined by disorder, signalled most particularly by the notion of *jāhiliyya* in its secular sense of the condition of a people bereft of political authority.[14] In addition, certain historical works refer to Persian legends of the emergence of polity and kingship under Gayomard as the direct result of human fractiousness and congenital propensity to enmity, envy, injustice, and violence.[15] This runs parallel to various Muslim interpretations of Jewish history which explain the genesis of Jewish kingship as an act of divine grace necessitated by the disarray and violence that had come to prevail amongst the Israelites when God sent Saul to rule over them with royal authority.[16] Such explanations also run parallel to the history of divine intervention in the affairs of the world as expressed in the general history of prophecy, although it is rare for this point to be brought out explicitly in writings about politics.[17]

Nevertheless, it would be hard to speak of the prevalence of a theory of social contract, notwithstanding medieval Arabic contractualist vocabulary.[18] Some authors speak explicitly of divine inspiration and innate pragmatic predisposition in contradistinction to reason as the efficient cause of sociality,[19] along lines reminiscent of certain discussions of the genesis of language in medieval literature. Some philosophical texts regard sociality as the acquisition of appropriate 'perfections' (in the Aristotelian sense of entelechy), or as the cultivation of complementary virtues.[20] In all, one gathers the impression of a quasi-natural process whereby natural disorder is coerced into the order of culture. And although there are occasional hints at the role of human reason in the formation of political collectivities which might yield a notion of social contract,[21] the prevalent drift of philosophical arguments on this matter indicates supra-mundane intervention: by emanation from the active intellect as with Fārābī,[22] or with prophecy as with Ibn Sīnā, who conceives of the prophet as one who demonstrates his prophecy by the performance of miracles, and who indicates to the multitude profound truth concerning order in the metaphorical or analogical form to which their intellect is receptive.[23] Ghazālī's dictum that God accomplishes with the sword what he does not accomplish with the force of reason (*burhān*)[24] expresses well the belief in the unnatural character of reasonable and just behaviour for humankind.

Inequality and unevenness are thus a natural condition, indeed the natural precondition of order. Just as not all individuals can be kings, nor all of them tradesmen,[25] moral differentiation is the precondition of sound morality, and the presence of ignorance the precondition for the cultivation of knowledge.[26] In order for natural differentiation to cohere into order, its elements need to be subject to politics: a form of husbandry, *siyāsa*, a term applied to both the management of humans and the husbandry of animals, also termed *tadbīr* in texts of a philosophical nature or utilising philosophical vocabulary.

The husbandry of humans employs as its main instruments enticement and threat, the carrot and the stick, both used in the management of animals, and their somewhat more complex human analogues of granting and withholding, distancing and holding near, elevating and demoting.[27] All these matters are ceaselessly repeated in works on government by courtiers, men of letters, historians, and jurists alike, and are amply demonstrated, as we shall see, in the practice of kingship. By using this staple repertoire of political techniques, statecraft maintains the body social according to its two axes of organisation, that of co-operation among different parts performing different functions, and that of the hierarchy superimposed upon this functionally concatenated order.[28] Hence it becomes quite natural that the functioning of this body-social fashioned and regulated by the king should be almost universally likened to a human body.

These analogies call to mind similar notions, with Sanskritic associations, available in a ninth-century Zoroastrian text which likens the four-fold division of society into castes with the four-fold division of the body into a hierarchy starting with the head (priests), descending to the belly (husbandmen) and the hands (warriors), and down to the feet (artisans).[29] The somatic analogy is alternatively conceived as the body regulated by its central point, the heart, which oversees the functional hierarchy of other organs, co-operation among which – and the regulation by the heart of which – assures the maintenance of life within the organism.[30]

Yet the heart and that to which it corresponds in the body politic is much more than a first among equals; the decisive moment in the analogy is not the moment of function but of hierarchy. This much is always indicated in the extended use of the somatic analogy: the heart is the first organ to be formed in the embryo; its primacy is perpetually underlined, not only for purposes of embryological information, but also to indicate that its existence is the pre-condition for the existence of other organs; that it is nobler than other organs; that it regulates and thus maintains their proper functioning.[31]

In fact, as the principal component in the body politic, the king is distinct from its other components and stands above their relations including their conformation into a body social: if they, in their functional interdependence and their hierarchy, constitute the body social, the existence of a king over and above their various networks constitutes them into a body politic, that is, one based on a principle of order. The analogy drawn by Miskawayh between the role of the king in a body-politic and the function of gold in economic transactions, in which gold forms an indispensable part yet exists apart from other currencies in a status of superposition, is therefore quite apt.[32] Gold acts not only as a measure of exchange, but also as a regulator and measure of each transaction, and thus as a standard of relative values. In much the same way, sociality is regulated, with its hierarchies and interdependences, by a certain vertical authority (*qayyim*), which is the king. Earlier, Qudāma b. Jaʿfar (d. ca 320/932) had correlated the two sides of this analogy and noted that the regular circulation of gold and silver currency was one of the conditions which provide for the imperative of kingship.[33]

Yet a third analogy often drawn between the human body and the body politic refers to the commanding position of the king rather than the functional interdependence and hierarchy over which the king is superimposed.[34] It likens the king to the mind, and the king's various officers to the senses which, together and under the direction of the mind, tend the body and assure its continued vitality, the performance of its various functions, and the fulfilment of its various needs. This same analogy is used also by some Ismāʿīlī thinkers to represent the myriad of relationships that bind the two aspects of imāmist epiphany, the *ḥujja* and the *nāṭiq*.[35] These analogies are implicit in Ibn Khaldūn's metaphysical formulation of the relationship between the body social and the state as one between matter and form:[36] the state, represented by the king, is primary and constitutive, while the body social is a formless mass of wild nature unless and until it is constituted as an orderly form by a state conceptually primary to it, or at least by a movement that telologically leads to the constitution of a state.

In other words, though what we might today call state and society are relative terms which are in practice inconceivable except in conjunction with each other,[37] the primary and conceptually anterior moment in the constitution of this relationship is the state and not society. In the medieval Muslim conception the body politic, whose locus is the king, constitutes the body social and maintains it. The relationship is not the other way round – one of the organic emergence of polity from society – not even in Ibn Khaldūn's conception, which is often misconstrued along these lines. It is rather premised on a specific and artificial condition of sociality brought about by kingship. Being artificial and unnatural, sociality requires constant maintenance, the constant manifestation of absolute power, the constant reminder of the unilateral activity of the king and passivity of his subjects. Not unnaturally in this perspective, when the subjects present themselves as an active force independent of the king, they are construed as pathological actors, mere rabble (*dahmāʾ*, *ruʿāʿ*, *awbāsh*, or simply *ʿāmma* in certain contexts, especially when personified by the *ʿayyārūn*). Independent commoners are an irrational, destructive force comparable to children, with a propensity heedlessly to follow any demagogue, a pure force of mindless transgression, a manifestation of disorderly nature resistant to the orderly culture of kingship.[38] It is thus not surprising that subversive statements, even criticisms of royal hubristic dereliction and predilection, when spoken in the royal presence, should often take the form of discourse by the insane.[39]

If social hierarchies are complex and involve functional interdependence, political hierarchy is essentially simple consisting of two major terms related by power and powerlessness: the king and his subjects, whose relationship mirrors that of God to His creation. The hierarchies among the body of subjects, as between elites and commoners, are transcended by kingship, which is beyond this hierarchy and exists on different terms. The fabric of sociality constitutes a unitary entity in relation to the king, whose status as king can only be conceived in distinction from this entity. Domination is, as it were, ontologically built into the very constitution of the body social, which constitutes the zero degree of a simple hierarchy in which the king, like the One in the Neo-Platonic scheme of things, by being its very principle, holds the full plenitude of the hierarchy.[40]

This relationship is constantly reiterated by means of the analogy continually drawn by Muslim authors of all persuasions, between the unicity of God and that of the king, along lines reminiscent of Eusebius. Power can only be exercised uniquely, and command is unilateral and indivisible; otherwise the result will be dissension, division, and the dissolution of order, as the Sasanian king Ardashīr is supposed to have said.[41] Many Muslim authors postulated the dilution of absolutism as the primary cause for the decline of the state. Thus, associating subalterns in the signs and titles of sovereignty, and allowing them to use royal symbols, are customarily read as signalling the decline of Abbasid caliphal power.[42]

This reasoning is used in the interpretation of the Koranic verse (al-Anbiyā', 22) which states that the cosmos would be corrupted if more than one God existed:[43] the necessity of the unicity both of God and of kingship are derived from this argument in works of dogmatic theology[44] no less than in *Fürstenspiegel* and works of *siyāsa sharʿiyya*.[45] One Ismāʿīlī author, ʿAlī b. Muḥammad b. al-Walīd, the *dāʿī muṭlaq* of Yemen (d. 612/1215 f.), used this also in the inverse sense, as an argument for proving the unicity of God.[46] Political and other proverbial maxims were also produced to sustain this conception: the saying attributed to the Buyid ʿAḍud ad-Dawla Fanā-Khusraw (r 949-983) that the world is too small to accommodate two kings, or the sayings that a scabbard can hold no more than one sword, that more than one captain would sink a ship, or that a heart can no more sustain two loves than the heavens two gods.[47] It therefore stands to reason that a late Abbasid caliph should be enjoined to relate himself to God as his own officers are related to him.[48] In metaphysical terms, this very same notion is expressed by saying that consummate being is One, and that plurality is radically other, as it is a privation emerging from non-existence, just as goodness is partaking of the One, and evil is sheer privation of the Good.[49]

The unicity of power, its unilateral character, and therefore the imperative of absolutism, is the hinge of this artificial human assembly which constitutes the body social. Hence the ubiquitous maxims that the well-being and indeed the rectitude of subjects is the unmediated result of the rectitude of their king, that time is corrupted with the corruption of the king, that the shepherd's doctrinal and other leanings become those of his flock, that customs and beliefs change with the change of rulers, that the dispositions of subjects follow those of rulers.[50] Indeed, the saying is attributed to Ardashīr that the sobriety of a king is more beneficial to his subjects than times of fertility and prosperity.[51] Just rulers were thought even to produce beneficent weather,[52] a point which will be discussed more fully later. It is therefore no mere hyperbole to state that in the notion of kingship under consideration, a king is the root of all matters, the very substance of order, the pole of both worldly and religious affairs, the shadow cast by God upon his worshippers, the pillar of justice.[53]

Indeed, virtually the entire repertoire of metaphors familiar from Middle Eastern kingship was deployed and considered fundamental in references to and descriptions of Muslim sovereigns. The king is as a *pater familias* to his subjects; he also stands to them as does a soul to a body, he affects them as fire treats and properly fashions shapeless and uneven metals, he sustains them as water sustains land otherwise fallow.[54] The king stands to his subjects as a sea to rivers, the saltier the sea the saltier the rivers; he is likened to the heart while the subjects represent the limbs, he is likened to a pole to which they relate as the extremities and as external points.[55] The metaphor of light is ubiquitous, most potently in poetry: the king's justice is like a sun that illuminates the world, while he, as God's shadow, provides shade under which peace and security can flourish.[56] Needless to say, much is invariably said about the analogies between the king and God, even of a mimetic relationship that binds them by analogy.[57] All these and other matters are clearly organised in panegyric poetry, whose structure of strophe/antistrophe indicates the ruler as sheer energy with positive effect: he rejuvenates, fertilises, brings life from the slaughter of enemies, and order and prosperity where chaos and barrenness once reigned.[58]

Given these quasi-demiurgical attributes of kingship in relation to the order of the social world, it is hardly surprising that the relation of activity and passivity that links kings and subjects [59] should yield the imperative of obedience as *modus operandi*, endlessly and almost invariably reiterated and supported with Koranic authority (an-Nisā', 59). The only condition imposed is that the king cannot be obeyed if he orders a matter contrary to divine command, although even this condition is occasionally ruled out as a disobedience of disobedience. Indeed the question is never consequentially tackled or resolved; the injunction to absolute obedience is emphasised and even regarded as part of obedience to God himself, and the theoretical possibility of disobedience is left open, albeit with much ambiguity.[60] There is in principle no solution to this problem, in which the theoretical possibility of a contradiction between the practical and the legitimate is offered or mooted. What is on offer is a series of sententious reflections on the inexorable entrapment of the courtier, leading in cases of conflict to inevitability of the sort of resolution reminiscent of Greek tragedy, where hubris and innocence are together implicated in the making of doom.[61] Order is dependent upon obedience, for obedience maintains the basis of order which is kingship, and the felicity and good fortune of subjects consists primarily in obedience to kings and in their veneration.[62]

Kingship conceived in its ideal mode, in works of *Fürstenspiegel* no less than in *adab* more widely conceived, in philosophical writing, and in juristic manuals, is geared towards the enunciation and the maintenance of absolutism in the relentless form discussed so far. There is also much cross-referencing between theory discursively enunciated and royal practice recollected and contemporary. The primary topic enunciated both in theory and in practice is royal distance from the passive object of its absolute and unilateral activity. It is on such distance that obedience and veneration are premised, and it is across the space of this distance that the relationship of activity and passivity operates, as between two entirely independent substances. Although full cognisance is made of the differentiation amongst the subjects, particularly between the king's entourage (the *khāṣṣa*) and the *ʿāmma*, the former are by no means exempt from considerations and rules affirming distance.[63] Even royal offspring are required to behave towards the king with the same veneration as other subjects, a deference of such exclusive remit that it overrides the normal sentiments and patterns of filiality and paternity. The example of Sasanian, Umayyad, and Abbasid offspring is cited in support of this position.[64] Kings are benighted creatures, and pay no normal human heed to family or progeny (*arḥāmuhum maqṭūʿa*) to whom they should act as unsentimentally as they do towards other subjects.[65] In his *Fürstenspiegel*, the fourteenth-century Zayyānid king of Tlemcen, Abū Ḥammū, who knew Ibn Khaldūn and employed his brother, warned against sharing knowledge of the private apartments of a king's castle or its other secrets with even the closest of children.[66] In keeping with the same principle of impersonal distrust, Murādī advised kings never to divulge the extent of their wealth to their children who, he maintained, would hold them in contempt if they thought it too meagre, and would disparage the amounts spent on them if they thought it ample.[67]

Similarly, although kings are enjoined, by God in the Koran as by their advisers, to seek advice, such advice as they might accept from a courtier should never be attributed to its authors,[68] for to do so would be to admit to plurality within a royal attribute and prerogative, that of indivisible decisiveness. Again, when in audience, a king should distribute his gaze equally among those present and not display favour by word or gesture to any individual, for in the august presence all subjects are equal and homogeneous in comparison to the transcendence of the king.[69] The appointment of a vizier is likewise seen to be necessary so that the king's majesty will not be soiled or debased by too direct contact with the detailed affairs of state,[70] for he needs to affirm his majestic distance by remaining beyond their flow as their supreme regulator. It is unsurprising, therefore, that those entering the royal presence should so often be warned against greeting the king or otherwise addressing him, as such a greeting is a presumption upon the will of the king to respond.[71]

Just as kings are enjoined to maintain a superior distance, so also are officers of kings likewise enjoined to maintain and nurture this distance from its lower terminus and subaltern perspective. The leitmotif of this is the necessity of observing unusual care and circumspection in the unnatural presence constituted by the king. Just as kings are outside the normal conventions that bind relations within a family, so too are their courtiers similarly denied human warmth. A courtier is exhorted to exaggerate even further the deference shown to his king if the king were to display to him signs of intimacy, and to reserve his very partial reciprocation to strictly private occasions.[72] This nurture is exercised as canny obsequiousness, as conduct mindful of the fact that kings are unaccountable, absolute, and therefore unpredictable. A ruler is likened to a storm, which would not harm trees supple enough to bend before it, and the saying is attributed to Muʿāwiya that a ruler has the anger of a boy and the covetousness of a lion.[73] In keeping the company of a king, a courtier should be wary in much the same way as he would be with a lion or among venomous serpents, for the dispositions of kings are erratic and irregular.[74] In a compendium of miscellaneous narratives, Ibn Qutayba devotes a whole section to the topic of royal caprice and inconstancy,[75] and in his manual for viziers, Māwardī includes a long chapter on the caution to be observed in the service of kings[76] mindful, presumably, of the example of the unfortunate Ibn al-Muqaffaʿ who appears to have been the first to have formulated this maxim firmly in Arabic letters and to have himself been a victim of its reality.

Caprice is of course a primary correlate of absolute power, and indeed a manifestation of it if proof were needed. The emphasis placed on it, over and above considerations of canniness and utility on the part of the courtier, results from its status as a conceptual prop of the topic of absolutism. The author of the 'Greek Testaments' produced a diagrammatic representation of sixteen possible permutations of royal moods and dispositions and recommended corresponding ways of conduct for the courtier.[77] Moreover, the rule of precariousness and distrust – reflecting political realities – works in both directions. The king should be ever vigilant, and his spies should be constantly active among his subjects.[78] Correlatively, if, as mentioned, a king should be inscrutable and divide his gaze equally among his audience, his secret gaze should make a register of the scene before him, down to its minutest detail, noting particularly presences and absences.[79]

It is as if the entire art of ruling, and of playing court, consists of prophylactic speech, observation, and behaviour in a situation where individuals find themselves entrapped by a precariousness stemming from a power whose arbitrariness, like that of God, is a manifestation of its boundlessness. A courtier should be ever on his guard,[80] and the king should be omniscient and omnipresent, through his own gaze and through that of his spies. Yet such omniscience should not be disclosed or betrayed, but deployed politically in times of need,[81] thus accentuating the inscrutability and unpredictability that goes with absolutism.

The only certainty for a courtier seems to have been that the king's ire would be aroused and punishment provoked if three (or four) matters intimately connected to the royal person and his inscrutability were betrayed: divulging a secret, speaking ill of the king and his dynasty, and corrupting the king's private domain, to which was later added, in times of relative need, the collection of insufficient revenue.[82] Although kings are almost invariably advised to be clement, patient, and not to act hastily – particularly when angry – on lofty moral grounds and to accentuate their aloofness, the Machiavellian benefits of morality are also underlined: the deferment of punishment induces fear in the soul of the person deserving punishment and deters further maleficence.[83]

Royal hubris is also a natural corollary of absolutism. Power entrances its holder, it intoxicates him as intensely as a youth can be intoxicated.[84] The disposition power induces in kings is such that some 'are enraged by rains and winds … if they happen to go contrary to their wont' or might threaten to fill the sea with mountains if a ship eagerly awaited were late, or might curse the moon if its light disturbed their sleep.[85] This is why self-control, especially control of desire, anger, and other passions, is invariably considered to be a primary royal virtue by Muslim authors, and why the deliberate training of the character of kings is regarded as a matter of prime importance. Māwardī's and Ṭurtūshī's *Fürstenspiegel*, among others, devote very lengthy sections to this subject and to hubris and the ephemeral character of mundane life.[86] After all, the failings of kings, who can limitlessly unleash the most unbridled of passions, contrary to the failings of commoners, are hidden from their own eyes by fawning courtiers, and are invariably accentuated by the power at their disposal.[87] The king's character is, according to an expression which somehow overdraws on its zeal for the improvement of character, the very instrument of his power.[88] A king ought to be too proud to allow any of his subjects to be more righteous than he is, in the same way as he would not allow a subject to be more authoritative than he.[89] A gracious and just king is thus one who shoulders a tremendous responsibility and who sacrifices his comfort for the common weal – pleasure derived from the corrective exercise of power is likened in one text to the pleasure a lover derives from inflicting pain on his beloved.[90]

Responsibility and inscrutability are therefore central. The reason of state is known only at its apex. According to sayings attributed to Ardashīr, a king might treat his subjects severely, and might even deliberately corrupt some of them, in his desire to improve them collectively and preserve their best interests. Hence both violence and leniency, the two modalities of exercising power, should really be understood as variants of leniency and indulgence for the subjects by their king.[91]

Everything in this hyper-purposive perspective, in this sublimated *Zweckrationalität*, leads back to the image and idea of the king as fashioner of the body social into which his subjects are organised by means of politics. In one extended analogy of Abū Zayd al-Balkhī (d 934), which recalls Aristotelian notions of causality, the craft of politics is compared to the crafts of building and of medicine which have a material, a form, an actor employing a technique, a purpose, and an instrument. In the case of politics, the active party is the king who, like a physician treating a body in distemper, acts upon the lives of his subjects with the purpose of perpetuating the common weal. In so doing, he uses as his instrument the two techniques to which the political art is reducible – the proverbial *targhīb wa tarhīb*, the carrot and the stick,[92] the one employing manipulation and the other distanciation. Subjects are defined by their pliant subjection, as objects subject to royal action and correction. Both are constantly necessary given the pessimistic anthropology which requires the maintenance and continuity of human collectivity to be unnatural, and thus constantly in need of action from above and from without through sultanic surveillance.

It is universally maintained that the order which assures the continuity and stability of the body social, and signals its viability, is one defined by *ʿadāla*, justice. Both in its Greek and Persian acceptations and in the Arthaśastric tradition, and indeed according to the Muslim inheritors of the Near Eastern patrimony, the notion of normative equity intended a notion not of equality or equivalence, but of optimal proportionality among the unequal and uneven components of a composite. The essentially Pythagorean formulation of this notion is particularly well brought out in the discussion by Miskawayh of the concept of justice, a discussion which is by no means idiosyncratic or unusual but is distinguished by its clarity and explicitness.[93] Justice is the maintenance of the mean or of the just middle.[94] All virtues can be reduced to this mean which consists of the maintenance of order, that is to say of stable proportionality composed of hierarchy and functional interdependence between the elements of the body social. In this way, justice consists of a teleological state of assembly of unequal parts whose purpose is unaccounted for by the separate components of this assembly,[95] but is known to the external agency of its cohesion, royal power.

This was not a solely philosophical notion, although it was most explicitly formulated in philosophical works. It constituted the implicit spontaneous philosophical scaffolding of all discussions of justice in other fields. Injustice, according to a theological text, is transgression pure and simple.[96] According to Sasanian notions in circulation, any permutation among the hierarchy of castes has dire effects upon the stability of kingship, for it necessarily implies heads turning to tails, or tails to heads.[97] The legal definition of justice and injustice is not premised on a metaphysic of equality or inequality as such, and not even necessarily on a notion of equity, but rather on a technical conception of rule-boundedness; Muslim law did not assume legal persons to be equally subject to all rules, but legally differentiated women, slaves, non-Muslims, and other categories. A legal text describes the equity exercised by the Prophet in the distribution of booty as proportionality related to need, bereft of all notions of equivalence.[98] The stupendous work on social and political philosophy by Naṣīr ad-Dīn at-Ṭūsī, *The Nasirean Ethics*, resorts, like Ibn Khaldūn's more celebrated *Muqaddima*, to a medical metaphor. This metaphor construes social hierarchy according to groups adapted from the quadripartite Sasanian model,[99] and the analogy of each to the four elements of fire, water, air, and earth. It then posits justice as the analogue of humoural balance between them, whose stability is maintained by the dominance of the king.[100] Fārābī, for his part, famously regarded the injustice to be found in imperfect polities as the disturbance of hierarchy.[101] Overall, justice is the maintenance of order and of the stable equilibrium of unequal parts.[102]

It is precisely in this sense that the celebrated 'circle of justice' operates, a circle that is the axis of all orderly political collectivities. Existing in many variant redactions, variously attributed to Persian and Greek authors, and sometimes to Muslim personalities such as ʿAlī b. Abī Ṭālib, it finds its classic formulations in causally connecting the maintenance of kingship with the proper management of an army, itself dependent on sufficient revenue and thus on prosperity and industry which in turn requires justice for its maintenance.[103] Conversely, if kingship were to be sought for unsalutary reasons, it would inevitably lead to the emergence of a negative of this circle: greed, envy, and mendacity will bring injustice, which yields to dissension and dispute, hence to conflict and the ruination of organised social life (*ʿimāra*, which bears comparison to Ibn Khaldūn's *ʿumrān*).[104] A transition from the political to the ethical, and indeed occasionally an identification between political action that is ethical and action that is politically rational, almost always takes place at this juncture in the discourse on absolutism.

The rationally optimal conduct of absolutism is at once the ethically optimal. The canny methods of distanciation and manipulation that subtend political wisdom need not only be used for the selfish purposes of the king, nor simply for the maintenance of sheer power unrelated to other considerations. This lies at the heart of the classification of polities, first set down by Ibn al-Muqaffaʿ, later endlessly repeated and finally expressed in a very well-known form by Ibn Khaldūn a little over six centuries later, an expression which took to their logical conclusions centuries of reflection on this matter by legists, historians, and philosophers.[105] This classification divides polities into the rational – in the expression of Ibn al-Muqaffaʿ, polities built on just firmness – the religious, and the irrational or polities based on passion and arbitrariness (*mulk hawā*) leading to 'short-lived play and an eternity of ruin'.[106] The first, identified proverbially with Persian kingship, is one in which the circle of justice is pursued, with firmness and justice, leading to the perpetuation of kingship. The religious polity, which will be taken up in detail in the next chapter, has an otherworldly sanction and was historically represented, uniquely, by the caliphate as long as this institution remained intact. The caliphate, moreover, was equivalent in many ways to the rational polities of the Persians, except that it derived most of its working principles from divine inspiration mediated by the Prophet. It thus married the course and principles of rational kingship in accordance with the nature of human, as distinct from supernatural, collectivities by implementing divine commands and prohibitions designed to further the interests of human collectivities in this world and the next.[107] But in all cases, we have the self-same vertical relation between sovereign and subject, and the same methods of manipulation and distanciation that make effective the maintenance of both justice and tyranny.

The equivalence between this conception and that of Muslim philosophers, who sublimate justice in identification with a metaphysic of optimal and definitive reason corresponding to the workings of the macrocosm, is a matter which merits attention. Interpreting Plato's taxonomy of constitutions with reference to regimes contemporary with him – in contrast to the bookish and over-rated Fārābī and indeed in contrast to the considerations of Muslim thinkers in general, with the exception of Ibn Khaldūn – Ibn Rushd takes up forms of natural kingship based on honour, plutocracy, democracy, and tyranny as so many variations on deficient rule based on the workings of human nature rather than divine command.[108]

Suffice it to say, for the purposes of the present argument, that the distinction between the purely natural and the religious polities is, therefore, technical and not substantive, much like the distinction between kingship and the caliphate, a matter to be discussed further in the next chapter. In a certain perspective, the superiority of a religious polity is not only to be accounted for by reference to the afterlife, but also to mundane efficiency. For a king, 'albeit in control of people's necks', holds his subjects in obedience for a variety of reasons: fear, inclination, affection, or religion, the last being the best.[109]

'Control of necks' is the axial *modus operandi* of an absolutist polity. Religious, rational, or purely arbitrary, power is exercised absolutely and unilaterally from one point of command. Subjects are mere objects for the activity of the sole subjectivity at play, that of the king. As a result, when Muslim political literature discusses the relationship between the king and various grades of his subjects, it appears as a body of manipulative prescriptions centering on the obligations the king expects each category to fill.[110] All polities, rational, religious, or irrational, just or tyrannical, legitimate or illegitimate, rest on the unilateral action by the king on his subjects. The techniques of this action are reducible to the twin methods of distanciation – which can go as far as physical elimination – and manipulation, which in its turn can go as far as indulgent patronage. At the limit, as a sanction both for distanciation and for mystifying incorporation, the king becomes a figure of terror as in Sasanian iconography where he is portrayed in apotropaic motifs 'radiating terror'.[111]

Power Manifest

The conceptual enunciations of absolute power in Muslim polities were correlative with deliberate forms of visual and aural display, like all enunciations of power in human societies. Specific manners and colours of dress, particular rhythms of activity, visual prerogatives, the exclusive possession of emblematic objects, titles, specific charismatic manifestations, and the combination of all these with a particular etiquette and the specific spatial and temporal disposition of the bodies, manners, gaze, and speech of various classes of subjects in relation to the position and aspect of the king – all were deployed in the enunciation of royal power, or power fashioned after the model of kingship, and were integral to its constitution. They serve to dramatise the locus of power, to diffuse the enunciation of kingship among a populace that may have no access to formal and emblematic enunciations spoken and written in courtly circles, to amplify absolutism by entrancing its beholders at court and enchanting those beyond, and to reaffirm in ritual both the unilaterality and indivisibility of power and the hierarchy of its attendant personnel. Indeed, it is often the case that the visual mystification of power and its transformation into a sheer spectacle of charisma serves not only to amplify the enunciation of absolute power, but also to lodge it in the hearts of men as a force of nature whose location is beyond nature.

The dramaturgy of kingship, moreover, does not simply enhance distance and vertical exclusivity by transforming it into a visual and somatic habitus, or display the unique majesty and splendour of the royal person. Ceremonial and other visual representations of power have, in a manner analogous to that of dogmatic expression, the effect of appearing in a constant state of perfection, thus tending to accumulate not only loftiness, but also an idolatrous sanctity, a totemic consummateness, an emblematic plenitude. Ceremonial is akin to a mobile iconography, representing kingship and not actual kings. Similarly, panegyric poetry at the Abbasid court, in the patterns of its composition, in its imagery and in its setting, constitutes ceremonial ritual.[112] Power, therefore, ritualised and thus enchanted, is placed outside negotiation and transaction, as the very measure of all negotiation and transaction, like gold in transactions of the market.

The fetishisation of power in this manner in turn feeds from and leads back to the naked exercise of immediate force. Both force and royal ornament are interdependent, as Ibn al-Muqaffa' noted, and the one generates the other, though utlimately depending on the maintenance of force.[113] Some centuries later, this same notion was adapted by another author, its two terms being 'the politics of force' and 'the politics of splendour'.[114] The illustrious Niẓām al-Mulk believed pomp and circumstance to be a constituent element of kingship although, as he added, the king is personally far too lofty to be in need of such display.[115]

Yet force can itself also be an ornament. The manifestations of naked power are not only means of manipulative and exemplary terror, nor just political acts of immediate practical effect like the elimination of a foe. They are also negative ornaments of power, a display of arbitrariness, not necessarily in the choice of the person to be eliminated or disgraced, but in the discretion used in artfully carrying out an execution or making a foe destitute. Here, arbitrariness and uncommon harshness or brutality in the infliction of punishment manifests unaccountability and unapproachability.

To take the Baghdad caliphate as a case in point of matters

that were by no means unusual in other Muslim polities as in royal practices everywhere: the caliphs, and sometimes their central or provincial officers, held real or nominal power, according to circumstances, over the lives and fortunes of their subjects, without recourse to judicial processes of any kind. Al-Muʿtaṣim maintained a pit of wild animals to which at least one man was condemned.[116] Al-Muʿtaḍid (r 892–902) had notorious torture chambers, for the construction of which many properties had been confiscated from their owners.[117] It also seems that when three senior officials, including the famous Muʾnis, were executed in 321/933, their heads were 'according to usual procedure' (*ʿalā al-rasm*) consigned to a special cabinet maintained at the caliphal palace,[118] not so much as trophies or spoils of war as an accumulation of a macabre capital of power by successive masters of the caliphal palace. Al-Hādī (r 785–86) and al-Rashīd are not the only ones known to have ordered the execution of persons who they thought to have slighted them before their accession.[119] Later on al-Qāhir (r. 321–22/933–34), who was extraordinarily cruel and vindictive and was himself deposed and blinded, had two men put to death who, before his accession, had bid against him at auction for the purchase of concubines.[120]

The torture, destitution, and often finally the execution of viziers and other senior officials occupies a notable place in the chronicles of the Abbasid caliphate, especially in the period of military anarchy. During the reign of al-Muqtadir (r 908–32), the confiscation of wealth accumulated by senior officials seems to have constituted the major source of caliphal income and a special bureau was established by Muʾnis to manage moneys seized in this way. Wealth was later extracted under torture from the mother and children of al-Muqtadir by al-Qāhir.[121] The practice had apparently started with al-Maʾmūn who, however, confiscated the property of only one of his viziers, and then only upon the vizier's death. It was intensified under al-Mutawakkil (r 847–861). The famous vizier Ibn al-Zayyāt died in 233/838 enduring a device of torture he had himself invented for use on persons required to divulge and give up their wealth.[122] Later, the equally famous vizier Ibn al-Furāt (d 924), who had destituted his predecessor and his predecessor's children, brothers, officers, and representatives, was himself made destitute three times under al-Muqtadir and eventually executed, together with his son, on the orders of the caliph.[123]

It might have been argued, of course, but it never was to be argued in contemporary texts, that over and above the pragmatic political and financial logic of confiscation was another, which regarded destitution as simply the revocation of caliphal favour arbitrarily granted and equally arbitrarily withdrawn. The aura of absolute power was as alluring as it was fatal: between fortune and extinction lay the arbitrary will of the sovereign, whose beneficence, like the notion of *amān*,[124] was a proof *a contrario* of absolutism. Accounts of *taghayyur*, unexpected reversals of royal favour and mood through sometimes unexplained ill-disposition, also tend to communicate and amplify the singular prerogatives of the sovereign. The only locus which is changeless despite changes of mood is the sovereign.

With the exception of al-Muhtadī (r 869–70), the Abbasids, like their predecessors, assiduously accumulated and later systematised royal prerogatives and ceremonial. It will be recalled that the earlier Abbasids, roughly until the time of al-Mahdī (r 775–85), had not been terribly aloof in daily practice from their subjects, and had been enmeshed within the networks of kin and alliance with other Arabs. Not a century had elapsed before Abbasid caliphs and members of the caliphal family confirmed – like many other dynasties, including the Ottomans after their establishment in Istanbul[125] – the practice of anisogamy, of marriage with inferiors, specifically women of servile origin, thus affirming their location beyond social relations, most particularly beyond any relations of reciprocity.

Highlighting this are a variety of practices. It was not uncommon at assemblies such as weddings or the circumcision of royal sons to throw gold and precious stones and even titles to land, to be caught or collected.[126] The circumcision of princes was sometimes accompanied by the mass circumcision of commoners' sons at royal expense.[127] One telling anecdote well-illustrates the transcendence by the royal aura of all reciprocity: it was considered particularly impolite to ask for or to be given water at the caliphal palace. On one occasion, however, a man requested and was given water, after which he was told to take away as his own the page-boy who served him, as 'that which is given away here is not to be returned'.[128] Being beyond reciprocity is a token of uniqueness and of indivisibility.

With the increasing elaboration of caliphal households came the acquisition of yet more signs of private magnificence, which in themselves bespoke distance, although not very much is known about the actual procedures of private audience at court, most particularly from the beginning of the Sāmarrā period.[129] To a daughter of Abū Jaʿfar al-Manṣūr, the mother of the caliph al-Amīn (r 809–13), are attributed important innovations in the disposition of royal apartments, the acquisition of golden utensils and various kinds of textiles and clothing, and the organisation of an androgynously clothed and coiffed corps of slave girls (*al-ghulāmiyyāt*).[130] Her taste in furniture differed markedly from that of her grandfather, who on receiving guests ordered skins to be placed on the ground for them to sit upon.[131] The acquisition of chess by al-Rashīd, the game of *ṭabṭāb*, somewhat akin to tennis, and various other marks of distinction were of course passed down to the aristocracy, as were various fashions first appearing at court. Presumably other practices were similarly passed on, such as the maintenance by al-Mutawakkil of assorted court jesters, buffoons, keepers of fighting cocks and dogs, and performers of far coarser entertainments.[132] It should be added that the enjoyment by caliphs of common entertainments conveys not so much possession of the common touch as omniscience conveyed by certain knowledge of all worlds, no matter how far removed from the palace, even the world of the street that is brought into the palace by its entertainments or by caliphal spies. Indeed, stories of Abbasid caliphs eavesdropping on their servants or walking the streets in disguise are not confined to *The Arabian Nights* but were widely current in Abbasid Baghdad.[133]

Where activities were shared by caliph and subjects alike, the distinction of the caliphal or royal court would be maintained by scale rather than substance. Yet the very substance of royalty is distinctive, and this distinctiveness is marked by insignia. It is well known that the Abbasids possessed, and wore on certain ceremonial occasions, three objects attributed to the Prophet – a cloak, a stave (probably a special rendition of the sceptre), and a ring. It is reported that the same objects were previously in the possession of the Umayyads,[134] but this is doubtful given the lack of direct reports and accounts of the manner in which these objects came into the possession of the Abbasids. Detailed research might well demonstrate a connection between the appearance of these objects and the crystallisation of the notion of a binding corpus of prophetic *sunna*. Later, the Koran of ʿUthmān was added to the repertoire of holy relics, and was placed before the caliph at ceremonial occasions, but this is not attested before the end of the tenth century.[135] It is noteworthy that the same Koran was later said to be found in Cordoba,[136] and that these same relics as well as others, including the turbans of Joseph and of Abū Ḥanīfa, and the Prophet's sword, standard, and bow, were later acquired by the Ottomans and kept in a special room at Topkapi palace. The standard, brought from Damascus in 1596, was hoisted in battle in Hungary and displayed on the streets of Istanbul in times of unrest.[137] The other Muslim dynasty of œcumenical ambition, the Fatimid, possessed Dhu'l-fiqār, the sword of ʿAlī, which tradition says had been brought to them from the caliphal palace in Baghdad and was used with miraculous success in battle.[138] To these holy relics, the Fatimids added, as a sign of kingship, the parasol, for which there are no Muslim precedents.[139] The parasol and other Fatimid insignia were retained by the Ayyubid and Mamluk sultans of Egypt and Syria as signs of their own royalty.

The other prerogatives of the caliphate were, as is well known, mention in the Friday *khuṭba*, the ancient practice of embossing or otherwise writing the royal name on coins and military standards and embroidering it on the edge of *ṭirāz* textiles produced by caliphal factories in Baghdad, Cairo, and Cordoba and used for furnishings and clothing for the caliph or for robes of honour (*khilʿa*, pl. *khilaʿ*) given away by the caliph. All these privileges were to be encroached upon and shared by sultans, as we shall see in the next chapter. So was the privilege of having drums play outside the palace gate at the five times of prayer.

Other indices of royalty were left as exclusive caliphal prerogatives. The wearing of red footwear, for instance (an old Byzantine practice), was always to remain the exclusive preserve of the caliph.[140] Black was, of course, the colour of the Abbasids, with only an episodic interregnum: when al-Maʾmūn in defiance of Abbasid outrage named the ʿAlīd ʿAlī ar-Riḍā as his heir apparent and granted him his daughter in marriage, he ordered the substitution of the ʿAlīd colour green for black. This only lasted for as long as the heir apparent was alive; black was re-adopted after his mysterious death.[141] With time, the caliphs came to wear black clothing and turbans of specific materials and of particular description at ceremonial occasions, as did the various other categories of courtiers, who were obliged to wear black if they represented the caliph in their capacity as office holders on his behalf, such as military officers and judges of Baghdad. After judges were invested with their offices and their letters of investiture were read out, they wore black and rode out in procession.[142] Other categories of people would wear different colours and be dressed in a different style. Robes, for instance, were the preserve of secretaries and of those employed outside the court while remnants of the Medinan aristocracy were allocated the colour yellow.[143]

Black and white came to represent the Abbasids and the Fatimids (and occasionally other Ṭalibids) respectively: when al-Mustaʿīn (r 862–866) secured the naming of his brother as his successor, he invested him with a black standard in his capacity as heir apparent and a white standard in his capacity as custodian of the holy sites at Mecca and Medina, thus investing him with the charisma both of Abbasid legitimism and of prophetic sanction.[144] When in the early tenth century Ibn Faḍlān made his journey to the Volga Bulgars to seal their anti-Khazar alliance with Baghdad as clients of the caliph, their king was made to wear black as the caliph's letter was read out before him.[145] When anti-Fatimid warfare raged in Syria, black standards were hoisted.[146] In contrast, when in 1058–59 Baghdad was briefly overrun by the general Basāsīrī acting as a nominal vassal of the Fatimids, preachers and other officials were made to wear white, the colour of the Fatimids.[147] And when in 1012 the illustrious Shīʿī aristocrat, litterateur, and divine, al-Sharīf al-Raḍī, was invested with the office of Syndic of the Ṭalibids, in addition to superintendent of the Baghdad mosques and leader of the pilgrimage procession, he was granted black robes of honour, becoming the first Ṭalibid to be so dressed,[148] reflecting the position of the Ṭalibid aristocracy of Baghdad within the caliphal regime. The colour stood for the person of the caliph and delivered his metaphorical and indexical presence and, through him, that of his dynastic charisma.

Caliphal prerogatives over and above single indices of the office cohered in the Sāmarrā period where in the first half of the tenth century their concatenation and institutionalisation crystallised in palatine institutions that have been compared in their complexity to those of Byzantium.[149] These remained more or less constant, and although they occasionally frayed, they maintained their magnificence, sumptuousity, and visual grandiloquence even at the Abbasids' darkest of hour, under the earliest Buyids. Indeed, it was in this period that they seem to have grown more grandiose than ever, although Abbasid ceremonial seems always to have been somewhat less hallucinatory than that of the Fatimids.[150]

Our knowledge of daily etiquette as of the physical structure and layout of Abbasid palaces is still slight,[151] although Ṣābī's description of ceremonial and other etiquette, written during the reign of al-Qā'im (1031–1075), was based on first-hand instruction from the author's grandfather, who had witnessed ceremonial in full splendour. Ṣābī thought his manual was necessitated by the need to fix on paper matters which, he said, were being forgotten.[152] This was doubtless connected with the increasing self-consciousness of the caliphate in its relations to the Buyids, and a prelude for the caliphal resurgence which was to take place not long after the time of al-Qā'im.

It should be noted that the insignia of kingship, its colour codes, its manifestations of violence, munificence, and of splendour, were signs which were, with very few exceptions as far as the Abbasids were concerned, displayed principally, almost exclusively, in private. Apart from references to the introduction of certain procedures for caliphal movements outside the palace involving the display by guards of swords and bows, or of saddles ornamented with gold and silver,[153] there seems to have been little by way of processional procedures. They were palatine, not public ceremonies. Unlike the Fatimids' display of magnificence on the streets of Cairo – the Nilometer procession, processions to prayers on days of the two main feasts of the Muslim calendar, the new year, the beginning of Ramaḍān[154] – Abbasid caliphs from the Sāmarrā period onwards almost never appeared in public. Only two public processions are on record for this entire period, and from the time that al-Muqtadir ascended to the caliphate in 907, seven years were to elapse before he appeared before his subjects.[155] Caliphal appearances in public seem only to have occurred when public disturbances were fuelled by rumours of the caliph's death, and they were brief and purely functional.[156] Given the axiality of the caliphate, and the notion of disorder correlative with its absence, it was natural that such rumours should always provoke disturbances, inflate prices, lead to a scarcity of goods and so on.[157]

The invisible caliph was occasionally made officially visible to members of his court, though we do not have information on his routine daily visibility to his officials and courtiers. Just as discourse on kingship sketches its impeccable conditions, so does history record virtually only those occasions of visibility which are ceremonial or otherwise extraordinary. We have already had occasion to speak of the *ḥijāb*, a screen hiding the caliphal person from the gaze of his courtiers, and used by both the Sasanians and the Byzantines.[158] It seems this was retained except when the caliph appeared in his aspect of giver: dispenser of money, or of robes of honour, and later, of titles. In this visible aspect the caliph was seated on a cushioned and carpeted dais, *takht* or *sarīr*, reputedly as high as seven spans in Baghdad, and made of marble after the Abbasid caliphate was set up in Cairo following the Mongol sack of Baghdad in 1258.[159] Fatimid caliphs sat ceremonially upon a golden throne.[160]

The whole aspect of the caliphal appearance bespeaks distance. Ghazālī stresses that the very glimpse of the caliphal person should be such as to strike terror in the hearts of his subjects, even at great distance.[161] Such of course presupposes not only physical ornament, but a terrible aura, projected in the rules that govern behaviour in the caliphal presence, and in turn confirmed by them. These constitute essentially a repertoire of restraint, mixed with regulations of distance from the caliph to be kept by different categories of courtiers, and the circumscription of the movement of the different categories of bodies in contiguity with the caliphal presence.

Silence and solemnity of aspect were fundamental to this whole disposition. Caliphal audiences were marked by the presence of pages carrying fly-whisks flanking the caliph, and others wielding slings, with which crows and other birds were shot lest they should crow or chirp.[162] Silence was also fundamental to Fatimid, Sasanian, and Byzantine audiences; Byzantine authors referred to an imperial audience as a *silention*.[163] All speech was to be conducted in subdued voices, with no gesticulation, and to be confined to brief statements made without flourish, in full humility and clarity.[164] People before the caliph were to speak only when commanded to do so by the caliph, who normally relayed the command through one of his pages or chamberlains. People attending an audience may look only at the caliph. Laughter and other unseemly behaviour that might pollute the purity of the silence engulfing the caliph, like clearing one's throat or sneezing, was to be avoided.[165]

Physical movement was also dependent on the caliphal gesture.

Apart from standing in their appointed places in a spatial expression of social and political hierarchies[166] – the right to be seated was reserved for the commander of the armies and the chief chamberlain, at caliphal invitation – members of an audience could move only at caliphal command. Movement was permissible only to approach the caliph when beckoned to do so for a private exchange of words, or to leave the audience, which had to be done without turning one's back to the caliph, and walking at a normal pace only once out of caliphal sight.[167] The very possibility of physical movement, and indeed any move that might cause some slight perturbation to eddy through the iconic order of an audience, was dependent on the gesture and gaze of the sovereign.[168]

Another gesture accentuating subjection to the caliph was that of kissing the ground before him. There is scattered reference to the possibility that the caliph's hand was kissed as early as the time of al-Ma'mūn,[169] and al-Jāḥiẓ at more or less the same time had prescribed the Sasanian custom of kissing the sovereign's extremities when a noble person is commanded to approach the royal person.[170] It is clear that not very long after, in 247/861, both the hands and feet of al-Mutawakkil's heir apparent, al-Muʿtazz (r 866–69), were kissed after he had delivered a Friday sermon on behalf of his father by the illustrious vizier al-Fatḥ b. Khāqān, the caliph's closest ally and drinking companion. It therefore seems that Ṣābī's contention that courtiers had 'previously' not humbled themselves to the person of the caliph, but had at most been offered his hand, covered with his sleeve, to kiss,[171] should be relegated to a past conjured by anti-hubristic piety, or to very early Abbasid practice.

Yet by Ṣābī's time the caliphal person had grown in loftiness and unapproachable sanctity, and the practice of humbling oneself and demonstrating awe for the caliph had been transformed to the practice of kissing the ground before his seat, to which those particularly privileged were allowed the added honour of kissing the hem of the caliph's cloak, and sometimes even his hand and foot. Al-Qāḍī al-Nuʿmān (d 974), chief courtier of the early Fatimids, clearly draws out some of the unspoken symbolism of kissing the ground in response to the religious polemic against it by saying it did not imply bowing as one bows before God in prayer, but rather that the caliph was far too elevated and lofty a person to be physically touched by a kiss of the hand.[172] There are very rare occurrences of people not kissing the ground, without incurring retaliatory sanction, and of kissing the caliph's ring instead of his hand and foot, but these are to be seen in the light of their immediate political context,[173] as indeed are the exaggerated gestures of moral mortification before the caliph that we will encounter in a moment. In any case, kissing the ground and its elevation into touching the caliphal person was the preserve of persons of the highest seniority,[174] although the Ṭalibids and the Qaḍīs of Baghdad were in principle exempt.[175] Occasionally the very presence of a caliphal object, or metonym, would provoke such a gesture of humility: when, for instance, Saladin received caliphal greetings despatched with an ambassador of an-Nāṣir (1180–1225), he promptly knelt and kissed the ground.[176]

The accent on impersonality and iconicity is completed by manners of address. Unlike earlier Abbasids, caliphs and kings were never referred to by their patronymics (*kunya*) or given names; nor were others referred to by patronymics in royal presence unless so honoured by the caliph or king himself. Given or patronymic names were particularly avoided if they were shared with the caliph.[177] Kings and caliphs were, after all, not only beyond reciprocity, but beyond overlap; they were absolutely unique and, as far as subjects were concerned, a mere objective presence, an epiphany of sublimity. Hence the profusion not only of titles, like the famous *amīr al-mu'minīn*, but of locational metaphors, especially used in correspondence in which the caliph and other grandees were referred to by such titles as 'the abode of clemency', 'the noble prophetic chamber', 'the second Ka'ba', and so forth.[178]

The inimitability and inviolability that underline the sanctity of the caliphal person were also expressed in more mundane and less routine incidents. When al-Muqtadir graced someone with a visit to his estate, a silver-plated dome was built over the spot where the caliph had sat, as if that particular spot had been sanctified. The same caliph is reported to have once, while visiting, refused to sit upon furniture especially laid out for him, telling his entourage that the carpet might subsequently be used by others and thus be defiled.[179] The Fatimids had particular variations on the theme of sanctity attributed to the caliphal body.[180] This entailed not only a veneration for objects emanating from the caliph or destined to be received by him, including letters, but also a propensity to prostration at the very mention of the caliph's name. Saladin's gesture referred to above is reminiscent of this:

he had been, after all, the last vizier of the Fatimids before he overthrew the dynasty and installed himself as a representative of the Baghdad caliphate. In addition, when the Fatimid caliph needed to don a turban, the task was performed by a particular officer, *shādd at-tāj ash-sharīf*, who was removed from both the sociality and the physical integrity that might pollute the caliphal head or otherwise compromise it. This office was reserved for eunuchs, inconsummate as physical persons and, by slavery, inconsummate as social beings, and therefore outside relations among persons and indeed, as persons owned by the caliph, part of his subjectivity.

The inviolable transcendence of the caliphal person is also expressed in spatial terms. This is enunciated above all in the invisibility of the caliph and in the remoteness and physical elevation of his visible aspect, accentuated by the silence required in his presence and the control, by his gaze and gesture, of physical movement in the space surrounding him, a space specifically allocated to display his person in ceremonial perfection and impeccability. The inviolability of the caliph's private quarters also reflects the sanctification of space. The inviolability of domestic space was shared with fellow Muslims, but particularly intensified in the case of the caliph, whose aura rendered it doubly inviolable, almost sacred. An episode will illustrate the conceptual force of this: when in 364/975 the caliph at-Ṭāʾiʿ found himself backing the wrong side in an inter-Buyid dispute which ended with the victory of ʿAḍud ad-Dawla, he was forced to flee his palace, which the curious victor wished to inspect. ʿAḍud ad-Dawla's judgement – other examples of which we shall presently see – was highly praised when, having been conducted around the palace by the chamberlain Muʾnis, he desisted from entering the private quarters which 'no fecund man', with the exception of caliphs, had ever entered previously.[181]

Though the caliphal complex in Baghdad was plundered on several occasions by unruly soldiers during the period of military anarchy and after, it was still regarded as to some degree inviolable, and in moments of uncertainty various people would move their valuables there.[182] Much can also be said for the design and relative position of the earliest Abbasid palace in the Round City of early Baghdad, which might be interpreted as symbolically standing at the centre of the world as the personal space of the caliph from whence radiated absolute power.[183] But it is difficult to construe a stable pattern for the spatial relation between the palace and the city in subsequent periods.

Like the Ottoman Sultan in Topkapi palace, the Abbasid caliph was 'an invisible signifier of pure potency',[184] in contrast both to the early caliphate and to most other regimes of Muslim sovereignty in which the connection between sovereign and the feudal or crypto-feudal aristocracies was closer, or in contrast to the Baghdadian civic populism of later Abbasids, most specifically an-Nāṣir, which will be taken up shortly. Yet within the confines of the palace, and most particularly within the great reception hall, *ṣaḥn as-salām*, where the great ceremonies of state took place, the august subject of absolutism manifested himself in a manner which pulled together magnificently all the strands and displays of perfection and of charisma in ceremonies of investiture.

The investitures referred to here are not the simpler ceremonies for officials such as viziers, or lower officials who were often invested by the viziers themselves, acting on behalf of the caliph. They are the investitures of independent kings who had first overpowered the caliphate, then acted as its protectors, most specifically the Buyids[185] and the Saljuqs, until the recovery of a vigorous caliphal absolutism over Iraq and parts of Mesopotamia. These ceremonies have their origin in the triumphs accorded to the caliph's victorious generals, who were granted robes of honour, bracelets, necklaces, belts, swords and horses, and crowned either with solid crowns or turbans to which was attached an aigrette studded with jewels, for which the word *tāj* was also used.[186] Robes of honour were not specific to investiture with public office, but were routine favours granted by the caliph to courtiers of various categories, even to poets and drinking and boon companions.[187] Merging with the ceremonies during which viziers were invested,[188] most particularly after the second quarter of the tenth century, when army commanders took over the functions and prerogatives of the vizirate and merged the military with the civil and financial administrations, these ceremonies invested the incumbents with the affairs of state and took the form of a delegation of absolute power by the caliph, a delegation which was itself regarded as a manifestation of caliphal dignity.

In his capacity as representative of the caliph, the king so crowned and invested was also granted a black turban, which marked his incorporation into the system of the caliphate which represented the legitimate Muslim polity. The entire symbolic repertoire of sublime absolutism was thus deployed. The fullest account of this ceremony in existence is that describing the crowning and investiture of the Buyid ʿAḍud ad-Dawla in 367/977f.[189] Having come to an understanding with at-Ṭāʾiʿ (r 974–991) who, as mentioned, had earlier fled his palace, the Buyid king petitioned him to be crowned and invested with caliphal political and administrative prerogatives and with insignia of office. His petition was duly granted, and the Buyid proceeded to the caliphal palace, and asked to be distinguished with the unique privilege of entering the palace gate on horseback. This was also granted, but a wall had been erected just inside the gate to bar any but the shortest possible mounted access.

The caliph had meanwhile seated himself on his dais in the *ṣaḥn as-salām*, dressed in black and bearing the Prophet's sword and cloak, with ʿUthman's Koran before him and the Prophet's stave by his side, surrounded by about a hundred of his private guard, armed and clad in coloured tunics and belts, and his senior pages. Thirty-one of the caliph's chief and assistant chamberlains, dressed in black tunics and bearing swords, were also present, as were officials, judges, and the Ashrāf, all standing in their appointed stations. Also in attendance were members of the Buyid king's entourage, unarmed.

ʿAḍud ad-Dawla asked for permission to enter, and permission was conveyed by a page, whereupon the drape hiding the caliph was removed. The mighty king was then told that the caliph's gaze was now upon him, and he approached the throne, kissing the ground nine times as he did so, and stopped. At-Ṭāʾiʿ then commanded Khāliṣ the page to bid the king approach the dais and ʿAḍud ad-Dawla ascended it, kissing the ground twice as he did so. He was then gently commanded by the caliph to come nearer; he bent down and kissed the caliph's foot, but desisted from sitting on a seat to the right of the caliph. When the latter insisted and swore that he must, he kissed the seat, and sat. The formula of investiture was then pronounced by the caliph,[190] who subsequently ordered that the crowning should proceed, and the king was taken away to an adjacent portico by courtiers and tailors, who dressed him in his robes of honour and other accoutrements, and set upon his head a crown into which precious stones were woven.

It might be well the practice of hyperbole, or indeed a *topos* in accounts of investiture ceremonies, which led descriptions of this ceremony to add that the weight of the crown and other accoutrements were such that ʿAḍud ad-Dawla's attempts to kiss the floor upon his re-admission to the caliphal presence were thwarted. Be that as it may, the king was invested with a sword in addition to that he had already received with his robes of honour and honoured with the bestowal of two further standards, one signalling his dominion over the east and another over the west. Finally, upon his petition, ʿAḍud ad-Dawla was accorded the privilege of not exiting by walking backwards, which he regarded as an omen of evil (the Buyids were, by all accounts, exceptionally superstitious), but was allowed to leave the hall by a side entrance.

Later Buyids also followed this ceremonial procedure[191] as did Saljuq Sultans.[192] The overall pattern was repeated in 1056 by the niece of Ṭughrul Beg when received by al-Qā'im (r 1031–75) to conclude a marriage contract witnessed by al-Māwardī: she too kissed the ground several times, and was crowned.[193] Slight variations can be noted in the investiture by al-Qā'im of the ageing Ṭughrul Beg in 449/1057. The sultan arrived at the caliphal palace on board a riverine boat accompanied on shore by two elephants, and rode on horseback all the way from the palace gate to the entrance of *ṣaḥn as-salām.* He asked for and was granted the privilege of shaking the caliphal hand after he had kissed it.[194] The other crucial innovation introduced later, under an-Nāṣir, reflected this caliph's attempt at incorporating his office and the Baghdad aristocracy into the civic institutions of the city. Having made himself the head of the *futuwwa* brotherhoods,[195] he wore the distinctive trousers of these brotherhoods, and made them into an element in the robes of honour he granted, whether in person or to faraway kings: Ayyubids in Syria and Egypt, Khwārāzm-Shāhs in eastern Iran and Turkestan, Ghūrids in India, Saljūqs in Anatolia, and others, a practice continued after an-Nāṣir by al-Mustanṣir (r 1226–42).[196] This was carried over to the Cairo caliphate, which included the trousers in the vestiment-ary repertoire of honour granted to Mamluk sultans upon their investiture and at other ceremonial occasions.[197] Mamluk investitures, like those of the Ayyubids before them, incorporated, however, many of the insignia (the parasol most particularly) and processions that had been introduced by the Fatimids and subsequently distinguished Cairene kingship, in addition to the banqueting traditions that had been brought from the steppes and had earlier been in use in Ṭūlūnid Egypt.[198] It must be noted, however, that Mamluk sultans demonstrated over the centuries individual versions of ceremonial etiquette.[199]

It is noteworthy that the full splendour of caliphal distance was reserved for outsiders. If the caliph was an invisible signifier of potency, his visibility to those not privileged to enter his palace had to amplify the august measure of his distance. Such an amplification is recorded in detailed descriptions of the audience accorded by al-Muqtadir to an ambassador of the Byzantine emperor Constantinus VII Porphyrogennetos in 305/917–18.[200] Here, distance from the awesome caliph was expressed not only in space separating him from the ambassador in the reception area (which was distinct from *ṣaḥn as-salām*), but in distances traversed before entry to the caliph and before the approach to the palace gate itself. It was also expressed in temporal terms, with periods of extended sequestration and waiting that had to be endured both before and after the visitor's entry into Baghdad, as if time itself were dilated before the office of the caliph. For all this, the encounter with the caliph was exceedingly brief and almost entirely impersonal; it constituted only the spatial and temporal terminus of a journey conducted elsewhere, amongst awesome and wonderful manifestations of the caliphal person.

Overall, amplifications of measure – of distance, time, numbers, sumptuosity – constituted a scale which expressed the mystique of the caliph and, through him, the Muslim in contradistinction to the Byzantine polity. The elements of this scale of amplification were power, made visible in arrayed soldiers and wealth, sumptuosity that increased as the ambassador approached closer to the abode of the magnificent caliph, and distance made visible by both time and space. The first audience was granted by Ibn al-Furāt the vizier, who seated himself on a great seat in an enormous pavilion sumptuously hung with drapes and with gilded roofing, surrounded by his guards, pages, and chamberlains. He had the ambassador and his entourage conducted in procession between a continuous line of soldiers connecting the ambassador's residence and that of the vizier and then through porticoes, hallways, and a garden which led to the pavilion where he received them and their message.

The same was repeated on a much grander scale once permission to appear before the caliph was given. This involved such amplification and exoticism as to render the mystical person of the caliph manifest through the surreality of his distance and of his ambient space, a surreality which further amplifies the hyperbolic amplitude of his distance. The ambassador and his entourage were again conducted between rows of liveried soldiers, numbering in the thousands, through streets, gardens, hallways, porticoes, antechambers, all hung with over 38,000 drapes, some ornamented with the pictures of horses, camels, elephants, and wild beasts woven with gold thread, others with pious sayings woven into them, and yet others manufactured at the time of al-Ma'mūn, al-Mutawakkil, and al-Muktafī (r 902–908), and bearing their names. Twenty-two thousand rugs were used to cover the floors, and thousands of shields, lamps, and other objects, many made of gold, were on display. The Romans were also conducted between two rows of 100 wild felines in iron collars, each restrained by a trainer, amongst herds of domesticated animals, past four elephants and two giraffes. They traversed thirteen buildings within the caliphal compound, before they were finally admitted to the caliphal residence itself, where array upon array of liveried guards, soldiers, pages, and chamberlains conducted them from portico to hall to corridor to pavilion, until they found themselves in the presence of the caliph, dressed in black, with a *ṭawīla* (long, pointed turban) upon his head, seated on an ebony chair between two lines each having nine strings of jewels knotted in the form of rosaries, through which sunlight was refracted, with the pages, guards, vizier, courtiers and officials all standing in their appointed places.

There they were made to stop and, after kissing the ground, to stay standing at a distance of some 100 cubits from the august person. Various automata were operated, including fountains spraying water scented with musk and rose essence, and mechanical birds attached to the trees that chirped as the breeze blew. All the while, the ambassadorial party delivered their message through translators, and then received the caliph's response. After their dismissal, they were granted robes of honour. The ambassador himself and his translator were in addition granted 20,000 dirhams each and were conducted back to their residence along the same wondrously surreal way, with its soldiers, furnishings, exotic animals and wild beasts.

The entire ambassadorial procession was a metonym for the person of the caliph who became visible, very briefly, only at the end, as a sort of token verification of the reality of all these awesome wonders. The accentuated impersonality of the caliph rendered by the awesome and surreal amplitude and plenitude of his ambience, and by the brevity of the encounter with him, rendered his person a token of an impersonal polity rather than the reality of a personal despotism. He was beheld as an icon of his office.

It was in this capacity that the Abbasid caliphate, like other caliphal regimes, particularly the Fatimids, construed itself as an œcumenical polity. This was not only an echo of the late antique trope of universal kingship, which was never absent although it was, in practice, relegated to eschatology as a regime which will come to be realised at the end of time, when Islam will reign throughout the world.[201] Nor was it just an echo of the trope of great kings, which then included the kings of the Byzantines and of the Chinese. It was an essential component of the very notion of the caliphate, whose theory will be taken up in the next chapter. It reflected the reality that caliphal politico-cultural and administrative norms were copied throughout the actual or erstwhile provincial domains of the caliphate, whether subordinate, as was the case in the early Abbasid period, or practically autonomous or semi-autonomous, as was the case later, when outside dynasties overpowered the caliphate, or coexisted with it, all the while regarding themselves as instruments of this august office and members of the same polity. When the Buyids overran Baghdad, their chanceries were, at least initially, integrated with that of the caliph,[202] doubtless reflecting both the administrative inexperience of these arrivistes no less than certain practices and conceptions of caliphal centralism, no matter what power relations subtended it. In all, we witness in the field of administrative, ceremonial, and architectural practices the same classicising and literarising trends witnessed in the discourse on power.

The international style of the Abbasid court, ceremonial, administrative, and conceptual, was by no means confined to the immediate environs of Iraq.[203] The layout of ceremonial space seems to have been reproduced, for instance, by the Umayyads of Spain at Madīnat az-Zahrā' outside Cordoba.[204] The Almohads and their Merinid successors instituted courtly norms directly derived from the Baghdadian models, including drums beating outside palace gates, albeit in a rudimentary form that reflected both provincialism and arrivism.[205] The Saljuq court also appears to have remained rather basic in its ceremonial, veering more towards the steppe than Baghdad, and one can clearly see in the

Fürstenspiegel of Niẓām al-Mulk an attempt to rectify this condition by the didactic introduction of the standard norms derived from Baghdadian example.[206]

More elaborately, the Mamluk sultans adopted many of the standard marks of royal distinction, such as a sequestered prayer space, the weaving of the sovereign's name on the *ṭirāz* (which they extended to the Sultan's parasol), the granting of robes of honour, manners of organising distance from the sovereign in receptions, the beating of drums at the palace gate, and much else.[207] Caliphal and other royal regimes in medieval Muslim polities being patrimonial and tributary, it was natural that various ceremonial matters were copied down the line. The palace of ʿAḍud ad-Dawla copied many of the conventions of seating and standing current in caliphal audiences.[208] The overall disposition was also copied at other Buyid courts, most particularly that of Abū Kālījār who in 1032 received al-Māwardī on an ambassadorial mission from the caliph of which a record is extant.[209] The Buyid Ṣamṣām ad-Dawla received a Byzantine embassy in a manner similar to the one described above, albeit far less sumptuous.[210] Kissing the ground was similarly not reserved for caliphs. Before his entry into the caliphal presence to receive his investiture in 404/1013f, Fakhr al-Mulk was received by chamberlains who kissed the ground before him.[211] Junior or supplicant Buyid princes kissed the ground before grander and more powerful ones.[212] Niẓām al-Mulk kissed the ground before his overlord Malik Shāh,[213] and Mamluk princes before the sultan.[214] Patriarchal authoritarianism was most widely expressed in kissing hands and feet, as in the state administration.[215]

The mention of the sovereign's name in the course of the official Friday sermon was equally a sign of sovereignty. This was initially the caliph's exclusive prerogative, but from the time of Ibn Rā'iq's tenure of the office of *amīr al-ʾumarāʿ* (935–38) when the military gained control over the treasury and the state administration, the names of effective co-sovereigns were mentioned in the Friday sermons throughout state domains, with the exception of Baghdad, where only the caliph's name was mentioned during the Friday sermon until the princely presumption to this prerogative crept in under ʿAḍud ad-Dawla. In between, this prerogative came to form a standard component of caliphal letters of investiture.[216] The removal of the caliph's name was almost invariably a sign of the intent to overturn the Abbasid dynasty and, on occasion, to replace it by a Talibid, as was the case with the Khwārazm-Shāhs in the early thirteenth century, who wished to take Baghdad as the Saljuqs did before them and to install a Ḥusaynid from Tirmidh in the caliphal office.[217]

When a sovereign prince whose name was mentioned in the Friday sermon by order of the caliph found himself in a precarious position, it was the case that the enemies seeking to overturn him would petition the caliph to revoke this order.[218] Similarly, such mention of a prince's or king's name was a sign of sovereignty more generally contested in political conflicts, and the order in which the names of princes were pronounced corresponded to relations of tributary seniority between them.[219] The sharing of sovereignty was also indicated in privileges fought over for very many years under the Buyids, of having drums beating outside the Sultan's palace. These disputes and quarrels concerned the granting of caliphal permission no less than, permission granted, the number of times a day drums were to be beaten. This uncertain situation lasted until either 418/1027 or 436/1044f, when Buyid princes seized and were consequently conceded the right to have drums beaten outside their palace gates at the time of all five daily prayers.[220]

Similarly, control over the mint expressed by embossing the name of a ruler on coinage was a universal sign of kingship, with the Baghdadian model being the conduit for the transmission of an ancient practice, as was the appearance of names on standards and on the *ṭirāz*. The names of sovereign princes again came to be engraved on coins (and printed on paper money when this was issued) along with that of the caliph. As was the case with the mention of individuals after the Friday prayer, this privilege was also specified in the letter of investiture.[221] But coins seem to have followed a rather less predictable course in many provincial areas, with elements of local or of ancient iconography present on some coins of the Saljuqs and their allies or successors in Anatolia and Mesopotamia, which did not always mention the name of the caliph, but the names of the lord in control of the mint and his immediate overlord.[222]

The œcumenical status of the Abbasid dynasty was such that contemporary kings, even those mightier than the Abbasids or in direct control of Baghdad and of the caliphate, represented themselves as vassals of the caliph. The only exception were the Fatimids, who were offered a deal by the caliph when they took

Alexandria and were clearly about to conquer Egypt, whereby they could keep the country as his representatives and vassals.[223] Even kings far removed from the affairs of western Asia reported their pious deeds on behalf of Islam to the caliph, and sought his ratification of their action and their investiture in by him. One such was Maḥmūd of Ghaznī (r 998–1030) who conscientiously reported to al-Qādir his exploits in India and his suppression of Ismāʿīlīs and Muʿtazilīs in Khurasan and elsewhere. He appears from correspondence quoted extensively by one chronicler to have habitually referred to himself as the caliph's slave, and construed his actions as undertaken on behalf of the caliphate.[224] Later, at the time of the Crusades, Nūr ad-Dīn (r 1146–74), ruler of Syria and Egypt and Saladin's erstwhile lord, reported his victories to Baghdad and sent the caliph various spoils, including Frankish shields, armour, and heads.[225] Ayyubid kings in their correspondence referred to themselves as the caliph's pages, servants, and slaves.[226] The same formulae were used by the Buyids,[227] whose international affairs such as wars and treaties, like those of other Muslim dynasts, were conducted in the name of the caliph.[228] The comparison by Qalqashandī (d 1418), writing at the time of the Mamluks, between the caliphate and the papacy,[229] is not as far fetched as might appear.

This notion of caliphal œcumenism entailed formal procedures, chief among which was investiture. In distant lands, and as a routine procedure in Ayyubid and Mamluk accession ceremonies, investiture with the sultanate by the caliph was the formal mark of accession to power and inclusion within the boundaries of caliphal legitimism. As was the case in Baghdad with the Buyids, this was the result of a petition to the caliph, who responded with a certificate of investiture that was ceremonially read before army commanders, senior officials, and judges, followed by the usual robes of honour, swords, standards, and necklaces, although crowns were replaced by black turbans in the case of the Ayyubids and the Mamluks.[230]

Certificates of investiture also included regnal titles conferred by caliphs upon the various sultans invested with caliphal authority. Most of these titles directly reflected the connection with the caliphate – first with the use of the term *dawla*, such as ʿAḍud ad-Dawla for the Buyid Fanā-Khusraw, reflecting notional vassalage to the Abbasid house (dawla), and somewhat later, possibly in connection with the increasingly formalised spiritualisation of the caliphate under Shi'i influence and under the Buyids and most particularly the Saljuqs, with the use of *dīn*, as with Ṣalāḥ ad-Dīn (Saladin).[231]

Other titles were used, often resulting in a string for a particular sultan, some reflecting not so much caliphal delegation as local or specific dynastic traditions or ambitions, such as the bestowal of the title Shāhān-Shāh upon 'Aḍud ad-Dawla and, after him, upon Ṭughrul Beg. The Saljuq Malik Shāh (r 1072–92) called himself Master of the World, King of Kings, Descendant of Afrāsiyāb, while the Saljuq Sanjar (r 1118–57) was, among other things, known by Alexander's title of Dhu'l Qarnayn,[232] of both Turkic and east Iranian incidence. Titles were often subject to negotiation, and were occasionally tokens used in political bargaining between caliphs and sultans,[233] for example the acquisition by Ṭughrul of the titles previously granted to the Buyid Fanā-Khusraw: King of Kings, 'Aḍud ad-Dawla, Tāj al-Milla, Abū Shujā'. Ṭughrul in addition used the Turkic Alp Arslān (Lion Heart), a title also adopted, more famously, by his nephew and successor.[234]

There was such a profuse accretion of titles in Buyid and Saljuq times that they became degraded and ultimately ceased to be seriously indicative of rank.[235] They later became routinised, and, under the Mamluks, were left for chancery officials to devise,[236] although they were, much later and much further east, to take on a renewed salience and magnificence under the Mughals. Ultimately also, titulature became more independent of the caliphate, and various sultans used in their correspondence titles that had not been specifically authorised. With the Mamluks, this reflected a trend which was later to be made even more illustrious by the Ottomans, namely, the incorporation of the entire Near Eastern repertoire of genealogies and notions of universal kingship. One Mamluk sultan was described thus: 'the victorious, in receipt of divine aid, the pillar of the world and of religion, sultan of Islam and of Muslims, sustainer of justice amongst mankind, the succour of those subject to injustice, the inheritor of kingship, king of Arabs and Persians and Turks, conqueror of lands, giver of lands and cities, Alexander of the age, king of the holders of pulpits, thrones, and crowns, the shadow of God on His earth, sustainer of His commands, lord of the two seas, servant of the two holy enclosures, lord of kings and sultans, unifier of Muslim opinion, protector of the Commander of the Faithful'.[237]

Thus were brought into close connection the rhetorical and conceptual apparatus of royal sublimity bequeathed upon Muslim polities in Late Antiquity, and specifically Muslim genealogical charters and accoutrements. And thus arose a specifically and identifiably Muslim redaction of absolutism. This last connection, between absolutism and Muslim religious representations, is the topic of our next chapter.

CHAPTER SEVEN

Absolutism Sublime

The notion of *khilāfa* is, in Muslim writings about politics, almost invariably brought out in conjunction with that of *istikhlāf*, derived from the Koranic verse (al-Baqara: 30) which ascribes to God the statement to his angels that, in creating Adam, He had set up a caliph in the world. The conjunction of this foundational act of humanity with the foundation of the authority of one over the multitude predominates in exegeses of this verse. A caliph represents God in the implementation of His will, designated by jurists as his 'rulings' (*aḥkām*), and is also the caliph of Adam, continuing his primal and archetypal establishment of order which is also the foundation of a human order fulfilling the divine purpose of creation. Koranic exegeses underline both the divine and mundane genealogies of the caliphate, as a vicarage of God with which Adam was invested, and was later invested in those who, after his death, fulfilled the same purpose with which he was charged – namely the maintenance through prophecy of satisfactory order.[1] The specification and merger of these genealogies in the prophetic line of Adam is clearly implicit in virtually all extant exegeses, and is brought out explicitly in some.[2]

In Ismā'īlī Islam, this takes the form of a systematic and consistent mythological narrative, describing the seven cycles which comprehend the entirety of human history in terms of eras of prophecy in both its esoteric and exoteric aspects. In each epoch there is a *nāṭiq* and a *ṣāmit*, that is to say, personalities who articulate, respectively, the exoteric letter of the prophetic mission and its esoteric register. These are, in turn, the couplets Adam/Seth, Noah/Shem, Abraham/Isaac, Moses/Aaron, Jesus/Simon, Muḥammad/'Alī, and in due course, from their line, the messianic figures of al-Qā'im/al-Mahdī.[3]

Attendant upon this narrative are two possible consequences, both of soteriological significance: either a distinctive and profane mundane order cognisant of divine design, or the mundane extension of a sacrality emanating from the primal act of foundation. In the latter case, the creation of Adam is conceived as an event conceptually coeval with the creation of all things, in which, as a consequence, the worldly order calques the divine order. This latter possibility in its turn yields two further eventualities. In one this correspondence of divinity and rightly-guided humanity is guaranteed by the observance of divine command. In the other it is expressed in a pantheistic vision which views affairs of the world as structurally equivalent to a cosmos conceived as emanation, as in the philosophy of Fārābī, or else conceives mundane matters as signatures of matters divine, best expressed in the pantheistic systems of Muslim mysticism, particularly that of Ibn ʿArabī.

Just order as an extended series of analogues of matters divine will be taken up later. But there is an essential implicit equivalence between the two positions, one well expressed by Ibn ʿArabī himself in texts that bear interpretation in both an esoteric and an exoteric register:[4] *istikhlāf*, equivalent to the imamate (which term designates both the Abbasid and Fatimid caliphs, in addition to Twelver imams and Sufi mystagogues), implies both the implementation of divine commands 'which He calls *al-sharʿ*', and a mimesis of divine attributes. Although the Koran neither prescribes nor describes a distinct political sphere,[5] in all instances we find that religious and mundane attributes and functions of political rule, specifically of just rule expressed in the caliphal regime, are consubstantial – irrespective of whether or not a just political regime could be described as theocratic. The play of analogies is perhaps most pointedly evident and articulated in Muslim oneirocriticism. Muslim manuals of dream interpretation represent kingship and divinity as displacements one of the other, as metonyms for one another, in which the appearance of a king in a dream must be interpreted as a representation of God, and in which a smiling king represents divine favour.[6]

The Sacral Caliphate

Not all statements on the secular moment of the caliphate played with the rhetoric which built analogies with divinity or with the divine order of things. We have seen that the enunciations of kingship, discursive and plastic, were by no means exclusively nor even largely religious, although they expressed themselves in tones of enchanting sublimity. Writing on kingship was not religious writing, and the ceremonial of the caliphate and its imitation in sultanic courts was not religious, though it contained religious elements and languages. Neither king nor caliph was the object of a cult, nor were their palaces sacred enclosures according to the criteria and lineaments of sacredness as defined by the vast majority of Muslim divines, which required the radical transcendence of divinity and its immediate attributes.

But, in varying degrees, matters mundane were sacralised in their own right. In Shiʿi Islam, the imam was a direct product of divine grace (*lutf*), and his attributes were such that, even though he was not divine (with the exception of beliefs held by certain marginal groups), he could without reservation be described as sacred. Notions of the imamate and the allied conception of Sufi eschatology will be taken up in the next chapter, and are mentioned here to underline the fact that Sunni notions of the caliphate, albeit distinctive in their jurisprudential foundations, are nevertheless not far removed from notions held by other Muslims. Both have in common not only a shared stock of sublime epithets, metaphors, attributes of power, notions of divine ratification and investment, but also idolatrous and sacralising practices and attitudes towards the person of the caliph.[7]

Needless to say, this body of attributes in Sunni Islam was not brought under the unitary ambit of an integrated soteriological theology of the caliphate, unlike Shiʿi and Sufi theories of the imamate, although eschatological elements were strong in the periods of dynastic foundation – of the Abbasids, the Almohads, and others – a matter expressed in early Abbasid regnal titles. Such elements were later to be strewn throughout the body of writings on political subjects, and disseminated in political and social practice. It will not do to privilege the most restrictive of puritanical and officious juristic writing on the subject in order to construe a purely formal, legal, and secular theory of the caliphal office and person. Though such a sober and legalistic construal of the caliphate without divine trimmings is possible, it was only one among many conceptions, and there is no evidence to suggest it predominated except in some circles of pietistic *ʿulamāʾ* and among the entourage of certain sultans of puritanical sharʿist disposition. Indeed, the very same authors sometimes wrote about the caliphate both legalistically and quasi-magically, not because of divided or hypocritical spirits, but because they were writing within different conventions, in different idioms, presupposing distinct audiences and æsthetics of reception.

At the most elementary level one would have to start with the quasi-magical qualities of the caliphal person. There is a saying, very widespread in medieval Arabic writings and attributed to Persian wisdom, that the justice of a king – *sulṭān*, a term frequently applied to caliphs as well – guarantees the proper functioning of the seasons, proper rainfall and irrigation, the proper reproduction of cattle and the proper functioning of trade.[8] This suggestion is not simply reducible to a statement on the structural worldly connections of prosperity detailed in the 'circle of justice' studied in the last chapter, but has interpretations over and above those of political wisdom and general advice to kings. It was regarded as empirically manifest that royal injustice not only produced deleterious mundane effects, but called forth supernatural forces that act ineffably, at a distance, to stop the sky from raining and cattle from breeding.[9] The natural effects of royal injustice are not simply metaphorical, for they have to do with *baraka* with the two shading into one another: *baraka* granted with justice, drying up with injustice.[10] *Baraka* was of course shared with Sufi sheikhs and Ḥanbalī divines. Many tangible wonderful acts and capacities were ascribed to Aḥmad b. Ḥanbal and others; but these were also sought from the remote caliph.

Such matters as the veneration of caliphal objects and the incommensurability of the caliphal – and royal – person have been encountered in the previous chapter. To these must be added less formal bestowals of supernatural favour. The caliphal shirt was used as a source of *baraka* by the prominent Ṭālibid, the Sharīf Abū Jaʿfar, leader of the Twelvers in eleventh-century Baghdad.[11] Earlier, al-Jāḥiẓ reported the belief in the therapeutic efficacy of royal or noble blood, which was reputed to cure rabies and madness.[12] Given that caliphal *baraka* was thought to inhere in caliphal objects, it is thus unsurprising to find one provincial governor soaking letters received from the caliph in water, which he used to mix dough and bake bread to feed his family.[13]

The tombs of Abbasid caliphs were regarded as sacred and inviolable, possibly ever since the death and burial of al-Muntaṣir (r. 861–62), the brother and successor of al-Mutawakkil, and people brought belongings and treasures to them for protection in times of chaos and plunder.[14] Muʿāwiya's grave in Damascus was reported in the middle of the fourth century of the Hijra to have been open to visitors on Mondays and Thursdays, and had earlier been much embellished by Ibn Ṭūlūn, the semi-independent Abbasid Governor of Egypt and Syria during the period 868–884, who had ordered lanterns to be lit and the Koran to be recited around it.[15] It was also a seemingly widely held opinion that the supplications of a just king are more readily answered by God than those of others.[16] And, of course, *baraka* was to be had not only from particular caliphs, but resided in lineages. The *baraka* of Ṭālibid and ʿAbbāsid alone according to al-Jāḥiẓ, was the cause for the recession of the plague which had afflicted the central Muslim lands prior to ʿAbbāsid rule.[17]

Not surprisingly, Shiʿi writings attribute *baraka* and miraculous doings to the imams far more systematically and relentlessly than do the Sunni. A curse by the Fatimid imam never went amiss, and the imam, like the Prophet among the Sunnis, can intercede (*shafāʿa*) with God on behalf of the faithful undergoing their final judgement.[18] Sand on which the Fatimid caliph sat, and apples granted by him, were thought to have beneficial effects.[19] Standard works of Twelver Shiʿism ascribe to ʿAlī and later imams quite spectacular miracles, ranging from foretelling the future and blinding enemies by the mere thought of a curse, to outdoing Joshua (who caused the sun to stand still), by making the sun retrace its path and the Euphrates flood abate.[20]

It is in the nature of miracles, however, to be irregular in their rhythm, for they are, after all, breaches in regularity. But miracle-working of this kind is premised on occult correspondences between things, between persons and inanimate objects, according to an implicit metaphysical conception that regards all existents to be, in some senses, signatures of one another.[21] It is this that makes possible the conception of auguries and portents which relate seemingly unrelated events, not least with respect to kings and caliphs. Thus the reigns and the deaths of caliphs are often foretold from dreams, meteorological phenomena, or occurrences seemingly random to the untrained eye, but portentous in their own occult way.[22] Courts were awash with *malāḥim* (sg.: *malḥama*), oracular poems foretelling the future of dynasties and the advent of new ones, ascribed in their origin to ʿAlid eschatology, but which were of far wider incidence.[23] Closely allied and equally premised on occult sympathies, but unmiraculously and with an iron regularity and inevitability, were astrological calculations of the life-spans of dynasties as of individual rulers[24] which were in vogue among the Abbasids from the time of al-Manṣūr.[25] Some of the most illustrious literati cultivated this art, among them the philosopher al-Kindī (ca 801–866), whose renown as an astrologer stretched as far as India, and whose pupil, Abū Maʿshar al-Balkhī (d. 885 f), was to become one of the most distinguished astrologers in the history of Islam.[26]

Although astrological prediction, which was quite commonplace, was not exclusive to kings and caliphs, it covered them in a particularly elaborate fashion, for the rise and fall of royalty were thought to be allied to the major conjunctions, most momentously of Jupiter and Saturn. It is unsurprising that the person and rule of individual kings, like that of dynasties, should have such a correlative cosmic signature. Since they were not simply the lynchpins of the mundane social order, but were appointed as part of the divine order, kings and caliphs were better endowed with instinctive virtues than other men. Thus Māwardī qualifies the sagely exhortation to kings to better themselves and seek to train their souls in temperance by adding that the effort required of them is small compared to that required of a commoner, since they are in substance better endowed with virtues.[27] Others, like the moral philosopher Yaḥyā b. ʿAdī (d.974) or the Sufi Ibn ʿArabī, confirm this unusual capacity for virtue by resorting to a notion of inner strength rather than to virtuous instinct,[28] while yet others, such as al-Jāḥiẓ, thought the inherent nature of caliphs to be superior, a view tinged with a slight hint of the notion of charisma that was later to develop into imamism.[29]

All these are variations upon capacities inherent in the person invested with sovereignty. It is not in vain that a king is so-called (*malik*), for this indicates that God Himself honoured sultans in his Book with an attribute (*mulk*) that he also applied to Himself, and made them superior to the rest of humanity, just as humanity is superior to the rest of perishable creation.[30] This is the sense of the ubiquitous description of kings as God's shadows, as the shepherds of humanity, husbanding their subjects who, like cattle, are incapable of managing themselves; and this is why, according to Māwardī, the ancient Arabs referred to their kings by the same term used for their gods, *arbāb* (sg. *rabb*).[31] Other variations on this theme of *de facto* election connect the notion of kingship as husbandry of the king's subjects with philosophical speculation which portrays the clement king as a manifestation of divine emanation and grace and the inclement king as deprived of these qualities: the analogy between a king's relation to his subjects and God's relation to his creation, and the royal mimesis of divinity, are well expressed in the contention of Abū Sulaymān as-Sijistānī (d. ca 1001) that a king, after all, is a human god.[32]

The force of these conceptions lies not in their technical rigour, but in their elusive quality, in their play of similes and analogies, in their construction of a self-conscious rhetoric of kingship which is thus impervious to all but the most officious of doctrinal or legalistic questioning. Although it is not a theoretical enunciation or regulation of sovereignty methodically systematised in a comprehensive and coherent statement, the rhetoric of sovereignty is a locus of significant conceptions that, in addition to their discursive consequence, have social and political effect. When conclusive doctrinal consequence was derived from this mimesis of divinity, or from the conception of the caliphate as the locus of divinity or its incarnation, the result was inevitably the establishment of a new religion. Such was the case of the Druze religion, which fused together literal interpretations of incarnation and of emanation, and divinised the Fatimid caliph al-Ḥākim bi Amr Allāh (r. 996–1021), thus provoking a very vigorous response, anathema, and repudiation from the mainstream of Ismāʿīlism.[33]

The belief, however, that the caliphate is an office arising from divine election, an office which betokens a representation and maintenance of divine interest in the world on the part of a vicar (*khalīfa*), need not entail dogmatic consequences. It could well be maintained, as it indeed was amongst both Sunni and Shiʿi Muslims, without detracting from the primacy of prophetic over caliphal missions. Prophets are indeed superior to kings, and Muḥammad superior to his caliphs, who stand to him in a mimetic relationship (*mushākala*).[34] But Muḥammad's superiority does not vitiate the contention that the caliph is God's caliph, nor does it necessarily interfere with the immediate and direct relationship between caliph and God.

In this, matters proceeded in continuity with the Umayyad enunciations explored in chapter four. The notion of the caliphate as a divine legacy, in which succession (*khilāfa*) of the Prophet and of previous caliphs does not exclude, but runs parallel to, the vicarage (*khilāfa*) of God, is the standard conception – reprehensible to many jurists though this direct connection with divinty might have been.[35] Some perfectly Orthodox jurists and other divines regarded caliphs as performing the same function as prophets, that of representing (*niyāba*) God.[36] This is a notion that ran parallel to the Shiʿi conception of the imamate, despite the predilection of modern as of late medieval scholarship to see Sunnism and Shiʿism as two entities born complete, intransitive, immutable, and incommensurable. The parallelism is particularly striking, even terminologically, in the formulae systematically deployed by the Shiʿi divine al-Shaykh al-Mufid. (d. 1022), for instance, in referring to successive imams, his 'Commanders of the Faithful', as each in turn assuming the caliphate in the double sense indicated: succession to predecessors, and vicarage (*khilāfa*) of God.[37] The theology of vicarage and the jurisprudence of succession are of course distinctive in Shiʿism. But this did not sully the semantic equivalence and the sublime, indeed, holy status of the Shiʿi imam or the Sunni caliph who was, after all, frequently referred to as imam, or their conceptual equivalence from the perspective of aesthetics of reception.

The caliphate is customarily described as a holy office (*muqaddasa*), at the very least from the era of al-Muqtadir. Official documents are replete with the use of this term, sometimes on its own, sometimes in conjunction with the connections between this office and the prophecy of Muḥammad.[38] The second Abbasid caliph al-Manṣūr already described his family as God's vicars and as the holders of the Prophet's legacy.[39] The poem of Kulthūm b. ʿUmar addressed to al-Maʾmūn, in which the caliph is told that right, orthodox, religion is inseparable from his person is well known.[40] Al-Amīn, al-Rashīd, no less than at-Ṭāʾiʿ, al-Mustarshid (r. 1118–1135), and al-Mustaḍīʾ (r. 1170–1180) described themselves, or were described, as God's vicars and legatees.[41] Ibn al-Jawzī told his caliph al-Mustaḍīʾ that affection for the Abbasid house was the pillar of all faith.[42] Others had told earlier caliphs that loyalty and obedience to them were essential to salvation.[43]

Moreover, al-Mustaḍīʾ and an-Nāṣir were described in terms normally associated with what later came to be identified as Shiʿi notions of the imamic prerogatives, such as intercession (*shafāʿa*), right-guidedness (*hudā*), mastery of the epoch (*ṣāḥib az-zamān*), lordship of the epoch (*rabb az-zamān*), and endowment with messianic attributes (*al-imām al-mahdī*). Obedience to al-Mustaḍīʾ was described as integral to faith just like belief in God; disobedience in contrast constituted unbelief, since the caliph was the fount and guardian of religion.[44] And with explicit reference to verse by Ibn Hānī' (934f–973), the prominent Fatimid panegyrist of earlier times, who famously described the caliph as the master of destiny and ascribed to him the divine attributes of unicity and power,[45] Sibṭ Ibn at-Taʿāwīdhī (d. 1188) described al-Mustaḍī' with the same attribute of mastery over destiny.[46] Similar descriptions of the Umayyad caliph at Cordoba are also in evidence.[47]

Like the Shiʿi imams, the caliphs were, moreover, radiant sources of light; this was a constant trope used in describing both their inner and outward aspects.[48] Throughout, the Abbasid house, like the line of ʿAlī, was thought to be particularly privileged, as a holy lineage representing divine interests on earth, the locus of sublime charisma which permits the order of the world to be maintained. In clear counterposition to Shiʿi advocacy, moreover, the Abbasid family is termed a *shīʿa* which inherits from the Prophet not only the office of the caliphate, but knowledge (*ʿilm*) as well.[49] The full integration of the caliphate and crypto-Shiʿi notions of the imamate put forth in terms of Sufi sheikhdom and of supremacy in terms of the popular fraternities of *futuwwa*, with the one enfolded in the other, was accomplished only by an-Nāṣir.[50]

There were of course no systematic institutional or strictly and bindingly devotional or theoretical and dogmatic consequences for these views within the Sunni legal and theological traditions. But they had very real discursive and political effects, and very real effects on the political unconscious of polities which sanctified the absolute ruler, irrespective of strictly theological specifications. In all, the rhetorical and visual assimilation of the caliph to prophecy, to divinity, to a charismatic line, and his conception in terms of inviolability, incommensurability, ineffability, and sheer potency, produced a critical mass creative of a sublime and holy authoritarianism, one which flows in the social and imaginary-conceptual capillaries of Muslim political traditions. Rhetorical hyperbole does not have necessary dogmatic consequence; but it is nevertheless constitutive of the conception of absolutism, for which theological and dogmatic statements are neither the exclusive nor necessarily the central enunciative location. The utilisation of specific descriptions and attributes and the contexts of this deployment, be they discursive, verbal, or ceremonial, are of course a matter for specific and detailed historical and sociological investigation, varying with context and setting.

Caliphal Kingship

Most of the matters dealt with in the preceding section applied both to caliphs and to kings who had the same repertoire of attributes, of relations to subjects, and of relations to divinity. Both the caliph and the king were represented as incommensurable, omnipotent, beyond reciprocity and measure. Were caliph and king to coexist within the boundaries of the same polity, the king would stand to the caliph, in principle, as subjects stand to kings, a relationship of subordination which recapitulates the standing of a king as of a caliph before God. [51] Both king and caliph are God's shadows, elected by God, God's vicars, for the very fact of political authority is a manifestation of the divine, of vicarage first bestowed upon Adam.

Caliphs are subordinate only to prophets, and kings are also second only to prophets, for both they and caliphs fulfil the political role of prophets in the maintenance of an order divinely sanctioned. When fast distinctions are made between prophets on the one hand and caliphs or kings on the other, they are formulated in terms of a division of labour, with the prophets revealing the right way to go about organising society, and caliphs and kings maintaining the order of this sociality by stemming the proclivities inherent in human beings who, left to themselves, would wage a war of all against all.[52] There is an implicit parity between caliph and king, as between caliph and prophet, in terms of social order. But this parity is rarely articulated in an explicit way as it was, for instance, by Abū Ḥayyān at-Tawḥīdī (d. circa 1009) who conceived it in terms of an apostolate, the one visible and explicit in prophets, the other implicit in kings.[53]

The Koranic injunction for the institution of order for subjects under the domination of their rulers (an-Nisā': 58) does not specify a particular title for or description of rulers. Kings may also be described as God's vicars (*khalīfa*).[54] Yet distinctions between kingship and the caliphate are made, and are made in two specific ways: through the pietistic and ultimately eschatological vision of history as a history of salvation, and through the designation of legitimate order by the juristic elaboration of public life, that is, by juristic legitimism in its conception of the caliphate.

The pietistic and, in certain of its shades, eschatological notion of the caliphate in relation to kingship was developed with the utmost consequentiality in imami writings, both legal and theological, which will be discussed in some detail in the next chapter. There were yet profound, albeit legally or theologically inconsequential, echoes of the absolute and irrevocable division between the legitimate vicarage of God and the profane kingship of the Umayyads and the Abbasids, with a vision of a perfect caliphate in Medina unsullied by the corruption and luxury of later times, to which whimsical reference is made in melancholic tones, and which is counterposed in a vast body of writing to the actually existing practices of the caliphate.[55] Sheer kingship (*mulk*) is often used in a derogatory sense that betokens the corruption of early prophetic models, although the term is applied more usually in the normal sense conveying elevation, sublimity, and might. [56]

Such a normative antithetical use of the terms caliphate and kingship formed part of a pessimistic notion of history, common to Sunnis and Shīʿis. It was most systematically developed by the Ismāʿīlis who conceived of the flow of time as the arhythmic succession of prophetic missions, each followed by degeneration, followed by further correction and the intervention of God in the affairs of the world with the despatch of another apostle, the last of whom was Muḥammad. In each of these arhythmic cycles, the caliphate turns to kingship, and the most assiduously quarried histories in the investigation of this process were those of Islam and of the Israelites.[57] But though the time of the Medinan regime was regarded by the Sunnis as ideal, it was not thought of as utopian in the sense of an order that was integrally repeatable. This notion did not in fact arise in any serious sense before political Islamism in the twentieth century.[58] The Medinan regime was an unrepeatable miraculous or semi-miraculous irruption in the natural course of human history,[59] and the Medinan example, though always thought of as salutary and a source of almost binding individual example in the construction or justification of legal and ethical norms, was not integrally repeatable, except in the context of chiliastic expectations. The Medinan period, for all its brevity, was a quarry of moral and religious perfection, of altruism, unwordliness, and pure justice which, according to the rigorous Sunnism of Ibn Khaldūn, it shared with later, brief periods of the fully sharʿist caliphate,[60] in which it was copied.

In some dispute, under Shīʿi and Abbasid influence, was the legitimacy of the Umayyad regime. Authors working under the Abbasids normally avoided addressing this question, or of singling out the Umayyads for charges of degeneration and illegitimacy. ʿUmar b. ʿAbd al-ʿAzīz and Yazīd b. al-Walīd were singled out for praise, while the rest were passed over in silence, as were, sometimes, the Abbasids after al-Wāthiq (r. 842–847).[61] Narratives about the excellence of Muʿāwiya, in the form of prophetic traditions parallel to those the Shiʿa attribute to him with respect to ʿAlī, were widespread.[62] But there was a strong feeling of anti-ʿAlid legitimism in all Sunni circles, and this entailed the valorisation – in the face of Shiʿi execration and anathema – of the integral line of legitimately-designated caliphs from Abū Bakr through the Umayyads and the Abbasids. Ibn Khaldūn, in his extended defence of Muʿāwiya, thus regards him as the last of the Rāshidūn, being also the last caliph who qualifies for belonging to the prophet's *ṣaḥāba*.[63] There were legalistic arguments, reticent but sometimes also, with the benefit of distance, quite categorical, concerning the legitimacy of the manner in which Marwān b. al-Ḥakam (r. 684–685) and his son ʿAbd al-Malik acceded to the caliphate, and the correlative question of the legitimacy of ʿAbd Allāh b. az-Zubayr,[64] who reigned in Arabia as anti-caliph during the period 683–692.

Questioning the juristic legitimacy of successive caliphs was sometimes, as with the weary mood of officious *Weltschmerz* that marked late Mamluk times, extended to almost all caliphs except the Rāshidūn, in addition to al-Ḥasan, Muʿāwiya, Ibn az-Zubayr, ʿUmar b. ʿAbd al-ʿAzīz, and al-Muhtadī.[65] In all, this line was in direct counterposition to and consequent upon the ʿAlid legitimism of the Shiʿi divines (but by no means all Shiʿa, whose official connections with the Abbasids and with their caliphal prerogatives and attributes have been noted) who stripped all but ʿAlī of legitimate title to the caliphate. This defence most often took the form of strong defence of ʿUthmān.[66] Yet these strictures remained without doctrinal, dogmatic, or indeed political consequence in Sunni circles but had the status of statements of piety and discomfort with a radically imperfect world which, despite its imperfection, was still legally regulated and legitimately run on behalf of God

In the case of what was to become the Sunni caliphate as distinct from the imamite caliphate of the Fatimids, the legal definition of a legitimate caliphal regime, which will be discussed presently, seems to have been a necessary but by no means sufficient source of legitimation. Thus in the fifteenth century, al-

Qalqashandī described not only the Fatimids, but also the Umayyads of Cordoba and his contemporary Ḥafsids in Tunis as pretenders to the caliphate, whose properly legitimate line was defined by the Medinan caliphs first, followed by the dynasties of the Umayyads and the Abbasids. The legitimacy of these lines was assured by the legal integrity of succession to the caliphal office, whose legal forms were either designation by the preceding caliph (*ʿahd*) or designation by a council (*bayʿa*); the latter sometimes followed the former. All other dynasties claiming the caliphal title were seditious.[67]

Legitimacy is, strictly speaking, a legal and not a religious or moral category, and a legitimate caliphate is one which obeys certain legal conditions. That many caliphs were deposed, blinded, or assassinated, is irrelevant from the point of view of the jurist, for whom the crucial matter was proper juristic form and procedure for the accession of caliphs following legal incapacitation of a previous incumbent, however caused – by death, by mutilation resulting in loss of sight, or by acts of abdication. Documents of abdication were invariably properly signed by caliphs forcibly deposed and witnessed by judges and senior officials. Failing abdication, caliphs might be legally deposed by a document of impeachment issued by judges and senior officials.[68] That the murderers of caliphs normally went unpunished was a matter legally distinct from the question of succession, whatever the politics or events that resulted in the legal document. Technically, the legal effects of a murder were relative to the person of the regicide, not the office of the caliphate, in much the same way as the turpitude and depravity of a caliph had legal effect upon his own person, not on his capacity as office holder.[69]

Caliphs belonging to lines other than the three centrally accepted ones, like the Almohads (1130–1269) and their Ḥafṣid successors (1228–1574) in different parts of the Maghreb and of Spain, had their own ideologues. Thus the grandfather of the celebrated Ibn Khaldūn spoke of the recession of the caliphate in the Maghreb and its atrophy in the East as a justification for the transference of its œcumenical seat to North Africa by the Almohad founder Ibn Tūmart (d. 1130).[70] For other authors, mainly Easterners, these caliphs were only pretentiously so-called, 'following the usage' of Abbasid sovereigns,[71] but also, as Ibn Khaldūn noted, signalling their great might.[72] This is why references to caliphs other than the Abbasids most often took the form of a formula referring to the pretentious rather than the legitimate use of the title (*al-mutalaqqib bi'l-khalīfa*).[73] A prominent scholar working under the Ḥafṣids referred to Ibn Tūmart in one book by the title he claimed (al-Mahdī), which was the basis for the claim to the caliphate by his successors in a semi-official history of that dynasty, while in a later work of biography he used the term 'al-Mahdī so-called', and in the semi-official history referred to Ibn Tūmart's Almohad successors as kings of the 'Abd al-Mu'min line, not as caliphs.[74] Needless to say, different neo-caliphal lines were judged differentially, with the Fatimids being a target for particularly bitter and almost universal vilification, on the grounds of dogmatic deviance no less than a false claim to descent from the line of the Prophet. To this, the Fatimids responded in kind, most particularly by reaffirming their 'Alid descent and their inheritance of the imamate from him, and by accusing the Cordoban Umayyads and the Abbasids of impiety and even of apostasy.[75] However, no dynasty claiming the caliphate had the longevity (749–1516) and originality of the Abbasids, and no other could make credible œcumenical claims with the same force, or be the focus of an œcumenical legitimacy, irrespective of the power it wielded or did not wield.

Alongside the legalist notions of caliphal legitimacy were other views, equally juristic, which legislated for new conditions, disassociated the office from the imperative of political œcumenism, and made legal the coexistence of more than one caliphal regime in the lands of the Muslim œcumene. The argument, correlative with the manifest simultaneous existence of many caliphates, and with refutations of the widely-held imperative that a caliph should stem from the Quraysh, is a legal one, based on the criticism of prophetic traditions. It was particularly prevalent from the eleventh century in both East and West[76] and deployed the normal equipment of legal argumentation – namely interpretation and criticism of foundational texts, in this case, prophetic tradition.

The well-known narratives attributed to the Prophet, stating that the sovereigns (*mulūk*, *a'imma*) should be of Quraysh,[77] were ubiquitous, and formed an integral part of legal treatises on the caliphate. But the central narrative does not answer to the rigorous standards of criticism of authenticity, as it is a *ḥadīth* which is not concomitant (*mutawātir*) and therefore not binding. The same Qurayshite imperative does not, additionally, arise necessarily from the nature of politics: the fact that God chose the house of the

Prophet is a favour granted to this House and is irrelevant to the legal position on matters concerning caliphal lineage; the fact that the authenticity of a prophetic narrative is widely accepted does not thus render it technically beyond such criticism.[78] This argument was not novel, and Muslim scholars were widely aware of the tenuous authenticity of prophetic narratives, but were equally conscious of a need to suspend judgement out of respect for traditionalism and for established practice and jurisprudence based on traditionalism.[79]

If we exclude the earlier traditions of the Khawārij, there was nevertheless available, from the ninth century (as evinced by its occurrence in the *Musnad* of Aḥmad b. Ḥanbal), another prophetic narrative concerning dynastic lines. The Prophet is reported to have indicated that the Quraysh should rule only so long as they did so properly.[80] Yet the exclusive title of the Quraysh was a tenacious idea; when it was discounted or qualified by political decentralisation, this was done by making it the centre of concentric circles of wider social amplitude: if no Qurayshite were qualified, then a Kinānite, failing whom another Isma'ilite would be chosen. Only if all else failed did a small number of scholars envisage the possibility of investing a non-Arab with sovereignty.[81] Yet there was also the legal principle that the leadership of the œcumene is not only exclusively vested in Quraysh, but that it was impossible that Quraysh should be devoid of an individual worthy of the caliphal dignity.[82] The tenacity of the Qurayshite imperative was such that Maqrīzī, the student of Ibn Khaldūn, writing in a mood of terminal melancholy, declared that it was God himself who removed the caliphate from the Quraysh: not because they had fallen out of favour, but rather as an act of grace granted this noble lineage who were thus saved by God from association with the degenerate kingship of his time.[83]

The tenacity of the belief in the divine election of the Quraysh, and of the Hāshimids within Quraysh (to whom both the Abbasids and the 'Alids belong),[84] was therefore evident. Yet this general consensus could be breached both by juristic innovation and by manifest political and œcumenical realities. This stands as just one example of the way in which the legal conception of the legitimate caliphate developed and changed over time. It is a conception that shares mutability with all histories, although modern scholars of Islam in the West have taken Muslim legal development and innovation for the metaphysical symptoms of decline and of a childish sense of unreality. The caliphate, sublime as it may be, was also, as of the eleventh century, juristically construed after a systematic manner subjecting it to legal rules which at one and the same time provided for its necessity, regulated its workings, and guarded its integrity and prerogatives in relation to the Buyid and other dynasties which had come to subdue its erstwhile dominions.

Systematic juristic statements of the caliphate were an innovation of the eleventh century, normally associated with the name of Māwardī but also including the twin work of his contemporary courtier and Ḥanbalī scholar and judge, Abū Yaʿlā b. al-Farrāʾ. Such systematic treatments were also common as final chapters in treatises on dogmatic theology which in disputes with imamism over the legitimacy of non-ʿAlid caliphs repeat much of the legal material, but preserve substantive features of their origin. These statements do not constitute a political theory as they are often construed, but are legal discourses on the subject of government and public authority in general, discourses ultimately sustained by the absolutist principles and theories of authority examined throughout this book. They are technical legal specifications of the caliphal office and its prerogatives and should not be given a remit wider than that of law. They do not provide theories of authority, but assume such theories.

Legal discourses on the regulation of the caliphate do not, moreover, as common scholarship has it, 'reconcile' the 'theory' of the caliphate with its practice, for there was no systematic legal theory of the caliphate prior to them, only scattered statements on taxation, investiture, war, and other matters, treated under these separate headings in legal compendia, narratives of the Arab conquests, and collections of prophetic narratives. The eleventh-century efforts of Māwardī and others were legislative efforts which, like all such efforts, were made by practising jurists working with matters both *de facto* and *de jure*. They were concerned with regulating the affairs of the world of social, political, and administrative practices. Māwardī systematised this material under a novel topic of legal discourse, that of public authority in its widest systematic sense, in the form standard in other compendia of Muslim jurisprudence. That is, to each topic are adduced a number of opinions, some discordant, others related by various shades of difference and distinctiveness. Māwardī thus brought to bear on the various topics of public authority various textual and other precedents from which contemporary legal judgements could be made by the discretionary legal power of the caliph. Although Māwardī often indicates preferences for certain positions, there is no implication that these were in any way binding on the caliph, who had the same capacity for legal decision as does a judge. *Aḥkām* works were legal treatises, not political theories or theories of government, although implicit in them were conceptions of government that have already been explored.[85]

Thus the first condition to be fulfilled in examining the legal theory of the caliphate is to be mindful of its complexity and of its technical nature,[86] rather than to assume its simplicity. The theory is formulated within the rules of composition of a particular genre – legal compendia, books of *aḥkām* or of *fiqh* – and must thus be read within this genre, which must not be confused with general treatises on political theory. It is premised on the absolutism of the caliphate, and it seeks to provide systematic and comprehensive legal material for regulating the detailed functions and delegations of this absolutism.

The net result is not a theory that subordinates the caliphate to the power of the Buyids, but one that regulates the caliph–sultan relation as one possible form for the delegation of power among others which range from the minimal to the maximal. Nowhere does Māwardī, or any other contributor to this literature, countenance a division of sovereignty.[87] The absolutist powers of the caliphate were not derogated, but delegated, and this delegation was to be withdrawn and full executive power re-appropriated when the caliphate in Baghdad regained its vigour and independence in the twelfth and thirteenth centuries, although it was no longer an imperial power. Thus we see in the legal treatise on caliphal regulations written for an-Nāṣir a restatement of caliphal functions and prerogatives that had become classical in the formulation of al-Māwardī, with somewhat different emphases and a few novel topics.[88] The legal articulation of the caliphate treated in a comprehensive way the delegation of powers: to overpowering Sultans no less than to the viziers of independent and powerful caliphs.

We should not, therefore, be speaking in terms of 'political realism' in the narrow sense of the term although, like all jurists at all times and places, had he not been a realist Māwardī would have been no jurist at all. Neither should we construe the legal theory of the caliphate as utopian or idealistic,[89] except in so far as all legal theories are, to some extent, statements of an optimal measure for reality. Such echoes of the standard positions on Māwardī are entirely unnecessary, and if one were in search of a theory of political ideals, one must turn to the exemplary and salutary narratives which form the bulk of *Fürstenspiegel*, be they Machiavellian or altruistic, where an idealistic utility and an idealistic morality are conjoined, as are the affairs of the world generally. Juristic theories of the caliphate can not be classified as realistic or idealistic, or properly understood in terms of idealism or realism; they are strictly and rigorously legalistic.

Three elements are crucial to the juristic discourse on the caliphate: the proposition that its establishment is a religious duty, the legal means and conditions of designating a caliph, and the functions that a caliph must discharge personally or delegate to others. The establishment of the caliphate is a duty – but unlike the Shi'i notion, not a fundamental dogmatic article of faith (*aṣl i'tiqādī*) – collectively incumbent upon Muslims. It is a duty to be shouldered by one particular individual as his particular responsibility, which is what Muslim jurisprudence, in its classification of legal duties, terms *farḍ kifāya*, as distinct from *farḍ 'ayn*, the latter being an obligation, like prayer, incumbent upon all individuals. It is, moreover, according to the majority of Muslim jurists and theologians whose opinion became the classical theory, a duty made imperative by traditional and not by rational argumentation, the source of the traditional argument being a consensual interpretation of textual material.

Several elaborations and refinements are attendant upon this proposition. There is, first of all, the proposition that some of the functions of a caliph or imām are founded not in reason but in religious obligation technically unrelated to any other consideration of rational argumentation for utility.[90] One would presume that reference is here being made to a category of arbitrary divine obligation, such as various devotional rites, like the precise order of prayer or of pilgrimage, which are universally regarded by Sunnis to have no justification in human reason and to derive their obligatory character from divine command.[91] Thus the caliphate may indeed be an institution of human society whose necessity is ascertainable by the use of reason. But this runs parallel to the autonomous and self-sufficient technical legal requirement on which this argument from human nature and its need for husbandry has no necessary impact.

Correlatively, another argument is adduced, but in theological not in legal works: namely the proposition that the institution of a caliph is rationally of the same order as the institution of all authority. The necessity of authority for the good order of human society is coterminous with the necessity of absolute power. Such good order is in keeping with what, after Ghazālī, came to be known as nomothetic intent (*maqāṣid ash-sharʿ*), or the mundane aims of the *sharīʿa*,[92] which run parallel to the requirements of human nature, and presume a natural law[93] that requires the institution of kingship. Thus, it can most plausibly be argued that Māwardī's was a theory of caliphal kingship.[94] In a further refinement, of Muʿtazilī inspiration by a prominent Twelver theologian, the rational necessity of the imamate is regarded as one known to God only and not to Muslims.[95]

Furthermore, the Sunni imamate or caliphate is legally construed as the result of a contractual procedure or *bayʿa* effected through an *ad hoc* electoral body of uncertain definition and composition generally referred to as *ahl al-ḥall waʾl-ʿaqd* ('those who bind and unbind'), designating the *de facto* authorities in a position to appoint or ratify the appointment of a caliph. This body almost invariably comprised religious and other dignitaries in addition to representatives of the court and military. In return, the caliph undertook to fulfil his legal obligations to the commonwealth of Muslims present before him as *ahl al-ḥall waʾl-ʿaqd*.

The erection of the caliphate is an obligation thus addressed to two categories of people: those in a position to choose consequentially (*ahl al-ikhtiyār*), and men of religion (*ahl al-ijtihād*).[96] It is clear that residents of the capital, though in principle not distinguished above provincials, have a priority in their inclusion among the appointing body.[97] The *bayʿa* is additionally the result of either the actual election by this body of a caliph, or their ratification of appointment (*ʿahd*) by a ruling caliph of a successor, both of which are long-standing procedures in Muslim history, embodied in standard testamentary and documentary forms[98] and buttressed with verbal and other ritual formulae and with the distribution of gifts, both money and robes of honour.[99] These documents of *ʿahd* were sometimes sent to be displayed at the Kaʿba in Mecca, as in 261/875 for instance.[100]

Only slightly after the formulation of Māwardī, compulsion – that is, the forcible installation of a caliph by a powerful prince – was regarded as a means of appointment on a legal par with the original two. Māwardī himself did not disallow this, and adduced legal opinion for this position as well as for its opposite.[101] After all, Abū Yaʿlā had already attributed to Aḥmad b. Ḥanbal the saying that such a forcible appointment was perfectly legitimate.[102] The justification for this view is that the caliphate must continue regardless of the means of appointment, and that the caliphate and the means for enforcing its authority are inseparable.[103]

It cannot be maintained, as do prevalent views on Muslim discourses of the caliphate, that this was originally a theory which described a far-fetched ideal, and then degenerated into coarse opportunism. We have seen that the theory was not idealistic, but rather a legal theory which systematised past practice in juristic form. Moreover, there was no process of degeneration, but the almost immediate and contemporary formulation, with Juwaynī and with Abū Yaʿlā, of different juristic innovations, the latter very much attuned to the Abbasid legitimism of certain Ḥanbali traditions, the former highly critical of Māwardī for insufficient adherence to Shāfiʿī legal positions. To assume that Māwardī was in his day canonical and unique is entirely unjustified.

The imperative of absolutism was also the *leitmotif* behind the universal aversion to the idea of contesting a ruling power. Sedition in Muslim law books is a legal offence of great consequence, attendant upon which is a particularly rigorous statutory penalty (*ḥadd*). In the final analysis, though the caliphate involves the assent of prominent subjects, it is a right pertaining primarily to the caliph rather than to his subjects.[104] There is great ambivalence in juristic writings on the subject of unjust rulers, the prevailing approach being to defer this question to the broader and more diffuse topic of impeachment. The subject of impeachment is also particularly serviceable in this strategy of diffusing points of tension, as it legislates in the same stroke for the unjust, but not necessarily illegal, removal of caliphs by mighty princes and their legal replacement by others. The lesser of two evils seems the preferred choice,[105] although the general categorical statement is almost invariably made that a ruler who causes the breakdown of order, whose markers of legitimacy are the maintenance of the legal system, should be resisted. The detailed treatment of the legal means for removing a ruling caliph from office is not one that is common. It does not occur in legal treatises, and is mooted only in a general way in theological discussions of the caliphate and in pronouncements and writings of a pietistic or of an ethical nature. That Māwardī and other jurists did not propose a legal theory for sedition is unsurprising, and does not imply, as modern Western scholarship generally assumes, the opportunistic legalisation of injustice.

The fundamental concern in establishing an imam and resisting sedition is that he deputises for the Prophet in guarding the faith and regulating the affairs of the world: '*ḥirāsat ad-dīn wa siyāsat ad-dunyā*' is the classical formula.[106] Following from this are the duties of the caliph and the public functions of the caliphate, duly classified into ten legal topics: the preservation of religion according to generally agreed principles; implementation of legal regulations governing relations between individuals so that justice prevails; keeping the peace and assuring private security so people might go about their business peaceably and travel in safety; enforcement of statuary punishments so that the rights of God and of his creation are guaranteed; enforcement and protection of borders to assure overall security; pursuance of war on behalf of Islam to spread religion or achieve relations of protection and patronage (*dhimma*) for non-Muslims; the collection of charitable donations and of legal land taxes (*fay'*) without fear or injustice; the assessment and payment of state remuneration to those entitled to it; the appointment of advisors and deputies in the performance of various administrative and financial functions, and finally, the personal and close discharge or supervision of these functions, for the caliph is the ultimate authority who holds responsibility for the actions of his subordinates.[107] In return for these public duties, the caliph must expect obedience and succour.[108] It is true that in theological writings on this subject ample emphasis is placed upon the necessity for the caliph to listen to advice,[109] but this is nowhere counterposed to the imperative of obedience or made a condition for obedience.

The caliph's person must additionally meet a number of criteria. These are such as might be required of a man of full legal responsibility, like majority and sanity, in addition to what might be required of a political leader: disposal of power, integrity of senses, and good judgement. And as a caliph is called upon to run the legal system and to safeguard the faith, he should also have the qualifications required of an accomplished religious scholar. The primary concern, explicitly brought out in one text, is an independence of opinion which is beyond relations of parity, although this is not meant to preclude the solicitation of advice.[110] Finally, Qurayshite origin is imperative in the classical statements of the legal discourse of the caliphate. However, there is no necessary connection between this and the functions to be discharged. This was used as an argument justifying, as we have seen, non-Qurayshi caliphates particularly at a time when Qurayshi origins had receded into the mists of time, and persons of other origins were qualified for the caliphate.[111]

We have seen that much of this legal regulation was a record of usage and precedent, sustained by interpretations of the Koranic text and the adduction of statements attributed to the Prophet, as was the normal procedure of Muslim jurisprudence. No sooner had this been systematically recorded by Māwardī than a process of revision and qualification set in, most particularly in the East, but also in Baghdad, by Isfarāʾīnī (d. 1078), Juwaynī and his pupil Ghazālī. This process, however, simply accentuated various tendencies already present in the legal record of precedent. The long-standing contention, counterposed to Shiʿi claims for ʿAlī and for the imams in general, was that the caliph need not necessarily be the very best man (*al-afḍal*) in his time, provided he fulfilled other conditions of the caliphate, including descent.[112] There is here a departure not only from Shiʿism, but also from the notion current in the Near East for over a millennium, of the ruler as *ipso facto* the best man. We have seen that this notion had been incorporated into Muslim writings on kingship, from which al-Jāḥiẓ extrapolated the necessity for the caliph to be the best man, but based this position on the argument that the caliph is after all a mimesis of the prophet.[113] The argument seems to have been quite widely-available, to the extent that one eleventh-century theologian felt the need to refute it, possibly also under the impetus of an anti-Shiʿi polemic.[114] But we must be aware that this disassociation of rule from prophetic or divine mimesis was located in the context of technical legal theory, without necessarily being prevalent outside this discursive field.

Here, the standard legal position was that although the reign of the best man was indeed optimal and ideal, its realisation was contingent on its being possible and practicable.[115] Sayings attributed by Abū Yaʿlā b. al-Farrāʾ to Aḥmad b. Ḥanbal[116] – a near contemporary of al-Jāḥiẓ – anticipate explicit statements by Ghazālī and others that the failure to fulfil the legal requirements of religious erudition and good character do not render a person disqualified for the office of the imamate. Māwardī's position on these matters was to deny the disqualification of the *fāsiq*, or person of low character. This position seems to derive by analogy from the permission to minors, slaves, and persons of poor character to lead public prayers,[117] or for the leadership of prayer to be assumed by a debauched person.[118] Necessity justifies matters which should be regarded illicit, as Ghazālī said, and is a matter sometimes indicated and affirmed in general terms, but very seldom indicated in detail, contrary to the common interpretations of Muslim jurisprudence of the caliphate. [119]

The different Sunni schools of law, which were definitively crystallising at that time, traditionally adopted distinctive positions towards matters relating to the caliphate. Laxity was not normally identified with Shāfiʿīs, including Ghazālī, who generally adopted a position of rigourism. Thus, for instance, the insistence on Qurayshi origin for the caliph and on matters relating to his character and qualifications. Not all Shāfiʿīs adopted a rigourist attitude on this question. Nevertheless, the Shāfiʿi reputation was such that a Ḥanafī scholar in Mamluk times quoted it as discreditable to their standing, yielding the denial of legitimacy to Mamluk rule. Mamluk sultans were therefore urged to favour Ḥanafī over Shāfiʿī jurists.[120] Another such point of contention was the matter of disqualification: while Māwardī, in line with Byzantine and earlier Baghdadian precedent, rendered the loss of sight an automatic legal disqualification from holding the caliphate, more than one caliph was still recognised after his eyes had been put out, in Iran and in Ḥamdānid Mesopotamia.[121] Likewise Juwaynī did not disqualify from rule eunuchs or men who had lost extremities on the grounds that what mattered was capacity, empowerment, and good judgement.[122] Clearly, the office was invariably greater and more exalted than the man.

It is, after all, the office that allows the man to delegate authority to subordinates. Some of these subordinates, like Buyid princes or Seljuq sultans, were far mightier than the caliph. Others, like Ghaznavid or Ayyubid kings, were entirely independent and not even geographically proximate. In all cases these kings were delegated the authority of the caliphate, although they were not necessarily actual subordinates of his person except in formal visual, verbal, and written statements which personify the legal office in the form of an individual caliph. It is often stated that we have here a perpetuation of a fiction. But this is far too crude a portrayal of the interplay between naked power, symbolic capital, political ritual, legitimacy, religious authority and charisma, and administrative practice. Even if the thesis of a fiction were to be conceded, it was clearly one with sufficient material force to require that it be elaborately sustained. It was the caliphal regime that was permanent, not the succession of kings who ruled in its name.

This relationship was articulated as a jurisprudence of devolution which took the form of a statement of delegation, in the due legal form, augmented with official verbal and chancellorial formulae. The original form of the jurisprudence of delegation resided in the documents by which the vizirate was conferred. This last office fell into two types, like the legal category of mandated agency (*wikāla*), which could be either absolute, constituting a general mandate, or restricted, entailing specific functions which are entirely and narrowly executive in nature, and which due to this could even be, in the controversial opinion of Māwardī, entrusted to a non-Muslim or to a slave.[123] This division reflects the two legal forms of the vizirate in Abbasid historical practice.[124] The paradigm of the absolute delegation of power led to the transference of powers. The first instace of such transfer was to *amīr al-ʾumarāʾ* Ibn Rāʾiq in the second quarter of the tenth century and came to constitute the paradigm of delegation of powers to sultans, Buyid and Saljuq kings, and to kings farther away. Powers so delegated had constituted the prerogatives of the caliphate – fiscal, financial, and military – which the caliph could no longer discharge, but which the caliphate discharged by legally delegating them to others.[125]

The paradigm of power fully delegated formed the legal basis of the famous *imārat al-istīlāʾ* in Māwardī, which others, such as Juwaynī, preferred to regulate under the original legal title of the vizirate.[126] Strictly speaking, the office of vizirate ought to be classified under *imārat al-istikfāʾ*, powers delegated voluntarily and at caliphal initiative. The term *istīlāʾ* is commonly rendered as 'usurpation', but should more appropriately be rendered in terms of compulsion and coercion, as the suggestion – or, even more rare, the practice – of the illegal tenure and discharge of caliphal prerogatives by others is so very infrequent as to be inconsequential.

The analogies with the vizirate of the absolute kind, *wizārat at-tafwīḍ*, the historical precedent for which was the vizirate of al-Faḍl b. Sahl under al-Maʾmūn, were never absent from Māwardī's mind. The supervisory and appellate functions of caliph over the vizirate are here stressed.[127] The practical primacy of the sultanate over the caliphate, formalised through documentary and ritual acts of investiture, was perfectly legal, although it may have been at variance with previous salutary practice.[128] The practical incapacitation of the person of the caliph had, as a legal consequence, the necessity of delegation to ensure that the functions of the caliphal office remained active. Delegation would be fully in keeping with the purpose of the caliphate if the overpowering sultan fully demonstrated religious deference to the caliph in the form of legality of action in terms of caliphal delegation. If this condition did not obtain, the caliph would not be empowered legally to invest a sultan with the powers of the caliphate, and would be legally bound to resist him with the aid of other powers of the time, which was not always possible.[129]

With very few exceptions, caliphs did not find themselves in a situation where they had to face a decision of this sort. It occasionally arose under the Buyids when they played off one Buyid prince against another, with the exception of the short period of centralisation under ʿAḍud ad-Dawla, who prevented at-Ṭāʾiʿ from adopting the role of 'umpire'.[130] The earlier Buyids were particularly rapacious, extorting the caliph, systematically robbing him and interfering even with the expenses of the caliphal table. ʿAḍud ad-Dawla restored the financial dignity of the caliphal palace, which had been repeatedly plundered by unruly soldiers, as had many parts of Baghdad since the period immediately preceding the advent of the Buyids.[131] Upon the entry of the Buyids into Baghdad in 334/946, the caliph was humiliated and manhandled in the presence of Muʿizz ad-Dawla (r. 945–967) by two of the latter's soldiers, and was subsequently blinded. One of the last Buyids compelled the caliph al-Qādir, who was later to come very much into his own and even to become a Buyid king-maker,[132] to take the unprecedented step of leaving his palace to receive Musharrif ad-Dawla (r. 1021–1025) on the Tigris, although the latter had the good grace to leave his boat, move to the caliph's, and kiss the ground before his lord.[133]

Other caliphal prerogatives were encroached upon, over and above financial control and interference with the detailed workings of the caliphal palace under the cover of caliphal investiture. One was intermarriage, which removed the caliph from the relations of social incommensurability. At-Ṭāʾiʿ married a daughter of ʿAḍud ad-Dawla, and al-Qādir married a daughter of Bahā' ad-Dawla.[134] This further empowered the caliphs in their implication with inter-Buyid conflicts.[135] With the conquest of Baghdad by the Saljuqs, the caliph had to succumb to intense and prolonged pressure to give his own daughter in marriage to the ageing Ṭughrul Beg, who was himself to expire three weeks after the marriage contract was concluded but before his new bride arrived before him.[136] At least one later marriage between a caliph and a Saljuq princess involved humiliating negotiations over bride-price payment.[137] Māwardī played an important role in many such negotiations.

Matters persisted precariously in this way until the reign of al-Muqtafī (r. 1136–1160) which also saw the revival of the traditional vizirate in the person of Ibn Hubayra (1106–1165). The reigns of al-Muqtadir and al-Qādir veered significantly towards the re-assertion of caliphal pre-eminence and independence.[138] The period was also characterised by symbolic tug-of-war over the matter of titles, of drums playing outside palace gates, of names mentioned or ignored during the Friday sermon, and of the appearance of names on coins minted in Baghdad and elsewhere. In times that witnessed the recession of sultanic pre-eminence in Baghdad, the name of the Sultan was dropped from benedictions of the Friday sermons altogether.[139]

In Mamluk Cairo in 1412, during an interregnum between the reigns of two sultans, the caliph ruled alone for a brief period and was the sole formal source of all state actions. He alone was mentioned in the course of Friday sermons and on currency minted during that period.[140] Correlatively, when the Baghdad caliphate disappeared after the fall of Baghdad to the Mongols, Egyptian coins minted by Quṭuz (r. 1259–1260) and Baybars (r. 1260–1277) dropped the caliphal association and substituted impersonal formulae for it, reflecting an interruption in the source of ultimate authority. But the caliph's name reappeared as soon as the Abbasid caliphate was restored in Cairo.[141]

It is well known that caliphs in the Cairo period were exceedingly feeble. Some stooped so low as to make the round of visits to notable houses on feast days, and were occasionally scolded by the sultan for bad behaviour.[142] One Cairo caliph at least was held a virtual prisoner in a tower, and his name was not minted on contemporary coins.[143] A nickname, al-Mustaʿṭi Billāh (beggar in the name of God), given to at least one caliph by the common run of people, betrays profound contempt.[144] Representing the formal personality of the state in a period of interregnum is reminiscent of a similar role for chief judges throughout many periods of Muslim history.

Orientalist scholarship generally and inappropriately describes the Baghdad caliphate under the Buyids in terms more appropriate to that of Cairo: it would have been unthinkable in Baghdad that the sultan should, as Barqūq (r. 1382–1389, 1390–1399) did in Cairo, assume titles such as 'Partner of the Commander of the Faithful' (*qasīm amīr al-mu'minīn*), or 'Guarantor of the Commander of the Faithful' (*kāfil amīr al-mu'minīn*).[145] It is not entirely inappropriate, therefore, that a Turkish historian in the second quarter of the fifteenth century should compare the role of the caliph in Cairo to that of the patriarch in Constantinople.[146] This is a far cry from the comparison of the caliph to the Byzantine emperor that Ibn Rushd proposed two-and-a-half centuries earlier.[147]

The Baghdad caliphs maintained their dominance over the religious and religio-judicial institution (as distinct from the state–legal *mazālim* institution) even at their moments of greatest weakness, which cannot be said of the Cairo caliphs who delegated to the sultan all powers and prerogatives relative to these matters.[148] This entailed control over appointments to the religious offices deriving from the caliphate,[149] most particularly judges, syndics of the 'Alids, leaders of the Meccan pilgrimage, preachers at state mosques as distinct from civil mosques, and inspectors of markets. Buyid interference in these matters, most particularly in Baghdad, was episodic and almost invariably met with caliphal resistance and the refusal to ratify appointments made by the princes.[150] Such interference was sometimes written into the letters of investiture: the investiture by the caliph al-Ṭā'i' of the Buyid Fakhr ad-Dawla in 366/January 977, for instance, specified leadership at prayer among the caliphal functions transferred to the king, but excluded the legal system from these functions.[151] Disagreements between the various Sunni law schools over the legitimacy of Friday prayers without specific authorisation from the caliph reflected different conceptions of public authority;[152] but the caliph in Baghdad nevertheless authorised such prayers in some mosques and on occasion withdrew his permission.[153] Investiture with leadership of Friday prayers in Baghdad involved the command to offer prayers for the caliph,[154] was associated with the wearing of black by preachers and judges,[155] and was specific to state rather than to private mosques.[156] The caliph also felt empowered to withdraw authorisation to teach at the Niẓāmiyya College although, technically, the acts of foundation of this and similar colleges vested such authority in their founders.[157] In all, it seems that the *concordat* which constituted the investiture of sultans, which involved empowerment to appoint judges and preachers, did not apply to such appointments in Baghdad.

Caliphal involvement in matters of doctrine, most particularly the adoption of official creeds of Ḥanbalī inspiration in the Buyid era by al-Qā'im and most importantly by al-Qādir, were crucial components in the crystallisation of Sunnism and had, as correlative movements, the professionalisation and corporatisation of the *ʿulamā'* as a priestly sodality under caliphal control. Under the Saljuqs and even more firmly under the Mamluks, this professionalisation was sustained by specific educational and career itineraries supported by very substantial financial endowments and resources.[158] The process amounted ultimately to the formation of a state clerisy which was to find its most consummate form under the Ottomans. Credal control by the caliphate had antecedents in the policies of al-Ma'mūn and al-Muʿtaṣim,[159] whose doctrinal commitment to Muʿtazilism has been misconstrued and much exaggerated and must be thoroughly reviewed in the light of recent research.[160]

Baghdad caliphs also habitually tried to stem independent popular religiosity, most particularly the activities of street-corner preachers, whose activities they banned on occasion. These matters were closely allied to Sunni–Shiʿi disputes, and disputes between theological schools.[161] Credal orthodoxy was finally crystallised in the Ashʿarīte creed of al-Taḥāwī, which was later to become the official creed of the Ottomans and which, in Mamluk times, Ḥanafī clerics sought to render mandatory and to impose upon others, most particularly on the theologically-suspect Ḥanbalī divines. It was in this connection that the wayward Ibn Taymiyya was subjected to an inquisitorial procedure.[162]

The Sultanic Shadow of God

With the crystallisation of an *ʿulamā* sodality throughout the lands of Islam, the saying that the *ʿulamā* were really the vicars of prophecy was increasingly repeated. We have already seen how *Fürstenspiegel* written by the *ʿulamā* were full of exhortations to piety, the cultivation of religious knowledge, and the need, with a Koranic sanction, to take advice. Juwaynī also had the audacity to exhort obedience to the *ʿulamā* upon Niẓām al-Mulk,[163] a great patron of their sodality who was highly influential in its institutionalisation and the provision for it of an infrastructure. This indicates the prior conceptualisation of a notion of priestly authority in matters of belief and practice. When al-Qāʾim appointed a chief judge in Muḥarram 423/ December 1031, the act of investiture acknowledged the interposition of the judge between God and the caliph in matters of law.[164] The notion of *ʿulamā* guardianship of the faithful became widespread, as was indeed the idea that the existence of the *ʿulamā*, personified in *mujtahids*, was imperative, because their non-existence entailed the atrophy of legal obligations divinely prescribed.[165] The analogy with the imperative for the existence of the Shiʿi imam is self-evident, although the Sunni notion, when expressed by jurists rather than by courtiers, is bereft of the cosmic parameters in which the Shiʿi imam is implicated. The analogy with the mystical notions of the imamate and of the Pole of the Time (*quṭb*) as the direct inheritance of prophecy in preserving the order of the world, visible and invisible, is also clear.[166]

As has already been suggested, what this represents is a displacement, or at least the statement of the possibility for a displacement, of caliphal charisma by the corporate charisma of the *ʿulamā* sodality. The implication is a movement within the regime whose legislative bases were set out in legal discourses on the caliphate and on public life in general, whereby competence was divided into the normative or sharʿist, and the executive, with the latter making possible the maintenance of the former. Whereas the former is the province of the *ʿulamā*, the latter is the province of the sultan. God would render a king victorious provided he upheld the fundamental obligations of Islam. Yet he is at the same time the shadow of God on earth and is described by a host of other characteristics which have been discussed on more than one occasion.[167] The maintenance of an order in the world which might win God's favour is assured not only by the maintenance of God's rights, but by the sustenance of this through the principle, first adumbrated by the Muʿtazilī theologians as one of the five pillars of the creed and which then went into general circulation, of 'enjoining good deeds and forbidding reprehensible ones' (*al-amr biʾl-maʿrūf waʾn-nahī ʿan al-munkar*).

This was the *leitmotif* of the intervention by the *ʿulamā* in public life: when Abū Yaʿlā b. al-Farrā' declared, with the Muʿtazilites, that it was an obligation incumbent upon everyone, he was not simply referring to the position he was refuting, namely the Shiʿi view that it was the exclusive prerogative of the imam, [168] but was imposing upon the corporate body of the *ʿulamā* a collective obligation. In view of the prevalent mood of these times, it cannot be assumed that he was making this obligation incumbent upon all individuals, most particularly the *ʿāmma*, commoners; his saying is more likely to be correctly interpreted with reference to the particular collectivity of the *ʿulamā*.

Yet there was never any question to the mind of Sunni *ʿulamā* that this in any way implied sedition. The empowering agency which held ultimate responsibility for maintaining the sort of order that the *ʿulamā'*, following their interpretation of God's will, found desirable, was always and forever the king. The saying that years of iniquity are preferable to a single night without a king is everywhere to be found, for the king was the condition of the possibility of right order. If such order were in keeping with revelation and with divine will, the more fortunate both for the king and for his subjects.

The prototype of sultanic power answering to the exigencies of sharʿism was that invested by the caliphs, first in the Buyid and the Ghaznavid polities in Afghanistan, India, and Khurasan (ca. 997–1186), and later in Saljuq, Ayyubid, Mamluk, and other, less consequential, states. The investiture of these kings, a general commission to all-powerful kings, was contained in texts of a more or less standard form which differed from Baghdad to Cairo only in the sense that investitures from Baghdad caliphs were formulated as commands, whereas those of Cairo took the form of invocations, exhortations, and implicit directives.[169] The component of these letters most germane to the present discussion is the king's absolute vicarage of the caliphate in all matters except the caliph's private matters and 'what lies behind his door', as in the investiture of ʿAḍud ad-Dawla.[170] This sultanic vicarage of the caliphate was consummated under the Mamluks, when the caliph habitually and explicitly handed over to the sultan all his religious prerogatives over territories the sultan controlled or might come to control in the future.[171] Yet it was the caliphal ratification that appointed the Mamluk Sultan legally.

If the sultanate, albeit the shadow of God on earth, was not the caliphate, it was yet coeval with it in the perspectives both of the present and of eternity. Neither prophecy nor its vicarage could exist without the application of force, and the terrain of force was termed *siyāsa* which was sharʿified under the auspices of the sharʿified caliphate. It was also sharʿified under the auspices of the sultanate, whence the legal discourse upon the prerogatives of the caliphate devolved to a legal discourse of sharʿist politics whose guarantor was to be the sultan. The sultan not being caliph, the impersonal organisation of public life in the sharʿist mode under sultanic direction became the substitute for the person of the caliph and his charisma. In this regime, the vigilant *ʿulamā* acted out their vicarage of the Prophet by permission and grace of the sultan, but in turn mediated the prophetic charisma that was no longer mediated by the caliph, and in a context in which the Prophet had come to be cast after the image of the imam. Thus emerged the genre of *siyāsa sharʿiyya* not requiring caliphal vigilance, of which many treatises are extant, and whose most celebrated representative is undoubtedly Ibn Taymiyya.

Siyāsa sharʿiyya thus took over the tasks of caliphal legitimism. The organisation of public life along lines instituted under the caliphate and continued by the latter-day vicars of the Prophet, the *ʿulamāʾ*, had no need of the caliphate. In this perspective the caliphate appears as an ephemeral form of polity whose institutes are by and large devolved to other authorities, but the overall sum of whose institutes can be maintained through the impersonal machinery of the legal system. The caliphate thus construed appears merely as a technical specification, as a regime whose distinctiveness is technical, expressed in terms of law, and not substantive in any way.

When Ibn Khaldūn spoke, therefore, of the detachment or devolution of certain erstwhile caliphal functions pertaining to matters sharʿist, and their incorporation into the sultanic register of functions and prerogatives,[172] he was indicating in a precise formulation the way in which the institutes of the caliphate were devolved. It will have become clear that these institutes were not an integral code, but a body of legal preferences, precedents with legal force, and interpretations of Koranic statements pertaining to public life, which, at a certain point in time, were integrated vertically by the office of the caliphate. The caliphate, though an imperative institution according to Māwardī and many others, is not indispensable given the transference of enchantment to the

ʿulamā and the legal system they oversee, a legal system alive with the suggestion of God.

Māwardī himself had already stated that though the vizirate was not strictly an office required on religious authority, the politics giving rise to it is admixed with religious requirements. They are geared towards the well-being and rectitude of Muslims, the task of a vizier being performed by a person who, legally, is required to possess all the personal qualities of the caliph barring Qurayshi descent.[173] Legalism is the overriding criterion here as elsewhere in this discourse. Yet sharʿist legalism requires that leadership in public life, under which both kingship and the caliphate are subsumed, should be the task of the leader in matters of religion.[174] This leader is the caliph and, through delegation by him, the formally subaltern sultan. The functional equivalence in terms of public life is completed in the form of a general investiture, and the distinction is entirely technical.

The theorists of *siyāsa sharʿiyya* were not, therefore, sheer opportunists, but jurists cognisant of the technical organisation of legal life. When Ibn Jamāʿa, the prominent Mamluk jurist and judge, used the terms *imām* and *sulṭān* almost interchangeably,[175] it was not the result of some sleight of hand, but a reference to the decisive authority in public affairs, including religion. It is, in fact, in keeping with the reference by loyalist writers to the caliphs throughout the Abbasid period as sultans, a term which eventually came to designate the top authority in matters of state. Māwardī not only notes this, but expostulates on the terminological equivalence involved, stating among other things that the majesty of kings led Muslims to apply the term *imām* to supreme kings in recognition of obeisance due to them and implied in the linguistic sense of the word, and that the majesty of kingship is such that both language and religion apply the term *sulṭan* to them, in recognition of the definitive and final authority it implies.[176]

The technical distinction between the two, when they came to designate distinctive offices, is the contractual *bayʿa* relationship of the caliph to his electors which can be, we have seen, either voluntary or compulsory.[177] Otherwise, the offices are equivalent, and are classified as guardianship of the public, as two genera of kingship, the general (caliphate, implying œcumenism) and the specific, whose holders are called kings or sultans.[178] The fact that holders of the two offices are described by the same repertoire of metaphors, that they relate to their subjects as a head to a body, that God termed sultans kings (sg. *malik*) as He termed himself *malik* and prescribed the same obedience of subjects to them as He did to himself and his apostle Muhammad, is crucially indicative of a register of equivalences distinct from, but corresponding to, the shar'ist register.[179] Later caliphal investiture documents under the Mamluks describe the sultan in terms which we have encountered in encomia for caliphs, but which were also very common in the secular writings on kingship we have examined.[180]

The historical and legal imbrication of the two offices, and the shading of the one into the other, including their coalescence in the caliphate in its effective moments, was thus well noted, and its legal consequences well brought out by jurists, including Māwardī, whose work constitutes the first statement of *siyāsa shar'iyya.* The displacements that relate the one to the other are clearly stated by Ibn Khaldūn,[181] and a glossator of Ibn Khaldūn's text states that the historical transition from caliphate to kingship is not only a matter in keeping with the nature of human societies, but is also one that does not sully the purpose for which the two offices are instituted, [182] in the sense that the transition from the one to the other does not disturb the equivalent public functions they perform. Laoust made the correct observation that the work of Ghazālī constituted a 'mixed theory' of the imamate, which incorporated both the caliphate and the sultanate.[183]

But we should go further and make it clear that there was never a pure theory of the caliphate, only a jurisprudence of the public sphere which comprised the two historically, ceremonially, and technically distinctive, but functionally and legally concordant, offices of caliph and sultan. Indeed, the distinction of functions and offices is not fast and stable even within its legal expression, as the functions relating to war, finance, and the legal system are legally interdependent and combined, albeit in origin religious and shar'ist offices.[184]

Though there were some apologetic writings in the shar'ist defence of sultanism,[185] most were legal, indeed, legalistic. Ghazālī had already stated that the main pillar of *siyāsa,* of the husbandry of people, was *fiqh.*[186] In the Mamluk era, statutory punishments were seen as the fundamental means for enjoining good deeds and forbidding reprehensible ones,[187] thus instituting a regime of public punishment as a personified manifestation of the impersonal primacy of a public life legally instituted, much as is being advocated today by political Islamism. Ibn Taymiyya regarded these punishments as a form of *jihād* incumbent upon the collectivity of Muslims.[188]

Indeed, the whole body of writing on sharʿist politics is, like that of Māwardī, a topical account of various preferences, obligations, and precedents pertaining to the management of ritual, public offices, and financial and military administration. Much of it was in response to calls for co-operation by the state which also entailed, on the part of the *ʿulamāʾ*, a certain criticism of laxities and even major transgressions by state officials,[189] in which the co-operation of senior *ʿulamāʾ* was sometimes obtained.[190] Among the royal (and caliphal) transgressions often pointed out, and not only in Mamluk times, were cruel and severe punishments beyond those required by statutory punishments specified in Muslim jurisprudence, except for the provision made for them in Mālikī jurisprudence.[191] By extension the Mamluk judge and divine Subkī (d. 1369–70) criminalised executioners who carried out orders for the execution of innocent men.[192] Other objects of complaint and objection were the inaccessibility of kings and caliphs, the use of golden utensils and clothing,[193] and the kissing of the ground before the king.[194] Māwardī felt it necessary to outline the juristic differences of opinion against imbibing alcoholic drinks, and to indicate opinions on the legitimate consumption falling short of inebriation of some kinds of intoxicants, but enjoined the king to choose the more pious and elevated of legal options.[195] Ostentatious sharʿist political practices were often performed by various kings, most particularly on their accession, such as the suppression of drinking and prostitution.[196] When the Fatimid general Jawhar first addressed the populace of al-Fusṭāṭ, he put himself forward as the restorer of sharʿist institutes and the enemy of iniquity, most particularly of taxes without sharʿist sanction.[197] When in 638/1240–41 the Ayyubid sultan allowed the Franks to enter Damascus and to purchase arms, this led to a serious confrontation with many elements within the city, and the sultan's name was dropped, without authorisation, from the Friday sermon.[198]

In all this, the partnership of the *ʿulamāʾ* as the representatives of prophetic continuity, and of sultans as the guarantors and worldly patrons, is fundamental in the absence of an exclusive caliphal point of religious authority and competence. Legal provisions do not become redundant if they are broken: thus Māwardī[199] expressed the rationale of all legal systems which continue impersonally. But over and above a certain number of tokens of shar'ist legitimacy, made visible by the infliction of statutory punishments, the world in the shar'ist mirror is many worlds, with different notions of the precise regulation of a sovereign's authority and rights – these being far wider, including a wider freedom of economic action according to Ḥanafi than to Shāfi'ī traditions. This formed the basis for the bid by the Ḥanafi priesthood to achieve primacy at the Mamluk court, at a time when the priesthood had taken over from the caliphate in matters of legitimation: reminding the sultan that he has wider latitude in the distribution of land and the raising of money in time of war, in the imposition of *jizya*, in the authorisation of public prayer and the exaction of punishment, and much more.[200] In all, the Ḥanafi legal tradition seems far more apprised of the idea of a strong state than the more demotically pietistic Shāfi'ī which appears far more bookish. It was perfectly suited to the Ottoman state. But none of this detracts from the essential equivalence of the notions of authority held by the different schools, although the absolute exercise of authority according to the Shāfi'ī traditions is more minutely regulated by knowledge whose custodians are the *'ulamā'*.

CHAPTER EIGHT

Political Soteriology

The previous chapters have shown the concrete manner in which universal tropes of kingship were reworked in the context of Muslim polities. We have seen how these tropes were adopted in direct emblematic continuity, how theories of absolutism were articulated in terms of a *philosophia perennis* ascribed to a universal sagely corpus and to salutary precedent often speciously construed as Machiavellism by modern commentators. We have also seen how some of these universal tropes were endowed with specifically Muslim genealogies or were reinforced and revalidated by such genealogies, and how specifically Muslim regulations of power premised on the principle of absolutism were enunciated in terms of jurisprudence. It has been noted that this impersonal jurisprudential treatment of power, in formal or informal association with fetishistic notions of sovereign persons, tended from the thirteenth century to drain away the direct charisma of the sovereign into avenues that, in the Maghrib, led to the emergence of mahdistic and maraboutic kingship and, in the East, to the charismatisation of shar'ism and of the *'ulamā'* sodality that carried and legalistically routinised it in succession to the defunct caliphate.

Yet there were other lines of enunciating power and of relating it to sacrality in which late antique tropes were in their essentials continued without serious conceptual disturbance. Messianic and quasi-messianic movements, sometimes allied to a pantheistic or emanationist metaphysic, at others rigorously guarding the absolute transcendence of God by transmuting His presence in the world to the presence of His will as revealed impeccably to an imam, are fundamental cases in point. They were represented respectively by Ismā'īlism in its propagandistic and agitational phase and subsequently its caliphal phase under the Fatimids, and by Sufi messianism associated with the Almeria school of Ibn

Barrajān and Ibn Qasī and further theorised in its metaphysic by Ibn ʿArabī, and by Twelver Shiʿism.

Allied to Ismāʿīlism and Sufi messianism, but in an altogether different setting, is the neo-Platonic position of Fārābī on the perfect state as the analogue of the order of the universe. All these positions, with the relative exception of Twelver Shiʿism in its pre-Safavid phase, share forms of pantheism and/or of emanationism, and all inscribe the sacral status of the sovereign within a certain order of the cosmos, not in his capacity as king, but as a sovereign with a primarily soteriological mission and with gifts transcending what human nature sustains naturally. All operate according to notions of structural analogy between the mundane and the supra-mundane orders, in which the special knowledge of an imam or accessible to a philosopher recapitulates and assimilates the form of the universe. At the same time, all are premised on the idea of the necessity of a regulator without whom the order of the world would disintegrate, an idea which, we have seen, is directly related to the absolutist imperative. Twelver Shiʿism fully shared the views of the supra-mundane character of the sovereign imam and regulator, without necessarily aligning this with a cosmology. The Abbasid caliphate shared these notions although, as we have seen, their expression was figuratively or poetically enunciated, without theorisation.

Hierocratic Saviours

Cosmology apart, imamist Islam in both its Twelver and its Ismāʿīlī forms, and indeed Sufism in its activist form,[1] conceived sovereignty in the affairs of the world as the preserve of persons not only divinely appointed in the most direct and deliberate way, but also preconceived in sempiternity and specifically designated as part of the process by which God created the world. The coming to be of a political regime adequate to this soteriological task, characterised by the absolute authority of a ruler pre-elected by God, is dependent on the appearance of such an individual. The conception of a just political order was for this reason always associated with messianic ideas and movements, and with correlated ideas about the impeccability and the inerrant nature of the worldly leader.

Like all messianism, Shiʿi (as well as Sunni[2]) eschatology held notions of an ultimate order presided over by a pre-designated deliverer – an imam, a mahdī or a combination of the two – irrespective of whether he be regarded as actually existing or as a messiah about to come. The advent of the deliverer takes place in a register of an history of the future, proximate or indeterminate; and the order over which he presides is conceived as a re-enactment of a primal innocence which had once been Adam's, and which had been repeatedly renewed by divine and prophetic interventions – for example, the reversion of the world to a primal *tabula rasa* after the flood. It was later definitively and integrally typified in Muḥammad and, after him, the imams who for the Shīʿa replaced the charisma of the caliphate and later of sharʿism.

It must be stressed, before this point is developed further, that there is no question here of subscribing to the common view that the Twelvers considered all government to be illegitimate and unjust in the absence of the imam. This may have been the case with some Ṭālibid legitimist elements before the Occultation of the Twelfth Imam in the tenth century. But the situation among the pro-Ṭālibid parties was highly complex and cannot be characterised with reference to a monolithic position.[3] Ṭālibid legitimism, whose intricate history is little understood, emerged out of a merger of Arab notions of a leading house, of the responsibilities of a legatee (*waṣī*), and the religious status of the keeper of holy places and fetishes (*sādin*).[4] It is well-known, although it has often been a topic for wild misinterpretation, that from very early on this legitimism constituted an important focus for the expression discontent, piety, and ambition. Ṭālibid charisma was such that the Umayyad ʿAbd al-Malik was reported to have ordered his lieutenant al-Ḥajjāj to avoid shedding ʿAlid blood, which he considered an act that precipitated divine revenge.[5]

The Ṭālibids constituted an aristocratic party and a corporate group in Baghdad and elsewhere, ostensibly under the direction of their imams, although the chronology of the ascription of classical imamist attributes to them is obscure. What is clear is that imamist ideas had taken shape amongst marginal groups by the middle of the second Muslim century, but that the idea of twelve imams constituting the full and definitive complement of the line was not known at the time of the occultation of the twelfth imam Muḥammad b. al-Ḥasan al-ʿAskarī in 940. The idea of twelve imams had a complex history which included elements from the Sunni tradition.[6] Be that as it may, it is well-known that Ṭālibids were prominent at the Abbasid caliphal court, and that they participated in the ratification ceremonies of caliphal accession (*bayʿa*) and enjoyed a multitude of financial, fiscal, and ceremonial privileges. Some wrote elegies (*rithāʾ*) of caliphs; the illustrious al-Sharīf al-Murtaḍā was the first person to offer *bayʿa* to al-Qāʾim in 422/1031.[7]

In all, it is clear that the Twelvers, or at least the great majority among them, had taken full cognisance of the absence of direct imamic intervention, just as the Sunni divines had been aware that direct prophetic intervention and direction was not available after the Prophet's lifetime. In both cases there is a self-ratified devolution of ultimate religious authority to the corps of the *ʿulamāʾ* in whom the power of interpretation was vested. The Twelver priesthood underwent a process similar to that noted among the Sunni clergy in Chapter 7, resulting in the emergence of a science of the principles of jurisprudence (*uṣūl al-fiqh*), not unlike its Sunni counterpart, after apparently centuries of traditionalist doubt concerning the very possibility of judicial activity independent of received opinion attributed to the imams. The development was accompanied by their acceptance, much like their Sunni counterparts, of the admissibility of judgements in law that are probable rather than infallible.[8] Analogously, the absence of the imam did not invalidate all government, nor preclude just government, which was defined in terms similar to those we have already encountered in the context of sharʿist politics.[9] Not unlike Sunni divines, their Shiʿi counterparts produced formulations of principles allied to specific regulations regarding particular sectors of life. But these did not theorise injustice in political terms, nor did they identify the legal regulation of the political as a sphere distinct from that of ethical procedures.

Yet the *ʿulamāʾ* as an imperfect figure of the imam were by all accounts an equally imperfect substitute for him. It was only later, in the Safavid period, that they began to assume a general custody of his prerogatives (*niyāba ʿāmma*)[10] and to transmute it into the ratification of Safavid imamist pretensions by a wide variety of means, including the coronation of Safavid monarchs.[11] But the relation between imams and *ʿulamāʾ*, like that between caliphs or indeed the Prophet and *ʿulamāʾ*, is one of devolution by default. In contrast, the relation between Prophet and imam, like that between the Prophet, earlier apostolic prophets (*rusul*) and Adam, is one of typology, a re-commencement and re-enactment of beginnings that have their ultimate type inscribed in the Tablet on which God ordered the inscription of the register of destiny (*al-lawḥ al-maḥfūẓ*). Thus was consummated the notion we have already encountered of *istikhlāf*, with Koranic support.

The Twelvers made only limited and textually episodic use of the mythological lore concerning creation, widely available in works of prophetic tradition, Sunni and Shi'i. Thus al-'Allāma al-Ḥillī (d. 726/1325)[12] quoted a tradition transmitted by Aḥmad b. Ḥanbal, in which the statement is attributed to the Prophet that both he and 'Alī were a light in the hands of God, created 14,000 years before Adam, and that when the latter was created, this light was deposited in his seed, whence it produced the line of prophecy and only divided into two individual lights in the seed and line of 'Abd al-Muṭṭalib. For his part, al-Shaykh al-Mufīd (d.413/1022) had earlier quoted a Shi'i tradition of uncertain date and provenance that Gabriel handed over to the Prophet a tablet containing the names of all twelve imams that were to follow him. He also cited another, in which it is related that the Prophet also received from Gabriel a folder with twelve seals, each of which was to be opened by one imam and then handed over to the next one.[13]

This divine pre-election of cosmic proportions was far more systematically, and to greater consequence, deployed by the Ismā'īlīs. The same repertory of mythological narratives was used, although it must be stressed that Ismā'īlī cosmology and cosmogony existed in many variants.[14] The Fatimid caliph al-Mu'izz is reported to have stated that the imams pre-existed creation in the form of ghosts, that they were the first of ideas and would be the last of material facts, divine creations all of them, and that they were transmitted from seed to seed from the time of Adam, and had been indicated by all prophets.[15] He also declared that he and the other imams had been mentioned in an inscription at the base of the divine throne which had been read by Adam.[16]

This seminal continuity is unadulterated, just as the lines of animal species are specific, so that horses cannot be begotten of donkeys.[17] It is, moreover, unaffected by spiritual impurity.[18] It is a typology manifested in the space of human temporality by a hiero-history dividing human time into seven eras. Each of these eras is enunciated by a speaker-prophet (*nāṭiq*) who commences a period which closes with the emergence of the next speaker-prophet who, in his turn, introduces a new legal regime. There are many local variants of Ismā'īlī hiero-history, although there is a fundamental structural concord which specifies it.[19] The first of the speaker-prophets was Adam,[20] followed by Noah, Abraham, Moses, Jesus, Muḥammad, on to the messiah, al-Qā'im who, according to standard Ismā'īlism, will commence the seventh and final cycle of world history.[21] For one early Ismā'īlī author, Muḥammad was the sixth Adam; for others, the Mahdī will renew the original religion of Adam.[22]

For the Fatimids, the actual foundation of their mighty and prosperous state and the very tangible and unapocalyptic reign of their caliphs necessitated the formulation of means for dealing with messianism, which had to be relegated to an accomplished past. This naturally resulted in grave doctrinal complications and led to schismatic dissent (most notably, with the formation of the Druzes). It was therefore not unnatural for al-Qāḍī an-Nu'mān to evade this issue in his account of the penultimate and terminal cycles of human history, and for other theorists of Fatimid Ismā'īlism, most particularly al-Kirmānī (d.ca 1020), to admit ever more complex heptadic arrangements of varying ingenuity.[23]

Just as these audible prophets are correspondent types,[24] so are their silent companions who carry forth the esoteric sense of the mission: these are, in order (and with some variation between sources), Seth, Shem, Ishmael, Aaron, Simon, and 'Alī. They perform their missions as allegories of that which is enunciated – allegories that denote a meaning more pristine than that declared in the exoteric enunciation, being an esoteric meaning prior to its audible pronouncement. The Koran stands in the same type of relationship to the Fatimid caliph as do the silent to the audible propagators of the divine *logos*. The Book is the silent text, and the imam its audible articulation,[25] that is to say, its infallible interpretation in the form of a particular reading. Inversely, the Qur'ān, according to al-Kirmānī, relates to the Mahdī as does matter to form.[26] Within each cycle of the imamate reign seven manifestations of the enunciatory and the silent types.

This strongly proportionalist mythography organised on an heptadic principle was, as might be expected, associated with the cosmic and numerological correspondences widely found in Arab-Muslim thought of the period. [27] The relevance here of the astral conjunctions – which, as we have seen, correspond to the onset of particular reigns and to the circulation of peoples in and out of history – as cyclical phenomena for the cycles of the imamate is readily apparent.[28] While there are contradictory reports about the use of astrology by the Fatimid caliphs, the more plausible appear to indicate a keen interest,[29] and the disclaimers of Fatimid courtiers suggest apologetic and defensive positions.[30] The assertion of an astrological justification for the naming of Jawhar's Egyptian colony, al-Qāhira (Cairo), one connected with the ascendancy of Mars, is very plausible,[31] and would not have gone amiss or been at all unusual at a time when certain astrological predictions could precipitate mass panic.[32] The assertion by a prominent Ismāʿīlī theoretician of the immunity of the imamate from auspicious and inauspicious astral signs was geared to asserting the inevitability of an imamic order transcending nature.[33]

This supra-mundane order is metaphysical, one in which the imamate and the various hierarchies it subtends correspond to the prime structure of the cosmos, physical and metaphysical. Altogether, the systematic elaboration of this soteriological metaphysic of a neo-Platonic emanationist character was commenced in Persia in the early part of the tenth century by divines of a proto-Ismāʿīlī tendency, and first elaborated into classical forms by Abū Yaʿqūb as-Sijistānī (d.ca 1000).[34] The earlier Fatimids were initially unreceptive to the metaphysics of such divines who came, after all, from circles that did not specifically recognise their imamate, and they had a preference for hieratocratic mythography and gnostic soteriology some of whose features are indicated above.[35] But emanationist philosophical doctrines were later well-received in Cairo, most particularly from Ḥamīd ad-Dīn al-Kirmānī.[36]

The emanationist neo-Platonism which became official Fatimid cosmography, postulates the emanation from God of ten intellects. There are many ambiguities and ambivalences concerning the divinity of the First Intellect, at once created and in possession of attributes normally associated with the divinity.[37] In any case, the first and the second are transcendent, and the subsequent seven, which emerge serially from the first and second by emanation, correspond to the seven heavenly spheres. The tenth and lowest, the Active Intellect, *al-ʿaql al-faʿʿāl*, creates the sublunary material world.[38] To the first and second rungs of humanity, the enunciatory prophet and his legatee, correspond respectively the first two intellects, although it is stressed that the one is prior to the other in the order of existence only, not in the order of excellence.[39] To the third intellect corresponds the imam, and lower intellects correspond to lower positions in the worldly hierarchy of Ismāʿīlism. To the heavenly spheres correspond spheres of religious representation; to the third sphere, for instance, which is that of Saturn, corresponds the *shahāda*, the fundamental Muslim formulaic profession of faith, and to the last four in Kirmānī's system, comprising the four elements, correspond obedience, prohibition, permission, and legal judgements.[40]

Correlative with this parallelism and mutually transferable allegorism, the heavenly spheres correspond to the rungs of the Ismāʿīlī hierarchy: the first to *tanzīl* (the Book) followed in turn by *taʾwīl* (esoteric interpretation) *al-amr* (command) and by kingship.[41] These are the functions that direct the common weal towards its soteriological ends and in this manner the imam, who is the Fatimid caliph, comes to organise and to relate to his subordinates in a hierarchical manner that calques that of the subtle universe. Prophets command a divine politics (*siyāsa ilāhiyya*) according to what is dictated by an attempted mimesis of the Maker, and the practical regulation of worldly affairs according to the *sharʿ* can thus produce a form which corresponds to this mimesis and is correlative with it.[42] Prophets and other imamist legatees instruct humanity in the act of mimesis and with the practice of the Two Devotions – knowledge (for the elect) and exoteric ritual. Salvation and felicity can be attained after the resurrection, which is the Second Beginning.[43] For the commoner such instruction takes the standard form of correction, using the usual means of correction, such as enticement, the rod, or the sword.[44] In a less mimetic and cosmographic frame, Nāṣir ad-Dīn Ṭūsī also spoke of divine laws which comprise devotions, punishments, transactions, and politics, which can be arrived at with divine assistance by a prophet or an imam.[45]

Thus the only access that a person of lower rank has to the esoteric truths of religion, whose acquisition is the primary soteriological activity, is by emanation from the imam, who receives direct divine inspiration filtered through the first two intellects. Unauthorised learning, or any form of learning without explicit imamic command, may lead to perdition and is prohibited.[46] In this way the socio-religious hierarchy and cosmic hierarchy are conjoined through correspondence: the one is the detailed signature of the other. Hierolatry becomes cosmolatry conceived as logolatry, and obedience to the imam becomes the act of acquiring such knowledge as is required as a condition for salvation.

The correspondence of macrocosm and microcosm, thus

achieved, carries into the realm of metaphysics, the correspondence of desired present – or future – with the primeval and paradigmatic past as these are construed in eschatology. Except that here, primevalism and originality are given a strongly ontological redaction, which coexists with the temporal notion of primevalism sustaining the mythological narrative of origins. Indeed, originality across the entire space of medieval Arab-Muslim thought was a strongly normative notion, which could be expressed in ontological, temporal, logical, normative and other terms, in all of which sequence and hierarchy were inseparable.[47]

Altogther, it seems that the introduction of the Neoplatonic sublimation of mythological typology, and the construal of typology as the impersonal signatures of the microcosm and the macrocosm each on the face of the other rather than a succession of personalised sparks of divinity, was one way in which the Fatimids immunised themselves against the mystagogic abandon immanent in messianism and messianic typologies – an abandon which led in 1017 to the Druze schism, with the assumption that al-Ḥākim bi-Amr Allāh was God incarnate, the very matter which al-Kirmānī addressed and refuted, re-affirming the absolute transcendence of God.

Similar to these motifs and themes were those elaborated with great luxuriance and magnificence in the theosophical and pantheistic theories of Sufism, most particularly as they were developed by the Almeria school,[48] which must be considered as a broad current with very significant internal differentiations.[49] In this trend were combined metaphysics and messianism centred around the idea of a mystical imam, 'the pole of the time' (*al-quṭb*), who carried the same charismatic and divine charge as did the imams of the various Shi'i sects, but without the notion of genealogical election and pre-ordination carried by imamism. In other words, this concerns a Sunni current carried by mystagogues and chiliasts. The two most outstanding – and unfortunate – political figures in this current were Ibn Barrajān (d.536/1141) and Ibn Qasī, but the most outstanding theoretician was Ibn 'Arabī. It must also be emphasised that, with the expansion and organisation of mystical orders in the Mashriq from the thirteenth century onwards, the primacy given to poles – specifically so identified, and therefore not identified with the *'ulamā'* – invaded even the works of conservative authors. An example can be found in the Koranic exegesis by Suyūṭī in fifteenth-century Egypt of verse 251 from the *sūra* of al-Baqara, where the Poles are seen in a soteriological or at least radically revivalist light.[50]

The revivalist sentiment that characterised Shiʿi and other messianisms also characterised the Sufi notion of the role of the saint as true *khalīfa*, in his capacity as one who will restore the condition of primeval innocence binding humanity and divinity, thus repeating the origin of man in divinity and fully performing the task of vicarage. Ibn ʿArabī stated quite explicitly that he expected the just ruler to 'return' things to God in the condition in which they were originally conceived.[51] By the play of metonyms normal in the analogical transferences that mark Ibn ʿArabī's work, the just ruler could be an ordinary caliph or a king who, when unjust, should be removed and replaced. Yet even in his secular condition, the just king must display the manifestations of God whose legatee he is, and must therefore 'encompass' all divine attributes.[52] To this practically political position reminiscent of that generally held in terms of a very different vocabulary by the *ʿulamāʾ*, is added another, properly eschatological one, which was not altogether absent from the world of the *ʿulamāʾ*, who fully validated eschatological *hadīth* though generally without accepting activist chiliastic propositions.

However, there is no ambiguity, still less ambivalence, in Ibn ʿArabī regarding the profane or sacred nature of the deliverer and of the order of primal, Edenic innocence delivered by him. There is, in his writings, a play of correspondences, of analogies, of types microcosmic and macrocosmic, which might endow an ordinary, albeit just, king with the charisma that properly belongs to the saint. Although he affirms apostolic prophets as the most superior members of humanity who possess the attributes of prophecy over and above those of sainthood, for Ibn ʿArabi saints and their hierarchies of *aqṭāb*, *awtād*, *aʾimma*, perform this very same preservative and soteriological function, and are therefore correspondent with the same cosmic type as prophets. Indeed, saints can be regarded as apostolic by virtue of their axial position as *aqṭāb*, for an apostle is, after all, a *quṭb*.[53] A *quṭb* is thus the genus comprehending the species of apostle. The order of the cosmos corresponds to the order of a polity run according to justice as defined in the *Fürstenspiegel* tradition. Ibn ʿArabī's sagely advice to kings, enjoining generosity, justice, and other traits of character conducive to the well-being of the state, as well as his description of the offices of the vizirate, the chancery, and the military, are formulated according to the usual conventions of content and sentiment.[54]

Yet these offices and traits of royal character have macrocosmic analogies in a cosmos conceived as manifestations and attributes of God. The world, after all, is the Kingdom of God, a space for his *khilāfa*, the location wherein reigns his deputy (*nā'ib*) who, according to Ibn 'Arabi, is manifest with the manifestation of judgements implied by the attributes of God[55] – a passage difficult to interpret unless one notes the author's statement elsewhere: that the *shar'* is the name God gave to the command which explicated in material form the thrust of His attributes.[56] Almost as an allegory of this truth, but also a manifestation of God's ontological ubiquity, somewhat earlier the illuminationist metaphysician Shihāb ad-Dīn als-Suhrawardī (d.1191) had not dissimilarly held, in a Persian work, that a properly illuminated royal person would receive by illumination the light of kingship (*farra-yi īzadī, kiyān kharra*), a notion that we have encountered in the earlier part of this book in an earlier linguistic form. Persons thus enlightened, who in other texts are identified with the Active Intellect, are caliphs of God, among whose number he includes the first four Medinan caliphs no less than Sufi divines like Bisṭāmī and Tustarī; all are capable of performing wonders.[57]

This *khilāfa* of God indicated by Ibn 'Arabī was primeval, and indeed, as a type, coeval with the very act of creation. Ibn Barrajān, quoted approvingly by Ibn 'Arabī, held that the *khilāfa* also corresponds to the Tablet of Fate which, when created, was granted a kingdom over which to reign, which kingdom is materiality on which the writ of the Tablet is inscribed as the unfolding of time.[58] Thus an analogy is established between a series of dyads: command and passivity, spirit and matter, caliphate and its subjects, primeval command and subsequent order. Absolutism is therefore affirmed with the affirmation of the primacy of the caliphate over the charges of the caliphate, to which it is ontologically and temporally anterior. The body politic, like all material entities, is soiled and therefore in need of salvation and of constant maintenance by a saviour who is the representative of a Type synonymous with the comprehensive and definitive command of God which is the Tablet of Fate. The world, according to Ibn 'Arabī, is never devoid of a living apostle who, unlike the Twelver imam, is physically present (*ḥayy bi-jismihi*),[59] a *quṭb* who is functionally equivalent in this preservative respect to the caliph, the *'ulamā'* sodality, or the impersonal *shar'* of Sunnism. A heavily Shi'ified Sufism of this turn was to develop among Turkic communities in Iran and contributed to the rise of the Safavid dynasty (1501–1722).[60]

Ibn Qasī expressed the same universe of types in a somewhat more mythologising mode, reminiscent in certain respects of early Ismā'īlism. In this, he used the tradition attributed to the Prophet concerning immanence within Adam's seed. But Ibn Qasī amplified its scale to comprehend the entire fate of humanity. God extracted humanity from Adam's back, which is the location of his seed. He covenanted them, allocating destinies as salvation and damnation, before returning them to Adam's body. He subsequently created a variety of spirits followed by the rest of creation.[61] A complex prophetology, duly analogised with theosophical and pantheistic notions and with a theosophy of historical cycles, finally yields to the present. The present age for Ibn Qasī was the Muḥammadan era, 'gist of the sempiternal light' (*'uṣārat nūr ad-dahr*), the 'post-cosmic cycle' which initiates the era in which humanity repossesses its cosmic innocence. Muḥammad, the most perfect man and the light of God, thus initiates the end of the world.[62] He does so by initiating the repossession of its Beginning.

That Ibn Qasī, and probably also Ibn Barrajān, were manifestly chiliastic in comparison with Ibn 'Arabī is clear, the latter having conceived of salvation as in some sense a condition in steady state, cosmically and politically, although he was not averse to apocalyptic predictions using numerological and astrological calculations.[63] Yet the imminence of the End is readily derivable from these notions of soteriology. The End has well-established signs in Muslim eschatological lore, Sunni no less than Shi'i, and the use of these motifs in the course of messianic movements was invariable. Ibn Qasī repeated the standard traditions about the fall of Constantinople, about a general antinomianism of nature itself auguring the end.[64] So did the Twelver tradition, speaking of human conflagrations and cosmic catastrophes and wonders, including a sunrise from the west and war, carnage, and depravity.[65] Similar narratives are common in the traditions of the Sunnis, which also include the rise of the sun from the west, and all manner of calamities both cosmic and human, in addition to preternatural behaviour of animals no less than of anomalous humans like the Gog and Magog.[66] Similarities and concordances in this eschatological lore point further, of course, for they are also shared, among other elements in the legacy of the Middle East, with Byzantine apocalyptic traditions.[67]

Antinomian belief and behaviour precipitated by the imminence of the Apocalypse, ascribed to and enjoined by certain sections and offshoots of the Ismāʿīlīs, are well-known, and were shared by other movements in the same culture area. They are of indeterminate ancient provenance, though conceptually they are anything but mysterious. One of the best-studied phenomena of this kind originated in the seventeenth-century Ottoman domains and spread farther afield – the movement initiated by Sabbatai Zevi the Jewish Messiah and his prophet Nathan of Gaza. Zevi called for the utterance of the Ineffable Name of God, called upon women to read the Torah, and abolished all fasts commemorating the Exile and the destruction of the Temple, thus seeking with antinomianism (which has Ismaʿīlī parallels) to signal the end of an era.[68]

Apocalyptic expectation and apocalyptic association were legion in Muslim history, and apocalyptic traditions concerning the Mahdī were very widespread. Among the Sunnis, the Mahdī was not associated with the ʿAlid house, with some rare and seemingly odd exceptions.[69] The Abbasids, the Fatimids, the Almohads[70] and lesser dynasties all claimed a mahdistic soteriological mission, and North Africa and Spain proved to be especially fertile ground for such movements.[71] The surprising appointment by al-Maʾmūn of ʿAlī al-Riḍā as heir apparent has been linked with messianic expectations,[72] although other matters are equally germane to the interpretation of this event. Various authors wrote on apocalypses and on political divination, including the philosophers al-Kindī and Ibn Sīnā.[73] An apocalypse attributable to Ibn ʿArabī is also extant.[74] Mahdistic expectations were legion among many Shīʿi communities, and were used to interpret the Mongol invasions no less than the advent of the Saljuqs before them.[75]

In all cases, practice incorporated the choreography of theory. It is not known precisely how Ibn Barrajān managed his public appeal at the 150 Andalusian domains which are reported to have recognised him as imam.[76] But Ibn Qasī, during his short-lived state in Algarve (ca 1144–1151), not only claimed thaumaturgic powers such as clairvoyance and the same ability as the Prophet to translate himself to Mecca and back in the course of a single night, but also proclaimed himself Mahdī. In keeping with his statement[77] that Jesus (who plays a very important role in Muslim eschatology) and John would together be on a throne in preparation for the apocalypse, he introduced the practice of placing two men on the pulpit, alongside the preacher, the one representing John and the other Jesus.[78] At the other side of the domains of Islam, in a mid-fourteenth-century 'Republic' in Iran, a caprisioned horse was brought to the city gates twice a day in expectation of the appearance of the Mahdī. The Safavids later kept a stable for the Mahdī, and permanently had harnessed two horses, one for him and another for Jesus.[79]

In all instances, the one awaited to save and restore, the messiah, is the Mahdī, a term for which Shiʿa of both the Twelver and Ismāʿīlī variety substituted the term al-Qāʾim. Even the Ẓāhirīte Sunni Ibn ʿArabī refers to a just king who re-establishes divine justice by the term *al-Qāʾim biʾl-ḥaqq*.[80] In all cases, his activities are registered in advance in a kind of history of the future, much of it military, involving the defeat of the Dajjāl, the Anti-Christ, and a true Islamity comprehending the whole of mankind.[81] It is interesting to compare here the belief, widespread among world Jewry during the Sabbataian movement, that the Lost Tribes of Israel were encamped in the Arabian desert and were about to take Mecca, and the belief later in the history of this movement that they had actually taken the city.[82] Also in all cases, the saviour is thought to pre-exist the present: primevally in the case of mythological narratives, historically (but without excluding the notion of cosmic sempiternity) in the case of the Ismāʿīlīs and Twelvers. The imam who is to rise to save humanity is not dead, but simply in occultation. This is a belief similar to very ancient lore preserved today in the idea of Christ resurrected. It is also much like the belief among some Greeks after the fall of Constantinople that the last emperor Constantine Palaeologus had not actually been killed during the Turkish conquest of the city, but was saved by an angel who turned him to marble and hid him in a subterranean cavern (like the Twelfth Imam Muḥammad b. al-Ḥasan al-ʿAskarī), located under the Galata bridge, from whence he would, in time, be re-animated and rise to chase away the Turks.[83]

Be that as it may, the idea of an individual redeemer and saviour is fundamental to the idea of redemption and of salvation, the imminence of which is formative of messianic movements of state formation and of chiliastic claims. The imam is the carrier of this salutary function, the direct performance of divine decree unmediated and unrefracted by merely human agency. The general outline of his worldly charge is identical with the repertoire of world-regulating function encountered above in detailed discussions of Sunni enunciations on kingship: the imam, in his capacity as ruler, manages human sociality as does any ruler, by keeping fractious and violent humanity in an order of civility, and by directing them towards common endeavours. He thus founds a collective will for them, by exacting the rights of God as stated in expressions of His will, by enjoining good and combating its opposite, and by establishing and controlling a proper legal system.[84]

The imam thus has general leadership in matters religious and secular in his own right.[85] This is a pregnant statement and may be interpreted as implying a general deputyship of God without prophetic mediation, although the role and status of the Prophet is in no way diminished, much like the notions of God's caliph discussed above. This Twelver distinction between imamate and prophecy is construed with conceptual instruments derived from Muʿtazilite theology, which holds the two to be the recipients of divine grace (*luṭf*) of differential amplitude. Whereas the grace given to the Prophet is particular (*khāṣṣ*), that received by the imam is general (*ʿāmm*), so much so that al-ʿAllāma al-Ḥillī was moved to conclude that the denial of particular grace is a lesser evil than the denial of general grace.[86] The imamate is the bestowal of this divine grace which assures the preservation of the human species.[87] The imam is the *khalīfa* of God and of the Prophet at one and the same time,[88] but is such in two distinct ways which mutually reinforce each other, much like the Abbasid caliph.

Being a species-preserving grace which is itself a divinely ordained obligation, the imamate is an office whose inevitability and necessity is rationally necessary. This is unlike arguments propounded by Sunni jurists concerning its traditional as distinct from its rational bases. The ground for this assertion, according to standard Twelver arguments, is that grace is a rational obligation incumbent upon God, and an obligation which antedates the Muslim *sharʿ*. To assume, therefore, that it emerges from sharʿist tradition is self-contradictory.[89]

The Ismāʿīlī arguments took a different turn, in accordance with their prophetology and imamology, which construed the prophecy and the imamate as related by the delivery by the one of the exoteric, enunciated, text of divine mission, and by the other of the esoteric sense and by his assumption of God's legacy (*khilāfa*). The distinction between the one and the other is thus a distinction of modality, and also of station, with the enunciator-prophets being the more elevated.[90] Clearly, Fatimid dogmatics, most particularly after the establishment of the state, did not have the leeway for metaphysical and mystagogic abandon it enjoyed previously. It is therefore unsurprising that the primacy of Prophet over imam is repeated, and given a metaphysical sanction, being the unmediated access by the Prophet (unlike the imam) to higher substances.[91] It appears altogether that the attributes of proximity to God of the Twelver imam are far more accentuated, unmediated, and anthropomorphic than those of the Ismāʿīlī imam.

Yet in all cases it is universally emphasised that the obedience due to the one is due to the other, and that this is coterminous with obedience to God. In the words of al-Qādī an-Nuʿmān, obedience is a 'continuous unity (*wāḥida mawṣūla*)'.[92] Alternatively, the imam is said to issue commands that are God's, and to order interdictions which are equally those of God.[93] Mediators between God and humanity,[94] imams cannot, in the Sunni manner, be subject to choice or ratification. An Ismāʿīlī thinker proposed that the idea of choosing an imam is self-contradictory, as the imam is by definition more knowledgeable than his community, and to introduce the idea of selection is to assume a parity of knowledge which is inadmissible.[95] The imamate is neither optional nor elective, al-ʿAllāma al-Ḥillī asserted, because it is a fundamental article of faith with Koranic sanction. The imamate is, moreover, of such moment that God could not leave it to mere humans to decide, especially as He had explicitly revealed rules and regulations of even far less moment. Imputing an elective character to the matter is, further, contrary to its purpose, the leadership of fractious humanity. Other arguments are deployed in this context, the most important of which are related to the properties and endowments of the imam. His superhuman qualities are esoteric and known to God only, as are his impeccability and infallibility.[96]

The imam is impeccable and infallible; he is immune from error and iniquity, from birth to death. This is an assertion for which 1,038 separate arguments, both positive and apologetic, were adduced in a fundamental Twelver text.[97] Chief among them is the assertion that the imam is the keeper of God's law and will, and that he is the axis of good order. In this spirit, the Fatimid caliph al-Mu'izz declared that it was impossible that he might be capable of injustice and rapacity.[98] The same applies to Prophets, both before and after their personal reception of prophecy. Sunni accounts of the sheer fallible humanity of Muḥammad are refuted by recourse to arguments from the rational necessity of impeccability and infallibility.[99] The entire argument is allied to the Shiʿi requirement that the imam be 'the best man (*al-afḍal*)', thus going counter to the Sunni allowance of sinfulness and all manner of other defects in the ruler, and arguing that it is rationally demonstrable that none but the best of men could rule his flock.[100]

Correlative with the superhuman elevation of the imam is the question of his commission. An imam is appointed either by the direct commission of God, the Prophet, or a previous imam, as the consequence of a manifest miracle.[101] This is demonstrated with respect to ʿAlī by the rational argument that he was the best man and that his virtues were outstanding, and by the textual and traditional arguments that he had been specifically appointed by Muḥammad, and that the Koran can be correctly interpreted to indicate his appointment by God.[102] His miracles include clairvoyance, among others mentioned above. All such arguments were long resisted and refuted by Sunni authors. The superiority of ʿAlī over his contemporaries was early refuted by, among others, al-Jāḥiẓ.[103] His express appointment by Muḥammad as his successor was also the subject of detailed refutations, not least because the tradition to this effect ascribed to the Prophet was regarded as spurious.[104] It is interesting to note the Fatimid tendency to minimise the imams's knowledge of the unseen, except such knowledge as God chose to grant them, and their apologetic criticism of the 'deviations' of some of their supporters who were making unfounded claims on behalf of the imams, unduly mixed philosophy with matters of religion.[105] Finally, Sunni legalism blandly refuted the claims of the Twelvers (without mentioning them explicitly), who yield authority to an imam in occultation, to one who disappeared and is merely presumed to be alive and waiting to emerge as saviour, by saying that the imamate cannot legitimately be conferred upon an absent person about whose life or death no information could be ascertained.[106]

There is in fact no immanent reason for the flow of divine grace within one particular line, and Ibn ʿArabī showed a clear awareness of this by affirming that genealogy is relevant only insofar as it betokened a Muḥammadan connection,[107] which could, presumably, be made in a variety of other ways. Even in the field of genealogy, there was no immanent need for the charisma of Muḥammad to flow through the line of ʿAlī. This is why the Abbasids were also supported in their caliphate by traditions ascribed to the Prophet, purporting to appoint not ʿAlī as his successor and vicar, but the progeny of al-ʿAbbās, who were also said, on Muḥammadan authority, to rule the world until such a time in the future that they can transfer their power and authority to the Mahdī or to Jesus.[108]

Both Twelver and Ismāʿīlī notions of a just political order sought messianic discourses in order to inscribe within them notions of a world refashioned by a politico-religious authority in such a manner that a restoration of primeval humanity is achieved. This order is variously conceived: it is cosmologico-philosophical with the Ismāʿīlīs, with an important admixture of the narrative and mythological; nomocratic with equally important components of the narrative and the mythological with the Twelvers; pantheistic immanence with certain mythological and narrative elements with Sufi messianic activism, which often construes even its philosophical discourse in terms of allegorising narratives.

Both the Ismāʿīlīs and the Sufis conceived a just and proper order to be one of structural homology with an extra-terrestrial order: pantheistic, based on analogies and comprehensive correspondences in the case of the Sufis or, with the Ismāʿīlīs, in overall correspondence with the cosmic architectonic. More central to the Twelvers is a point they share with these two other tendencies: the accent on nomothetic divine command which assures a correspondence with divine will, without this implying, for the Twelvers, a system of structural and analogical correspondences between the microcosm and the macrocosm. In this scheme the microcosm, when perfected, is an allegory of its ambient parent. For the Twelvers as well as the Sunnis analogy, if at all conceivable, was between divine command and its implementation. There is no structural or architectural form which comprehends the terrestrial and extra-terrestrial orders and is the criterion for structural correspondences or perfect allegories and typologies. The only typology at play with the Twelvers, as with the Sunnis, is one which links carriers of the divine message, regardless of whether or not mythological narratives have them pre-existing the rest of humanity.

Logocratic Sages?

Structural correspondence between the order of the world and that of the cosmos, or between the order of the cosmos and the sagely intelligence, is also the centrepiece of notions of adequate political authority in certain philosophical discourses. Such correspondence was construed mythographically and anthropomorphically and also according to an implicit assumption of consubstantiality (as with Ibn 'Arabī). We have seen how these correspondences were metaphorised and sublimated into allegories and philosophical concepts, chief among which are emanation and intellect. All these, in their different ways, could be construed as renditions of the notion of *khilāfa* as the type of relation that binds God to his creation represented by its best, namely, its worldly apex.

As with the imamate, one crucial aspect of *khilāfa* is that, although it is a patrimony devolving to humanity in general, humans participate in it differentially. There is a severe elitism in the manner of conducting this charge, one which differentiates kings, caliphs, imams and saints from the common run of humanity by the fact that they discharge their duty by mimesis of the divine and the cosmic and by devolution of cosmic or divine functions. Commoners, on the other hand, discharge their task in the universe of *istikhlāf* by obedience. The former category carry a knowledge correlative with their mimetic, allegorical and representative role, be this Sunni *ijtihād* (directly as with caliphs, by consultation with the *'ulamā'* in the case of sultans) or the esoteric *'ilm* of the Shi'i imam. At one end of the scale, as in Sunnism, there exists a unitary form of knowledge, part of which needs to be censored as it would disturb the common mind. Sunni authors wrote much about the limits of the common understanding, and produced special treatises arguing that commoners should be debarred from access to theological arguments. Correlatively, the control of folk religiosity at a more basic social level was sought by determining the boundaries of permissible popular preaching.[109] Clearly, there were particular circumstances for the ebb and flow of learned interest in the limits and boundaries of public communication which can not be taken up here; the same might be said of the historical circumstances governing a seemingly reverse position – namely the seductive but deceptive deferral by the learned to 'old women's religion'.[110]

At the other end of the scale, we have a specifically esoteric knowledge available only to the imams by divine inspiration and the legation of previous imams. In the Sufism of Ibn 'Arabī, access to esoteric knowledge is barred by specific modes of encoding texts, the key to which is supplied orally by a Sufi shaykh to chosen acolytes.[111] Finally, we have the knowledge with which specially favoured individuals are graced by emanation from the cosmic intellects. Commoners also carry a form of knowledge appropriate to their station which, when perfected, can comprise no more than a few fundamental professions of faith and articles of devotional obligation.[112]

Germane to the present argument is that this cognitive elitism, some of whose consequences will be examined presently, was not peculiar to those claiming inspired knowledge, divine grace, or fusion with the divine substance. It was, rather, a natural corollary of the fundamental distinction between the rulers and the ruled attendant upon the absolutist imperative. In this perspective, the commoners, albeit mentally in possession of 'quasi-minds', are nevertheless the mud of the earth, as it were, who attend markets and extinguish fires,[113] and in this patronising perspective, are by no means as wanting in intellect as children or the insane.[114] Yet the commoners are a sheer sign of disorganisation, and whatever salty earthiness is attributed to them is there to be regulated and husbanded, directed to various trades, to manning armies, and standing to the elite as do sensations to the brain.[115] Indeed, the descriptions relating the contrast between commoners and elite are very reminiscent of those relating the contrast – and complementarity – between king and subjects, most particularly of the contrast of order and chaos: thus the commoners, if left to themselves, would according to the restricted measure of their minds, attribute knowledge to the ignorant, follow the ignoble, think no further than anticipating the spectacle of an execution, of an acrobatic bear, or of a performing monkey, and claim, moreover, to be able to settle points of doctrine.[116] In a milder vein, Ibn Rushd contrasted the views of felicity held by the commoners and the elect: to the former, the good and felicitous king is the triumphant one, while to the initiate into reason, he is the just and truthful one.[117]

This contrast of discrimination and disorder is transposed by Muslim philosophers of a peripatetic bent into a hierarchy with definable epistemological properties which follow specific criteria of reason and are not fully subject to the divine will to inspire. It is generally assumed in current scholarship that the leitmotif of philosophical writing on public life and on politics is the notion of *sa'āda*, felicity, rather than salvation in its specifically religious profile of bodily punishment or deliverance. But it must be stressed at the outset that this is too narrow and selective a reading, as it tends, erroneously, to identify a paradigm represented by Fārābī and does not allow for the eccentricity of the Fārābīan project. It also impoverishes his output by simplifying it unduly and seeing in it a univocity, uniformity, and constancy it does not possess.[118] The standard approach, in keeping with an implicit historiography of Muslim philosophy which regards it under the aspect of the transmission of Greek patrimony to the West, also implicitly renders irrelevant the very interesting positions on actual politics held by Muslim writers of philosophical texts, and their positions on Muslim soteriology in relation to the order of the world. At best, it holds these positions to be purely casuistical and cautionary in a sense construed as at once insincere and somewhat pathetic.

Matters that we have seen to be implicated in the soteriological tropes of Muslim thinking on politics and the sacred are equally present in Muslim philosophical discourse on politics: mimesis, allegory, participation and sheer obedience as modalities of living *istikhlāf* and therefore of salvation. After all, salvation is the grand recursive loop of the world, by which original perfections and pristine conditions are retrieved. Finally, philosophy and philosophical thinking can not be legitimately confined to philosophers.[119] This is so not least because philosophical ideas were widely used outside the specific paradigmatic conformation of topics and concepts which constituted philosophy. These same ideas had analogues in metaphorical and allegorical discourses no less than in the mythological narratives of various strands of Shi'ism and mysticism, and not unnaturally had concordances and parallelisms in Muslim conceptions of the organisation of public life in general.

The concordances between theories of consummate worldly – and spiritual – leadership put forth in philosophical texts, and in texts concerning the imamate and sainthood, centre not only on the assumption shared with other expressions of the absolutist imperative – which entail the notion of a particular election and favour of the man who consummates the regime of *khilāfa* in its various acceptations and the instantiation of God's legacy – but also involve consideration of correspondences between the manner in which the election is exercised and the way it is inserted into the order of the cosmos. Such election is exercised in its turn by concordances of various orders of the cosmos, among them the concordance between the rational modus operandi characterising the mind of the ruler or the philosopher, and the cosmic intellects that populate and animate the Neo-Platonic universe. Also at work is the allegorical as well as the consubstantial correspondence between saint and God pantheistically conceived, no less than the formal correspondence between worldly and cosmic hierarchies as in the Neo-Platonic expressions to be found in Fārābī and the Ismāʿīlīs. It is therefore appropriate that this discussion should start with highlighting the virtually interchangeable character of this kind of ruler when expressed in different mythographic and metaphysical idioms.

The Shiʿi divine Nāṣir ad-Dīn aṭ-Ṭūsī brought out these parallels and equivalences clearly and explicitly. Basing himself on the assumption that the social world invariably requires a regulator, he put forward the proposition that when the affairs of humanity are managed in accordance with divine regulation, the worldly regulator will, according to what he characterised as contemporary parlance, be an imam. He will also – according to what Ṭūsī called the terminology of the Ancients (by which the Greeks in general are intended) – be an absolute king. Other terminological equivalences are suggested in accordance with a particular inflection given them by Ṭūsī: this same office of divinely-guided regulation is the self-same Demiurge of Plato, and the civic man of Aristotle. To the notion of absolute kingship he ascribed to the ancients and to the imam, he adjoins the Ismāʿīlī notion of *nāṭiq* and *asās*.[120]

To this imputation of essential equivalences between various terminological protocols and conceptual fields concerning kingship active in the Near East before and after the rise of Islam, Ṭūsī added a further notion derived from philosophical terminology further specified with religious notions. He established a synonymy between a possessor of the true *khilāfa* of God on earth and consummate humanity as such, this person being the best and ideal man. He further proposed the equivalence between this and the *wilāya*: a term used to designate at once sainthood and custody of the world, very much in the manner of Sufism, presaging the fusion that, as has been indicated, was systematised in currents out of which the Safavids emerged. Neo-Platonism may indeed have been used to construe the cosmic function of kingship, but it was not essential to it; it was possible to construe perfect men without neo-Platonic metaphysics, and Abbasid caliphs may indeed be designated as such.

Philosophically expressed, this amounts to saying that these heights are attained once a man had realised his perfection *qua* man within the Great Chain of Being, in which man is a microcosm encompassing in himself analogues of the rest of creation both higher and lower.[121] Such a person will have fulfilled the teleological purpose of humanity. In this context, such a purpose is presented analogously to the attainment of eternal happiness and, in the afterlife, a place in the divine presence without the intervention of veils separating the resurrected mortal and his Creator. The term 'felicity'(*saʿāda*), common in philosophy and outside, is used to describe this condition. [122]

There is, in this bold play on equivalences and analogies and in this creative trans-disciplinary abandon, a clear realisation of two specific motifs that permeate enunciations of power in Muslim as well as in previous Near Eastern civilisations, motifs variously denominated and embellished, sometimes with the utopian colours of Muslim paradise.[123] These are the variously mimetic connections between perfected humanity and divinity or at least the divinely-ordained order, and the centrality of the regulator-king in this mimetic scheme. In the same context, but not in the public and religious articulation, it matters little whether prophecy is conceived philosophically as divine illumination or some other form of rational inspiration mediated by cosmic intellects, or as inspiration anthropomorphically pictured. The distinction between prophet, imam, and inspired philosopher is of the dogmatic and not of the conceptual order that describes a relation between the two terms, the divine and the consummately human.[124]

In the Fārābīan scheme of things, this leader becomes the locus wherein the Active Intellect inheres. When this intellect illuminates the perfect man's Passive Intellect, he becomes a philosopher. He becomes a prophet with respect to the illumination by the same Active Intellect of his imaginative faculty; this endows him with knowledge of particulars, including the capacity for particular prognostication[125] associated with Muḥammad as a sign of his prophecy. Such knowledge may, in the standard way, be received in the form of visions made available in dreams or in wakefulness, indifferently to prophets and other seers.[126] It is evident that this is a position very much analogous to the Ismāʿīlī scheme.[127]

To this also belongs the saying attributed to Abū Sulaymān as-Sijistānī, that the divine emanation received by a king makes him into a human god[128] – a statement that might seem shocking, even from the hand of a philosopher. Such a statement needs to be metaphorically interpreted in a manner which regards as central the essential structural equivalence of notions at play, when taken, as it should, as part of an inextricable structural relation between divinity and elected humanity. The essential structure of the relationship is preserved regardless of the denominative and conceptual terms in which the separate elements are expressed. It thus becomes possible to understand the various enunciations of the same relationship as specific to particular discursive communities, and to conjugate them according to a pragmatics of discourse, which is not our task here.

Suffice it to mention two further inflections of the conceptual physiognomy of the regulator-ruler. Abu'l-Ḥasan al-ʿĀmirī (d.922), who belonged to the Fārābīan school of Baghdad, insisted that the regulator-leader should be a sage in possession of knowledge of particulars and precedents (*sunan*) and of a Pythagorean turn of mind – that is, possessing knowledge of the sciences of proportion (arithmetic, geometry, and music), as it is only knowledge of the sciences of number, and hence of proportion, that makes possible the proper regulation of the world;[129] we have seen that the world is best governed by justice, which is a relation of proportionality guaranteed and regulated by the ruler. Thus the mind of the ruler is made mimetic of the just order of the universe, which in this perspective consists of proportionality hierarchically conceived and as such comes to regulate optimally the affairs of the world by maintaining an order based on principles of proportionality. Just as al-ʿĀmirī saw in the leader power no less than virtue,[130] so al-Ābilī, the teacher of Ibn Khaldūn,[131] concurred with his own mystical master, Ibn al-Bannā', in the statement that the Mahdī was, after all, a sultan-scholar.[132]

It is clear then that virtue, scholarship, receipt of emanation and of inspiration in states of consciousness or of somnolescence, sainthood, the imamate, and cognate phenomena, are different ways of inscribing the notion of political transcendence in different discursive regimes. For Fārābī, indeed, the terms philosopher, ruler, king, lawgiver and imam are of the same conceptual order.[133] That Fārābī regarded philosophical activity as the archetype of governance of which political rule is a metaphor does not necessarily entail a belief in an utopian philosopher-king. Standard interpretations, until very recently, have restricted the range of his conception of rulership to the utopian philosopher-king without serious textual justification from his works which, in fact, yield a more variegated and tense texture of conceptions. Among other things Fārābī invokes worldly political experience for its didactic philosophical value, which thus contributes to the perfection of practical philosophy itself.[134]

One should therefore be wary of restrictive, literal, and fanciful interpretations of the pronouncements, ubiquitous in Muslim writings on kingship and public authority in general, concerning the mimetic task of philosophy 'according to human capacity', as a conservative Ashʿarite theologian put it in a dictionary of technical terms.[135] This mimesis, as we have seen, can take many forms and can be variously conceived, ranging from substantive participation at one end of the spectrum, to the mere execution of divine commands at the other, through to analogies with the order of the cosmos. Furthermore, the various mimetic functions and moments need not be encompassed in one person, not even to the mind of Fārābī. Unlike some of his modern interpreters, Fārābī was clearly capable of envisaging functional specialisation in the capacities required for rule, which comprise practical and ethical virtues no less than metaphysical knowledge, knowledge of jurisprudence and of precedent, and of the arts of war.[136] For Ibn Sīnā, three distinctive fields of virtue exist. Justice, which he conceives according to the classic ethical theory as the three means of wisdom, courage, and temperance, is not and need not necessarily be associated with the second field, that of theoretical virtue brought about by philosophy. If an individual were to combine these two with prophetic inspiration, he would approximate the status of a human god, and would come close to meriting worship, after the worship of God. Such a rare individual becomes, fully and truly, God's caliph on earth.[137]

Ibn Rushd enriches these ideas still further. In his characteristic way he shows an acute awareness of the bearing of philosophical activity and of ethics upon practical political reality. He allocates wisdom and courage to the state, and spreads temperance all across the populace, conceiving of justice as the all-encompassing virtue which assures continuity and stability by keeping people in the stations for which they are fit.[138] This is a matter that takes us back to some of the prime constituent elements of the notion of order as enunciated by Muslim polities, namely the bearing of state wisdom upon public order whose emblem is justice – that is, the preservation of the status quo, the prevalent hierarchy of command, as the best of all possible worlds. The question which devolves from the exclusivist possession of true knowledge – inspiration, illumination, or the logicalist fundamentalism according to which Ibn Rushd interpreted Aristotle – is that concerning the way in which public interest and the virtues required for it come to be translated to a commoners' patois. This translation from the language of those knowledgeable in philosophy and learned in the religious sciences needs to be effective in its primary aim, which is the preservation of order and the realisation of divine purposes, including salvation.

Clearly the question here does not devolve to a double-truth theory, dear as this may be to modern scholarship on medieval Muslim philosophy. The mediation required is one that aims to translate the truth of matters revealed to those chosen for this particular receipt of divine beneficence or emanation, or those capable of attaining it by rational application, into the regulation of the behaviour of the unruly, irrational and vulgar demos in accordance with the ordinances of God and of reason combined. This is not a movement between two types of truth of distinctive substance, but is in a rigorous and technical sense a rhetorical and linguistic translation. The idea was not new: Ibn Sīnā had already interpreted the 'translation' in terms of symbolism and of sensuous representation for the vulgar.[139] The epistemological and the political are not necessarily either continuous or intransitive, but are symbolically connected. The relationship is of a very specific order mediated by the standard Arabic linguistic and rhetorical theories of enunciation, in which a single enunciation can have different forms of expression – literal, symbolic, metonymic, graphic and others – none of which derogates from its truth, all being part of a pragmatics of discourse which writers in Arabic in the Middle Ages took very much for granted.[140]

We do not therefore have a chivalric contest of faith against reason after the fashion which emerged in the eighteenth and nineteenth centuries. What we have, best articulated by Ibn Rushd and Ibn Sīnā, is the crossing of a perennial philosophy driven by theodicy, and of practical institutes called the *sharʿ*. The *sharʿ* makes possible the realisation of the order of theodicy whose ultimate end is salvation in its various forms and acceptations, bodily as well as spiritual. It is in this sense that the ubiquitous statements concerning the socially-specific articulation of eternal verities, the expression of truths in terms suitable to the comprehension of respective listeners or readers – the elect or the initiated, and the commoners – should be understood. This is expressed in terms of the self-same pessimistic anthropology that was taken up in detail elsewhere in this book, according to which there are limits inherent to the capacity of the common understanding and judgement.

It is in view of the imbrication of this matter with Arabic linguistic theory that Ibn Rushd made his famous and frequently misunderstood statement that, if any contradictions seem to exist between the literal enunciation of canonical statements and the truths accessible to demonstrative reason, the solution to them must lie in pursuing the rules of Arabic hermeneutics (*qānūn at-ta'wīl al-ʿarabī*).[141] Such contradictions are inadmissible and impossible because 'truth can never contradict truth',[142] for truth is indivisible, albeit variously expressed and articulated. Commonly misconstrued as a casuistical euphemism this is, in fact, simply a statement made in the light of full acquaintance with the Arab linguistic and rhetorical theories which formed an integral part of the literacy of the Middle Ages. The Rushdian position was specified in the normal way, by recourse to the notion that sensuous representation and illustration by example – as in the justification for *Fürstenspiegel* – is the appropriate form into which eternal verities are translated for them to be accessible to the multitude, unlike demonstration and the handling of abstract categories.[143]

What is sometimes regarded as a characteristically or peculiarly Rushdian position was not by any means specific to Ibn Rushd. It was widely shared in its general outline, and was indeed incorporated into the conception of philosophy held by personalities as unlikely as the conservative but formidably sober-minded Ibn Ḥazm[144] and Ibn Taymiyya.[145] Multiplicity is inadmissible with respect to the truth.[146] Fārābī, for one, proposed that eternal verities, like transcendent entities, celestial essences, the generation and corruption of bodies, emanation and other metaphysical topics philosophically accessible to those who can attain them, are the very same topics that are known by analogy and figural representation to commoners. Even among the latter there are different manners of such representation and analogy. These depend on the proximity of a particular people to the abstract entities, measured in the degree of abstraction, but also according to national and religious conventions. Hence it is possible that cities of excellence, equal in their perfection (a notion, as mentioned, to be understood teleologically), could be set up by various communities of varying religions and histories.[147] Ibn Rushd expressed the same theme by emphasis on the linguistic means of delivery. He spoke in terms of using rhetorical and poetical syllogisms when communicating with commoners, rather than the demonstrative syllogisms that yield demonstrative certainty which are accessible only to the philosophically instructed.[148] Another manner of expressing the same relation was proposed by Fārābī, who regarded Muslim jurisprudence as comprising two broad thematic categories, the one being particulars pertaining to the abstract generalities of philosophy, the other sensuous representations of elements of the same body of generalities.[149] At the lowest end of this scale we find idolatry.[150]

Yet nowhere does the reader encounter a specific listing of these various analogies and particularities in the manner that one finds them especially in Muslim jurisprudence, where specific rulings in works of jurisprudential epistemology are related to general principles, textual and otherwise, as in Ibn Rushd's great legal work *Bidāyat al-mujtahid wa nihāyat al-muqtaṣid*.[151] Yet the same author differentiates between his unwritten, natural law, which though natural to human collectivities in general is explicitly accessible only to the elect like himself, and the written law, which is revealed and involuntary and may not always be beneficial, as it is changeless.[152] The latter, in which one would include the *sharʿ*, seems to fulfil the double purposes of figuration, as text, and of social control of the inchoate demos. There was always, moreover, a serious tension, even in the work of Fārābī, between the claims of philosophical reason to exclusivity and epistemological priority,[153] and the utopian project of generalising virtue as such, as distinct from sheer obedience built upon exemplars, analogies, and other sensuous representations of virtue. Fārābī had even envisaged a division of labour at the top, with the possibility of nonphilosophical statesmanship, and had not always spoken for the inseparability of theoretical and deliberative excellences.[154]

It is this tension which accounts for the puritanical cognitive moralism of certain thinkers, most notably Ibn Bāja in Spain but also Fārābī in some texts, who gave up on the multitude and stressed the need for spiritualising self-cultivation. This was conceived after a manner similar to mystical and certain other forms of pietism which conceived the perfected man as a stranger among his countrymen.[155] Such a position was often criticised on the grounds of contradicting the necessary sociality of just humanity.[156] It was also countered with the argument that such spiritual and intellectual excellence as may be cultivated by a solitary sage, when directed at neither good nor evil transcending the sage himself, renders their holder akin to the dead or to inanimate matter, as it is only in association that virtues can be truly perfected.[157]

All this takes us back to the necessity of kingship, with or without philosophical cultivation, and hence to the contrast between the ethical reveries of Fārābī and the worldly realism of Ibn Sīnā, who re-introduced into this discourse of practical philosophy the centrality of prophecy and its progeny to the constitution of political entities. Ibn Sīnā had indeed admitted the possibility of individual rational and spiritual cultivation to an extent that it makes possible the attainment of felicity as construed philosophically. Whereas Fārābī's conception of political life at its best is one which, *grosso modo*, ignores the limitations of the commoners and sets out to prepare them for perfection, Ibn Sīnā distinguishes the lesser from the better commonwealth by the ability of the better to secure stability and continued sociality in a manner which creates a morality of moderation overall. In this perspective it could be said that whereas for Fārābī cities exist in order to make men good, Ibn Sīnā postulates that subjects ought to be driven to do good in order for their commonwealth to exist.[158] Politics with Ibn Sīnā being no longer moral action on a grand scale, as it was with Fārābī, the primacy for him of the just commonwealth over the idea of a virtuous city, and the consequent redundancy of the Platonic ideal of a philosopher-king, become understandable.[159]

For Ibn Sīnā it is prophets, not philosophers, who with miraculous testaments to their prophecy, are capable of symbolising and otherwise sensuously representing the sublime truths to the multitude. Such symbolic representation and apprehension, for persons endowed with appropriately receptive souls, may even be a starting point for philosophical speculation.[160] On occasion, such truths symbolised are thought to be conducive to the moralisation of the public sphere, one almost akin to the Kantian notion of *Sittlichkeit*, for which love between fellow-countrymen is emblematic, a bond between persons which was deemed by Ṭūsī to be a natural sentiment, in contrast to the artificiality of justice.[161] Yet over and above private and public ethics stands religion adopted by kings as a primary regulator and agency of legislation and consequent regulator of sociality.[162] Various ways of articulating this complex of themes have been studied above. The imamate in general is defined in a philosophical text as the nomocratic and ethical behaviour of a king, who consequently becomes a paragon to his subjects and thus conducts them to felicity.[163] When this is achieved, by whichever means described, we have a world perfected by ethics and by religion under the regulation of a just ruler. In cosmological terms the human microcosm and the heavenly macrocosm come to correspond structurally in such a way that the hierarchical order of the one corresponds to the hierarchical order of the other.[164]

The degree to which philosophical texts themselves make the effortless transition between vocabularies in the manner described above is astonishing. They move, for instance, from a conception of politics as a practical philosophy to establish a discourse on kings as God's caliphs and legatees, quoting in support the well-known statements attributed to Persian sages about the indissoluble bond between religion and state.[165] All this goes to show that there is always, barring a few exceptional and intransigently utopian texts by Fārābī, a residual irrationalism at work bridging the gap between statements of rationalism and statements on politics and the order of human sociality.

Miskawayh, for instance, spoke of education into moderation as conducive to the reception in maturity of all that reason and the *sharʿ* would separately prescribe.[166] Matters that obtain from demonstrable sharʿist consensus, for Ibn Rushd following the standard line of Sunnism, are beyond the reach of theorisation.[167] Indeed, if the philosopher correcting a city were to be likened to a physician healing a body, this analogy must encompass the necessity for all manner of coercion, as the physician's prescriptions and remedies will not win ready assent, but rather provoke resistance.[168] Yet this view does not preclude rationalist notions of the *sharʿ*, holding it to be analogous to a natural law conceived in terms of theodicy,[169] although this notion is equally obtainable from strictly traditionalist redactions by the *ʿulamāʾ* of the legal notion of public interest.[170] This tallies with more detailed anthropological interpretations of Muslim ritual which is generally regarded as sheer divine command without connection to reason. Such, for instance, was the interpretation of the injunction to collective Friday prayers as an instrument of sociality,[171] or the interpretation of prayer akin to standard anthropological theories of ritual, as repetitive actions meant as 'reminders', as distinct from sheer sharʿist ruling.[172] Overall, Muslim philosphers were not the agents for sophistical courtesies and the rhetorical resolution of positions in principle irreconcilable. They exercised philosophical reason within a set of political and religious ideas that they fully shared with their times, traditions, and polities.

Notes

Preface

1 For a contiguous field of public sphere representation, that of justice, see Robert Jacob, *Images de la justice. Essai sur l'iconographie judiciaire du Moyen Age à l'age classique*, Paris, 1994

2 Cf. the statement that Judaism indicates that monotheism alone does not generate universalism: Garth Fowden, *Empire to Commonwealth. Consequences of Monotheism in Late Antiquity*, Princeton, 1993, p. 71.

3 K. W. Whitelam, *The Invention of Ancient Israel*, London, 1996; T. L. Thompson, *Early History of the Israelite People from the Written and Archaeological Sources*, Leiden, 1992

4 See particularly Thompson, *Early History of the Israelite People*, pp. 415 ff.

5 Gilbert Dagron, 'Frontières et marges: Le jeu du sacré à Byzance', in idem., *La romanité chrétienne en Orient*, London, 1984, ch xii, p. 166

6 Jacques Le Goff, 'Aspects religieux et sacrés de la monarchie française du xe au xiiie siècle' in *La royauté sacrée dans le monde chrétien*, ed. Alain Boureau and Claudio-Sergio Ingerflom, Paris, 1992, p. 19

7 For an exploration of possibilities, with reference to the Umayyad dynasty of Cordoba, see G. Martinez-Gros, *L'Idéologie Omeyyade. La construction de la légitimité du Califat de Cordoue (X-XIe siècles)*, Madrid, 1992

Chapter 1

1 C. Geertz, *Negara. The Theatre State in Nineteenth-Century Bali*, Princeton, 1980, p. 13.

2 S. Tambiah, *World Conqueror and World Renouncer. A Study of Buddhism and Polity in Thailand against a Historical Background*, Cambridge, 1976, ch. 7; idem., 'The Galactic Polity in Southeast Asia', in S. J. Tambiah, *Culture, Thought, and Social Action*, Cambridge, Mass., 1985, pp. 252–86.

3 G. Coedes, *The Indianized States of Southeast Asia*, Honolulu, 1968, pp. 252, 3–4.

4 M. G. S. Hodgson, *The Venture of Islam*, Chicago and London, 1974,

vol. 1, pp. 61–2.

5 N. R. Ray, *Maurya and Sunga Art*, Calcutta, 1945, pp 4–5, 10–11.

6 Coedes, *Indianized States*, pp. 15–16, 33–4.

7 Arnold Toynbee, *A Study of History*, 2nd edn, vol. 1, London, 1951, pp. 72 ff.

8 Carl Becker, *Islamstudien*, Leipzig, 1924, p. 201.

9 Garth Fowden, *Empire to Commonwealth: Consequences of Monotheism in Antiquity*, Princeton, 1993, pp. 7–8, 10, 138, and ch. 1, passim.

10 Ibid., p. 21.

11 F. Millar, *The Roman Near East, 31 – 337*, Cambridge , Mass., 1993, p. 172.

12 Ibid., p. 334.

13 Ibid., pp. 325–7, 504–5, and passim.

14 See M. Rodinson, *The Arabs*, London, 1981, pp. 54–5. The account of Millar, *The Roman Near East*, esp. pp. 505 ff., is cast in a hyper-sceptical mode which claims fidelity to material available, designed to deny any Arab character to the peoples, cultures, or institutions in the area.

15 F. Dvornik, *Early Christian and Byzantine Political Philosophy. Origins and Background*, Washington, DC, 1966, pp. 558–9.

16 Ibid., p. 448.

17 G. Tarn, *Alexandre*, vol. 1, p. 138, quoted in translation by R. Lane Fox, *Alexander the Great*, Harmondsworth, 1986, p. 460.

18 Coedes, *Indianized States*, p. 25.

19 Millar, *Roman Near East*, pp. 172–3, 301. Hadad/Baal, a god common throughout Canaanite and Aramean Syria, also dwelt on a mountain, and the associations with the sun-god Shamash are also strong, as were those of the roughly analogous Mesopotamian god Anu, whose own messenger was Shamash.

20 N. Cohn, *Cosmos, Chaos and the World to Come. The Ancient Roots of Apocalyptic Faith*, New Haven, 1994, p. 128.

21 A. Kuhrt, 'Usurpation, Conquest, and Ceremonial: From Babylon to Persia', in *Rituals of Royalty. Power and Ceremony in Traditional Societies*, ed. D. Cannadine and S. Price, Cambridge, 1987, pp. 40, 48–9.

22 Fox, *Alexander*, p. 277.

23 Dvornik, *Political Philosophy*, pp. 462–3.

Chapter 2

1 J. Stargardt, 'Social and Religious Aspects of Royal Power in Medieval Burma (From the Inscriptions of Kyansittha's Reign, 1084–1112)', in *Journal of the Economic and Social History of the Orient*, 13 (1970), p. 305.

2 Coedes, *Indianized States*, p. 26.

3 A. Grabar, *L'Empereur dans l'art byzantin*, Paris, 1936, pp. 4, 99.

4 Berlin, Aegyptisches Museum, Inv. No. 14 503.

5 Dvornik, *Political Philosophy*, p. 524.

6 P. Schramm et al., *Herrschaftszeichen und Staatssymbolik*, Stuttgart, 1954–6, vol. 2, p. 380.

7 R. Ettinghausen, *From Byzantium to Sasanian Iran and the Islamic World. Three Modes of Artistic Influence*, Leiden, 1972, pp. 30–2.

8 Ibn az-Zubayr, *Kitāb al-dhakhā'ir wa't-tuḥaf*, ed. M. Ḥamīd Allāh, Kuwait, 1984, p. 198.

9 Schramm et al., *Herrschaftszeichen*, vol. 2, p. 380.

10 J. Nelson, 'The Lord's Anointed and the People's Choice: Carolingian Royal Ritual', in *Rituals of Royalty*, ed. Cannadine and Price, p. 137.

11 Schramm et al., *Herrschaftszeichen*, vol. 1, p. 146, vol. 2, pp. 538 ff.

12 Fox, *Alexander*, pp. 428, 449.

13 E. E. Herzfeld, *Iran in the Ancient Near East*, London and New York, 1941, p. 258.

14 Ibn Ḥamādū, *Akhbār mulūk Banī 'Ubayd*, ed. M. Vonderheyden, Paris, 1927, pp. 15, 28, quoted in J. Johns, 'The Norman Kings of Sicily and the Fatimid Caliphate', in *Anglo-Norman Studies, XV. Proceedings of the 1992 Battle Conference on Anglo-Norman Studies* (Palermo, 1992), pp. 146–7.

15 L. A. Mayer, *Saracenic Heraldry, A Survey*, Oxford, 1933, pp. 22–4.

16 A. Lombard-Jourdan, *Fleur de lis et oriflamme. Signes célestes du royaume de France*, Paris, 1991, quoted in Jacques Le Goff, 'Aspects religieux et sacré de la monarchie française du xe au xiiie siècle', in *La royauté sacrée dans le monde chrétien*, ed. A. Boureau et al., Paris, 1992, pp. 21 and 21n3.

17 J. Auboyer, 'Symbols of Sovereignty in India according to Iconography', in *Indian Arts and Letters*, 12(1938), pp. 26–8.

18 Johns, 'The Norman Kings of Sicily', pp. 133 ff.

19 Ettinghausen, *From Byzantium to Sasanian Iran*, p. 15; Jean Seznec, *The Survival of the Pagan Gods. The Mythological Tradition and its Place in Renaissance Humanism and Art*, tr. Barbara F. Sessions, Princeton, 1972, pp. 163–4, 291.

20 Dvornik, *Political Philosophy*, p. 525; O. Treitinger, *Die oströmische Kaiser- und Reichsidee nach ihre Gestaltung im höfischen Zeremoniell* [1938], Darmstadt, 1956, p. 49.

21 Dvornik, *Political Philosophy*, pp. 119–20.

22 Janet Nelson, private communication.

23 M. Tardieu, 'Théorie de la mémoire et fonction prophétique', in *La mémoire des religions*, ed. P. Borgeaud, Geneva, 1988, pp. 108 and see 112–3.

24 S. Weinstock, *Divus Julius*, Oxford, 1971, p. 19.

25 F. Reynolds, 'The Two Wheels of Dhamma: A Study of Early Buddhism', in *The Two Wheels of Dhamma*, ed. L. Bardwell Smith, Chambersburg, 1972, p. 13.

26 B. A. Uspenskij, 'Tsar and Pretender: *Samosvastvo* or Royal Imposture in Russia as a Cultural-Historical Phenomenon', in *Semiotics of Russian Culture*, ed. A. Shukman, Ann Arbor, 1984, p. 264.

27 M. Bloch, *Les rois thaumaturgues*, Paris, 1983.

28 J. Le Goff, 'Preface' to Bloch, *Les rois thaumaturgues*, p. xvii; idem.,

'Aspects religieux et sacrés de la monarchie française', p. 20.

29 Cf. G. Widengren, *The Ascension of the Apostle and the Heavenly Book*, Uppsala, 1950, p. 10.

30 Cohn, *Cosmos, Chaos, and the World to Come*, pp. 38, 43.

31 C. Brett, 'The Priest-Emperor Concept in Japanese Political Thought', in *Indian Journal of Political Science*, vol. 23, no. 1(1962), p. 19.

32 H. J. Wechsler, *Offerings of Jade and Silk. Ritual and Symbol in the Legitimation of the T'ang Dynasty*, New Haven, 1985, p. 32.

33 Ettinghausen, *From Byzantium to Sasanian Iran*, p. 34.

34 Johns, 'The Norman Kings of Sicily', pp. 149–51.

35 For instance, B. G. Gokhale, 'Dhammiko Dhammarājā. A Study in Buddhist Constitutional Concepts', in *Indica. The Indian Historical Institute Silver Jubilee Commemoration Volume*, Bombay, 1953, p. 163; Weinstock, *Divus Julius*, pp. 204–5.

36 Dvornik, *Political Philosophy*, p. 36.

37 Ibid., p. 526.

38 Ibid., p. 95.

39 See in general E. Peterson, *Der Monotheismus als politisches Problem. Ein Beitrag zur Geschichte der politischen Theologie im Imperium Romanum*, Leipzig, 1935, pp. 66 ff., 71 ff., and passim, and N. H. Baines, 'Eusebius and the Christian Empire', in idem., *Byzantine Studies and other Essays*, London, 1955, pp. 168–72. The fundamental text of Eusebius is well-translated and thoroughly annotated by H. A. Drake, *In Praise of Constantine: A Historical Study and New Translation of Eusebius' Tricennial Orations*, Berkeley and Los Angeles, 1976.

40 Dvornik, *Political Philosophy*, pp. 524, 620–1, 631–3.

41 H. P. L'Orange, *Studies on the Iconography of Cosmic Kingship in the Ancient World*, Oslo, 1953, pp. 28 ff.

42 H. Frankfort, *Kingship and the Gods. A Study of Ancient Near Eastern Religion as the Integration of Society and Nature*, Chicago, 1948, p. 237.

43 R. Burghart, 'Gifts to the Gods: Power, Property and Ceremonial in Nepal', in *Rituals of Royalty*, ed. Cannadine and Price, p. 237.

44 Frankfort, *Kingship and the Gods*, p. 237.

45 Wechsler, *Offerings of Jade*, pp. 12–13.

46 G. Coedès, 'Le culte de la royauté divinisée, source d'inspiration des grands monuments du Cambodge ancien', in *Instituto Italiano per il Medio ed Estremo Oriente. Conferenze = Serie Orientale*, No. 5 (1952), pp. 3–4, 12–13, 16; idem., *Indianized States*, pp. 98–101; Tambiah, *World Conqueror and World Renounce*, p. 99–100.

47 Geertz, *Negara*, p. 106.

48 R. Heine-Geldern, 'Conceptions of State and Kingship in Southeast Asia', in *Far Eastern Quarterly*, 1(1942), pp. 22–3; Tambiah, *World Conqueror and World Renouncer*, p. 100 n. 18.

49 Coedès, 'Le culte de la royauté', p. 15.

50 M. Aung-Thwin, *Pagan: The Origins of Modern Burma*, Honolulu, 1985,

pp. 47–9; Heine-Geldern, 'Conceptions of the State and Kingship', pp. 23–4.

51 Brett, 'The Priest-Emperor Concept', p. 24.

52 Bīrūnī, *Taḥqīq mā lil-Hind min maqūla, maqbūla fi'l-'aql aw mardhūla*, 2nd rev. ed., Hyderabad, 1958, p. 84.

53 S. R. F. Price, *Rituals and Power. The Roman Imperial Cult in Asia Minor*, Cambridge, 1984, esp. Pt. I, passim, and p. 242.

54 Ibid., p. 26, and cf. Dvornik, *Political Philosophy*, p. 208.

55 Dvornik, *Political Philosophy*, pp. 184 ff., 195 ff., 221.

56 Cf. the brief pertinent remarks of T. I. Oizerman and A. S. Bogolomov, *Principles of the Theory of the Historical Process in Philosophy*, Moscow, 1986, pp. 120–1.

57 Dvornik, *Political Philosophy*, pp. 227–30.

58 Ibid., pp. 232–40.

59 Ibid., pp. 255–8.

60 Weinstock, *Divus Julius*, on which the following account will depend for its factual material, unless otherwise stated.

61 Fox, *Alexander*, passim.

62 G. Dumézil, *L'Héritage Indo-Européen à Rome*, Paris, 1949.

63 Price, *Rituals and Power*, p. 57.

64 Ibid., pp. 71–91.

65 Ibid., pp. 215–6.

66 Dvornik, *Political Philosophy*, pp. 495–6; Weinstock, *Divus Julius*, p. 303.

67 Weinstock, *Divus Julius*, pp. 303–5.

68 Dvornik, *Political Philosophy*, pp. 498 ff.

69 Ibid., pp. 117–8.

70 Price, *Rituals and Power*, pp. 97–8.

71 Dvornik, *Political Philosophy*, pp. 583–4.

72 Ibid., pp. 558–65.

73 G. Ostrogorsky, 'The Byzantine Emperor and the Hierarchical World Order', in *The Slavonic and East European Review*, 35 (1956–57), p. 2.

74 Fowden, *Empire to Commonwealth*, pp. 52–3 and ch. 3 and 4, passim.

75 Dvornik, *Political Philosophy*, p. 648.

76 Treitinger, *Reichsidee*, pp. 38–40.

77 Grabar, *L'Empereur dans l'art byzantin*, pp. 98–9.

78 Dvornik, *Political Philosophy*, pp. 61–4, 71.

79 This matter is distorted by the requirements of latter-day doctrines, a distortion reflected in the normal course of translations that render the term *basileus* as king with reference to God, and emperor with reference to the Byzantine emperor: see Drake, *In Praise of Constantine.*

80 Uspenskij, 'Tsar and Pretender', p. 261.

81 K. Setton, *Christian Attitudes towards the Emperor in the Fourth Century*, New York, 1941, ch. 1, passim.

82 M. McCormick, 'Analyzing Imperial Ceremonies', in *Jahrbuch der*

österreichischen Byzantinistik, 35(1985), p. 10.

83 Grabar, *L'Empereur dans l'art byzantin*, pp. 1–2.

84 H. Belting, *Likeness and Presence. A History of the Image before the Era of Art*, tr. E. Jephcott, Chicago, 1994, pp. 36–7.

85 G. Dagron, 'Frontières et marges: le jeu du sacré à Byzance', in idem., *La romanité chrétienne en Orient*, London, 1984, p. 160.

86 Grabar, *L'Empereur dans l'art byzantin*, pp. 2–3, 99; McCormick, 'Imperial Ceremonies', pp. 2, 7; A. Cameron, 'The Construction of Court Ritual: The Byzantine *Book of Ceremonies*', in *Rituals of Royalty*, ed. Cannadine and Price, p. 131.

87 Belting, *Likeness and Presence*, p. 106.

88 Grabar, *L'Empereur dans l'art byzantin*, pp. 5–8.

89 H. Ahrweiler, *L'Idéologie politique de l'empire byzantin*, Paris, 1975, p. 141.

90 Dvornik, *Political Philosophy*, p. 652–4.

91 Treitinger, *Reichsidee*, pp. 84 ff.

92 Ibid., pp. 88–9.

93 Ostrogorsky, 'The Byzantine Emperor', p. 3.

94 Treitinger, *Reichsidee*, pp. 7 ff.

95 L'Orange, *Iconography*, pp. 88–90, 103 ff.

96 Ostrogorsky, 'The Byzantine Emperor', p. 4; Dvornik, *Political Philosophy*, pp. 693–5.

97 Treitinger, *Reichsidee*, pp. 1–2, 40, and pt. 1, ch. 2, pt 2., ch. 1, passim.

98 Ibid., pp. 49–51, 227–8.

99 Ibid., pp. 39–40.

100 Dvornik, *Political Philosophy*, pp. 618–9.

101 Treitinger, *Reichsidee*, p. 46.

102 Wechsler, *Offerings of Jade*, p. 122.

103 Peterson, *Der Monotheismus*, pp. 23–30.

104 R. C. Zaehner, *The Dawn and Twilight of Zoroastrianism*, London, 1961, p. 298.

105 Peterson, *Der Monotheismus*, pp. 57, 61 ff., 81n135.

106 The reader is referred, most particularly, to the fundamental article of E. R. Goodenough, 'The Political Philosophy of Hellenistic Kingship', in *Yale Classical Studies*, 1(1928), pp. 55–102, and to Dvornik, *Political Philosophy*, ch. 8, passim., and pp. 717–23.

107 Drake, *In Praise of Constantine*, p. 87 n. 15.

108 Treitinger, *Reichsidee*, p. 216.

109 Dvornik, *Political Philosophy*, pp. 622–3.

110 Ibid., pp. 662–3.

111 I. H. Robinson, 'Church and Papacy', in *The Cambridge History of Medieval Political Thought*, pp. 287–8.

112 On monotheistic and pagan equivalences and inflections of the same idea, see J. Croissant, 'Un nouveau discours de Thémistius', in *Serta Leodiensa (Bibliothèque de la Faculté de Philosophie et des Lettres)*, Liège,

XLIV(1930), pp. 9 ff., 20–1.

113 Eusebius' text in Drake, *In Praise of Constantine*, p. 89.

114 Dvornik, *Political Philosophy*, p. 723.

Chapter 3

1 See the overall considerations in A. Al-Azmeh, 'Chronophagous Discourse', in *Religion and Practical Reason*, ed. F. Reynolds and D. Tracy, Albany, 1994, pp. 164 ff.

2 Frankfort, *Kingship and the Gods*, pp. 319–26; Cohn, *Cosmos, Chaos, and the World to Come*, pp. 38–9; Kuhrt, 'Usurpation, Conquest, and Ceremonial', p. 31.

3 Kuhrt, 'Usurpation, Conquest, and Ceremonial', p. 30.

4 Dvornik, *Political Philosophy*, pp. 29–42, 299.

5 Frankfort, *Kingship and the Gods*, bk. I, passim., Dvornik, *Political Philosophy*, pp. 10–14.

6 See A. J. Festugière, 'Les inscriptions d'Ašoka et l'idéal du roi héllenistique', in *Mélanges Jules Lebreton: Recherches de Science Religieuse*, xxxix/2–4, pp. 38–9, who adopts, however, notions of East and West which are no longer tenable. Cf. Goodenough, 'Hellenistic Kingship', p. 85.

7 R. Gombrich, *Theravada Buddhism. A Social History from Ancient Benares to Modern Colombo*, London, 1988, p. 23.

8 L. Bardwell Smith, 'The Ideal Social Order as Portrayed in the Chronicles of Ceylon', in *The Two Wheels of Dhamma*, ed. L. Bardwell Smith, p. 52.

9 Stargardt, 'Social and Religious Aspects of Royal Power', p. 290.

10 B. G. Gokhale, 'The Early Buddhist View of the State', in *Journal of the American Oriental Society*, 89 (1969), pp. 736–7.

11 Tambiah, *World Conqueror and World Renouncer*, pp. 77–8n.

12 Gokhale, 'The Early Buddhist View', p. 736.

13 Sarkisianz, *Buddhist Background*, pp. 44–7; Reynolds, 'The Two Wheels of Dhamma', p. 29; Bardwell Smith, 'The Ideal Social Order', pp. 38–9; Tambiah, *World Conqueror and World Renouncer*, pp. 39, 73.

14 Gokhale, 'Dhammikō Dhammarājā', pp. 164–5; Reynolds, 'The Two Wheels of Dhamma', p. 20.

15 Tambiah, *World Conqueror and World Renouncer*, p. 45.

16 Sarkisianz, *Buddhist Background*, pp. 93 ff.; Aung-Thwin, *Pagan*, pp. 58 ff.

17 Heine-Geldern, 'Conceptions of State and Kingship', pp. 25–6.

18 Bardwell Smith, 'The Ideal Social Order', p. 55.

19 Tambiah, *World Conqueror and World Renouncer*, p. 43.

20 Eusebius' text in Drake, *In Praise of Constantine*, pp. 93–4.

21 See in general H. Lewy, *Chaldean Oracles and Theurgy. Mysticism, Magic, and Platonism in the Late Roman Empire*, ed. M. Tardieu, Paris, 1978, and A. Al-Azmeh, *Arabic Thought and Islamic Societies*, London, 1986, pp. 69 ff.

22 Heine-Geldern, 'Conceptions of State and Kingship', pp. 16, 20; Coedès, 'Le culte de la royauté', p. 5.

23 Tambiah, *World Conqueror and World Renouncer*, pp. 111 ff.

24 Heine-Geldern, 'Conceptions of State and Kingship', pp. 17–18; Tambiah, *World-Conqueror and World Renouncer*, p. 258.

25 Tambiah, *World Conqueror and World Renouncer*, pp. 102–8, 113–14, 123.

26 Ibid., pp. 19–22.

27 Widengren, *The Ascension of the Apostle*, pp. 18–19, 22 ff.

28 Cohn, *Cosmos, Order, and Chaos*, pp. 82 f., 100 ff., 114; Zaehner, *Zoroastrianism*, p. 299.

29 For apocalyptic conceptions, writings, and associated notions overall, both Pagan and monotheistic (though Islam is, regrettably but not uncharacteristically for studies in the history of religion, excluded), see the voluminous *Apocalypticism in the Mediterranean World and in the Near East*, ed. D. Hellholm, Tübingen, 1983.

30 M. Boyce (tr.), *The Letter of Tansar*, Rome, 1968, p. 37.

31 A. Christensen, *Les gestes des rois dans les traditions de l'Iran antique*, Paris, 1936, ch. 1 & 2, passim.

32 Al-Azmeh, 'Chronophagous Discourse', pp. 166 ff.

33 Weinstock, *Divus Julius*, p. 183.

34 Christensen, *Les gestes des rois*, p. 75; Dvornik, *Political Philosophy*, pp. 95–100.

35 K. Erdmann, 'Die Entwicklung der Sāsānidischen Krone', in *Ars Islamica*, 1951, pp. 87–8 and passim.

36 Wechsler, *Offerings of Jade*, pp. 222–3, 98–9.

37 Peterson, *Der Monotheismus*, pp. 77, 79–80.

38 See in general the limpid account of E. Auerbach, 'Figura', in idem., *Scenes from the Drama of European Literature*, Manchester, 1984, pp. 42 and 11–76, passim. On the distinction between typology and allegory, see Ibid., pp. 69 ff. and J. N. D. Kelly, *Early Christian Doctrines*, 5th ed, London, 1977, p. 54.

39 H. Schraeder, *Moskau, das Dritte Rom. Studien zur Geschichte der politischen Theorien in der slawischen Welt* [1929], Darmstadt, 1957, pp. 40, 49–50.

40 E. H. Kantorowicz, *The King's Two Bodies. A Study in Medieval Political Theology*, Princeton, 1957, pp. 88–9 and passim.

41 Grabar, *L'Empereur dans l'art byzantin*, pp. 95–7.

42 Treitinger, *Reichsidee*, pp. 4, 37, 125–7; Ostrogorsky, 'The Byzantine Emperor', p. 4.

43 A. Cameron, 'Eusebius of Caesarea and the Rethinking of History', in *Tria Corda. Scritti in onore di Arnaldo Momigliano*, ed. E. Gabba (*Biblioteca di Athenaeum, I*), Como, 1983, pp. 76 and passim.

44 Treitinger, *Reichsidee*, p. 45.

45 Dvornik, *Political Philosophy*, pp. 614–7.

46 Cameron, 'Eusebius of Caesarea', p. 78.

47 Dvornik, *Political Philosophy*, p. 585.

48 Ibid., p. 725; Peterson, *Der Monotheismus*, pp. 57–78, 81–91.

49 Schraeder, *Moskau, das Dritte Rom*, pp. 14–15.

50 Ibid., pp. 16–17; Ahrweiler, *L'idéologie politique*, p. 51.

51 Ahrweiler, *L'idéologie politique*, pp. 35–45; P. Brown, *The World of Late Antiquity*, London, 1971, pp. 174, 184–6.

52 G. Dagron, 'Minorités ethniques et religieuses dans l'Orient byzantin à la fin du dixième et au onzième siècles: l'immigration Syrienne', in idem., *La romanité chretienne*, esp. pp. 182–4, 198–9, 214–6.

53 Text in Drake, *In Praise of Constantine*, p. 103.

54 Zaehner, *Zoroastrianism*, p. 298.

55 Dvornik, *Political Philosophy*, p. 643.

56 Schraeder, *Moskau, das Dritte Rom*, pp. 1–2.

57 Ostrogorsky, 'The Byzantine Emperor', p. 6.

58 Ibid., p. 10.

59 Ibid., pp. 7–8.

60 G. Necipoğlu, *Architecture, Ceremonial, and Power. The Topkapi Palace in the Fifteenth and Sixteenth Centuries*, New York and Cambridge, Mass., 1991, p. 249.

61 Schraeder, *Moskau, das Dritte Rom*, pp. 21, 117 ff.

62 Ibid., pp. 112, 128 and cf. Ostrogorsky, 'The Byzantine Emperor', p. 8–9; D. M. Nicol, *The Immortal Emperor. The Life and Legend of Constantine Palaiologos, Last Emperor of the Romans*, Cambridge, 1994, pp. 105, 115.

63 J. M. Lotman and M. Uspenskij, 'Echoes of the Notion 'Moscow as the Third Rome' in Peter the Great's Ideology', in *Semiotics of Russian Culture*, ed. Shukman, p. 55.

64 Ibid., pp. 53–4.

65 Ahrweiler, *L'idéologie politique*, pp. 79–80.

66 Ibid., p. 103 and ch VI, passim.

67 Ibid., pp. 123–5; S. Runciman, *The Fall of Constantinople, 1453*, Cambridge, 1990, pp. 71–2, 131–2.

68 Nicol, *The Immortal Emperor*, pp. 37 ff.

69 Ibid., pp. 71–2.

70 Schraeder, *Moskau, das Dritte Rom*, pp. 12–13.

71 J. H. Burns, 'The Barbarian Kingdoms', in *The Cambridge History of Medieval Political Thought*, ed. Burns, p. 127.

72 Ibid., p. 129.

73 Ibid., pp. 144–7.

74 Ibid., pp. 136–7; J. Nelson, 'Kingship and Empire', in *The Cambridge History of Medieval Political Thought*, ed. Burns, pp. 151–3.

75 Ibid., pp. 156–7, and cf pp. 164, 169.

76 Burns, 'The Barbarian Kingdoms', pp. 124–5, 147.

77 E. R. Curtius, *European Literature and the Latin Middle Ages*, tr. W. R. Trask, London, 1953, p. 29.

78 Kantorowicz, *The King's Two Bodies*, p. 193.

79 I. S. Robinson, 'Church and Papacy', in *The Cambridge History of*

Medieval Political Thought, ed. Burns, pp. 302–3.

80 Ibid., p. 304.

81 Treitinger, *Reichsidee*, pp. 71 ff.

82 S. Runciman, *The Byzantine Theocracy*, Cambridge, 1977, p. 4.

83 Nelson, 'Kingship and Empire', pp. 146–7.

84 For instance, by Isidore of Seville: Burns, 'The Barbarian Kingdoms', pp. 143–4.

85 A. Boureau, 'Un obstacle à la sacralité royale en Occident. Le principe hiérarchique', in *La royaté sacrée*, p. 32.

86 Le Goff, preface to Bloch, *Les rois thaumaturgues*, p. xxii.

87 D. E. Luscombe, 'Introduction: The Formation of Political Thought in the West', in *The Cambridge History of Medieval Political Thought*, ed. Burns, p. 105.

88 Ibid., p. 171.

89 Ibid., pp. 168–9.

90 Robinson, 'Church and Papacy', pp. 281, 289; R. A. Markus, 'The Latin Fathers', in *The Cambridge History of Medieval Political Thought*, ed. Burns, pp. 93–102; J. Nelson, personal communication.

91 Robinson, 'Church and Papacy', p. 296.

92 Dvornik, *Political Philosophy*, p. 848; Luscombe, 'Introduction', pp. 166–7; Nelson, 'Kingship and Empire', p. 221.

93 Robinson, 'Church and papacy', pp. 299 ff.

94 A. Boureau, 'Un obstacle à la sacralité royale en Occident. Le principe hiérarchique', in *La royaté sacrée*, pp. 29, 31–2.

95 Ibid., p. 32.

96 Dvornik, *Political Philosophy*, pp. 817 ff.

97 J. L. Nelson, 'Symbols in Context: Rulers' Inauguration Rituals in Byzantium and the West in the Early Middle Ages' in *Studies in Church History*, 13 (1976), pp. 105, 111.

98 Treitinger, *Reichsidee*, p. 8.

99 Ibid., ch. I, sec. 1.b.a, passim; Nelson, 'Symbols in Context', pp. 100 ff. and idem., 'The Lord's Anointed', pp. 142 ff.; Cameron, 'The Construction of Court Ritual' pp. 117–8.

100 Nelson, 'Symbols in Context', p. 107.

101 Treitinger, *Reichsidee*, p. 35.

102 Runciman, *The Fall of Constantinople*, pp. 155–7.

103 Ahrweiler, *L'idéologie politique*, pp. 130 ff.; A. W. Ziegler, 'Die byzantinische Religionspolitik und der sogenannte Cäsaropapismus', in *Festgabe für Paul Diels*, ed. E. Koschmieder, München, 1953, pp. 81–3.

104 Dvornik, *Political Philosophy*, p. 643.

105 L. Bréhier, 'Hiereus Kai Basileus', in *Mémorial Louis Petit. Mélanges d'histoire et d'archeologie Byzantines (Archives de l'Orient Chrétien, 1)*, Bucharest, 1948, pp. 4–45.

106 Ibid., p. 41.

107 Treitinger, *Reichsidee*, p. 220.

108 Ibid., pp. 128–130.
109 Ziegler, 'Die byzantinische Religionspolitik', p. 94.
110 Treitinger, *Reichsidee*, pp. 137, 139; Dvornik, *Political Philosophy*, p. 645; Bréhier, 'Hiereus Kai Basileus', pp. 42–5
111 Cf. Le Goff, preface to Bloch, *Les rois thaumaturgues*, p. xxxiv.
112 Bréhier, 'Hiereus Kai Basileus', p. 44.
113 Treitinger, *Reichsidee*, p. 41.
114 Ahrweiler, *L'idéologie politique*, pp. 136–44.
115 Reynolds, 'The Two Wheels of Dhamma', p. 18.
116 Ibid., p. 14; idem, private communication.
117 Tambiah, *World Conqueror and World Renouncer*, p. 83.
118 Smith, 'The Ideal Social Order', pp. 35, 37.
119 Gokhale, 'The Early Buddhist View of the State', p. 737.
120 Reynolds, 'The Two Wheels of Dhamma', pp. 16–17.
121 Tambiah, *World Conqueror and World Renouncer*, p. 24.
122 Ibid., p. 93.
123 See, among others, Gokhale, 'The Early Buddhist View of the State', pp. 732–3.
124 Tambiah, *World Conqueror and World Renouncer*, p. 73.
125 Ibid., p. 70.
126 On this see Michael Mann, *The Sources of Social Power*, Cambridge, 1986, ch. 5, and cf. ch. 10 and 11.
127 Tambiah, *World Conqueror and World Renouncer*, p. 70.
128 Ibid., p. 259.
129 Reynolds, 'The Two Wheels of Dhamma', p. 20.
130 See the detailed account of H. L. Shorto, 'The Mon Genealogy of Kings: Observations on *The Nidana Arambhakatha*', in *Historians of South Asia*, ed. D. G. E. Hall, London, 1961, pp. 63–72.
131 Stargardt, 'Social and Religious Aspects of Royal Power', p. 295.
132 Tambiah, *World Conqueror and World Renouncer*, pp. 77 and 77–8 n.
133 Ibid., ch 9 and 10, and cf. Aung-Thwin, *Pagan*, pp. 28, 144 ff.
134 Geertz, *Negara*, p. 126.
135 Gokhale, 'The Early Buddhist View of the State', pp. 737–8.
136 On the vexed question of authorship and date of composition, see the detailed review of R. P. Kangle, *The Kauṭilīya Arthaśāstra*, Delhi 1986, pt. 3, ch. 4.
137 Tambiah, *World Conqueror and World Renouncer*, pp. 52, 52n21
138 Ibid., p. 57.
139 Gokhale, 'Dhammikō Dhammarājā', p. 163.
140 Tambiah, *World Conqueror and World Renouncer*, pp. 25, 50, 61–2.
141 Ibid., p. 30.
142 Smith, 'The Ideal of Social Order', pp. 42, 47–8.
143 See Reynolds, 'The Two Wheels of Dhamma', pp. 18–19; Gokhale, 'The Early Buddhist View of the State', p. 731; Gombrich, *Theravada Buddhism*, p. 85.

144 Gokhale, 'Dhammikō Dhammarājā', pp. 161–2; idem., 'The Early Buddhist View of the State', p. 733.

145 As far as I know, the only other concrete indication to affinities between Muslim and Indian political notions in modern scholarship is the reference to Arabic analogues to Kautliyan ideas in M. Manzalaoui, 'The Pseudo-Aristotelian *Sirr al- Asrār*. Facts and Problems', in *Oriens*, 1974, pp. 211 ff.

146 See Gokhale, 'The Early Buddhist View of the State', pp. 733–5.

147 Boyce, *Letter of Tansar*, p. 44; Zaehner, *Zoroastrianism*, p. 285.

Chapter 4

1 See M. Lombard, *The Golden Age of Islam*, tr. J. Spencer, Amsterdam and New York, 1972 ; A. al-ʿAẓma, *al-ʿArab wa'l-barābira*, London, 1991, ch. 1.

2 Terry Allen, 'The Arabesque, the Beveled Style, and the Mirage of an Early Islamic Art', in *Tradition and Innovation in Late Antiquity*, ed. F. M. Clover and R. S. Humphreys, Madison, 1989, pp. 221 ff. and passim.

3 The controversial work of ʿAlī ʿAbd al-Rāziq, *al-Islām wa uṣul al-hukm*, Cairo, 1925, is still unsurpassed.

4 Personal communication from Dr Sebastian Brock.

5 On the historicity of the traditional narrative canon on early Islam, see S. al-Bashīr, *Mūqaddima fi't-tārīkh al-ʿākhar. Fī naqd ar-riwāya al-islāmiyya*, Jerusalem, 1984. For an overview, see A. Al-Azmeh, 'The Muslim Canon: Typology, Utility and History', in *Canonizationand Decanonization* (Supplement to *Numen*, Leiden, 1998, pp. 191–228.

6 For instance, M. Fakhry, *A History of Islamic Philosophy*, New York, 1970, pp. 52–4.

7 Miskawayh, *Tahdhīb al-akhlāq* , ed. Q. Zūrayq, Beirut, 1966, p. 141.

8 Māwardī, *Naṣīḥat al-mūlūk*, ed. J. al-Ḥadīthī, Baghdad, 1986, p. 360.

9 For instance, Ibn Khaldūn , *Les Prolégomènes d'Ebn Khaledoun*, ed. E. Quatremère, Paris, 1858, vol. 2 pp. 3–4.

10 K. A. C. Creswell, *A Short Account of Early Muslim Architecture*, rev. J. W. Allan, Cairo, 1989, pp. 110–13, and O. Grabar, 'The Painting of the Six Kings at Quṣayr ʿAmrah', in *Ars Orientalis*, 1(1954), pp. 185–7.

11 Ibn az-Zūbayr, *Kitāb al-dhakhā'ir wa't-tuḥaf*, ed. M. Ḥamīd Allāh, Kuwait, 1984, pp. 127 ff, 159 ff.

12 Ibid., p. 203.

13 Ibid., p. 229 and 204.

14 Ibid., p. 231; Maʿsūdī, *Mūrūj adh-dhahab*, ed. Ch. Pellat, Beirut, 1965, § 3070.

15 For confirmation of his historicity in the light of recent research, see ʿĀdil Furayjāt, 'Jadhīma al-Abrash al-Azdī fi'l-maṣādir al-ʿarabiyya', in *Dirāsāt Tārikhiyya*, No. 47–48 (1993), pp. 23–36.

16 Qalqashandī, *Ṣubḥ al-aʿshā fī ṣināʿat al-inshā*, Cairo, 1915, vol. 1, p. 416;

M. Morony, *Iraq after the Muslim Conquest*, Princeton, 1984, p. 72.

17 L'Orange, *Iconography*, p. 24.

18 Ibn az-Zubayr, *Dhakhā'ir*, p. 160.

19 Mār Ighnāṭiūs Ifrām Barṣūm, 'al-Alfāẓ as-sūryāniyya fi'l-ma'ājim al-'arabiyya', in *Majallat al-Majma' al-'Ilmī al-'Arabī*, 23(1948), p. 331; *Tāj al-'arūs*, q.v.; R. Blachère et al., *Dictionnaire Arabe-Français-Anglais*, Paris, 1970, q.v.

20 Dominique Sourdel, 'Questions de cérémonial 'Abbaside', in *Revue des Etudes Islamiques*, 28 (1960), pp. 143–4.

21 For instance, Mas'ūdī, *Mūrūj*, §§ 2809, 2815.

22 Ibid., pp. 2801 ff.

23 J. G. Frazer, *The Golden Bough*, 2nd. ed., London, 1899, vol. 1, pp. xxi–xxii. See the critical comments on Frazer's interpretation in Frankfort, *Kingship and the Gods*, ch. 14 n. 11 and ch. 22 n 14.

24 Abū Hilāl al-'Askarī, *al-Awā'il*, ed. W. Qaṣṣāb and M. al-Miṣrī, Damascus, 1975, vol. 1, pp. 34, 38, 50; Ibn az-Zūbayr, *al-Dhakhā'ir*, p. 4.

25 Cf. Robert Hillenbrand, 'The Symbolism of the Rayed Nimbus in Early Islamic Art', in Emily Lyle (ed.), *Kingship (Cosmos, vol. 2)*, Edinburgh, 1986, pp. 27–9.

26 Qalqashandī, *Ṣubḥ al-a'shā*, vol. 4, p. 6; idem.,*Khilāfa*, ed. 'A. A. Farrāj, Kuwait, 1964, vol. 2, pp. 228–9; Ibn az-Zūbayr, *Dhakhā'ir*, p. 290; Mas'ūdī, *Mūrūj*, § 2154; al-Ya'qūbī, *Mushākalat an-nās li-zamānihim*, ed. W. Milward, Beirut, 1980, p. 16; al-Jāḥiẓ, *Kitāb at-tāj fī akhlāq al-mūlūk*, ed. A. Zakī, Cairo, 1914, pp. 23–4, 28, 32 [the attribution of this book to al-Jāḥiẓ is a matter of dispute. See the Editor's introduction (ibid., pp. 37–60) for confirmation of this attribution, and the doubts of Ch. Pellat, *Le livre de la couronne attribué à Gāhiz*, Paris, 1954, pp. 11–17, which do not seem altogether convincing.]

27 al-Jāḥiẓ, *Tāj*, pp. 151–3; O. Grabar, 'Note sur les cérémonies umayyades', in *Studies in Memory of Gaston Wiet*, ed. M. Rosen-Ayalon, Jerusalem, 1977, p. 58.

28 'Askarī, *Awā'il*, vol. 1, p. 364; Qalqashandī, *Khilāfa*, vol. 3, p. 344.

29 Grabar, 'Cérémonies umayyades', pp. 53, 59–60.

30 Mas'ūdī, *Murūj*, §§ 2219, 2248–50, 3449.

31 Ibid., §§ 2333, 2418.

32 Ibn 'Abd Rabbih, *al-'Iqd al-Farīd*, ed. M. M. Qumayḥa, Beirut, 1983, vol. 2, pp. 6–8.

33 Mas'ūdī, *Murūj*, §§ 2308, 2446.

34 For a full list of royal pilgrimage convoys and of their commanders, ibid., §§ 3630–56.

35 Jāḥiẓ, *Tāj*, pp. 46, 46–9.

36 Richard Ettinghausen, *From Byzantium to Sasanian Iran and the Islamic World. Three Modes of Artistic Influence*, Leiden, 1972, p. 15.

37 Ibn 'Abd Rabbih, *Dīwān*, ed. Riḍwān al-Dāya, Beirut, 1979, p. 182; Sibṭ Ibn at-Ta'āwīdhī, *Dīwān*, ed. D. S. Margoliouth, Cairo, 1903, pp. 1, 3.

38 Hillenbrand, 'Symbolism of the Rayed Nimbus', pp. 1–3, 7–8, and passim; Morony, *Iraq after the Muslim Conquest*, p. 30; Said Amir Arjomand, *The Shadow of God and the Hidden Imam. Religion, Political Order, and Societal Change in Shi'ite Iran from the Beginning to 1890*, Chicago, 1984, p. 93.

39 Hillenbrand, 'Symbolism of the Rayed Nimbus', pp. 31–5, for instance, for such over-interpretation.

40 F. Barry Flood, 'The Iconography of Light in the Monuments of Mamluk Cairo', in Emily Lyle (ed.), *Sacred Architecture in the Traditions of China, India, Judaism and Islam*, Edinburgh, 1992, pp. 186, 182–6.

41 The relationship between the design of Kūfa and Hellenistic, Babylonian, and Persian cities is extremely complex. An exemplary study is to be found in H. Djaït, *al-Kūfa. Naissance de la ville islamique*, Paris, 1986, pp. 139 ff., 157 ff., 311 ff.

42 J. Lassner, *The Topography of Baghdad in the Early Middle Ages*, Detroit, 1970, pp. 133–6.

43 Charles Wendell, 'Baghdād: *Imago Mundi* and other Foundation Lore', in *International Journal of Middle East Studies*, 2(1971), pp. 103–5, 109–10, 117–20.

44 Ibid., pp. 122–5.

45 Hans Peter L'Orange, *Studies on the Iconography of Cosmic Kingship in the Ancient World*, Oslo, 1953, pp. 9 ff., 18 ff.; Herzfeld, *Iran in the Ancient Near East*, pp. 1 ff.

46 See Morony, *Iraq after the Muslim Conquest*, p. 29.

47 Qalqashandī, *Khilāfa*, vol. 1, pp. 22, 110. For a comprehensive list of titles used in the histories of Muslim polities, see Ḥasan al-Bāshā, *al-Alqāb al-Islamiyya fi't-tārīkh wa'l-wathā'iq wa'l-āthār*, Cairo, 1957, pp. 117–544.

48 Mas'ūdī, *Mūrūj*, § 2386.

49 Of numerous possible citations relative to the Umayyad period: Mas'ūdī, *Mūrūj*, §§ 1912, 1914, and passim; 'Abd al-Ḥamīd al-Kātib, 'Risālat 'Abd al-Ḥamīd al-Kātib Fī naṣīḥat walī al-'ahd', in *Rasā'il al-būlaghā'*, ed. Mūḥammad Kurd 'Alī, 4th ed., Cairo, 1954, p. 173. For citations indicating the constancy of these motifs throughout the histories of Islam (Umayyad, Abbasid, Andalusian Umayyad, and others) see Emile Tyan, *Institutions du droit public Musulman, tome premier: Le Califat*, Paris, 1954, pp. 440 ff; Patricia Crone and Martin Hinds, *God's Caliph. Religious Authority in the First Centuries of Islam*, Cambridge, 1986, pp. 6 ff. Cf. Morony, *Iraq after the Muslim Conquest*, pp. 33–5.

50 Mas'ūdī, *Mūrūj*, § 1914.

51 Tyan, *Le Califat*, passim.

52 Crone and Hinds, *God's Caliph*, passim.

53 Bernard Lewis, *The Political Language of Islam*, Chicago, 1988, pp. 45–6.

54 H. Ringgren, 'Some Religious Aspects of the Caliphate', in *Sacral Kingship* (Supplement to *Numen*, IV) , Leiden, 1959, p. 738.

55 For instance, *Alf layla wa layla*, Būlāq ed., nights 18, 435, and passim.

56 For instance, Hilāl as-Ṣābī, *Rūsūm dār al-khilāfa*, ed. M. ʿAwwād, Baghdad, 1964, pp. 4, 5.

57 Qalqashandī, *Khilāfa*, vol. 2, pp. 325–5.

58 For instance, ibid., 262–4.

59 Ibid., vol. 1, pp. 8–9; and cf. William Montgomery Watt, 'God's Caliph. Qur'ānic Interpretations and Umayyad Claims', in *Iran and Islam. In Memory of the Late Vladimir Minorsky*, ed. E. Bosworth, Edinburgh, 1971, pp. 568, 571.

60 Illustration and description in *al-Maskūkāt al-Islāmiyya. Majmūʿa mūkhtāra min ṣadr al-Islām ḥattā al-ʿahd al-ʿūthmānī* , Beirut, n.d., p. 16.

61 Paris, Bibliothèque Nationale, Cabinet des médailles, inv. L 256.

62 *al-Maskūkāt al-islāmiyya*, pp. 18, 24, 26, 38, 40; P. Grierson, 'The Monetary Reforms of ʿAbd al-Malik', in *Journal of the Social and Economic History of the Orient*, 3(1960), pp. 242, 245–6.

63 'Risāla', and see Iḥsān ʿAbbās, *ʿAbd al-Ḥamīd b. Yaḥyā al-Kātib*, Amman, 1988.

64 For instance Akhṭal, *Dīwān*, poems 2, 7, 19, 21 and passim.

65 Muḥammad Ismāʿīl as-Ṣāwī, *Sharḥ dīwān Jarīr*, Cairo, AH 1354, p. 275.

66 The reference here is to the early Abbasid al-Hādī (785–6): Ṭabarī quoted in Tyan, *Le Califat*, p. 446 n.

67 Ibid., p. 442 n.

68 Crone and Hinds, *God's Caliph*, pp. 27–8.

69 S. Marmon, *Eunuchs and Sacred Boundaries in Islamic Society*, New York, 1995, pp. 31–4, 52–3.

70 at-Ṭūrṭūshī, *Sirāj al-mūlūk*, ed. Jaʿfar al-Bayyātī, London, 1988, p. 148.

71 ʿAbd al-Ḥamīd al-Kātib, 'Risāla', p. 179.

72 *ʿAhd Ardashīr*, ed. Iḥsān Abbās, Beirut, 1967, 'Aqwāl mutafarriqa', p. 16, and cf. Morony, *Iraq after the Muslim Conquest*, pp. 34–5.

73 For instance, Akhṭal, *Dīwān*, poem 24; Sāwī, *Dīwān Jarīr*, pp. 16–17, 274.

74 Ringgren, ' Some Religious Aspects of the Caliphate', p. 740.

75 *Fragmenta historicorum arabicorum*, ed. M. J. de Goeje, Leiden 1869–71, vol. 3, p. 101.

76 Masʿūdī, *Mūrūj*, § 2397.

77 S. Sperl, 'Islamic Kingship and Arabic Panegyric Poetry in the early 9th Century', in *Journal of Arabic Literature*, 8(1977), pp. 20–35, passim.

Chapter 5

1 Some of these questions are raised in J. Sourdel-Thomine, 'L'Expression symbolique de l'autorité dans l'art islamique', in *La notion de l'autorité au môyen-age – Islam, Byzance, Occident*, Paris, 1982, pp. 273–86. I am not in accord with all the views expressed in this article.

2 Masʿūdī, *Mūrūj*, §§ 1836, 2288.

3 Manzalaoui, 'The Pseudo-Aristotelian *Kitāb Sirr al-Asrār*' pp. 165, 170 ff.

4 Abdel Hakim H. A. M. Dawood, 'A Comparative Study of Arabic and Persian Mirrors of Princes from the Second to the Sixth Century AH', unpub. PhD thesis, University of London, 1965, ch. IV; Albert Dietrich-Heidelberg, 'Das politische Testament des zweiten ʿAbbasiden-kalifen al-Mansūr', in *Der Islam*, xxx(1952), pp. 133 ff. The genre was to persist, albeit faintly, well into the Ḥafṣid dynasty in North Africa in the 14th century: Brockelman, *GAL*, vol. 2, p. 254. The Zayyānid king of Tlemcen, Abū Ḥammū Yūsuf (d 1388), composed an entire *Fürstenspiegel* in the guise of a Testament to his son: *Wāsīṭat as-sūlūk fī sīyāsat al-mūlūk*, Tunis AH 1279 [1862]. The genre was to persist into Ottoman times.

5 Numerous examples in Qalqashandī, *Khīlāfa*, vols 2 and 3, passim.

6 For instance, Māwardī, *Kitāb naṣīḥat al-mūlūk*, ed. Muḥammad Jāsim al-Ḥaḍithī, Baghdad, 1986, pp. 381–3, for a typical statement well into the Muslim Middle ages.

7 Aḥmad b. Yūsuf, 'Kitāb al-ʿuhūd al-yūnāniyya al-mustakhraja min rumūz as-siyāsa li-Aflāṭun wa mā inḍāfa ilaihi', in *al-Uṣūl al-yūnānīyya līl-naẓarīyyāt as-sīyāsīyya fī'l-Islām*, ed. ʿAbd al-Raḥmān Badawī, Cairo, 1954, p. 3.

8 Morony, *Iraq after the Muslim Conquest*, p. 27.

9 Iḥsān Abbās, *Malāmīḥ yūnānīyya fī'l-adab al-ʿArabī*, Beirut, 1977, pp. 99–109.

10 Editor's Introduction to *ʿAhd Ardashīr*, p. 34.

11 Manzalaoui, 'The Pseudo-Aristotelian *Sirr al-Asrār*', p. 206, attributes this reference to a possible Babylonian textual origin describing the campaign by Antiochus III against Egypt.

12 'Kitāb as-siyāsa fī tadbīr ar-riyāsa al-maʿrūf bi Sirr al-asrār alladhī allafahu al-faylasūf al-fāḍil Aristạṭālīs li-tilmīdhihi al-malik al-muʿaẓẓam al-Iskandar bin Filibis al-maʿrūf bi dhi'l-qarnayn', in *al-Uṣūl al-yūnānīyya*, ed. Badawī, pp. 140–5, 147, 150, 154, 152–5, 159–64.

13 Gustav Richter, *Studien zur Geschichte der älteren arabischen Fürstenspiegel*, Leipzig, 1931, pp. 93–5.

14 Miskawayh, *al-Ḥikma al-khālīda*, ed. ʿAbd al-Raḥmān Badawī, Cairo, 1952, Editor's introduction, pp. 32–3.

15 See for instance, Abū Ḥayyān at-Tawḥīdī, *al-Baṣā'īr wa'dh-dhakhā'īr*, ed. W. al-Qāḍī, Beirut, 1988, vol. 8, §§ 228, 553.

16 Aḥmad b. Yūsuf, 'al-ʿUhūd al-Yūnānīyya', pp. 31, 32, and passim.

17 *Letter to Tansar*, tr. Mary Boyce, Rome 1968, Introduction, pp. 16–22.

18 See Jan Rypka et al., *History of Iranian Literature*, ed. Karl Jahn, Dordrecht, 1968 , pp. 44–5.

19 Richter, *Fürstenspiegel*, pp. 29–30.

20 Manzalaoui, 'The Pseudo-Aristotelian *Sirr al-Asrār*', pp. 159–83.

21 Zaehner, *Zoroastrianism*, p. 286, and cf. Richter, *Fürstenspiegel*, pp.

102–3.

22 Aziz Al-Azmeh, *Arabic Thought and Islamic Societies*, London, 1986, pp. 44–5 n 65.

23 For instance, Richter, *Fürstenspiegel*, pp. 97–9.

24 ʿAbbās, *Malāmīḥ Yūnānīyya*, pp. 140 ff.

25 Ibid., 65–75; Richter, *Fürstenspiegel*, pp. 29–30.

26 Miskawayh, *Ḥīkma*, pp. 5–6.

27 Al-Azmeh, *Arabic Thought*, pp. 159–60; Jean Jolivet, 'L'Idée de la sagesse et sa fonction dans la philosophie des 4è et 5è siècles', in *Arab Sciences and Philosophy*, 1(1991), 53 ff.

28 D. Chwolsohn, *Die Ssabier und der Ssabismus*, St. Petersburg, 1856, vol. 1, p. 643.

29 ʿAbbās, *Malāmīḥ yūnānīyya*, pp. 57 and passim.

30 al-Mubashshir b. Fātik, *Mūkhtār al-ḥikam wa maḥāsīn al-kalim*, ed. ʿA. Badawī, 1980, p. 10.

31 This subject is still in its infancy, but see A. Noth, *Quellenkritische Studien zur Themen, Formen, und Tendenzen frühislamischer Geschichtsüberlieferung*, Bonn, 1973.

32 See for instance Masʿūdī, *Kitāb at-tanbīh wa'l-īshrāf*, ed. M. J. de Goeje, Leiden, 1894, p. 196; Yaʿqūbī, *Tārīkh*, Beirut, 1960, vol. 1, p. 159.

33 See particularly the statement of Miskawayh, *Ḥikma*, pp. 5–6, 375–6.

34 Ibn al-Muqaffaʿ, *Durra*, pp. 17–18.

35 A. Al-Azmeh, *Ibn Khaldūn. An Essay in Reinterpretation*, London, 1982, ch. 1, passim.

36 Idem., *Arabic Thought and Islamic Societies*, pp. 106 ff.

37 Azīz al-Azma, 'As-Siyāsa wa'l lā-siyāsa fi'l fikr al-ʿarabī', in idem., *al-Tūrāth bayn as-sūlṭān wa't-tārīkh*, Beirut-Casablanca, 1990, pp. 42–3.

38 For instance: Ibn Ṭabāṭabā, *al-Fakhrī fi'l-ādāb as-sūlṭānīyya wa'd-duwal al-islāmīyya*, Cairo, 1962, p. 14.

39 Al-Azmeh, *Ibn Khaldūn*, pp. 48 ff.

40 *Mūkhtār al-ḥikam wa maḥāsin al-kalim*, ed. ʿAbd al-Raḥmān Badawī, 2nd ed., Beirut, 1980.

41 *Kalīla wa Dīmna*, ed. Louis Shaikhū, 11th ed., Beirut, 1973, pp. 19, 21, 59.

42 Abū Hilāl as-Ṣābī, *Rūsūm Dār al-Khilāfa*, ed. M. ʿAwwād, Baghdad, 1964, pp. 46–8.

43 Ibn Rushd, *Talkhīṣ al-Khaṭāba*, ed. M. S. Sālim, Cairo, 1967, pp. 453–4, 622, and idem., *Talkhīṣ Kitāb Arīṣṭūṭālīṣ fi'sh-Shiʿr*, ed. M. S. Sālim, Cairo, pp. 101, 154 . The affinity between Ibn Rushd's view of the social rhetoric of Homer has a clear affinity with the notion of modern scholarship that the Greek epics were an Homeric encyclopedia for ancient Greek heroic *Bildung*: Havelock, *Preface to Plato*, passim.

44 For instance: *Kitāb alf-layla wa layla*, ed. M. Mahdi, Leiden, 1984, pp. 11 ff., and cf. F. Ghazoul, 'Poetic Logic in the Panchatantra and the

Arabian Nights', in *Arab Studies Quarterly*, 5 (1983), pp. 14–20.

45 For instance, Abū Ḥammū, *Wāsiṭat as-sulūk fī siyāsat al-mulūk*, Tunis, AH 1279, pp. 111 ff.

46 'Abbās, *Malāmiḥ Yūnāniyya*, p. 77; Richter, *Fürstenspiegel*, pp. 33–5.

47 *Ḥikāyat al-asad wa'l-ghawwāṣ* , ed. Riḍwān as-Sayyid, Beirut, 1978, p. 39.

48 Jāḥiẓ, *Tāj*, Editor's Introduction, p. 69.

49 *'Ahd Ardashīr*, Editor's Introduction, pp. 34–8, The Appendix to this edition contains 55 other sayings attributed to the Persian king

50 'Abbās, *Malāmiḥ Yūnāniyya*, pp. 126–7, 133, 149 ff, 156 ff, 165 ff; idem., *Tārīkh an-naqd al-adabī 'ind al-'Arab*, Beirut, 1971, pp. 243–50.

51 C. Bremond, J. Le Goff, and J.-C. Schmitt, *L'Exemplum*, Turnhout (Belgium), 1982, pp. 51–2; P. von Moos, *Geschichte als Topik. Das rhetorische Exemplum von der Antique zur Neuzeit und die historiae im 'Policraticus' Johanns von Salisbury*, Hildesheim, Zürich, New York, 1996.

52 M. R. Menocal, *The Arabic Role in Medieval Literary History*, Philadelphia, 1987, pp. 35–6, 49–50, and passim.

53 Ibn al-Khaṭīb, *al-Ishāra ilā adab al-wizāra, talīhā maqāmat as-siyāsa*, ed. M. K. Shabāna, Rabat, [1980–81] , and see A. Al-Azmeh, 'Mortal Enemies, Invisible Neighbours: Northerners in Andalusi Eyes', in *The Legacy of Muslim Spain*, ed. S. Khadra Jayyusi, Leiden, 1992, p. 263 and passim.

54 Abbās, *Malāmiḥ Yūnāniyya*, p. 125.

55 Ibn al-Farrā', *Kitāb rusul al-mulūk wa man yaṣluḥ lil-risāla was-sifāra*, ed. Ṣalāh ad-Dīn al-Munajjid, Beirut, 1972, passim. This person should not be confused with his famous Baghdadi Ḥanbali namesake. His biography is entirely obscure, except for the century during which he lived and that he came from either Mosul or Cordoba.

56 Māwardī, *Naṣīḥat al-mulūk*, passim.

57 al-Ghazālī, *al-Tibr al-masbūk fī naṣīḥat al-mulūk*, ed. Muḥammad Aḥmad Damaj, Beirut, 1987, passim. There are doubts regarding the attribution of this whole work to Ghazālī. See P. Crone 'Did al-Ghazālī write a Mirror for Princes? On the authorship of Naṣīḥat al-Mulūk' in *Jerusalem Studies in Arabic and Islam*, 10 (1987) pp. 167–191.

58 al-Murādi, *Kitāb al-ishāra ilā adab al-imāra*, ed. Riḍwān as-Sayyid, Beirut, 1981, Editor's Introduction, pp. 20–1, 31–2, and pp. 145–6 and passim.

59 Tha'ālibī, *Tuḥfat al-wuzarā'*, ed. Ḥabīb 'Alī al-Rāwī and Ibtisām Marhūn as-Ṣaffār, Baghdad, 1977, Introduction, pp. 11–16.

60 Muḥammad Bāqir Najm-i Sānī, *Advice on the Art of Governance (Maw'izah-i Jahāngīrī)*, tr. Sajida Sultana Alvi, Albany, 1989, Introduction, pp. 2–3, 10–12, 30.

61 *'Uyūn al-akhbār*, 4 vols, Cairo, 1925–30.

62 *al-'Iqd al-farīd*, ed. Mufīd Muḥammad Qumayḥa, 9 vols, Beirut, 1983.

63 Ibid., vol. 1, pp. 33–5.

64 *Kitāb al-akhlāq wa's-siyar*, ed. Eva Riad, Uppsala, 1980, Editor's

Introduction, p. 36.

65 *The Nasirean Ethics*, tr. G. M. Wickens, London, 1964.

66 *The Book of Government or Rules for Kings*, tr. Hubert Darke, London, 1978.

67 Ṭūsī, *The Nasirean Ethics*, p. 28; Ibn Sīnā, 'Fī aqsām al-'ulūm al-'aqliyya', in idem., *Tis' rasā'il*, Constantinople, AH 1298, pp. 73–4; al-Fārābī, *Iḥṣā' al-'ulūm*, ed. 'Uthmān Amīn, Cairo, 1968, p. 124; Miskawayh, *Tahdhīb*, p. 132.

68 *Averroes' Commentary on Plato's Republic*, tr.. E. I. J. Rosenthal, Cambridge, 1966, p. 112.

69 Ibn al-Azraq, *Badā'i' as-silk fī ṭabā'i' al-mulk*, ed. Muḥammad b. 'Abd al-Karīm, Tunis and Libya, 1977, vols 1 and 2, passim.

70 Māwardī, *Naṣīḥa*; and idem., *Tashīl an-naẓar wa ta'jīl aẓ-ẓafar fī akhlāq al-malik wa siyāsat al-mulk*, ed. Riḍwān as-Sayyid, Beirut, 1987.

71 Ibn Ẓafar, *Silwān al-muṭā' fī 'udwān al-atbā'* , ed. Aḥmad 'Abd al-Majīd Ḥuraydī, [Cairo] 1978.

72 For instance, Murādī, *Ishāra*, pp. 46 ff., 115 ff. 165 f.

73 Abū 'Abd Allāh Muḥammad b. 'Alī al-Qal'ī, *Tahdhīb ar-riyāsa wa tartīb as-siyāsa*, ed. I. Y. M. 'Ijjū, Zarqa, 1985.

74 Suhrawardī, *Taḥrīr al-aḥkām fī tadbīr ahl al-Islām*, MS Istanbul, Agia Sophia-Sultan Mahmūd, No. 2852, fol. 56 ff.

75 Manzalaoui, 'The Pseudo-Aristotelian "*Kitāb Sirr al-Asrār*", p. 160.

76 For instance, Ṭurṭūshī, *Sirāj*, ch. 1 and 2, and Māwardī, *Naṣīḥa*, pp. 63–8, 147–93, 223–6.

77 Ghazālī, *Maqāmāt al-'ulamā' bayn ayādī al-khūlafā' wa'l-'umarā'*, ed. Muḥammad Jāsim al-Ḥadīthī, Baghdad, 1988.

78 *al-Miṣbāḥ al-muḍī' fī khilāfat al-Mustaḍī'*, ed. Nājia 'Abd Allāh Ibrāhīm, Baghdad, 1976–77, vol. 1, p. 246.

79 For instance, Ibn al-Jawzī, *al-Mudhīsh*, ed. Marwān Qabbānī, Beirut, 1981.

80 Bremond et al., *L'Exemplum*, passim.

81 Henri Laoust, *La politique de Ǧazālī*, Paris, 1970, p. 83.

82 Ghazālī, *at-Tibr al-masbūk*, passim.

83 Ḥajjī Khalīfa, *Kashf az-ẓunūn 'an asāmī al-kutub wa'l-funūn*, ed. S. Yaltakaya and R. Bilge, Istanbul, 1942, vol. 1, p. 19.

84 Juwaynī, *Ghiyāth al-'umam fī't-tiyāth az-ẓulam*, ed. 'Abd al-'Aẓīm Dīb, [Cairo] , AH 1401[1980 f].

85 Al-Azmeh, *Arabic Thought and Islamic Societies*, pp. 211–28.

86 Ibn al-Muqaffa', in *Rasā'il al-bulaghā'*, ed. Kurd 'Alī, pp. 126–7.

87 See in particular Fahmī Jad'ān, *al-Miḥna. Jadalīyyat ad-dīnī wa's-siyāsī fī'l-Islām*, Amman, 1989, pp. 108, 153, 275–90, and passim; Dominique Sourdel, 'La politique religieuse du calife 'abbaside al-Ma'mūn', in *Revue des Etudes Islamiques*, 30(1962), pp. 27–48.

88 See particularly Ibn al-Jawzī, *al-Muntaẓam fī tārīkh al-mūlūk wa'l-umam*, ed. Krenkow, Hyderabad AH 1357–8, vol. 7, pp. 161, 268, 287–9, vol. 8,

pp. 109–111 (including text of the Qādirī creed). See George Makdisi, *Ibn 'Aqīl et la résurgence de l'Islam sunnite au XIe siècle*, Damascus, 1963, pp. 299–312.

89 Ibn Abī Ya'lā, *Ṭabaqāt al-Ḥanābila*, ed. Muḥammad Ḥāmid al-Fiqī, Cairo, 1952, vol. 2, p. 197, and see also p. 205.

90 Henri Laoust, 'La pensée et l'action politiques d'al-Māwardī (364/450–974/1058), in *Revue d'Etudes Islamiques*, xxxvi/1(1968), pp. 11–92 – the author talks of Sunnism 'resurgent'.

91 On this corpus, see Ibrāhīm Fawzī, *Tadwīn as-sunna*, London, 1994.

92 Aziz Al-Azmeh, 'Muslim Legal Theory and the Appropriation of Reality', in idem. (ed.), *Islamic Law: Social and Historical Contexts*, London, 1988, pp. 250–65.

93 For instance: Ibn Abī Ya'lā, *Ṭabaqāt*, vol. 1, pp. 18, 169, 81–2; Ibn Rajab, *al-Dhayl 'alā ṭabaqāt al-Ḥanābila*, ed. Muḥammad Ḥāmid al-Fiqī, Cairo, 1952, vol. 2, pp. 138, 164; Ibn al-Jawzī, *Manāqib al-Imām Aḥmad Ibn Ḥanbal*, Beirut, 1973, pp. 143, 168, 187, 276, 295–7, 483, 513.

94 *Ghiyāth*, §§ 540–2.

95 *al-Durra al-fākhira fī kashf 'ulūm al-ākhira*, ed. Lucien Gautier as *La perle précieuse* (1878), Amsterdam, 1974, p. 107.

96 Ibn Jamā'a, *Taḥrīr al-aḥkām fī tadbīr ahl al-Islām*, ed. H. Kofler, in *Islamica*, 6(1934), p. 360.

97 'dīnan wa qurban': Ibn Taymiyya, *as-Sīyāsa ash-shar'īyya fī iṣlāḥ ar-rā'ī wa'r-ra'iyya*, Beirut, 1966, p. 77.

98 Henri Laoust, *Essai sur les doctrines sociales et politiques de Taḳī ad-Dīn Aḥmad B. Taymīya*, Cairo, 1939, pp. 186–95, 202.

99 For instance: Juwaynī, *Ghiyāth*, § 560; al-Muṭahhar al-Ḥillī, *Tabṣirat al-mūta'allimīn fī aḥkām ad-dīn*, ed. Aḥmad al-Ḥusaynī and Hādī al-Yūsufī, Beirut, 1984, p. 115.

100 See Norman Calder, 'Friday Prayer and the Juristic Theory of Government: Sarakhsī, Shīrāzī, Māwardī', in *Bulletin of the School of Oriental and African Studies*, 49(1986), pp. 35–47.

101 For instance, Ibn Taymiyya, *As-Siyāsa ash-shar'īyya*, Beirut, 1966, p. 77.

102 Ibn al-Muqaffa', text in *Rasā'il al-bulaghā'*, ed. Kurd 'Alī, p. 56; Māwardī, *Naṣīḥa*, pp. 527–8; Wilferd Madelung, 'A Treatise of the Sharīf al-Murtaḍā on the Legality of Working for the Government', in *Bulletin of the School of Oriental and African Studies*, 43(1980), Arabic text, pp. 22–4, and pp. 30–1; Ibn 'Abd al-Barr, *Jāmi' bayān al-'ilm wa faḍlih wa mā yanbaghī fī riwāyatihī wa ḥamlih*, Cairo, AH 1346, vol. 1, pp. 170 ff, 179, 185. Creeds: for instance, Ibn Baṭṭa, *Kitāb ash-shūrūḥ wa'l-ibāna 'alā ūṣūl as-sunna wa'd-diyāna*, Arabic text in Henri Laoust, *La profession de foi d'Ibn Baṭṭa*, Damascus, 1958, pp. 67–8; Hans Daiber, 'The Creed ('*aqīda*) of the Ḥanbalite Ibn Qudāma al-Maqdisī. A Newly Discovered Text', in *Studia Arabica et Islamica. Festschrift for Iḥsān 'Abbās*, ed. Wadad al-Qadi, Beirut, 1981, Arabic text, p. 111.

103 For instance: *'Ahd Ardashīr*, § 4; Suhrawardī, *Taḥrīr al-aḥkām*, fol. 29;

'Sirr al-asrār', in *al-Uṣūl al-Yūnānīyya*, ed. Badawī, p. 77.

104 For instance, Riḍwān as-Sayyid, 'al-Khilāf al-fiqhī bayn tamāyuzāt al-manāhij wa'l-fikr as-siyāsi min khilāl ((*Tuḥfat at-Turk*)) lil Ṭarsūsī', in *Dīrāsāt 'Arabīyya*, 29/5–6(1993), p. 44.

105 This is the overall schematic and nominal plan of Tilman Nagel's *Staat und Glaubensgemeinschaft im Islam*, Zurich and Munich, 1981, vol. 1.

106 Ibn Abī Ṭāhir Ṭayfūr, *Kitāb Baghdād - al-jūz' as-sādis*, ed. H. Keller, Leipzig, 1908, pp. 36–7, 52. On this epistle's reputation and readership, see ibid., p. 54.

107 *Sīyāsa* (Beirut ed.), pp. 4–5. The Koranic text (an-Nisā', 58–9) reads as follows: 'God doth command you to render back your Trusts to those to whom they are due; and when ye judge between man and man, that ye judge with justice … O ye who believe! Obey God, and obey the Apostle, and those charged with authority among you. If ye differ in anything among yourselves, refer to God and His Apostle'.

108 Ibn al-Ḥaddād, *al-Jawhar an-nafīṣ fī siyāsat ar-ra'īs*, ed. Riḍwān as-Sayyid, Beirut, 1983.

109 *Baḥr al-favā'id*, pp. xi–xvi.

110 Qal'ī, *Tahdhīb ar-riyāsa*, passim.

111 Ṭurṭūshī, *Sirāj*, pp. 165 ff, 196 ff, 329 ff.

112 Māwardī, *Naṣīḥa*, pp. 197–238.

113 Laoust, *La politique de Ġazālī*, pp. 316 and passim.

114 Ghazālī, *Tibr*, pp. 109–110, 139–40.

115 *Siyāsa* (Beirut ed.), pp. 138–40.

116 *Baḥr al-Fava'īd*, ch. 4.

117 Ibn Riḍwān, *as-Shuhub al-lāmī'a fī's-siyāsa an-nāfi'a*, ed. 'Alī Sāmī al-Nashshār, Casablanca, 1984, pp. 56 ff.

118 Ibid., pp. 74–5.

119 Ibn Khaldūn, *Prolégomènes*, vol. 2, p. 3.

120 *Tibr*, pp. 172–5, and see the lucid account of Miskawayh, in Miskawayh and Tawḥīdī, *al-Hawāmil wa'sh-shawāmil*, ed. Aḥmad Amīn and Sayyid Aḥmad Ṣaqr, Cairo, 1951, p. 192.

121 For instance: Ibn al-Muqaffa', text in *Rasā'īl al-Bulaghā'*, ed. Kurd 'Alī, p. 49; Ibn Khaldūn, *Prolégomènes*, vol. 1, p. 344; *Alf Layla wa layla*, (Būlāq ed.), vol. 1, pp. 173–4; and see the particular inflection within the repertoire by Abū Ḥammū, *Wasīṭa*, pp. 23 ff.

122 For instance: Fārābī, *Mabādī' 'ārā' ahl al-madīna al-fāḍila* ed. R. Walzer, Oxford, 1985, , pp. 254–8 and passim; 'Āmirī, *Sa'āda*, pp. 265–8 and passim; *The Nasirean Ethics*, pp. 211–12.

123 For instance, Māwardī, *al-Aḥkām as-sulṭānīyya*, bk I.

124 For instance, Juwaynī, *Ghiyāth*, pp. 21 ff.

125 Taftāzānī, *Sharḥ al-maqāṣid*, ed. S. M. b. 'Umar, Beirut, 1989, vol. 5, pp. 213, 232.

126 Āmidī, *Ghāyat al-marām fī 'ilm al-kalām*, ed. Ḥusayn Muḥammad 'Abd al-Laṭīf, Cairo, 1971, p. 363.

127 Ibid., pp. 232–320.

128 For instance, Abū Ya'lā b. al-Farrā, *Kitāb al-Mu'tamad fī uṣūl ad-dīn*, ed. W. Z. Ḥaddād, §§ 431–64.

129 One exception which refuted 'Abbasid and all other claims to prophetic designation was Juwaynī, in *Ghiyāth*, §§ 29 ff. There is in this work an implicitly anti-Abbasid stance (§ 139) which could be pursued in terms of the political context of the time.

130 Cf. Al-Azmeh, *Arabic Thought and Islamic Societies*, pp. 211 ff.

131 Abū Ya'lā b. al-Farrā, *al-Aḥkām as-sulṭāniyya*, ed. Muḥammad Ḥamid al-Fiqī, 2nd ed., Cairo, 1966, p. 3.

132 Ghazālī, *al-Munqidh min ad-ḍalāl wa'l mūṣil ilā dhi'l-'izzah wa'l-jalāl*, ed. Jamīl Ṣalībā and Muḥammad Kāmil 'Ayyād, Beirut, 1967, pp. 85–6.

133 Laoust, *Ibn Taimīya*, pp. xiii, xxvii–xxix.

134 Ibn Taymiyya, *Siyāsa* (Beirut ed.), p. 3.

135 Ibn al-Jawzī, *Miṣbāḥ*, vol. 1, pp. 298–9.

136 Ibn al-Jawzī, *Talbīs Iblīs*, Cairo, AH 1368, p. 141.

137 Ibn Qayyim al-Jawzīyya, *al-Ṭuruq al-ḥikmīyya fi's-siyāsa ash-shar'īyya*, ed. Aḥmad 'Abd al-Ḥalīm al-'Askarī, Cairo, 1961, pp. 4–5, 15 ff; idem., *I'lām al-muwaqqi'īn 'an Rabb al-'ālamīn*, ed. Ṭāhā 'Abd al-Ra'ūf Sa'd, Beirut, n.d., vol. 4, pp. 375 and passim, and cf. Ṭurṭūshī, *Sirāj*, pp. 170–1.

138 Ibn Taymiyya, *Minhāj as-sunna an-nabawīyya fi naqd kalām ash-Shī'a wa'l-qadarīyya*, Cairo AH 1322, vol. 1, p. 3.

139 Al-Azmeh, 'Chronophagous Discourse', pp. 186 ff.

140 Ibn Jamā'a, *Taḥrīr*, p. 353.

141 See Subkī, *Mu'īd an-ni'am wa mubīd an-niqam*, ed. D. W. Myhrman, London 1908, p. 27.

142 Laoust, *Politique de Ğazālī*, pp. 88, 146; idem., 'Māwardī', p. 26.

143 For instance, Ṭurṭūshī, *Sirāj*, pp. 48–50; Māwardī, *Tashīl*, pp. 206, 207 n.1–2.

144 For instance, Ibn Riḍwān, *Shuhub*, pp. 415–22.

145 For instance: 'Hāğī Chalfa's Düstür'l-'amel. Ein Beitrag zur osmanischen Finanzgeschichte', tr. by W. W. A. Behrnauer, in *Zeitschrift der deutschen morgenländischen Gesellschaft*, xi(1857), pp. 118 ff.

146 Al-Azmeh, *Ibn Khaldūn: An Essay*, pp. 28–31, 39, and passim.

147 Idem., *al-Kitāba at-tārīkhīyya*, Beirut 1983, pp. 73 ff., 77 ff.

Chapter 6

1 'Abd al-Qāhir al-Baghdādī, *Kitāb uṣūl ad-dīn*, Istanbul, 1928, p. 271.

2 For instance: Ibn Khaldūn, *Prolégomènes*, vol. 1, p. 72-3, for a Sunnī argument, and Abū Ḥātim as-Sijistānī , *Kitāb ithbāt an-nubuwwāt*, ed. 'Arif Tāmir, Beirut, 1966, p. 173, for a Shī'i statement.

3 Ibn Rushd, *Talkhīṣ al-Khaṭāba*, pp. 213, 229 ff.

4 For instance: Māturīdī, *Kitāb at-tawḥīd*, ed. Fatḥ Allāh Khulayf, Beirut, 1970, pp. 182–3 and Fakhr ad-Dīn ar-Rāzī, *al-Mabāḥith al-mashriqiyya*,

Tehran, 1966 (photomechanical reproduction of the Hyderabad AH 1343 edition), vol. 2, p. 523.

5 Al-Azmeh, *Arabic Thought*, pp. 37–40 and ch. 1, passim.

6 For a classic statement very often referred to in modern writing, see Ibn Khaldūn, *Prolégomènes*, vol. 1, pp. 71–2.

7 Rāzī, *Mabāḥith*, vol. 2, pp. 409–10.

8 Ibn Sīnā, 'Athar majhūl li Ibn Sīnā [Kitāb at-tadbīr]', ed. Luwīs Ma'lūf, in *Al-Mashriq*, 9 (1906), pp. 971–3, very much amplified by Ṭūsī in *The Nasirean Ethics*, pp. 153 ff.

9 al-'Āmirī, *Sa'āda*, pp. 186–7.

10 Fārābī, *Al-Farabi on the Perfect State. Abū Nasr al-Fārābī's Mabādi' 'ārā' ahl al-madīna al-fāḍila*, ed. R. Walzer, Oxford, 1985, p. 228; Miskawayh, *Tahdhīb al-akhlāq*, ed. C. Zurayq, Beirut, 1966, pp. 14–15, 167–8.

11 *The Nasirean Ethics*, pp. 189, 212.

12 For example, respectively, Qalqashandī, *Khilāfa* vol. 2, p. 297, *Alf layla wa layla* (Būlāq ed.), vol. 1, p. 319, and al-Jāḥiz, *Rasā'il*, ed. 'Abd as-Salām Hārūn, Cairo, 1964, vol. 3, pp. 149–50.

13 For example, Ṭurṭūshī, *Sirāj*, pp. 145, 156–7, and 'Amirī, *Sa'āda*, p. 188.

14 Al-Azmeh, *Ibn Khaldūn*, p. 134; idem, 'Barbarians in Arab Eyes', in *Past and Present*, 134(1992), pp. 3 ff.

15 For instance, Mas'ūdī, *Murūj*, §§ 531–2.

16 For instance, Ya'qūbī, *Tārīkh*, Beirut, 1960, vol. 1, pp. 46–9.

17 One exception is Niẓām al-Mulk, *The Book of Government or Rules for Kings*, tr. Hubert Drake, London, 1978, p. 9.

18 Māwardī, *Tashīl*, p. 97.

19 Ibn Khaldūn, *Prolégomènes*, vol. 1, pp. 71–2.

20 Tūsī, *The Nasirean Ethics*, pp. 196, 200 ff.; *Averroes' Commentary on Plato's Republic*, pp. 113–4.

21 For instance, Miskawayh, *Tahdhīb al-akhlāq*, pp. 14–15.

22 *Madīna*, p. 244.

23 Ibn Sīnā, *as-Shifā': al-Ilāhiyyāt (2)*, ed. M. Y. Mūsā et al., Cairo, 1960, pp. 441–3.

24 al-Ghazālī, *al-Iqtiṣād fi'l-i'tiqād*, ed. I. A. Çubukcu and H. Atay, Ankara, 1962, p. 10.

25 Ibn Sīnā, 'Athar majhūl', p. 969.

26 al-Ghazālī, *al-Maḥabba wa'l-uns wa'sh-shawq wa'r-riḍā*, Cairo, 1961, p. 86.

27 'Āmirī, *Sa'āda*, p. 187; Ibn Sīnā, 'Athar majhūl', p. 972.

28 Tha'ālibī, *Tuḥfat al-wuzarā'*, ed. H. 'A. Rāwī and I. M. Ṣaffār, Baghdad, 1977, pp. 45–7.

29 Zaehner, *Zoroastrianism*, p. 285.

30 For instance: Fārābī, *Madīna*, pp. 230–6.

31 Ibid., pp. 234, 236.

32 Miskawayh, *al-Hawāmil wa'sh-shawāmil*, ed. A. Amīn and A. Ṣaqr,

Cairo, 1951, pp. 347–8.

33 Arabic text in Franz Rosenthal, *A History of Muslim Historiography*, Leiden, 1968, p. 543.

34 For instance, 'Sirr al-asrār', in *al-Uṣūl al-yūnāniyya*, ed. 'A. Badawī, p. 132, Māwardī, *Naṣīḥat al-Mulūk*, ed. M. J. al-Ḥadīthī, Baghdad, 1986, p. 77, and Tha'ālibī, *Tuḥfat al-wuzarā'*, p. 58, quoting a saying attributed to a Sasanian king. The two analogies are sometimes combined , as for instance in *Ḥikāyat al-asad wa'l-ghawwāṣ*, ed. R. as-Sayyid, Beirut, 1978, p. 65.

35 al-Qāḍī al-Nu'mān, *Asās at-ta'wīl*, ed. 'A. Tāmir, Beirut, 1960, pp. 43–4.

36 *Prolégomènes*, vol. 2, pp. 264–5 and passim, and see Al-Azmeh, *Ibn Khaldūn*, pp. 33 ff., 76 ff.

37 cf. Ibn Khaldūn, *Prolégomènes*, vol. 1, p. 340 and Abū Sulaymān as-Sijistānī quoted in Abū Ḥayyān at-Tawhīdī, *al-Imtā' wa'l-mu'ānasa*, ed. A. Amīn and A. Zayn, Cairo, 1953, vol. 3, p. 87.

38 For some eloquent characterisations of the common rabble, comparable in their overall sense with certain European writings of the 19th and 20th centuries (Gustave Le Bon being a good example), see for instance Jāḥiẓ, *Rasā'il*, vol. 4, pp. 36–8, 40–41 and passim, and Mas'ūdī, *Murūj*,§§ 1847–8 and passim.

39 On this see Muhammad Ḥayyān as-Sammān, *Khiṭāb al-junūn fi'th-thaqāfa al-'arabiyya*, London, 1993, pp. 93, 111, and passim.

40 cf. Waḍḍāḥ Sharāra, 'al-Malik/al-'āmma, at-ṭabī'a, al-mawt', in *Dirāsāt 'Arabiyya*, 16/12(1980), pp. 25–6; idem., 'al-Muqaddima, at-tārīkh, wa jasad as-sulṭān al-mumtali' ' in idem, *Hawla ba'd mushkilāt ad-dawla fi'th-thaqāfa wa'l-mujtama' al-'arabiyyayn*, Beirut, 1980, p. 33; Al-Azmeh, *Arabic Thought and Islamic Societies*, pp. 39–40.

41 *'Ahd Ardashīr*, ed. I. 'Abbās, Beirut, 1967, § 12, and cf. Tha'ālibī, *Tuḥfat al-wuzarā'*, p. 101 and Jāḥiẓ, *Rasā'il*, vol. 3, p. 151.

42 For instance, Tha'ālibī, *Tuḥfat al-wuzarā'*, p. 54; Qalqashandī, *Khilāfa*, vol. 1, p. 298 and al-Bīrūnī, *Al-Āthār al-bāqiya 'an al-qurūn al-khāliya*, ed. C. E. Sachau, Leipzig, 1923, p. 132.

43 For instance: Zamakhsharī, *al-Kashshāf 'an ḥaqā'iq at-tanzīl*, ed. W. Nassau Lees et al., Calcutta, 1856, ad loc.

44 For instance, Māturīdī, *Tawḥīd*, p. 20, and Ash'arī, *al-Luma' fir-radd 'alā ahl az-zīgh wa'l-bida'*, ed. R. J. McCarthy in *The Theology of Al-Ash'arī*, Beirut, 1953, pp. 20–1.

45 For instance: Ṭurṭūshī, *Sirāj*, p. 156 and Ibn Jamā'a, *Taḥrīr al-aḥkām fi tadbīr ahl al-Islām*, ed. H. Kofler, in *Islamica*, 6(1934), pp. 364–5.

46 *Tāj al-'aqā'id wa ma'din al-fawā'id*, ed. 'A. Tāmir, Beirut, 1967, p. 37.

47 Respectively: Miskawayh, *Tajārib al-umam*, ed. H. F. Amedroz, Cairo, 1914–16 and Oxford, 1920–21, vol. 3, pp. 39–40; Tha'ālibī, *Tuḥfat al-wuzarā'*, p. 53; Ibn Qayyim al-Jawziyya, *Rawḍat al-muḥibbīn wa nuzhat al-mushtāqīn*, rev. S. Yūsuf, Beirut, 1982, p. 231.

48 Abu'l-Ḥasan as-Suhrawardī, *Kitāb fīhi taḥrīr li-aḥkām fi's-siyāsa*, MS. Istanbul, Aya Sofia-Sultan Mahmud, No. 2852, fol. 20.

49 Miskawayh, *Risāla fī māhiyyat al-ʿadl*, ed. M. S. Khan, Leiden, 1964, pp. 12–13. For the wider bearings of this notion, axial in Islamic thought, see Al-Azmeh, *Arabic Thought and Islamic Societies*, pp. 3 ff.

50 For instance, respectively: ar-Rāghib al-Iṣbahānī, *Muḥāḍarāt al-udabā' wa muḥāwarāt al-bulaghā'*, ed. I. Zaydān, Beirut, n.d., p. 67; Ibn ʿAbd Rabbih, *al-ʿIqd al-farīd*, ed. M. M. Qumayḥa, Beirut, 1983, vol. 2, p. 8; Māwardī, *Naṣīḥa*, p. 45; Ibn Khaldūn, *Prolégomènes*, vol. 1, pp. 45, 266–7; Ghazālī, *at-Tibr al-masbūk fī naṣīḥat al-mulūk*, p. 197.

51 *ʿAhd Ardashīr*, § 3.

52 For instance, Ṭurṭūshī, *Sirāj*, p. 147.

53 For instance: Ibn ʿAbd Rabbih, *ʿIqd*, vol. 1, p. 9.

54 For instance, Ṭurṭūshī, *Sirāj*, pp. 162–3, and Yaḥyā b. ʿAdī, *Kitāb tahdhīb al-akhlāq*, ed. M.-T. Urvoy , Paris, 1991, p. 135.

55 Māwardī, *Tashīl*, pp. 135, 198.

56 For instance: Ibn ʿAbd Rabbih, *Dīwān*, ed. R. ad-Dāya, Beirut, 1979, p. 182; Sibṭ Ibn at-Taʿāwīdhī, *Dīwān*, ed. D. S. Margoliouth, Cairo, 1903, pp. 1, 3, and passim; Muhammad Bāqir Najm-i Sānī, *Advice on the Art of Governance*, tr. S. S. Alvi, Albany, 1989, p. 45.

57 For instance, *Sirr al-asrār*, p. 125.

58 Sperl, 'Islamic Kingship and Arabic Panegyric Poetry', pp. 27–31.

59 ʿAmirī, *Saʿāda*, p. 216.

60 See, for instance, Ibn al-Muqaffaʿ, text in *Rasā'il al-Bulaghā'*, ed. Kurd ʿAlī, pp. 120–21, Qalqashandī, *Khilāfa*, vol. 1, pp. 62–3, and Ṭurṭūshī, *Sirāj*, pp. 188–9, for classical statements. See also the widely circulated injunctions to unqualified obedience attributed to Aḥmad b. Ḥanbal, in Ibn al-Jawzī, *Manāqib al-Imām*, pp. 175–6.

61 The classical formulation, very widely quoted and adapted, is that of Ibn al-Muqaffaʿ, *Durra*, p. 29.

62 Jāḥiẓ, *Kitāb at-tāj fī akhlāq al-mulūk*, ed. Aḥmad Zakī, Cairo, 1914, pp. 2–3.

63 The composition and profile of the *khāṣṣa*, usually thought by no means exclusively defined as connection with the court, varied with time, place, and author. See, for instance, ʿAbd al-Ḥamīd al-Kātib, 'Risāla', p. 178, who limits the category to family members, Hilāl as-Ṣābī, *Rusūm dār al-khilāfa*, ed. M. ʿAwwād, Baghdad, 1964, p. 21, for a more complex picture, and Māwardī, *Naṣīḥa*, p., 297, who establishes categories of proximity and distance within the overall category of the *khāṣṣa*. See Maxime Rodinson, 'Histoire économique et histoire des classes sociales dans le Monde Musulman, in *Studies in the Economic History of the Middle East*, ed. M. A. Cook, London, 1970, p. 149.

64 Jāḥiẓ, *Tāj*, pp. 125–7. Cf. Sharāra, 'Al-Muqaddima', p. 41.

65 Ibn al-Muqaffaʿ, in *Rasā'il al-bulaghā'*, ed. Kurd ʿAlī, p. 58.

66 *Wāsiṭat as-Sulūk fī siyāsat al-mulūk*, Tunis AH 1279 [1862], p. 21.

67 Murādī, *al-Ishāra ilā adab al-imāra*, ed. R. as-Sayyid, Beirut, 1981, p. 77.

68 'Abd al-Ḥamīd al-Kātib, 'Risāla', in *Rasā'il al-bulaghā'*, ed. M. Kurd 'Alī, p. 193; Māwardī, *Tashīl*, p. 168; Tha'ālibī, *Tuḥfat al-wuzarā'*, p. 95.

69 'Abd al-Ḥamīd al-Kātib, 'Risāla', p. 184.

70 Tha'ālibī, *Wuzarā'*, p. 58.

71 For instance, Abū Hilāl al-'Askarī, *Al-Awā'il*, ed. A. al-Miṣrī and W. Qaṣṣāb, Damascus, 1975, vol. 1, p. 351.

72 For instance: Tha'ālibī, *Wuzarā'*, pp. 102–3.

73 Ibn 'Abd Rabbih, *'Iqd*, vol. 1, pp. 49–50.

74 Iṣbahānī, *Muḥāḍarāt*, p. 80.

75 *'Uyūn al-akhbār*, vol. 1, pp. 19 ff.

76 *Qawānīn al-wizāra wa siyāsat al-mulk*, ed. R. as-Sayyid, Beirut, 1979, pp. 165–89, and Ibn al-Muqaffa', in *Rasā'il al-bulaghā'*, ed. Kurd 'Alī, pp. 57–70. Cf. Ibn al-Khaṭīb, *Adab al-wizāra*, pp. 93 ff.

77 Aḥmad b. Yūsuf, *Al-'Uhūd al-yūnāniyya*, in *al-Uṣūl al-Yūnāniyya* ed. Badawī, pp. 44–5.

78 Jāḥiẓ, *Tāj*, pp. 167–72.

79 'Abd al-Ḥamīd al-Kātib, 'Risāla', p. 184.

80 For instance, Ibn al-Muqaffa', in *Rasā'il al-bulaghā'*, pp. 54 ff.

81 For instance, Jāḥiẓ, *Tāj*, pp. 61–6, 91–4.

82 *Ḥikāyat al-asad wa'l-ghawwāṣ*, pp. 115–6 and footnotes. Bizarre injustices and arbitrary behaviour were popularly and humurously attributed to Bahā' ad-Dīn Qarāqūsh, Saladin's governor of Acre and Tripolitania, (Ibn Khallikān, *Wafayāt al-a'yān*, ed. I. 'Abbās, Beirut, 1970, vol. 4, p. 92), who seems to have become the topos for such behaviour, and still remains proverbially so in the popular culture of many parts of the Arab World today.

83 Ibn Riḍwān, *Shuhub*, pp. 347–52.

84 This is a constant assertion: for example, *Kalīla wa Dimna*, ed. L. Shaykhū, Beirut, 1973, p. 18, and Ibn al-Jawzī, *Al-Miṣbāḥ al-muḍī' fī khilāfat al-Mustaḍī'*, ed. N. A. Ibrāhīm, Baghdad, 1976–7, vol. 1, p. 160.

85 Miskawayh, *Tahdhīb*, p. 203.

86 *Naṣīḥat al-mulūk*, pp. 147–287; *Sirāj al-mulūk*, pp. 169–305.

87 For instance, Ibn Sīnā, 'Athar majhūl', pp. 1037–8.

88 For instance: Māwardī, *Tashīl*, p. 104 and 'Abd al-Ḥamīd al-Kātib, 'Risāla', pp. 176–7.

89 Māwardī, *Tashīl*, p. 201.

90 *Ḥikāyat al-asad wa'l–ghawwāṣ*, pp. 42–3, and cf. Ṭurṭūshī, *Sirāj*, pp. 152–5.

91 *'Ahd Ardashīr*, §§ 9–10, 14.

92 at-Tawḥīdī, *al-Baṣā'ir wa'dh-dhakhā'ir*, vol. 9, § 475.

93 *Tahdhīb al-akhlāq*, pp. 113–5; idem., 'Risāla fī māhiyyat al-'adl', pp. 15–16, 18–20, and cf. 'Āmirī, *Sa'āda*, pp. 223–4.

94 For Persian formulations, see Zaehner, *Zoroastrianism*, pp. 285–7 ; for

literary elaboration, Ibn Qutayba, *'Uyūn al-akhbār*, vol. 1, pp. 325 ff.

95 Al-Azmeh, *Arabic Thought and Islamic Societies*, p. 36.

96 Ibn al-Farrā', *Kitāb al-mu'tamad fi ūṣūl ad-dīn*, § 195.

97 *'Ahd Ardashīr*, § 13.

98 Ibn Jamā'a, *Taḥrīr al-aḥkām*, p. 384.

99 Mary Boyce (tr.), *The Letter of Tansar*, Rome, 1968, pp. 37–9.

100 *The Nasirean Ethics*, p. 230.

101 Cf. 'Abd as-Salām Bin 'Abd al-'Ālī, *al-Falsafa as-siyāsiyya 'ind al-Fārābī*, Beirut, 1979, pp. 73, 82, and passim.

102 See Miskawayh, *Tahdhīb al-akhlāq*, p. 147.

103 For instance, at random:Māwardī, *Tashīl*, pp. 207 ff.; Abū Ḥammū, *Wāsiṭa*, pp. 118 ff.; Ibn al-Ḥaddād, *al-Jawhar*, pp. 67 and 66–7n. One of the most interesting formulations is to be found in *Sirr al-asrār*, pp. 126–8 and see 128n. Cf. Morony, *Iraq after the Muslim Conquest*, p. 28 and 28n5.

104 *Sirr al-asrār*, pp. 75–6.

105 Abdallah Laroui, *Islam et modernité*, Paris, 1987, pp. 23–4.

106 See Ibn al-Muqaffa' in *Rasā'il al-bulaghā'*, pp. 110 ff. and passim, and cf. *Sirr al-asrār*, p. 73.

107 See most particularly, Māwardī, *Aḥkām*, p. 5, Ibn Khaldūn, *Prolégomènes*, vol. 1, pp. 342–3, vol. 2, pp. 127–8, and Ibn al-Azraq, *Badā'i'*, vol. 1, Baghdad 1977, p. 194. Cf. Ṭurṭūshī, *Sirāj*, pp. 165 ff., who from the more restricted self-conscious standpoint of a Muslim jurist describes rational justice as 'quasi-justice' (*mā yushbih al-'adl*).

108 *Averroes' Commentary on Plato's Republic*, tr. E. I. J. Rosenthal, Cambridge, 1966, pp. 207 ff. See Fārābī, *Madīna*, pp. 292 ff. and idem., *Fuṣūl al-madanī*, ed. D. M. Dunlop, Cambridge, 1961, pp. 137–8.

109 Jāḥiẓ, *Rasā'il*, vol. 3, p. 147.

110 Cf. 'Izz ad-Dīn al-'Allām, 'Mafhūm al-ḥāshiya fi'l-adab as-siyāsī as-sulṭānī', in *Abḥāth*, 4/13(1986), p. 101. See, for instance, Māwardī, *Naṣīḥa*, pp. 360 ff. and passim, Aḥmad b. Yūsuf, *al-'Uhūd al-yūnāniyya*, pp. 6, 15 ff.

111 Herzfeld, *Iran in the Ancient Near East*, p. 320.

112 Sperl, 'Islamic Kingship and Arabic Panegyric Poetry', pp. 20, 33–4.

113 Ibn al-Muqaffa' in *Rasā'il al-bulaghā'*, p. 54.

114 Murādī, *Ishāra*, p. 149.

115 *The Book of Government*, p. 94.

116 Mas'ūdī, *Murūj*, § 3055. This caliphal order was not carried out. The beasts kept there were ordered killed by al-Muhtadī (Ibid., § 3130), an ascetic and pious figure who self-consciously tried to emulate the reputation of 'Umar b. 'Abd al-'Azīz.

117 Ibid., § 3358. These properties were returned to their owners, and the prisoners released, with the accession of al-Muktafī in late 289/911.

118 Miskawayh, *Tajārib*, vol. 1, p. 268. The assertion by E. Tyan (*Institutions du droit public Musulman. Tome premier: Le Califat*, Paris, 1954, p. 418n1) that to each head was attached a name label appears to be the

author's invention, although there is extant a report from Merv in 305/917f that an underground cabinet had been found containing labelled heads (Ibn al-Jawzī, *Muntaẓam*, vol. 6, p. 144).

119 For instance, Masʿūdī, *Murūj*, § 2473.

120 Miskawayh, *Tajārib*, vol. 1, pp. 284–5. See also pp. 253, 264–5.

121 Ibid., pp. 238–41, 244–5.

122 See Tyan, *Le Califat*, pp. 403 ff., 418 ff.

123 Miskawayh, *Tajārib*, vol. 1, pp. 20, 42, 110 ff., 128 ff.

124 Tyan, *Le Califat*, pp. 426–7.

125 Gürlu Necipoğlu, *Architecture, Ceremonial, and Power. The Topkapi Palace in the Fifteenth and Sixteenth Centuries*, New York and Cambridge, Mass., 1991, p. 161.

126 Ibn az-Zubayr, *Dhakhā'ir*, §§ 116, 119, 141, 149, and passim; Qalqashandī, *Khilāfa*, vol. 3, pp. 366–8.

127 One of the most lavish such mass circumcision was at the orders of the Fātimid al-Muʿizz (r 953–975): al-Qāḍī an-Nuʿmān, *Kitāb al-majālis wa'l-musāyarāt*, ed. H. Faqī et al., Tunis, 1978, pp. 556–9.

128 Ṣābī, *Rusūm*, p. 68.

129 For some glimpses: as-Ṣūlī, *Akhbār ar-Rāḍī Billāh wa'l-Muttaqī Lillāh*, ed. J. Heyworth-Dunne, London, 1935, pp. 47, 56; Masʿūdī, *Murūj*, § 2875.

130 al-Yaʿqūbī, *Mushākalat an-nās li-zamānihim*, ed. W. Milward, Beirut, 1980, p. 27.

131 Masʿūdī, *Murūj*, § 2418.

132 Ibn az-Zubayr, *Dhakha'ir*, § 304. Al-Muhtadī ordered fighting cocks and other fighting animals to be put down (Masʿūdī, *Murūj*, § 3130), and juristic opinion was divided over the legality of the hunt, polo, and other games, in addition to music. See Māwardī, *Naṣīḥa*, pp. 533–7.

133 Māwardī, *Naṣīḥa*, p. 388.

134 Masʿūdī, *Murūj*, §§ 2238, 2299; Qalqashandī, *Khilāfa*, vol. 2, pp. 232 ff.

135 Sourdel, 'Questions de cérémonial 'Abbaside', *Revue des Études Islamiques*, 28 (1960), p. 135.

136 al-Maqqarī, *Nafḥ aṭ-ṭīb min ghuṣn al-Andalus ar-raṭīb*, ed. I. ʿAbbās, Beirut, 1968, vol. 1, p. 606.

137 Necipoğlu, *Architecture, Ceremonial, and Power.*, pp. 141, 151.

138 al-Qāḍī an-Nuʿmān, *Majālis*, pp. 114–5, and see Maqrīzī, *Ittiʿāẓ al-ḥunafā' bi akhbār al-a'imma al-Fāṭimiyyīn min al-khulafā'*, ed. M. Aḥmad, Cairo, 1977 ff., vol. 1, p. 83.

139 A description of this parasol, termed by the Persian word transcribed as *al-chatr*, see Qalqashandī, *Ṣubḥ* vol. 4, pp. 7–8.

140 Ṣābī, *Rusūm*, p. 75.

141 Masʿūdī, *Murūj*, §§ 2746–8.

142 For instance, Ibn al-Jawzī, *Muntaẓam* , vol. 8, p. 2.

143 Ibid., pp. 79, 81, 90–92.

144 Masʿūdī, *Murūj*, §§ 3057, 3517. White also seems to have been the

colour worn in mourning: see Ibn al-Jawzī, *Muntaẓam* , vol. 8, p. 292, vol. 10, p. 120.

145 Ibn Faḍlān, *Risālsat Ibn Faḍlān fī waṣf ar-riḥla ilā bilād at-Turk wa'l-Khazar wa'r-Rūs wa's-Ṣaqāliba*, ed. S. ad-Dahhān, Damascus, 1978, p. 144.

146 Maqrīzī, *Ittiʿāẓ* , vol. 1, pp. 130–1 and passim.

147 Ibn al-Jawzī, *Muntaẓam*, vol. 8, p. 196. See also Farhad Daftary, *The Ismāʿīlīs. Their History and Doctrines*, Cambridge, 1990, p. 206.

148 Ibn al-Jawzī, *Muntaẓam*, vol. 7, pp. 260, 176; *Rasā'il aṣ-Ṣābī wa'sh-Sharīf ar-Raḍī*, ed. Muḥammad Yūsuf Najm, Kuwait, 1961, pp. 73, 78.

149 Sourdel, 'Cérémonial Abbaside', pp. 147–8.

150 On these, see Marius Canard, 'Le cérémonial fatimide et le cérémonial byzantin. Essai de comparaison', in *Byzantion*, 21 (1951), pp. 355–420; Paula Sanders, 'The Court Ceremonial of the Fatimid Caliphate in Egypt', PhD thesis, Princeton University, 1984.

151 Ibid., pp. 146 and passim.

152 *Rusūm*, pp. 5–6.

153 Masʿūdī, *Murūj*, § 3012; Yaʿqūbī, *Mushākala*, p. 24.

154 See Sanders, 'The Court Ceremonial', ch. 4–6, passim, and Qalqashandī, *Subh*, vol. 3, pp. 505–22. For a translation of medieval Arabic texts on this into a European language, see Marius Canard, 'La procession du nouvel an chez les Fatimides', in *Annales de l'Institut d'Études Orientales de la Faculté des Lettres d'Alger*, x(1952), pp. 364–98.

155 Sourdel, 'Cérémonial Abbaside', p. 145.

156 For instance, al-Muqtadir in 306/918 f.; Ibn al-Jawzī, *Muntaẓam*, vol. 6, p. 147.

157 For instance, Ibid., vol. 10, p. 192.

158 Jāḥiẓ, *Tāj*, pp. 23–4, 28, 32–5, 37–44.

159 Qalqashandī, *Ṣubḥ*, vol. 4, p. 6. Everyday sitting by Cairo Caliphs is described in Ibid., p. 7.

160 Maqrīzī, *Ittiʿāẓ*, vol. 1, pp. 136, 208.

161 *Tibr*, pp. 222–3.

162 Ṣābī, *Rusūm*, pp. 81, 91.

163 Canard, 'Cérémonial fatimide', pp. 384–6.

164 Jāḥiẓ, *Tāj*, pp. 112–8; Ṣābī, *Rusūm*, pp. 33–4.

165 Ṣābī, *Rusūm*, pp. 34–5.

166 Ṣābī, *Rusūm*, p. 34; Sourdel, 'Cérémonial Abbaside', pp. 141–2; J. Sadan, 'A propos de Martaba: Remarques sur l'étiquette dans le monde musulman médiéval', in *Revue des Etudes Islamiques*, 41(1973), pp. 51–69.

167 Ibid., pp. 34, 85. For Fatimid analogues, see Qalqashandī, *Ṣubḥ*, vol. 3, pp. 499–500.

168 Jāḥiẓ, *Tāj*, pp. 7–8, 22, 118–120.

169 Masʿūdī, *Murūj*, § 2704.

170 *Tāj*, pp. 7, 9.

171 *Rusūm*, p. 31.

172 *al-Himma fī ādāb atbāʿ al-a'imma*, ed. M. K. Ḥusayn, Cairo, n.d., p..

105; idem., *Majālis*, pp. 57, 59.

173 For instance, Ibn al-Jawzī, *Muntaẓam*, vol. 9, pp. 35–6.

174 Ṣābī, *Rusūm*, p. 32. For the Fatimids, see Sanders, 'Court Ceremonial', pp. 18–21.

175 Ṣābī, *Rusūm*, p. 31.

176 Maqrīzī, *Kitāb as-sulūk li-ma'rifat duwal al-mulūk*, ed. M. M. Ziyāda and S. 'A. 'Āshūr, Cairo 1956–71, vol. 1, p. 70.

177 Jāḥiẓ, *Tāj*, pp. 83–9; Ṣābī, *Rusūm*, pp. 57–9.

178 Ḥasan al-Bāshā, *al-Alqāb al-islāmiyya fi't-tārīkh wa'l-wathā'iq wa'l-āthār*, Cairo, 1957, pp. 80 ff.

179 Ibn az-Zubayr, *Dhakhā'ir*, § 127.

180 Canard, 'Cérémonial fatimide', pp. 374, 380–3.

181 Ṣābī, *Rusūm*, p. 87.

182 For instance, Ibn al-Jawzī, *Muntaẓam*, vol. 8, pp. 116–7.

183 Robert Hillenbrand, 'The Symbolism of the Rayed Nimbus in Early Islamic Art', in E. Lyle (ed.), *Kingship* (*Cosmos*, vol. 2), Edinburgh, 1986, pp. 18–19.

184 Necipoğlu, *Architecture, Ceremonial and Power*, p. 254. See also Ibid., pp. 29–30.

185 See Heribert Busse, *Chalif und Grosskönig. Die Buyiden im Iraq (945–1055)*, Wiesbaden, 1969, pp. 203 ff.

186 For instance, al-Afshīn after defeating the rebellion of Pāpak, which seems to be the first use of this ceremonial: Mas'ūdī, *Murūj*, § 2815. See also ibid, §§ 3306, 3337. For a chronology of these ceremonies, see Ṣābī, *Rusūm*, p. 94.

187 For instance, Miskawayh, *Tajārib*, vol. 1, p. 93.

188 On which see Sourdel, 'Cérémonial Abbaside', pp. 675 ff.

189 The most detailed account is to be found in Ṣābī, *Rusūm*, pp. 80–4. See also the somewhat briefer account Ibn al-Jawzī, *Muntaẓam*, vol. 7, pp. 98–9, which contains, however, minor variations and additions.

190 This is discussed in ch. 7 below.

191 For instance, Ibn al-Jawzī, *Muntaẓam*, vol. 7, pp. 120, 126, 135, 148, 266–7, vol. 8, p. 136.

192 Ibid., vol. 8, p. 235, vol. 9, p. 226.

193 Ibid., vol. 8, p. 170.

194 Ibid., pp. 181–3.

195 On this, Claude Cahen, 'Notes sur les débuts de la futuwwa d'al-Nāsir', in *Oriens*, 6(1953), pp. 18–23. On the incorporation of futuwwa in the theoretical equipment of the Caliphate, see Angelika Hartmann, *An-Nāṣir li-Dīn Allāh (1180–1225). Politik, Religion, und Kultur in der späten 'Abbasidenzeit*, Berlin and New York, 1975, pp. 112 ff.

196 Herbert Mason, *Two Statesmen of Medieval Islam: The Vizier Ibn Hubayra and the Caliph an-Nāṣir li Dīn Allāh*, Paris and The Hague, 1972, pp. 121–4, 131.

197 For instance, Maqrīzī, *Sulūk*, vol. 1, p. 459.

198 For instance, Ibid., p. 459; idem., *Khiṭaṭ* , vol. 2, p. 209. For Fatimid triumphs, which seem to have excluded the crown which was reserved for the Caliph, see, for instance, Maqrīzī, *Ittiʿāẓ*, vol. 1, p. 139.

199 D. Behrens Abou Seif, 'The Citadel of Cairo: Stage for Mamluk Ceremonial', in *Annales Islamologiques*, 24 (1988), pp. 26, 30.

200 Details in Ibn az-Zubayr, *Dhakhā'ir*, pp. 130–9, Ibn al-Jawzī, *Muntaẓam*, vol. 6, pp. 143–4, and Ṣābī, *Rusūm*, pp. 11–14.

201 See for instance, the formula of Māwardī, *Naṣīḥa*, p. 111.

202 Busse, *Chalif und Grosskönig*, p. 135.

203 On the reproduction of Abbasid norms at Buyid courts, see Ibid., pp. 222 ff.

204 Jerrilynn Dodds, *Architecture and Ideology in Early Medieval Spain*, London and University Park, Pennsylvania, 1990, p. 96.

205 Qalqashandī, *Ṣubḥ*, vol. 5, pp. 143–7, 203–9; Ibn Khaldūn, *Prolégomènes*, vol. 2, pp. 45–6.

206 *The Book of Government*, pp. 94, 120, 131, and passim

207 Qalqashandī, *Ṣubḥ*, vol. 4, pp. 7–9, 44–49, 52–6.

208 Ṣābī, *Rusūm*, pp. 77, 85.

209 Ibid., p. 65.

210 Ibid., pp. 14–17.

211 Ibn al-Jawzī, *Muntaẓam*, vol. 7, p. 266.

212 Ibid., p. 132.

213 Ibid., vol. 9, p. 73.

214 Maqrīzī, *Sulūk*, vol. 1, p. 461; idem., *Khiṭaṭ*, vol. 2, p. 209.

215 For instance, Hilāl b. al-Muḥassin as-Ṣābī, *Tuḥfat al-umarā' fī tārīkh al-wuzarā' – aqsām ḍā'iʿa* , ed. M. 'Awwād, Baghdad, 1948, p. 41.

216 Ṣābī, *Rusūm*, pp. 133–5; Qalqashandī, *Khilāfa*, vol. 1, p. 298; Busse, *Chalif und Grosskönig*, p. 185.

217 Mason, *Two Statesmen*, pp. 108–9; Vassili Vladimirovitsh Bartold, *Turkistān min al-fatḥ al-ʿArabī ilā al-ghazū al-Maghūlī*, tr. S. 'U. Hāshim, Kuwait, 1981, p. 535.

218 For instance: Ibn al-Jawzī, *Muntaẓam*, vol. 8, p. 89.

219 For instance: Qalqashandī, *Khilāfa*, vol. 2, p. 25; Maqrīzī, *Sulūk*, vol. 1 , p. 272.

220 Ibn al-Jawzī, *Muntaẓam*, vol. 8, pp. 30, 119; Ṣābī, *Rusūm*, pp. 136-7.

221 Qalqashandī, *Khilāfa*, vol. 3, p. 36. For Fatimid practice, see al-Bāshā, *Alqāb*, pp. 97–8.

222 For instance, some of the collection of the National Museum in Damascus: *al-Maskūkāt al-Islāmiyya. Majmūʿa mukhtāra min ṣadr al-Islām ḥattā al-ʿahd al-ʿUthmānī*, [Beirut, 1980], pl. 64–8.

223 Text in S. M. Stern, 'Al-Mahdī's Reign According to 'Uyūn al-Akhbār', in idem., *Studies in Early Ismailism*, Jerusalem and Leiden, 1983, pp. 122–3.

224 Ibn al-Jawzī, *Muntaẓam*, vol. 7, pp. 292–3, vol. 8, pp. 29–30, 38–40.

225 Ibid., vol. 10, p. 176.

226 Qalqashandī, *Khilāfa*, vol. 3, pp. 323–4.
227 Ibid., p. 284.
228 Busse, *Chalif und Grosskönig*, pp. 134–5.
229 *Ṣubḥ*, vol. 5, p. 472, and cf. the rather more doctrinaire contrastive comparison of Ibn Khaldūn, *Prolégomènes*, vol. 1, p. 415.
230 For instance, Maqrīzī, *Sulūk*, vol. 1, pp. 167–8, 219–20, 319, 323, 398, 407; Qalqashandī, *Khilāfa*, vol. 2, p. 59.
231 Cf. C. Edmund Bosworth, 'The Titulature of the Early Ghaznavids', in *Oriens*, xv(1962), pp. 216 and passim.
232 Nizām al-Mulk, *Book of Government*, p. 10; al-Bāshā, *Alqāb*, p. 64.
233 For instance: Maqrīzī, *Sulūk*, vol. 1, p. 437 and Qalqashandī, *Khilāfa*, vol. 3, pp. 86, 88ff.; Ṣābī, *Rusūm*, pp. 131–2; Ibn al-Jawzī, *Muntaẓam*, vol. 8, p. 65; Nizām al-Mulk, *Book of Government*, pp. 149–56.
234 Ibn al-Jawzī, *Muntaẓam*, vol. 8, pp. 223, 235.
235 Ṣābī, *Rusūm*, p. 105; Nizām al-Mulk, *Book of Government*, pp. 148 ff.
236 al-Bāshā, *al-alqāb al-islāmiyya*, pp. 90, 103 ff.
237 Maqqarī, *Nafḥ*, vol. 4, p. 394.

Chapter 7

1 For instance, Suyūṭī, *Tafsīr al-Jalālayn*, ad loc.; idem., *ad-Durr al-manthūr fi't-tafsīr bi'l-ma'thūr*, Beirut, 1990, ad loc.; Māwardī, *An-Nukat wa'l-'uyūn: Tafsīr al-Māwardī*, ed. K. M. Khiḍr, Kuwait, 1982, ad loc.; Ibn al-Jawzī, *Ẓād al-Masīr fi 'ilm at-tafsīr*, Damascus, 1964-68, ad loc.

2 Zamakhsharī, *al-Kashshāf 'an ḥaqā'iq at-Tanzīl*, ed. W. Nassau Lees et al., Calcutta, 1856, ad loc.

3 al-Qāḍī an-Nu'mān, *Asās at-ta'wīl*, p. 41.

4 Ibn 'Arabī, *al-Futūḥāt al-Makkiyya*, Cairo, AH 1293, vol. 4, pp. 3–4.

5 Cf. Said Arjomand, *The Shadow of God*, p. 32.

6 'Abd al-Ghanī an-Nābulsī, *Ta'ṭīr al-anām fi ta'bīr al-manām*, Cairo, n.d., s.v. 'sulṭān'; Ibn Sīrīn, *Muntakhab al-kalām fi tafsīr al-aḥlām*, printed on the margins of ibid., vol. 1, s.v. 'sulṭān' (the actual author of this work appears to have been one Abū Sa'īd (or Abū Sa'd) al-Wā'iẓ: see M. Steinschneider, 'Ibn Sirin und Ibn Shahin', in *Zeitschrift der Deutschen Morgenländischen Gesellschaft*, 17(1863), pp. 227 ff., quoted in F. Meier, 'Die Welt der Urbilder bei Ali Hamadani (+ 1385)', in *Eranos-Jahrbuch*, 18(1950), p. 122.

7 See the unfortunately not well-articulated study of the saintly and magical qualities of the caliphate by Armand Abel, 'Le Khalife. Présence sacré', in *Studia Islamica*, 7(1957), pp. 29–45.

8 For instance: Ṭurṭūshī, *Sirāj*, pp. 146–7; Māwardī, *Tashīl an-naẓar*, p. 247; Ibn al-Jawzī, *Miṣbāḥ*, vol. 1, p. 289.

9 For instance, Ibn al-Jawzī, *Miṣbāḥ*, vol. 1, pp. 289–91; Ibn Riḍwān, *Shuhub*, pp 95–7; Subkī, *Mu'īd*, p. 58.

10 Ibn Jamā'a, *Taḥrīr al-aḥkām*, p. 363. For the Koranic sanction of this

contention, see ibid., p. 355.

11 Ibn Abī Ya'lā, *Ṭabaqāt al-Ḥanābila*, ed. M. H. al-Fiqī, Cairo, 1952, vol. 2, p. 240.

12 *al-Ḥayawān*, ed. 'A. Hārūn, Cairo, 1965–8, vol. 2, p. 310.

13 Tyan, *Le Califat*, p. 473.

14 Mas'ūdī, *Murūj*, § 2989, and see Busse, *Chalif und Grosskönig*, p. 201.

15 Mas'ūdī, *Murūj* , § 1772; Ibn al-Jawzī, *Muntaẓam*, vol. 5, pt 2, p. 71. See Charles Pellat, 'Le culte de Mu'āwiya au IIIe siècle de l'Hégire', in *Studia Islamica*, 9 (1956), pp. 53–66.

16 Māwardī, *Naṣīḥā*, p. 360.

17 'Min kitāb al-amṣār wa 'ajā'ib al-buldān', ed. C. Pellat in *al-Mashriq*, 60(1966), p. 181.

18 al-Qāḍī an-Nu'mān, *Majālis*, pp. 55, 72, 419.

19 Ibid., pp. 157, 292–3. On Fatimid tombs in Cairo, see Sanders, *Court Ceremonial*, pp. 63–4.

20 as-Shaykh al-Mufīd, *al-Irshād*, Beirut, 1979, pp. 160–86, 273–5.

21 Al-Azmeh, *Arabic Thought and Islamic Societies*, pp. 69 ff.

22 For instance, Mas'ūdī, *Murūj* , §§ 2621–3, 2980–1, 3426–7.

23 Most particularly, Ibn Khaldūn, *Prolégomènes*, vol. 2, pp. 142 ff.; Qalqashandī, *Khilāfa*, vol. 3, p. 131.

24 Ibn Khaldūn, *Prolégomènes*, vol. 2, pp. 185–201; *The Astrological History of Māshā'allāh*, ed. E. S. Kennedy and D. Pingree, Cambridge, Mass., 1971; 'Risālat Ya'qūb b. Isḥaq al-Kindī fī mulk al-'Arab wa kammīyatuh', Arabic text in Otto Loth, 'Al-Kindī als Astrolog', in *Morgenländische Forchungen. Festschrift Heinrich L. Fleischer* [1875], Amsterdam, 1981, pp. 173–9; Bīrūnī, *Al-Athār al-bāqiya*, p 132. Examples of specific predictions: Ibn al-Jawzī, *Muntaẓam*, vol. 8, p. 171, vol. 9, p. 97; Miskawayh, *Tajārib*, vol. 1, p. 139. On the use of astrologers in courtly intrigue: Miskawayh, *Tajārib*, vol. 1, p. 286. On unsuccessful political astrology, and for a sceptical attitude towards it: Tawḥīdī, *Baṣā'ir*, vol. 6, § 332b.

25 Mas'ūdī, *Murūj* , § 3446.

26 Loth, 'Al-Kindī als Astrolog', pp. 264–5.

27 *Tashīl*, pp. 104–5.

28 Yaḥyā b. 'Adī, *Akhlāq*, p. 137; Ibn 'Arabī, *Kitāb al-akhlāq*, Cairo, n.d., p. 48.

29 *Rasā'il*, vol. 4, p. 43.

30 For instance, Māwardī, *Naṣīḥā*, pp 72–3 and Ibn al-Jawzī, *Miṣbāḥ*, vol. 1, pp. 143–7.

31 Ibid., pp. 74–5.

32 Tawḥīdī, *al-Imtā' wa'l-mu'ānasa*, vol. 3, pp. 99 and 86–91.

33 Daftary, *The Ismā'īlis*, pp. 196–9.

34 Māwardī, *Tashīl*, p. 134; Jāḥiẓ, *Rasā'il*, vol. 4, p. 43.

35 For the various views, see Māwardī, *Aḥkām*, pp. 22–3 and Qalqashandī, *Khilāfa*, vol. 1, pp. 14–17.

36 Ibn al-Jawzī, *Miṣbāḥ*, vol. 1, p. 93.

37 *Irshād*, pp. 267, 270, and passim.
38 For instance, Qalqashandī, *Khilāfa*, vol. 2, pp. 348, 351, vol. 3, p. 103; Tyan, *Le Califat*, p. 473.
39 Mas'ūdī, *Murūj* , § 2416.
40 Tha'ālibī, *Laṭā'if al-luṭf*, ed. 'U. al-As'ad, Beirut, 1980,§ 121.
41 Qalqashandī, *Ṣubḥ al-A'shā*, vol. 1, p. 415; Ibn al-Jawzī,*Muntaẓam*, vol. 7, p. 67, vol. 10, pp. 51, 163.
42 *Muntaẓam*, vol. 10, p. 264.
43 Tyan, *Le Califat*, pp. 456–7.
44 Sibṭ Ibn at-Ta'āwīdhī, *Dīwān*, pp. 3, 158, 165, 172.
45 Maqrīzī, *Itti'āẓ al-ḥunafā'*, vol. 1, p. 97.
46 *Dīwān*, pp. 173, 176.
47 Ibn 'Abd Rabbih, *Dīwān*, pp. 114, 122, and passim.
48 For instance, ibid., p. 182; Sibṭ Ibn at-Ta'āwīdhī, *Dīwān*, pp. 1, 3, and passim; al-Qāḍī an-Nu'mān, *Majālis*, p. 51.
49 Sibṭ Ibn at-Ta'āwīdhī, *Dīwān*, p. 161.
50 Angelika Hartmann, *An-Nāṣir li-Dīn Allāh (1180-1225). Politik, Religion, Kultur in der späten 'Abbāsidenzeit*, Berlin and New York, 1975 , pp. 112–6.
51 Cf. Ibn Jamā'a, *Taḥrīr*, p. 363.
52 Ghazālī, *at-Tibr al-masbūk*, pp. 171–2.
53 *Imtā'*, vol. 2, p 33.
54 Māwardī, *Tashīl*, pp. 198, 202. See also ibid., p. 202n3.
55 For instance, Ṣābī, *Rusūm*, p. 94, and Tawḥīdī, *Imtā'*, vol. 2, p. 76.
56 Cf. Ringgren, 'Some Religious Aspects of the Caliphate', in *Sacral Kingship* (Supplement to *Numen*, IV), Leiden, 1959, p. 738.
57 Azīz al-Aẓmah, *al-Kitāba at-tārīkhiyya wa'l-ma'rifa at-tārīkhiyya*, Beirut, 1983, pp. 116–24.
58 Cf. Al-Azmeh, 'Utopia and Islamic Political Thought', in idem., *Islams and Modernities*, London, 1993, pp. 97 ff.
59 Ibn Khaldūn, *Tārīkh*, vol. 3, p. 4; Ibn Ṭabāṭabā, *al-Fakhrī fi'l ādab as-sulṭāniyya wa'd-duwal al-islāmiyya*, Cairo, 1962, p. 60.
60 Māwardī, *Naṣīḥā*, pp. 119–22; Ibn Khaldūn, *Prolégomènes*, vol. 2, p. 249.
61 Māwardī, *Naṣīḥā*, pp. 133–40.
62 For instance, Abū Ya'lā b. al-Farrā', *Mu'tamad*, pp. 235–7; Suyūṭī, *Tārīkh al-khulafā'*, Beirut, n.d., pp. 212–3.
63 *Prolégomènes*, vol. 1, pp. 370 ff; idem., *Tārīkh*, vol. 2, pp. 1140–1.
64 For instance, Suyūṭī, *Khulafā'*, pp. 231, 234; Ibn 'Abd Rabbih, *'Iqd*, vol. 5, p. 148; Qalqashandī, *Khilāfa*, vol. 1, pp. 116, 123, 125.
65 Suyūṭī, *Khulafā'*, pp. 13–15, and cf. Ibn Khaldūn, *Prolégomènes*, vol. 1, pp. 375–6, 380.
66 For instance, Ash'arī, *Maqālāt al-Islāmiyyīn wa ikhtilāf al-muṣallīn*, ed. M. M. 'Abd al-'Amīd, Cairo, 1950–54, vol. 1, p. 49; Juwaynī, *Irshād*, pp. 428 ff.
67 *Khilāfa*, vol. 2, pp. 255–6.

68 For instance: Ibn al-Jawzī, *Muntaẓam*, vol. 7, p. 66, on the voluntary abdication of al-Muṭīʿ; Qalqashandī, *Khilāfa*, vol. 2, pp. 309–10, on an impeachment. Transitions from one live Caliph to another also involved the handing over the insignia of office, the Prophet's cloak, stave, and seal.

69 For instance: Abū Yaʿlā, *Aḥkām*, p. 4; Juwaynī, *Ghiyāth*, §§ 144–7, 150, 170–3, for variations and nuances.

70 Arabic text in E. Lévi-Provençal, 'Le traité d'*Adab al-Kātib* d'Abū Bakr Ibn Khaldūn', in *Arabica*, 2(1955), p. 285.

71 Qalqashandī, *Khilāfa*, vol. 2, pp. 25, 28.

72 *At-Taʿrīf bi Ibn Khaldūn wa riḥlatuhu gharban wa sharqan*, ed. M. b. Tāwīt at-Ṭanjī, Cairo, 1951, p. 336.

73 For instance: Ibn Khaldūn, *Tārīkh*, vol. 6, p. 225; ad-Dhahabī, *al-ʿIbar fī khabar man ghabar*, ed. Ṣ. al-Munajjid, Kuwait, 1960 ff., vol. 4, pp. 57–8, vol. 5, p. 36.

74 Ibn Qunfudh, *al-Fārisiyya fī mabādiʾ ad-dawla al-Ḥafsiyya*, ed. M. Shadhilī an-Nīfar and ʿA. Turkī, Tunis, 1968, pp. 99, 130; idem., *al-Wafayāt*, ed. ʿA. Nuwayhiḍ, Beirut, 1971, p. 273.

75 For instance, al-Qāḍī an-Nuʿmān, *Majālis*, pp. 92–3 and passim; Arabic Text in S. M. Stern, *Studies in Early Ismailism*, Leiden and Jerusalem, 1983, pp. 117–8. See P. H. Mamour, *Polemics on the Origin of the Fatimid Caliphs*, London, 1934.

76 Cf. Ibn Khaldūn, *Prolégomènes*, vol. 1, pp. 348–52 ; Ibn al-Azraq, *Badāʾiʿ*, (ed. Nashshār) vol. 1, pp. 77.

77 A convenient account is in Suyūṭī, *Khulafāʾ*, pp. 11–12

78 Juwaynī, *Ghiyāth*, §§ 106–9, and cf. Ibn Khaldūn, *Prolégomènes*, vol. 1, pp. 348–52.

79 Al-Azmeh, *Arabic Thought and Islamic Societies*, pp. 162–4.

80 Tawḥīdī, *Baṣāʾir*, vol. 5, § 777 and 777n.

81 Qalqashandī, *Khilāfa*, vol. 1, pp. 38–9; Taftāzānī, *Sharḥ al-maqāṣid*, ed. ʿA. ʿUmayra, Beirut, 1989, vol. 5, p. 233.

82 Abū Yaʿlā Ibn al-Farrāʾ, *Muʿtamad*, p. 241.

83 *an-Nizāʾ waʾt-takhāṣum fī mā bayna Banī Umayya wa Banī Hāshim*, ed. ʿA. Hāshimī an-Najafī, Najaf, AH 1368, pp. 38–9.

84 Details in Ibn al-Jawzī, *Miṣbāḥ*, vol. 1, pp. 95 ff.

85 Thus it is misleading to translate the word *aḥkām* occurring in the title of Māwardī's most famous book as 'statutes' (as in E. Fagnan (tr.), *Les statuts gouvernementaux*, Algiers, 1915) , for it is not a code of statutory rulings. The standard works on this matter in English (notably: T. W. Arnold, *The Caliphate* (1924), London, 1964; H. A. R. Gibb, 'Al-Māwardī's Theory of the Khilafah', in *Islamic Culture* , xi(1937), pp. 291–302, reproduced in idem., *Studies in the Civilization of Islam*, Boston, 1962, pp. 151–65; A. K. S. Lambton, *State and Government in Medieval Islam. An Introduction to the Study of Islamic Political Theory: The Jurists*, Oxford, 1981), propound theses that are tirelessly repeated. These should now be regarded as obsolete. They are marked

throughout by a conceptual crudeness and by historical naivete. Based on a far too restricted, truncated, and tendentious an acquaintance with the sources, including those directly discussed, they rest on 'an assumption which has never been substantiated and on basic research which has not yet been undertaken' (D. P. Little, 'A New Look to the *al-aḥkām as-sulṭāniyya*', in *The Muslim World*, 64(1974), p. 1). They display a grandiose peremptoriness, and a manifest contempt equally for their subject and for the requirements of scholarship. E. I. J. Rosenthal (*Political Thought in Medieval Islam*, Cambridge, 1958), though sharing many views and assumptions with these authors, is a far more scrupulous and careful scholar. H. Mikhail's *Politics and Revelation. Māwardī and After* (Edinburgh, 1995), fuller and based on better acquaintance with the subject, is yet captive to the academic ethos of the time in which it was composed, and was alas written without reference to the research of Henri Laoust. L. Gardet's *La cité musulmane* (2nd ed, Paris, 1961), is fairer in perspective, but shares many of the standard assumptions and propounds too monolithic, unhistorical, and schematic a view of the subject. T. Nagel's *Staat und Glaubensgemeinschaft in Islam* (2 vols, Zürich and Munich, 1981), more ample in scale and scholarship, also shares the standard assumptions. A recent quantitative scan of modern writing in Arabic on juristic discourses on the Caliphate has shown the proponderance of Māwardī's *Aḥkām* as a standard source and canonical statement, and an altogether very limited repertoire of other works consulted in this body of modern writing, much as in Western writing referred to. (M. N. 'Ārif, *Fī maṣādir at-turāth as-siyāsī al-islāmī*, Washington, 1994, pp. 59 ff.).

86 Rare considerations of complexity can be found in many passages of Henri Laoust's 'La pensée et l'action politiques d'Al-Māwardī (364/450–974/1058), in idem., *Pluralismes dans l'Islam*, Paris, 1983, pp. 177–258.

87 Ibid., p. 200.

88 Suhrawardī, *Taḥrīr al-aḥkām.*

89 Laoust, 'Al-Māwardī', pp. 181, 197.

90 Māwardī, *Aḥkām*, pp. 3–4.

91 Al-Azmeh, *Arabic Thought and Islamic Societies*, pp. 88–9. See also Abū Ya'lā b. al-Farrā', *Aḥkām*, p 3 and Ibn Khaldūn, *Prolégomènes*, vol. 1, pp. 345–6.

92 For instance, Ghazālī, *Iqtiṣād*, pp 234–7; Fakhr ad-Dīn ar-Rāzī, *Muḥaṣṣal afkār al-mutaqaddimīn wa'l-muta'akhkhirīn min al-'ulamā' wa'l-ḥukamā' wa'l-mutakallimīn*, Cairo, AH 1323, p 176; Ibn al-Jawzī, *Miṣbāḥ*, vol. 1, pp. 93–4, 148; Juwaynī, *Ghiyāth*, §§ 15–25.

93 See the argument of Ibn Rushd, *Talkhīṣ al-Khaṭāba*, pp. 229–30.

94 Jad'ān, *Al-Miḥna*, p. 303.

95 Al-'Allāma al-Ḥillī, *al-Alfīn fī imāmat Amīr al-Mu'minīn 'Alī b. Abī Ṭālib 'alayhi as-salām*, Beirut, 1982, p. 53.

96 Abū Ya'lā, *Aḥkām*, p. 19.

97 Māwardī, *Aḥkām*, p. 6.

98 Qalqashandī, *Khilāfa*, vol. 2, p. 261.

99 For instance, Mas'ūdī, *Murūj* , § 2995; Ibn al-Jawzī, *Muntaẓam*, vol. 9, pp. 197–8. Monetary gifts were on occasion extorted by riotous soldiers, as upon the accession of al-Qādir in 381/991: Ibn al-Jawzī, *Muntaẓam*, vol. 7, p. 157.

100 For instance: Ibn al-Jawzī, *Muntaẓam*, vol. 5, pt 2, p. 26.

101 *Aḥkām*, p. 8.

102 *Aḥkām*, p. 23.

103 For instance, Juwaynī, *Ghiyāth*, §§ 453 ff; Taftāzānī, *Sharḥ al-maqāṣid*, vol. 5, p. 233.

104 Qalqashandī, *Khilāfa*, vol. 1, p. 52.

105 For instance, Juwaynī, *Ghiyāth*, §§ 160–3, 180–9.

106 Māwardī, *Aḥkām*, p. 5.

107 Ibid., pp. 15–16.

108 Ibid., p. 25.

109 Laoust, 'Al-Māwardī', p. 204.

110 Juwaynī, *Ghiyāth*, §§ 113–6.

111 Thus, for instance, in justification of the Caliphate of the Merinid Abū 'Inān in fourteenth- century Maghreb: Maqqarī, *Nafḥ aṭ-ṭīb*, vol. 5, p. 282, and cf. Qalqashandī, *Khilāfa*, vol. 2, pp. 255 ff.

112 Māwardī, *Aḥkām*, pp. 8–9.

113 *Rasā'il*, vol. 4, pp. 305–6.

114 Al-Qāḍī 'Abd al-Jabbār, *al-Mughnī fi abwāb al-'adl wa't-tawḥīd*, ed. 'A. Maḥmūd and S. Dunyā, Cairo, n.d., vol. 20, pt 1, pp. 215 ff.

115 Juwaynī, *Ghiyāth*, §§ 643–9.

116 *Aḥkām*, p. 20.

117 Ibid., p. 102; Qalqashandī, *Khilāfa*, vol. 1, p. 36, but see also p. 72.

118 Juwaynī, *Ghiyāth*, §§ 438–43; Ghazālī, *Iqtiṣād*, pp. 237–40.

119 Ghazālī, *Iqtiṣād*, p. 240.

120 aṭ-Ṭarsūsī, *Tuḥfat at-Turk fi mā yajib an yu'mal fi'l-mulk*, ed. R. as-Sayyid, Beirut, 1992, pp. 63–5, 71.

121 Busse, *Chalif und Grosskönig*, p. 157.

122 *Ghiyāth*, §§ 102–5.

123 *Aḥkām*, p. 27, and Qalqashandī, *Khilāfa*, vol. 1, p. 75.

124 Tha'ālibī, *Wuzarā'*, pp. 75 ff.

125 See Ibn Khaldūn, *Prolégomènes*, vol. 2, pp. 3 ff. Under Ibn Rā'iq, the vizirate persisted, but in a purely ceremonial capacity: Miskawayh, *Tajārib*,vol. 1, p. 352.

126 *Ghiyāth*, §§ 223–4.

127 For instance, *Aḥkām*, pp. 27, 24.

128 Māwardī, *Aḥkām*, p. 33; Abū Ya'la, *Aḥkām*, p. 37.

129 Māwardī, *Aḥkām*, pp. 19–20.

130 Wilferd Madelung, 'The Assumption of the Title of Shāhanshāh by the Būyids and "the Reign of the Daylam (Dawlat ad-Daylam)"', in *Journal of Near Eastern Studies*, 28(1969), pp. 105 ff. The author's guess that

the demise of the ʿAbbasids would have been permanent had it not been for the premature death of ʿAḍud ad-Dawla is contrary to all evidence.

131 Miskawayh, *Tajārib*, vol. 2, pp. 307–8, 343–4, and passim; Ibn al-Jawzī, *Muntaẓam*, vol. 8, pp. 82 and vols 6–8, passim; az-Ṣūlī, *Akhbār ar-Rāḍī Billāh wa'l-Muttaqī Lillāh*, ed. J. Heyworth-Dunne, London, 1935, passim; Busse, *Chalif und Grosskönig*, pp. 148–52, 192–3. On the administrative rationality and firmness of ʿAḍud ad-Dawla, who was also a great builder, see Miskawayh, *Tajārib*, vol. 3, pp. 41–3, 58, and Ibn al-Jawzī, *Muntaẓam*, vol. 7, p. 117.

132 Busse, *Chalif und Grosskönig*, pp. 136–7.

133 Ibn al-Jawzī, *Muntaẓam*, vol. 6, pp. 342–3, vol. 8, p. 12; Busse, *Chalif und Grosskönig*, p. 153.

134 Ibn al-Jawzī, *Muntaẓam*, vol. 7, pp. 76, 172.

135 Busse, *Chalif und Grosskönig*, pp. 59–60.

136 Ibn al-Jawzī, *Muntaẓam*, , vol. 8, pp. 218–31.

137 Ibid., vol. 9, p. 2.

138 For instance, ibid., vol. 6, p. 68, vol. 8, p. 293; Qalqashandī, *Khilāfa*, vol. 2, pp. 37–9; Mason, *Two Statesmen*, pp. 22–3.

139 For instance, Ibn al-Jawzī, *Muntaẓam*, vol. 9, pp. 134, 144.

140 Qalqashandī, *Khilāfa*, vol. 2, pp. 205–6.

141 David Ayalon, 'Studies in the Transfer of the Abbasid Caliphate from Baghdad to Cairo', in *Arabica*, 7(1960), pp. 55–6.

142 For instance, Maqrīzī, *Sulūk*, vol. 1, p. 22, vol. 2, pp. 73–4 and passim.

143 Qalqashandī, *Khilāfa*, vol. 2, p. 118.

144 Ibn Ḥajar al-ʿAsqalānī, *ad-Durar al-kāmina fī aʿyān al-miʾa ath-thāmina*, Hyderabad AH 1348, vol. 1, p. 56.

145 Ibn Khaldūn, *Taʿrīf*, pp. 250, 283, 296.

146 Lewis, *The Political Language of Islam*, pp. 134–5.

147 Ibn Rushd, *Talkhīṣ al-Jadal*, p. 28.

148 Qalqashandī, *Khilāfa*, vol. 1, p. 80. See Sourdel, *Le vizirat ʿAbbaside de 749 a 936*, Damascus, 1960, pp. 617–9.

149 Ibn Khaldūn, *Prolégomènes*, vol. 1, pp. 349 ff.

150 For instance, Ibn al-Jawzī, *Muntaẓam*, vol. 7, pp. 2, 16, 226–7.

151 Qalqashandī, *Khilāfa*, vol. 3, p. 13.

152 Calder, 'Friday Prayer' , pp. 35–47.

153 Ibn al-Jawzī, *Baghdād*, p. 23.

154 Qalqashandī, *Khilāfa*, vol. 3, pp. 173–4.

155 For instance, Ibn al-Jawzī, *Muntaẓam*, vol. 6, p. 384, and see Māwardī, *Aḥkām*, p. 107.

156 Māwardī, *Aḥkām*, p. 100.

157 Ibn al-Jawzī, *Muntaẓam*, vol. 10, p. 142.

158 G. Makdisi, *The Rise of the Colleges*, Edinburgh, 1981, pp. 171 ff. A. Al-Aẓma *Al-ʿIlmāniyya min manẓūr mukhtalif*, Beirut, 1992.

159 See Sourdel, 'La politique religieuse' , pp. 27–48.

160 Fahmī Jadʿān, *al-Miḥna. Bahth fī jadaliyyat ad-dīnī wa's-siyāsī fi'l-Islām*,

Amman, 1989.

161 For instance, Ibn al-Jawzī, *Muntaẓam*, vol. 5, pt 2, pp. 122, 171, 312, 326, vol. 7, pp. 287, 289, and Ṣūlī, *Akhbār ar-Rāḍī*, pp. 62–3. See Aziz Al-Azmeh, 'Orthodoxy and Hanbalīte Fideism', in *Arabica*, 35(1988), pp. 153–66.

162 Ṭarsūsī, *Tuḥfat at-Turk*, pp. 81–5. See George Makdisi, 'Ash'arī and the Ash'arītes in Islamic Religious History', in *Studia Islamica*, 17(1962), pp. 37–58, 18(1963), pp. 19–39.

163 Juwaynī, *Ghiyāth*, §§ 540–2.

164 Ibn al-Jawzī, *Muntaẓam*, vol. 8, p. 62.

165 For a review of various opinions and statements of this matter, see the compendious review of the later Shawkānī, *Irshād al-fuḥūl ilā taḥqīq al-ḥaqq min 'ilm al-uṣūl*, Cairo, 1937, pp. 253–4.

166 Ibn 'Arabī, *Futūḥāt*, vol. 2, pp. 6–7.

167 Suhrawardī, *Taḥrīr al-aḥkām*, fol. 5–7.

168 *Mu'tamad*, pp. 194–5.

169 Qalqashandī, *Khilāfa*, vol. 3, p 2. Prior to 'Aḍud ad-Dawla, these commissions were letters delivered to the king in question, and 'Aḍud ad-Dawla's investiture introduced the new convention whereby these letters were read out in audience: Ibn al-Jawzī, *Muntaẓam*, vol. 7, p. 87.

170 Ibn al-Jawzī, *Muntaẓam*, vol. 7, p. 99; Ibn al-Zubayr, *Dhakhā'ir*, p. 83.

171 Qalqashandī, *Khilāfa*, vol. 2, pp. 242–4, vol. 3, pp. 55–6.

172 *Prolégomènes*, vol. 1, pp. 394 ff.

173 *Aḥkām*, p. 23.

174 Ibid., p. 5: 'jā' ash-shar' bi-tafwīḍ al-umūr ilā waliyyihi fi'd-dīn'.

175 For example, *Taḥrīr*, pp. 24, 26.

176 *Naṣīḥā*, pp. 78–9.

177 Ibid., pp. 356–8. Cf. Laoust, *Ibn Taimiyya*, p. 315.

178 Māwardī, *Naṣīḥā*, p. 367.

179 See for instance, Māwardī, *Naṣīḥā*, p. 78–9, and Ibn al-Jawzī, *Miṣbāḥ*, vol. 1, p. 143.

180 For example, Qalqashandī, *Khilāfa*, vol. 3, pp. 49–50.

181 *Prolégomènes*, vol. 2, p. 3: 'Insiḥāb ḥukm al-khilāfa ash-shar'iyya fi'l-milla al-islāmiyya 'alā rutbat al-mulk wa's-sulṭān.'

182 Ibn al-Azraq, *Badā'i' as-silk* (Nashshār ed.), vol. 1, p. 71.

183 Laoust, *La politique de Ǧazālī*, Paris 1970, p. 88.

184 Ibn Qayyim al-Jawziyya, *Siyāsa shar'iyya* , pp. 279–80.

185 For instance, in 14th-century Tunis, by the grandfather of the celebrated Ibn Khaldūn : 'Le traité d'Adab al-Kātib d'Abū Bakr Ibn Khaldūn', ed. E. Lévi-Provençal in *Arabica*, 11(1955), p. 281.

186 *Mīzān al-'amal*, ed. Sulaymān Dunyā, Cairo, 1964, p. 232.

187 Ibn Qayyim al-Jawziyya, *Siyāsa*, p. 311.

188 *as-Siyāsa ash-shar'iyya*, pp. 34–5.

189 See Laoust, *Ibn Taimiyya* , 'Introduction' , passim.

190 Al-Azmeh, *Arabic Thought*, p. 254 and notes.

191 For instance, Māwardī, *Naṣīḥā*, pp. 365–7; Juwaynī, *Ghiyāth*, §§ 321 ff.
192 *Muʿīd an-niʿam, wa mubīd an-niqam*, p. 294.
193 For instance, Māwardī, *Naṣīḥā*, pp. 529–31; Subkī, *Muʿīd an-niʿam*, pp. 69–70; Ṭurṭūshī, *Sirāj*, p. 182.
194 For instance, Subkī, *Muʿīd an-niʿam*, p. 33.
195 *Naṣīḥā*, pp. 532–3.
196 For instance, by Baybars in 667/1268–9: Maqrīzī, *Sulūk*, vol. 1, p. 578 – these measures were reversed 13 years later: ibid., p. 668.
197 Ibn al-Jawzī, *Muntaẓam*, vol. 7, p. 48.
198 Maqrīzī, *Sulūk*, vol. 1, p. 304.
199 *Aḥkām*, p. 259.
200 Ṭarsūsī, *Tuḥfa*, pp. 65–9.

Chapter 8

1 For copious material on the connections between Shīʿism and Sufism, See Muṣṭafā Kāmil ash-Shībī, *as-Ṣila bayn at-taṣawwuf waʾt-tashayyuʿ*, 2nd ed., Cairo, 1969.

2 On this: al-ʿAẓma, *al-Kitāba at-tārīkhiyya*, pp. 113 ff; Al-Azmeh, 'Chronophagous Discourse', pp. 169 ff.

3 See J. M. Hussain, *The Occultation of the Twelfth Imam. A Historical Background*, London, 1982, pp. 56 and passim.

4 Morony, *Iraq after the Muslim Conquest*, pp. 484 ff.

5 Tawḥīdī, *Baṣāʾir*, vol. 5, § 752.

6 E. Kohlberg, 'From Imāmiyya to Ithnā ʿAshariyya', *Bulletin of the School of Oriental and African Studies*, 39(1976), pp. 521 ff, 529 ff.

7 Ibn al-Jawzī, *Muntaẓam*, vol. 8, p. 58 and vol. 7, p. 224, where ash-Sharīf ar-Raḍī's poem on the occasion of the death of al-Ṭāʾiʿ is quoted. There is no mention in it of the usual tropes of panegyric for caliphs, but this must be set against the fact that what was possible to say about the defunct caliph must have been circumscribed by the fact of his recent deposition.

8 Wilferd Madelung, 'Authority in Twelver Shiism in the Absence of the Imam', *La notion d'autorité au moyen-age. Islam, Byzance, Occident. Colloques internationaux de la Napoule*, Paris, 1982, pp. 168–9. For Sunnism, Al-Azmeh, *Arabic Thought and Islamic Societies*, pp. 79 ff; idem., 'Chronophagous Discourse', pp. 181 ff.

9 Madelung, 'Authority in Twelver Shiism', pp. 170–1; Arjomand, *The Shadow of God and the Hidden Imam*, pp. 62–3, but contrast pp. 64–5.

10 Madelung, 'Authority in Twelver Shiism', pp. 166–7.

11 Arjomand, *The Shadow of God and the Hidden Imam*, pp. 177–8 and passim.

12 *Nahj al-ḥaqq wa kashf as-ṣidq*, with a commentary by F. Ḥusaynī and R. al-Ṣadr, Beirut, 1982, pp. 212–3.

13 *al-Irshād* , Beirut, 1979, pp. 262–3.

14 See Heinz Halm, *Kosmologie und Heilslehre der frühen Ismā'īlīya. Eine Studie zur islamischen Gnosis*, Wiesbaden, 1978, pp. 38 ff, 116–7.

15 Maqrīzī, *Itti'āẓ al-ḥunafā'*, vol. 1, pp. 190–1.

16 al-Qāḍī an-Nu'mān, *Majālis*, p. 210.

17 Abū Ya'qūb as-Sijistānī, *Kitāb ithbāt an-nubuwwāt*, ed. 'A. Tāmir, Beirut, 1966, p. 156.

18 al-Qāḍī an-Nu'mān, *Asās at-ta'wīl*, pp. 93–4.

19 Halm, *Kosmologie und Heilslehre* , pp. 18 ff, 31–7.

20 This specification was not universally adopted by the Ismā'īlīs and was a matter of controversy (Daftary, *The Ismailis*, pp. 236–8); the present reference is to the Ismā'īlism of the Fātimids.

21 For instance, Sijistānī, *Nubuwwāt*, p. 193; al-Qāḍī an-Nu'mān, *Ta'wīl*, ch.1–5.

22 Halm, *Kosmologie und Heilslehre*, p. 20. For Adamic topoi amply used by the Ismā'īlīs, see ibid., pp. 101 ff.

23 *Ta'wīl*, pp. 315 ff On Fātimid reactions to their own Caliphate and for the doctrinal consequences thereof, see Daftary, *The Ismailis*, pp. 126 ff, 177 ff, 218 ff.

24 Sijistānī, *Nubuwwāt*, p. 27.

25 Daftary, *The Ismailis*, p. 233.

26 al-Kirmānī, *Rāḥat al-'aql*, ed. M. K. Ḥusayn and M. M. Ḥilmī, Cairo, 1952, p. 126.

27 Al-Azmeh, *Arabic Thought and Islamic Societies*, pp. 69 ff.

28 See particularly, Yves Marquet, 'Les cycles de la souveraintè selon les épitres des Iḫwān al-Ṣafā', in *Studia Islamica*, xxxvi(1972), pp. 47–69, for an identification of the main lineaments of this question.

29 Maqrīzī, *Itti'āẓ al-ḥunafā'*, vol. 1, pp. 113, 231, and p. 93 for the horoscope of al-Mu'izz.

30 For instance, al-Qāḍī an-Nu'mān, *Majālis*, pp. 131–2, 433, 439, and cf. Arabic text in S. M. Stern, 'al-Mahdī's Reign According to 'Uyūn al-Akhbār', in idem., *Studies in Early Ismailism*, Jerusalem & Leiden, 1983, p. 105.

31 Maqrīzī, *Itti'āẓ*, vol. 1, pp. 112, 114, and Ibn al-Jawzī, *Muntaẓam*, vol. 7, p. 49. Sanders, *Court Ceremonial*, pp. 68 ff, seems to over-interpret the material somewhat.

32 For instance, Maqrīzī, *Sulūk*, vol. 1, p. 98.

33 Sijistānī, *Nubuwwāt*, p. 157.

34 See Walker, *Early Philosophical Shiism: Ismaili Neoplatonism of Abu Ya'qub al-Sijistani*, Cambridge, 1993.

35 See in general, Heinz Halm, *Kosmologie und Heilslehre* , passim.

36 For the the variety of Ismā'īlī works and their regional and temporal characteristics, see Halm, *Kosmologie und Heilslehre*, p. 16.

37 al-Kirmānī, *Rāḥat al-'aql*, pp. 59 f., 64 ff, 76 ff, 87–88. On the severely transcendentalist theology of divine attributes, see pp. 30, 42 ff, 49 ff.

38 It must be noted that Kirmānī (*Rāḥat al-'aql*, p. 154) does postulate

13 spheres in one discussion. But this seems to be the case because this scheme incorporates the four elements serially rather than together as a unit of materiality, starting with fire as the tenth sphere.

39 Ibid., p. 104.

40 Ibid., p. 154, and see n 38 above.

41 Ibid., pp. 134–5.

42 Ibid., p. 123.

43 Ibid., pp. 357, 364, 367.

44 ʿAlī b. Muḥammad, *Tāj*, pp. 49–50.

45 *The Nasirean Ethics*, p. 29.

46 Kirmānī, *Rāḥat al-ʿaql*, p. 18.

47 Al-Azmeh, *Arabic Thought and Islamic Societies*, pp. 3 ff.

48 See Miguel Asín Palacios, *The Mystical Philosophy of Ibn Masarra and his Followers*, tr. E. H. Douglas and H. W. Yoder, Leiden, 1978, pp. 119ff, 123 ff, with the discussion of Paul Nwiya, 'Note sur quelques fragments inédits et de la correspondance d'Ibn al-ʿArīf avec Ibn Barrajān', in *Hespéris*, 43(1956), pp. 217 ff, and Abul-Ala Affifi, *The Mystical Philosophy of Muhyid Din-Ibnul Arabi* [1939], Lahore, 1964, pp. 174 ff.

49 Ibn Khaldūn, *Shifāʾ as-sāʾil li-tahdhīb al-masāʾil*, ed. I. A. Khalifé, Beirut, 1959, pp. 51–3.

50 Suyūṭī, *ad-Durr al-manthūr*, ad loc.

51 Ibn ʿArabī, *Futūḥāt*, vol. 4, p. 4.

52 Ibid., pp. 3–4.

53 Ibid., vol. 2, pp. 6–7.

54 Ibn ʿArabī, *at-Tadbīrāt al-ilāhiyya fī iṣlāḥ al-mamlaka al-insāniyya*, ed. H. H. Nyberg in *Kleinere Schriften des Ibn al-ʿArabī*, Leiden, 1919, pp. 146–98.

55 Ibn ʿArabī, *Futūḥāt*, vol. 3, p. 328.

56 Ibid., vol. 4, p. 3.

57 H. Ziai, 'The Source and Nature of Authority: A Study of al-Suhrawardī's Illuminationist Political Doctrine', in *The Political Aspects of Islamic Philosophy*, ed. C. E. Butterworth, Cambridge, Mass., 1992, pp. 315, 315n29, 317, 329, 333–4.

58 Ibn ʿArabī, *Tadbīrāt*, pp. 125, 131–2, and cf. p. 120.

59 Ibn ʿArabī, *Futūḥāt*, vol. 2, p. 7.

60 Arjomand, *The Shadow of God*, pp. 80–1 and passim.

61 Ibn Qasī, *Kitāb Khalʿ an-naʿlayn wa iqtibās al-anwār min mawḍiʿ al-qadamayn*, Arabic text edited with an introduction by David Raymond Goodrich, *A 'Sufi' Revolt in Portugal; Ibn Qasi and his 'Kitab Khalʿ al-Naʿlayn'*, Ph.D. thesis, Columbia University, 1978, p. 77.

62 Ibid., pp. 84–5.

63 Ibn Khaldūn, *Prolégomènes*, vol. 2, pp. 168 ff; and cf. idem., *Shifāʾ as-sāʾil*, pp. 53–6.

64 Ibn Qasī, *Khalʿ an-naʿlayn*, pp. 90–1.

65 For instance, al-Shaykh al-Mufīd, *Irshād*, pp. 356–8.

66 For instance, Ibn Kathīr, *Nihāyat al-bidāya waʾn-nihāya fīʾl-fitan waʾl-*

malāḥim, ed. M. F. Abū 'Ubayya, Riyadh, 1968, vol. 1, passim.

67 P. J. Alexander, *The Byzantine Apocalyptic Tradition*, Berkeley and Los Angeles, 1975, pp. 151 ff, 185 ff, 193 ff, and passim.

68 Gershom Scholem, *Sabbatai Sevi. The Mystical Messiah 1626–1676*, London, 1973, pp. 402-3, 414.

69 Most notably, Sibṭ Ibn al-Jawzī: Wilferd Madelung, 'Mahdī', *Encyclopedia of Islam*, new ed., vol. 5, pp. 1236–7 and 1230–9, passim.

70 But care must be shown in handling this matter, in the light of remarks in Dominique Urvoy, 'La pensée d'Ibn Tūmart', in *Bulletin d'Etudes Orientales*, 27(1974), pp. 38–9.

71 For instance, Ibn Khaldūn, *Prolégomènes*, vol. 1, p. 290. On this entire matter, Ibn Khaldūn's account (Ibid., vol. 2, pp. 142–200) is indispensable and by far the fullest.

72 Wilferd Madelung, 'New Documents concerning al-Ma'mūn, al-Faḍl b. Sahl and 'Alī al-Riḍā' in *Studia Arabica et Islamica. Festschrift for Iḥsān 'Abbās*, ed. Wadād al-Qāḍī, Beirut. 1981, pp. 333–46.

73 Ḥajjī Khalīfa, *Kashf az-ẓunūn 'an asāmī al-kutub wa'l-funūn*, ed. S. Yaltakaya and R. Bilge, Istanbul, 1942, vol. 2, pp. 1812–3; Ibn Khaldūn, *Prolégomènes*, vol. 2, pp. 168, 170, 196; Loth, 'al-Kindī als Astrolog', passim.

74 This has been the subject of careful combing for references to contemporary events, and was thus uniquely studied, albeit in sheer philologico-historical manner: Richard Hartmann, 'Eine islamische Apocalypse aus der Kreuzzugszeit' in *Schriften der Königsberger Gelehrten Gesellschaft. Geisteswissenschaftliche Klasse*, 3(1924), pp. 89–106.

75 Heinz Halm, *Shiism*, Edinburgh 1991, pp. 62–3.

76 al-Sha'rānī, *aṭ-Ṭabaqāt al-kubrā al-musammāt bi-lawāqiḥ al-anwār fi ṭabaqāt al-akhyār*, Cairo, 1954, vol. 1, p. 15.

77 *Khal' an-na'layn*, pp. 250–1.

78 Goodrich, *Ibn Qasī*, pp. 17–8, 56–7.

79 Arjomand, *The Shadow of God*, pp. 69–70, 161.

80 *Futūḥāt*, vol. 4, p. 3.

81 For instance, al-Shaykh al-Mufīd, *Irshād*, pp. 346 ff and Ibn Kathīr, *Nihāya*, passim, for Sunnīte narratives.

82 Scholem, *Sabbatai Sevi*, pp. 334 ff, 347.

83 Donald M. Nicol, *The Immortal Emperor. The Life and Legend of Constantine Palaiologos, Last Emperor of the Romans*, Cambridge, 1994, pp. 101–2.

84 al-'Allāma al-Ḥillī, *al-Alfayn fi imāmat amīr al-mu'minīn 'Alī b. 'Abī Ṭālib*, introduced by H. al-A'lamī, Beirut, 1982, pp. 15–20.

85 Ibid., p. 12.

86 Ibid., p. 13.

87 Ibid., p. 15.

88 Ibid., p. 47.

89 Ibid., pp. 21–8, 32.

90 al-Qāḍī an-Nu'mān, *Ta'wīl*, pp. 50–1.

91 Ibid., p. 52. Cf. ʿAlī b. Muḥammad b. al-Walīd, *Tāj*, p. 65.
92 *al-Himma*, p. 39.
93 al-ʿAllāma al-Ḥillī, *al-Alfayn*, p. 55.
94 al-Qāḍī an-Nuʿmān, *Majālis*, p. 118.
95 ʿAlī b. Muḥammad b. al-Walīd, *Tāj*, p. 77.
96 al-ʿAllāma al-Ḥillī, *al-Alfayn*, pp. 36–46.
97 al-ʿAllāma al-Ḥillī, *Nahj al-ḥaqq*, pp. 56–445.
98 al-Qāḍī an-Nuʿmān, *Majālis*, p. 433.
99 al-ʿAllāma al-Ḥillī, *Nahj al-ḥaqq*, pp. 142–63.
100 Ibid., p. 168.
101 Ibid., p. 168.
102 Ibid., pp. 171–240.
103 *Rasāʾil*, vol. 4, pp. 19 ff.
104 For instance, Juwaynī, *Irshād*, pp. 419 ff; Suyūṭī, *Khulafāʾ*, pp. 9–11.
105 al-Qāḍī an-Nuʿmān, *Majālis*, pp. 84, 408, 419–20, 548–9.
106 Māwardī, *Aḥkām*, p. 11.
107 *Tadbīrāt*, p. 140.
108 Qalqashandī, *Khilāfa*, vol. 1, pp. 168, 170, vol. 2, p. 343, vol. 3, p. 41, and Suyūṭī, *Khulafāʾ*, p. 9.
109 For instance: Ghazālī, *Iljām al-ʿawām ʿan ʿilm al-kalām*, Cairo, AH 1351; Ibn al-Jawzī, *Kitāb al-quṣṣāṣ waʾl-mudhakkirīn*, ed. M. S. Swartz, Beirut, n.d.
110 Al-Azmeh, 'Orthodoxy and Hanbalite Fideism', passim.
111 Al-Azmeh, *Arabic Thought and Islamic Societies*, pp. 134–5.
112 For instance, Jāḥiẓ, *Rasāʾil*, vol. 4, pp. 36–40.
113 Tawḥīdī, *Imtāʿ*, vol. 1, pp. 205, 225.
114 Jāḥiẓ, *Rasāʾil*, vol. 4, p. 43.
115 Ibid, pp. 36–8.
116 For instance: ibid., pp. 40–1; Masʿūdī, *Murūj* , §§ 1847–50; ʿAmirī, *Saʿāda*, pp. 184–5.
117 Ibn Rushd, *Talkhīṣ as-safsaṭa*, ed. M. S. Sālim, Cairo, 1973, p. 96.
118 For the complexity of Fārābī, and the poverty of standard positions on his philosophy, see particularly Miriam Galston, *Politics and Excellence. The Political Philosophy of Alfarabi*, Princeton, 1990, ch 1 and passim. The philosopher's multivocality was clear to other Muslim philosophers, for instance, Ibn Tufayl, *Ḥayy b. Yaqẓān*, in *Ḥayy b. Yaqẓān li Ibn Sīnā wa Ibn Ṭufayl waʾl-Suhrawardī*, ed. A. Amīn, Cairo, 1958, pp. 62–3.
119 On the paradigmatic description of what constitutes philosophy in Muslim thought in the Middle Ages, see Al-Azmeh, *Arabic Thought and Islamic Societies*, pp. 205 ff.
120 *The Nasirean Ethics*, p. 192.
121 This is an idea of profound implication for medieval Muslim thought, one which is nevertheless very rarely considered. See Al-Azmeh, *Arabic Thought and Islamic Societies*, pp. 2 ff.
122 *The Nasirean Ethics*, p. 52.
123 On this: Aziz Al-Azmeh, 'A Rhetoric for the Senses. A Reading of

Muslim Paradise Narratives', in *Journal of Arabic Literature* , XXVI(1995), pp. 215–31.

124 Al-Azmeh, *Arabic Thought and Islamic Societies*, pp. 56 ff.

125 Fārābī, *Madīna* , p. 244.

126 Ibid., p. 240. Cf. Al-Azmeh, *Arabic Thought and Islamic Societies*, pp. 57, 61–2.

127 Cf. Hans Daiber, 'The Ismaili Background of Fārābī's Political Philosophy. Abū Hātim ar-Rāzī as a Forerunner of Fārābī', in *Gottes ist der Orient, Gottes is der Okzident. Festschrift für Abdoljavad Falaturi*, ed. Udo Tworuschka, Köln-Wien, 1991, pp. 143–150.

128 Tawḥīdī, *Imtā'*, vol. 3, p. 99.

129 *as-Sa'āda wa'l-is'ād*, pp. 189–90.

130 Ibid., pp. 196–200.

131 Nassif Nassar, 'Le maître d'Ibn Khaldūn: al-Abilī', in *Studia Islamica*, 20(1964), pp. 103–114.

132 Ibn Maryam, *al-Bustān fī dhikr al-awliyā' wa'l-'ulamā' bi-Tilimsān*, ed. M. Bencheneb, Algiers, 1908, p. 215.

133 Galston, *Politics and Excellence*, pp. 92–3 and passim.

134 Ibid., pp. 84 ff.

135 Jurjānī, *Kitāb at-ta'rīfāt*, ed. G. Flügel as *Definitiones*, Leipzig, 1845, p. 176.

136 *Madīna* , pp. 246–52.

137 *ash-Shifā' (Ilāhiyyāt, 2)*, p. 455. Two of the fullest and clearest statements of classical ethical theory based on the notions of justice and the mean, and in the context of philosophical psychology, can be found in Miskawayh, *Tahdhīb al-akhlāq*, pp. 16 ff, and Ṭūsī, *The Nasirean Ethics*, Bk 1, which incorporates interesting innovative twists.

138 *Averroes' Commentary on Plato's Republic*, pp. 159–60.

139 See D. Gutas, *Avicenna and the Aristotelian Tradition*, Leiden, 1988, pp. 300 ff, and P. Heath, *Allegory and Philosophy*, 1992, pp. 150.

140 Al-Azmeh, *Arabic Thought and Islamic Societies*, pp. 109 ff.

141 Ibn Rushd, *Faṣl al-maqāl fī mā bayna al-ḥikma wa'sh-sharī'a min ittiṣāl*, ed. Muḥammad 'Umāra, Beirut, 1981, p. 14.

142 Ibid., p. 13.

143 Ibn Rushd, *Talkhīṣ al-jadal*, pp. 8 and passim, and cf. the discussion of Dominique Urvoy, *Ibn Rushd (Averroes)*, London, 1991, pp. 75–80.

144 *al-Fiṣal fi'l-milal wa'l-ahwā' wa'n-niḥal*, Cairo, AH 1317, vol. 1, p. 94.

145 *Muwāfaqat ṣaḥīḥ al-manqūl li-ṣarīḥ al-ma'qūl*, ed. M. M. 'Abd al-Ḥamīd and M. M. al-Fiqī, Cairo, 1950–51, vol. 1, p. 181.

146 *The Nasirean Ethics*, p. 211.

147 *Madīna* , pp. 276–80; Galston, *Politics and Excellence*, pp. 144–5. Cf. *The Nasirean Ethics*, p. 214.

148 *Averroes' Commentary on Plato's Republic*, pp. 115–7.

149 *Kitāb al-milla*, ed. Muḥsin Mahdī, Beirut, 1968, § 10. See also *The Nasirean Ethics*, p. 214.

150 *The Nasirean Ethics*, p. 213. Cf. Bīrūnī, *Taḥqīq mā li'l-Hind min maqūla maqbūla fī'l-ʿaql am mardhūla*, Hyderabad, 1958, pp. 5–19.

151 ed. ʿA. Maḥmūd and ʿA. Ḥ. Maḥmūd, Cairo, n.d.

152 Ibn Rushd, *Talkhīṣ al-khaṭāba*, pp. 139–140, 213, 230–4.

153 Cf. ʿAbd as-Salām Bin ʿAbd al-ʿĀlī, *al-Falsafa as-siyāsiyya ʿind al-Fārābī*, Beirut, 1979, pp. 31–2.

154 Galston, *Politics and Excellence*, pp. 142–4. Cf. Miskawayh, *Tahdhīb al-akhlāq*, pp. 14–15, for a more radical statement on the necessary divisibility of excellences.

155 Ibn Bāja, *Tadbīr al-mutawaḥḥid*, in idem., *Rasā'il Ibn Bāja al-ilāhiyya*, ed. Mājid Fakhrī, Beirut, 1968, pp. 43, 49 ff, 55, 79 ff and passim; Galston, *Politics and Excellence*, pp. 175–7. Cf. the traditionalist, Hanbalite, rendition of this position in Ibn Rajab, *Kashf al-kurba bi-waṣf ḥāl ahl al-ghurba*, prepared by Jamāl Māḍī, Alexandria, 1983.

156 *The Nasirean Ethics*, pp. 194–5.

157 Miskawayh, *Tahdhīb al-akhlāq*, pp. 29–30, 167–8.

158 Miriam Galston, 'Realism and Idealism in Avicenna's Political Philosophy', in *Review of Politics*, 41(1979), p. 570. For a straightforward statement of the Fārābian position on the didactic function of the king: ʿAmirī, *as-Saʿāda wa'l-isʿād*, pp. 256 and passim.

159 Galston, 'Realism and Idealism', pp. 564, 577.

160 *ash-Shifā' (al-Ilāhiyyāt*, 2), pp. 442–3.

161 *The Nasirean Ethics*, p. 196, 215, 200 ff, and cf. Fārābī, *Fuṣūl al-madanī*, ed. D. M. Dunlop, Cambridge, 1961, pp. 140–1.

162 *The Nasirean Ethics*, p. 215.

163 ʿAmirī, *as-Saʿāda wa'l-isʿād*, pp. 212–5.

164 *The Nasirean Ethics*, pp. 47, 214; Fārābī, *Madīna* , pp. 236–8.

165 ʿAmirī, *as-Saʿāda wa'l-isʿād*, pp. 200–9.

166 *Tahdhīb al-akhlāq*, pp. 62, 102.

167 *Faṣl al-maqāl*, p. 15.

168 *Averroes' Commentary on Plato's Republic*, pp. 118–9, 129, 181.

169 Ibid., p. 185.

170 Al-Azmeh, 'Chronophagous Discourse', pp. 191 ff.

171 Miskawayh, *Tahdhīb*, pp. 140–1.

172 Ibn Sīnā, *ash-Shifā'* (*al-Ilāhiyyāt*, 2), p. 444.

Bibliography

Medieval Arabic and Ancient Sources

'Abd al-Ḥamīd al-Kātib, 'Risālat 'Abd al-Hamīd al-Kātib fī naṣīhat walī al-'ahd', in M. Kurd 'Alī, *Rasā'il al-bulaghā'*, Cairo, 1954, pp. 173–210.

'Abd al-Jabbār, al-Qāḍī, *al-Mughnī fī abwāb al-'adl wa't-tawḥīd*, vol 20/1:*Fī'l-imāma*, ed. 'A. Maḥmūd and S. Dunyā, Cairo, n.d.

Abū Ḥammū, *Wasīṭat as-sulūk fī siyāsat al-mulūk*, Tunis, AH 1279 [1862].

Abū Ya'lā b. al-Farrā', *al-Aḥkām as-sulṭāniyya*, ed. M. H. al-Fiqī, Cairo, 1966.

—— *al-Mu'tamad fī uṣūl ad-dīn*, ed. W. Z. Ḥaddād, Beirut, 1974.

'Ahd Ardashīr, ed. Iḥsān 'Abbās, Beirut, 1976.

Aḥmad b. Yūsuf b. al-Dāya, 'Kitāb al-'uhūd al-yūnāniyya al-mustakhraja min rumūz "as-siyāsa" li-Aflāṭun wa mā inḍāfa ilaihi', in *al-Uṣūl al-yūnāniyya li'l-naẓariyyāt as-siyāsiyya fī'l-Islām*, ed. 'A. Badawī, Cairo, 1954.

al-Akhṭal, *Shi'r al-Akhṭal Abī Mālik Ghiyāth b. Ghawth at-Taghlibī*, ed. F. Qabāwa, 2 vols, Aleppo, 1971.

Alf layla wa layla, 4 vols, Būlāq, AH 1279.

Alf layla wa layla, ed. M. Mahdi, Leiden, 1984.

'Alī b. Muḥammad al-Walīd, *Tāj al-'aqā'id was ma'din al-fawā'id*, ed. 'A. Tāmir, Beirut, 1967.

al-Āmidī, *Ghāyat al-marām fī 'ilm al-kalām*,ed. H. M. 'Abd al-Laṭīf, Cairo, 1971.

al-'Āmirī, Abu'l-Ḥasan, *as-Sa'āda wa'l-is'ād fī's-sīra al-insāniyya*, ed. M. Minovi, Tehran, 1957–58.

al-Ash'arī, Abu'l-Ḥasan, *al-Luma' fī'r-radd 'alā ahl az-zīgh wa'l-bida'*, ed. R. J. McCarthy in *The Theology of al-Ash'arī*, Beirut, 1953.

—— *Maqālāt al-Islamiyyīn wa ikhtilāf al-muṣallīn*, ed. M. M. 'Abd al-Ḥamīd, Cairo, 4 vols, 1950–54.

al-'Askarī, Abū Hilāl, *al-Awā'il*, ed. M. al-Miṣrī and W. Qaṣṣāb, Damascus, 1975.

Badawī: see *al-Uṣūl al-Yūnāniyya*.

al-Baghdādī, 'Abd al-Qāhir, *Kitāb uṣūl ad-dīn*, Istanbul, 1928.

Bahr al-Favā'id: The Sea of Precious Virtues. A Medieval Islamic Mirror for Princes, tr. from Persian by J. Scott Meisami, Salt Lake City, 1991.

al-Bīrūnī, *al-Āthār al-bāqiya 'an al-qurūn al-khāliya*, ed. C. E. Sachau, Leipzig, 1923.

—— *Taḥqīq mā li'l-Hind min maqūla maqbūla fi'l-'aql aw mardhūla*, rev. ed., Hyderabad, 1958.

Boyce, M. (Tr.), *The Letter of Tansar*, Rome, 1968.

al-Dhahabī, *al-'Ibar fī khabar man ghabar*, ed. S. al-Munajjid, 5 vols, Kuwait, 1960.

Daiber, H. 'The Creed (*'aqīda*) of the Hanbalite Ibn Qudama al-Maqdisī. A Newly Discovered Text', in *Studia Arabica et islamica. Festschrift for Iḥsān 'Abbās*, ed. W. al-Qāḍī, Beirut, 1981, pp. 105–25.

Drake, H. A. *In Praise of Constantine. A Historical Study and New Translation of Eusebius' Tricennial Orations*, Berkeley and Los Angeles, 1976.

Eusebius–see Drake.

al-Fārābī, *Fuṣūl al-madanī*, ed. D. M. Dunlop, Cambridge, 1961.

—— *Iḥṣa' al-'ulūm*, ed. 'U. Amīn, Cairo, 1968.

—— *Kitāb al-milla*, ed. M. Mahdī, Beirut, 1968.

—— *Mabādi' 'ārā' ahl al-madīna al-fāḍila*, ed. R. Walzer, Oxford, 1985.

Fragmenta historicorum arabicorum, ed. de Goeje, 3 vols, Leiden, 1869–71.

al-Ghazālī, *al-Durra al-fākhira fī kashf 'ulūm al-ākhira*, ed. L. Gautier as *La perle précieuse* [1878], Amsterdam, 1974.

—— *Iḥyā' 'ulūm ad-dīn*, 4 vols, Cairo, 1939.

—— *Iljām al-'awām 'an 'ilm al-kalām*, Cairo, AH 1351.

—— *al-Iqtiṣad fi'l-i'tiqād*, ed. I. A. Çubukçu and H. Atay, Ankara, 1962.

—— *al-Maḥabba wa'l-uns wa'sh-shawq wa'r-riḍā*, Cairo, 1961.

—— *Maqāmāt al-'ulamā' bayna aidī al-khulafā' wa'l-umarā'*, ed. J. al-Hadīthī, Baghdad, 1988 [doubt has been cast about the attribution of this book to this particular author].

—— *Mīzān al-'amal*, ed. S. Dunyā, Cairo, 1964.

—— *al-Munqidh min aḍ-ḍalāl wa'l-mūṣil ilī dhī'l-'izza wa'l-jalāl*, ed. J. Ṣalībā and K. 'Ayyād, Beirut, 1967.

—— *at-Tibr al-masbūk fī naṣīḥat al-mulūk*, ed. M. A. Damaj, Beirut, 1987.

Ḥajjī Khalīfa, *Kashf aẓ-ẓunūn 'an asāmī al-kutub wa'l-funūn*, ed. S. Yaltakaya and R. Bilge, 2 vols, Istanbul, 1942.

—— 'Hāğī Chalfa's Dustūr'l-amel. Ein Beitrag zur osmanischen Finanzgeschichte', tr. W. W. A. Behrnauer, *in Zeitschrift der Deutschen Morgenländischen Gesellschaft*, xi(1857).

Hartmann, R. 'Eine islamische Apokalypse as der Kreuzzugszeit', in *Schriften der Königsberger Gelehrten Gesellschaft, Geisteswissenschaftliche Klasse*, 3 (1924), 89–116.

Ḥikāyat al-asad wa'l-ghawwāṣ, ed. R. as-Sayyid, Beirut, 1978.

Hilāl aṣ-Ṣābī — see aṣ-Ṣābī.

al-Ḥillī, al-'Allāma, *al-Alfayn fī imāmat Amīr al-Mu'minīn 'Alī b. Abī Tālib 'alaih as-salām*, Beirut, 1982.

—— *Nahj al-ḥaqq was kashf aṣ-ṣidq*, Beirut, 1982.

al-Ḥillī, al-Muṭahhar, *Tabṣirat al-muta'allimīn fī aḥkām ad-dīn*, ed. A. al-

Ḥusaynī and Ḥ. al-Yūsufī, Beirut, 1982.
Ibn ʿAbd al-Barr, *Jāmiʿ bayān al-ʿilm wa fadlih wa mā yanbaghī fī riwāyatihi wa ḥamlih*, [ed. Muḥammad Munīr b. ʿAbduh al- Dimashqī] 2 vols, Cairo, [AH 1346].
Ibn ʿAbd Rabbih, *Dīwān*, ed. M. R. al-Dāya, Beirut, 1979.
—— *al-ʿIqd al-farīd*, ed. M. M. Qumayḥa, 9 vols, Beirut, 1983.
Ibn Abī Ṭāhir Ṭayfūr, *Kitāb Baghdād, al-juzʾ as-sādis*, ed. H. Keller, Leipzig, 1908.
Ibn Abī Yaʿlā, *Ṭabaqāt al-Ḥanābila*, ed. M. H. al-Fiqī, 2 vols, Cairo, 1952.
Ibn ʿArabī, *al-Futūḥāt al-Makkiyya*, 4 vols, Cairo, AH 1293.
—— *Kitāb al-akhlāq*, Cairo, n.d.
—— *at-Tadbīrāt al-ilāhiyya fī iṣlāh al-mamlaka al-insāniyya*, in *Kleinere Schriften*, ed. H. S. Nyberg, Leiden, 1919.
Ibn al-Azraq, Badāʾiʿ as-silk fī ṭabāʾiʿ al-mulk, ed. ʿA. S. an-Nashshār, vol. 1, Baghdad, 1977.
—— [another edition] ed. M. Bin ʿAbd al-Karīm, 2 vols, Tunis-Libya, 1977.
Ibn Bābawayh [Ibn Bābūyā], *Man lā yaḥdaruhu al-faqīh*, ed. Ḥ. al-Mūsawī, 4 vols, Beirut, 1981.
Ibn Bāja, *Rasāʾil Ibn Bāja al-ilāhiyya*, ed. M. Fakhrī, Beirut, 1968.
Ibn Baṭṭa, *Kitāb ash-sharḥ waʾl-ibāna ʿalā uṣūl as-sunna waʾd-diyāna*, ed. H. Laoust in *La profession de foi d'Ibn Batta*, Damascus, 1958.
——Ibn al-Dāya: see Aḥmad b. Yūsuf.
Ibn Faḍlān, *Risālat Ibn Faḍlān fī waṣf ar-riḥla ilā bilād at-Turk waʾl-Khazar waʾr-Rūs waʾṣ-Ṣaqāliba*, ed. S. al-Dahhān, Damascus, 1978.
Ibn al-Farrāʾ — see Abū Yaʿlā.
Ibn al-Farrāʾ, *Kitāb Rusul al-mulūk wa man yaṣluḥ liʾl-risāla waʾs-sifāra*, ed. Ṣ. al-Munajjid, Beirut, 1972.
Ibn al-Ḥaddād, *al-Jawhar an-nafīs fī siyāsat ar-raʾīs*, ed. R. as-Sayyid, Beirut, 1983.
Ibn Ḥajar al-ʿAsqalānī, *al-Durar al-kāmina fī aʿyān al-miʾa ath-thāmina*, Hyderabad, AH 1348.
Ibn Ḥazm, *Kitāb al-akhlāq waʾs-siyar, aw risāla fī mudāwāt an-nufūs wa tahdhīb al-akhlāq waʾz-zuhd fīʾr-radhāʾil*, ed. E. Riad, Uppsala, 1980.
—— *al-Fiṣal fīʾl-milal waʾl-ahwāʾ waʾn-niḥal*, 5 vols, Cairo, AH 1317.
Ibn Jamāʿa, *Taḥrīr al-aḥkām fī tadbīr ahl al-Islām*, ed. H. Kofler, in *Islamica*, 6(1934), pp. 349–414, 7(1935), pp. 1–34; translation: 7(1935), pp. 34–64, 1938, pp. 18–129.
Ibn al-Jawzī, *Manāqib al-Imām Aḥmad b. Ḥanbal*, Beirut, 1973.
—— *al-Miṣbāh al-muḍīʾ fī khilāfat al-Mustaḍīʾ*, ed. N. ʿA. Ibrāhīm, 2 vols, Baghdad, 1976–77.
—— *al-Mudhish*, ed. M. Qabbānī, Beirut, 1981.
—— *al-Muntaẓam fī tārīkh al-mulūk waʾl-umam*, ed. Krenkow, 10 vols, Hyderabad, AH 1357–58.

—— *Kitāb al-quṣṣaṣ wa'l-mudhakkirīn*, ed. M. S. Swartz, Beirut, n.d.
—— *ash-Shifā' fī mawā'iẓ al-mulūk wa'l-khulafā'*, ed. F. 'A. Aḥmad, Alexandria, 1978.
—— *Talbīs Iblīs*, Beirut, n.d. [after the edition of Cairo, AH 1368].
—— *Zād al-masīr fī 'ilm at-tafsīr*, 9 vols, Damascus, 1964–68.
Ibn Kathīr, *Nihāyat al-bidāya wa'n-nihāya fi'l-fitan wa'l-malāḥim*, ed. M. F. Abū 'Ubayya, 2 vols, Riyadh, 1968.
Ibn Khaldūn, Abū Bakr, 'Le traitée d'Adab al-Kātib d'Abū Bakr Ibn Ḫaldūn', ed. E. Lévi-Provencal, in *Arabica*, 11(1955), pp. 280–8.
Ibn Khaldūn, Abū Zayd 'Abd ar-Raḥmān, *Les Prolégomènes d'Ebn Khaledoun*, 3 vols, ed. E. Quatremère, Paris, 1858.
—— *Shifā' as-sā'il li-tahdhīb al-masā'il*, ed. I. 'A. Khalīfa S. J. Beirut, 1959.
—— *at-Ta'rīf bi-Ibn Khaldūn wa riḥtatuhu gharban wa sharqan*, ed. M. b. Tāwīt aṭ-Ṭanjī, Cairo, 1951.
—— *Tārīkh al-'allāma Ibn Khaldūn*, ed. Y. A. Dāghir, 7 vols, Beirut, 1956 ff.
Ibn Khallikān, *Wafayāt al-a'yān*, ed. I. 'Abbās, 8 vols, Beirut, 1970.
Ibn al-Khaṭīb, Lisān ad-Dīn, *al-Ishāra ilā adab al-wizāra*, ed. M. K. Shabāna, Rabat,1980–81.
Ibn Maryam, *al-Bustān fī dhikr al-awliyā' wa'l-'ulamā' bi Tilimsān*, ed. M. Bencheneb, Algiers, 1908.
Ibn al-Mi'mār, *Kitāb al-futuwwa*, ed. M. Jawād et al., Baghdad, 1958.
Ibn al-Muqaffa', *al-Adab al-kabīr*, *al-adab as-saghīr*, *al-Yatīma ath-thāniya*, and *Risāla fi'ṣ-ṣahāba* in M. Kurd 'Alī (ed.), *Rasā'il al-bulaghā'*, Cairo, 1954, pp. 1–241.
—— *al-Durra al-yatīma*, ed. A. R. al-Badrāwī, Beirut, 1974.
—— see also: *Kalīla wa Dimna.*
Ibn Qasī, *Kitāb khal' an-na'layn wa iqtibās al-anwār min mawdi' al-qadamayn*, Arabic text ed. and tr. by D. R. Goodrich in 'A "Sufi" Revolt in Portugal: Ibn Qasi and his 'Kitab Khal' al-Na'layn' (Arabic Text), Ph.D. dissertation Columbia University, 1979 (UMI).
Ibn Qayyim al-Jawziyya, *I'lām al-muwaqqi'īn 'an rabb al-'ālamīn*, 4 vols, Beirut, n.d.
—— *Rawḍat al-muḥibbīn wa nuzhat al-mushtāqīn*, ed. S. Yūsuf, Beirut, 1982.
—— *aṭ-Ṭuruq al-ḥikmiyya fi's-siyāsa ash-shar'iyya*, ed. A. 'A. al-'Askarī, Cairo, 1961.
Ibn Qudāma – see Daiber.
Ibn Qunfudh, *al-Fārisiyya fī mabādi' ad-dawla al-Ḥafṣiyya*, ed. M. S. an-Nīfar and 'A. at-Turkī, Tunis, 1968.
—— *al-Wafayāt*, ed. 'A. Nuwaihiḍ, Beirut, 1971.
Ibn Qutayba, *'Uyūn al-akhbār*, 4 vols, Cairo, 1925–1930.
Ibn Rajab, *al-Dhail 'alā ṭabaqāt al-Ḥanābila*, ed. M. M. al-Fiqī, 2 vols, Cairo, 1952.
—— *Kashf al-kurba 'an ḥāl ahl al-ghurba*, ed. J. Māḍī, Alexandria, 1983.
Ibn Riḍwān, *ash-Shuhub al-lāmi'a fi's-siyāsa an-nāfi'a*, ed. 'A. S. an-Nashshār,

Casablanca, 1984.
Ibn Rushd, *Bidāyat al-mujtahid wa nihāyat al-muqtaṣid*, ed. ʿAbd al- Ḥalīm Maḥmūd and ʿAbd ar-Raḥmān Ḥasan Maḥmūd, Cairo, n.d.
—— *Faṣl al-maqāl fī mā bayna al-ḥikma waʾsh-sharīʿa min al-ittiṣāl*, ed. M. ʿUmāra, Beirut, 1981.
—— *Talkhīṣ al-khaṭāba*, ed. Muḥammad Salīm Sālim, Cairo, 1967.
—— *Talkhīṣ kitāb Arisṭūṭālīs fīʾsh-shiʿr*, ed. Muḥammad Salīm Sālim, Cairo, 1971.
—— *Talkhīṣ as-safsaṭa*, ed. Maḥmūd Salīm Sālim, Cairo, 1973.
—— *Averroes' Commentary on Plato's Republic*, ed. and tr. E. I. J. Rosenthal, Cambridge, 1966.
Ibn Sīnā, 'Athar Majhūl li Ibn Sīnā [Kitāb at-Tadbīr]', ed. L. Maʿlūf S.J., in *al-Mashriq*, 9(1906), pp. 961–73, 1037–42, 1073–8.
—— *ash-Shifāʾ (al-Ilāhiyyāt, 2)*, ed. M. Y. Mūsā et al., Cairo, 1960.
—— *Tisʿ rasāʾil*, Istanbul, AH 1298.
Ibn Sīrīn, *Muntakhab al-kalām fī tafsīr al-aḥlām*, on the margins of Nābulsī: see Nābulsī, vol. 1.
Ibn Ṭabāṭabā (Ibn aṭ-Ṭiqṭaqā), *al-Fakhrī fīʾl-ādāb as-sulṭāniyya waʾd-duwal al-islāmiyya*, Cairo, 1962.
Ibn Taymiyya, *Minhāj as-sunna an-nabawiyya fī naqd kalām ash-Shīʿa waʾl-Qadariyya*, 4 vols, Cairo, AH 1322.
—— *Muwāfaqat ṣaḥīḥ al-manqūl li-ṣarīḥ al-maʿqūl*, ed. M. M. ʿAbd al-Ḥamīd and M. M. al-Fiqī, 3 vols, Cairo, 1950–51.
—— *as-Siyāsa ash-sharʿiyya fī iṣlāh ar-rāʿī waʾr-raʿiyya*, Cairo, AH 1322; another reprint: Beirut, [1966].
Ibn Ṭufayl, *Ḥayy Ibn Yaqẓān*, in *Ḥayy Ibn Yaqẓān li Ibn Sīnā wa Ibn Ṭufayl waʾs-Suhrawardī*, ed. A. Amīn, Cairo, 1958.
Ibn Ẓafar, *Sulwān al-muṭāʿ fī ʿudwān al-atbāʿ*, ed. A. A. ʿA. Huraydī, [Cairo], 1978.
Ibn az-Zubayr, *Kitāb adh-dhakhaʾir waʾt-tuḥaf*, ed. M. Ḥamīd Allāh, Kuwait, 1984.
al-Jāḥiẓ, *Kitāb al-ḥayawān*, ed. M. ʿA. Hārūn, 8 vols, Cairo, 1965–68.
——-*Kitāb at-Tāj fī akhlāq al-mulūk*, ed. A. Zakī Pāshā, Cairo, 1914; French translation by Ch. Pellat, *Le livre de la couronne, ouvrage attribué a Ǧāḥiẓ*, Paris, 1954.
—— 'Min Kitāb al-amṣār wa ʿajāʾib al-buldān', ed. Ch Pellat, in *al-Mashriq*, 60(1966), pp. 169–205.
—— *Rasāʾil al-Jāḥiẓ*, ed. M. ʿA. Hārūn, 2 vols, Cairo, 1964.
Jarīr: see as-Ṣāwī.
al-Jurjānī, *at-Taʿrīfāt*, ed. G. Flügel as *Definitiones*, Leipzig, 1854.
al-Juwaynī, *Ghiyāth al-umam fīʾt-tiyāth aẓ-ẓulam*, ed. ʿA. Dīb, [Cairo], AH 1401.
—— *Kitāb al-irshād ilā qawāṭiʿ al-adilla fī uṣūl al-iʿtiqād*, ed. M. Y. Mūsā and ʿA. ʿA. ʿAbd al-Ḥamīd, Cairo, 1950.
Kalīla wa Dimna , translated from Pahlavi by Ibn al-Muqaffaʿ, ed. L Shaykhū

S. J., 11th ed., Beirut, 1973.
Kauṭilīya: see Kangle.
al-Kindī: see Loth.
al-Kirmānī, *Rāḥat al-ʿaql,* ed. M. K. Ḥusayn and M. M. Ḥilmī, Cairo, 1952.
Kurd ʿAlī, Muḥammad (ed.), *Rasāʾil al-bulaghāʾ*, Cairo, 1954.
Loth, O. ʿal-Kindī als Asrtrologʾ, in *Morgenländische Forschungen. Festschrift Heinrich L. Fleischer*, Leipzig, 1875, pp. 263–309 (Arabic text, pp. 273–9).
al-Maqqarī, *Nafḥ aṭ-ṭīb min ghuṣn al-Andalus ar-raṭīb,* ed. I. Abbās, 8 vols, Beirut, 1968.
al-Maqrīzī, *Ittiʿāẓ al-ḥunafāʾ bi-akhbār al-ʿimma al-Fāṭimiyyīn min al-khulafāʾ*, ed. M. Aḥmad, 3 vols, Cairo, 1971 ff.
—— *an-Nizāʿ waʾt-takhāṣum fī mā bayna Banī Umayya wa Banī Hāshim* ed. ʿA. al-Hāshimī an-Najafī, Najaf, AH 1368.
—— *Kitāb as-Sulūk li-maʿrifat duwal al-mulūk*, ed. M. M. Ziyāda and S. ʿA. ʿAshūr, 3 vols, Cairo, 1956–71.
Māshāʾallāh, *The Astrological History of Māshāʾallāh*, ed. E. S. Kennedy and D. Pingree, Cambridge, Mass., 1971.
al-Maskūkāt al-islāmiyya. Majmūʿa mukhtāra min Ṣadr al-Islām ḥattāʾl-ʿahd al-ʿuthmānī, Beirut, The Arab Bank, 1980.
al-Masʿūdī, *Murūj adh-dhahab wa maʿādin al-jawhar*, ed. rev. by Ch. Pellat, Beirut, 1965.
—— *Kitāb at-tanbīh waʾl-ishrāf*, ed. M. J. de Goeje, Leiden, 1894.
al-Māturīdī, *Kitāb at-tawḥīd*, ed. F. Khulayf, Beirut, 1970.
al-Māwardī, *al-Aḥkām as-sulṭāniyya*, ed. M. Enger, Bonn, 1853.
—— *al-Aḥkām as-sulṭāniyya*, Cairo, 1973.
—— *Naṣīḥat al-mulūk,* ed. M. J. al-Ḥadīthī, Baghdad, 1986.
—— *an-Nukat waʾl-ʿuyūn: Tafsīr al-Māwardī*, ed. K. M. Khiḍr, 4 vols, Kuwait, 1982.
—— *Qawānīn al-wizāra wa siyāsat al-mulk*, ed. R. as-Sayyid, Beirut, 1979.
—— *Tashīl an-naẓar wa taʿjīl aẓ-ẓafar fī akhlāq al-mulūk wa siyāsat al-mulk*, ed. R. as-Sayyid, Beirut, 1987.
Miskawayh, *al-Ḥikma al-khālida*, ed. ʿA. Badawī, Cairo, 1952.
—— *Tahdhīb al-akhlāq wa taṭhīr al-aʿrāq*, ed. Q. Zurayq, 1966.
—— *Tajārib al-umam*, ed. H. F. Amedroz, 3 vols, Oxford, 1920–21.
—— *Risāla fī māhiyyat al-ʿadl*, ed. M. S. Khan, Leiden, 1964.
—— ʿTextes inédits de Miskawayhʾ, ed. M. Arkoun, in *Annales Islamologiques*, 5(1963), pp. 186–205.
—— and Tawḥīdī, *al-Hawāmil waʾsh-shawāmil,* ed. A. Amīn and A. Ṣaqr, Cairo, 1951.
al-Mubashshir b. Fātik, *Mukhtār al-ḥikam wa maḥāsin al-kalim*, ed. ʿA. Badawī, Beirut, 1980.
al-Murādī, *Kitāb al-Ishāra ilā adab al-imāra*, ed. R. as-Sayyid, Beirut, 1981.
an-Nābulsī, *Taʿṭīr al-anām fī taʿbīr al-manām*, 2 vols, Cairo, n.d.
Niẓām al-Mulk, *The Book of Government or Rules for Kings*, translated from

Persian by H. Drake, London, 1978.
an-Nuʿmān b. Muḥammad, al-Qāḍī, *Asās at-taʾwīl*, ed. ʿA. Tāmir, Beirut [1960].
—— *al-Himma fī ādāb atbāʿ al-aʾimma*, ed. M. K. Ḥusayn, Cairo, n.d.
—— *al-Majālis waʾl-musāyarāt*, ed. H. al-Fiqī et al., Tunis, 1978.
al-Qalʿī, *Tahdhīb ar-riyāsa wa tartīb as-siyāsa*, ed. Ibrāhīm Yūsuf Muṣṭafā ʿIjjū, Zarqā (Jordan), 1985.
al-Qalqashandī, *Maʾāthir al-ināfa fī maʿālim al-khilāfa*, ed. ʿA. A. Farrāj, 3 vols, Kuwait, 1964.
——-*Ṣubḥ al-aʿshā fī ṣināʿat al-inshā*, 14 vols, Cairo, 1915.
Qurʾān: *The Holy Qurʾan*, tr. ʿAbdallah Yusuf ʿAli, Kuwait, 1984.
ar-Rāghib al-Iṣbahānī, *Muḥāḍarāt al-udabāʾ wa muḥāwarāt ash-shuʿarāʾ waʾl-bulaghāʾ*, abr. I. Zaydān, Beirut, n.d.
Rasāʾil as-Ṣābī waʾsh-Sharīf ar-Raḍī, ed. M. Y. Najm, Kuwait, 1961.
ar-Rāzī, Fakhr ad-Dīn, *Kitāb asās at-taqdīs*, Cairo, AH 1328.
—— *al-Mabāḥith al-mashriqiyya fī ʿilm al-ilāhiyyāt waʾṭ-ṭabīʿiyyāt*, 2 vols, Tehran, 1966.
—— *Muḥaṣṣal afkār al-mutaqaddimīn waʾl-mutaʾakhkhirīn min al-ʿulamāʾ waʾl-ḥukamāʾ waʾl-mutakallimīn*, Cairo, AH 1323.
—— *at-Tafsīr al-kabīr*, Cairo, n.d.
as-Ṣābī, Hilāl b. al-Muḥassin, *Rusūm dār al-khilāfa*, ed. M. ʿAwwād, Baghdad, 1964.
—— *Tuḥfat al-umarāʾ fī tārīkh al-wuzarāʾ – aqsām ḍāʾiʿa*, ed. M. ʿAwwād, Baghdad, 1948.
—— see also: *Rasāʾil.*
Sānī, Muhammad Bāqir Najm-i, *Advice on the Art of Governance (Mauʿizah-i Jahāngīri)*, translated from Persian by S. S. Alavi, Albany, 1989.
as-Ṣāwī, M. I.ʿA., *Sharḥ dīwān Jarīr*, Cairo, AH 1354.
ash-Shaʿrānī, *aṭ-Ṭabaqāt al-kubrā al-musammāt bi lawāḥiq al-anwār fī ṭabaqāt al-akhyār*, 2 vols, Cairo, 1954.
ash-Sharīf ar-Raḍī — see Rasāʾil.
ash-Shawkānī, *Irshād al-fuḥūl ilā taḥqīq al-ḥaqq min ʿilm al-uṣūl*, Cairo, 1937.
ash-Shaykh al-Mufīd, *al-Irshād*, Beirut, 1979.
Sibṭ Ibn at-Taʿāwīdhī, *Dīwān*, ed. D. S. Margoliouth, Cairo, 1903.
as-Sijistānī, Abū Yaʿqūb, *Kitāb ithbāt an-nubuwwāt*, ed. ʿA. Tāmir, Beirut, 1966.
Sirr al-Asrār, *Kitāb as-siyāsa al-maʿrūf bi "Sirr al-asrār" alladhī allafahu al-faylasūf al-fāḍil Aristāṭālīs li-tilmīdhihi al-malik al-muʿaẓẓam al-Ishkandar b. Filibis al-maʿrūf bi Dhiʾl-Qarnayn*, ed. ʿA. Badawī in *al-Uṣūl al-yūnāniyya.*
Stern, S. M. (ed.), 'al-Mahdī's Reign according to "Uyūn al-Akhbār', in idem., *Studies in Early Ismailism*, Jerusalem and Leiden, 1983, pp. 96–45.
as-Subkī, Tāj ad-Dīn, *Muʿīd an-niʿam wa mubīd an-niqam*, ed. D. W. Myhrman, London, 1908.
——*Ṭabaqāt ash-Shāfiʿiyya al-kubrā*, ed. ʿA. Ḥilū and M. aṭ-Ṭanāḥī, 6 vols, Cairo, 1964 ff.

as-Suhrawardī, Abū Ḥafṣ 'Umar al-Baghdādī, *Taḥrīr al-aḥkām fī tadbīr ahl al-Islām*, MS Istanbul, Agia Sophia - Sultan Mahmoud, No. 2852.
as-Ṣūlī, *Akhbār ar-Rāḍī Billāh wa'l-Muttaqī Lillāh*, ed. J. Heyworth-Dunne, London, 1935.
as-Suyūṭī, *ad-Durr al-manthūr fi't-tafsīr bi'l-ma'thūr,* 6 vols, Cairo, 990.
—— *Tafsīr al-Jalālayn* (with al-Maḥallī) – numerous editions.
—— *Tārīkh al-khulafā'*, Beirut, n.d.
at-Taftāzānī, *Sharḥ al-maqāṣid,* ed. 'A. 'Umaira, 5 vols, Beirut, 1989.
Tansar — see: Boyce.
aṭ-Ṭarsūsī, *Tuḥfat at-Turk fī mā yajib an yu'mal fi'l-mulk*, ed. R. as-Sayyid, Beirut, 1992.
at-Tawḥīdī, Abū Ḥayyān, *al-Baṣā'ir wa'dh-dhakhā'ir*, ed. W. al-Qāḍī, 9 vols, Beirut, 1988.
——*Kitāb al-Imtā' wa'l-mu'ānasa*, ed. A. Amīn and A. az-Zayn, 3 vols, Cairo, 1953.
—— see also: Miskawayh.
ath-Tha'ālibī, *Laṭā'if al-luṭf*, ed. 'U. al-As'ad, Beirut, 1980.
—— *Tuḥfat al-wuzarā'*, ed. H. 'A. ar-Rāwī and I. M. as-Ṣaffār, Baghdad, 1977.
aṭ-Ṭurṭūshī, *Sirāj al-mulūk*, ed. J. al-Bayyātī, London, 1990.
Ṭūsī, Naṣīr ad-Dīn, *The Nasirean Ethics*, translated from Persian by G. M. Wickens, London, 1964.
al-Uṣūl al-Yūnāniyya li'l-naẓariyyāt as-siyāsiyya fi'l-Islām, ed. 'A. Badawī, Cairo, 1954.
Yaḥyā b. 'Adī, *Kitāb Tahdhīb al-akhlāq*, ed. M.-T. Urvoy as *Traité d'éthique d'Abū Zakariyyā' Yaḥyā Ibn 'Adī*, Paris, 1991.
al-Ya'qūbī, *Mushākalat an-nās li-zamānihim,* ed. W. Milward, Beirut, 1980.
—— *Tārīkh,* 2 vols, Beirut, 1960.
az-Zamakhsharī, *al-Kashshāf 'an ḥaqā'iq at-tanzīl*, ed. W. Nassau Lees et al., Calcutta, 1856.

Modern Works

Abbās, I. *'Abd al-Ḥamīd b.Yaḥyā al-Kātib*, Amman 1988.
—— *Malāmiḥ Yūnāniyya fi'l-adab al-'arabī*, Beirut 1977.
—— *Tārīkh an-naqd al-adabī 'ind al-'Arab* Beirut 1971.
Abd ar-Rāziq, 'A. *al-Islām wa uṣūl al-ḥukm*, Cairo 1925.
Abel, A. 'Le Khalife. Présence sacrée', *Studia Islamica*, 7 (1957), 29–45.
Affifi, A. E. *The Mystical Philosophy of Muhyid Din-Ibnul Arabi* (1939), Lahore, 1964.
Ahrweiler, Hélène. *L'idéologie politique de l'empire byzantin*, Paris, 1975.
al-'Allām, I. 'Mafhūm al-ḥāshiya fi'l-adab as siyāsī as-sulṭānī', *Abḥāth*, 4/13 (1986), 97–118.
al-'Aẓma, ,'A. *al-'Arab wa'l-barābira*, London 1991.
—— *al-'Ilmāniyya min manẓūr mukhtalif*, Beirut 1993.

—— *al-Kitāba at-tārikhiyya wa'l-ma'rifa at-tārīkhiyya. Muqaddima fī uṣūl ṣinā'at at-tārikh fi'th-thaqāfa al-'arabiyya*, Beirut 1983.
—— 'as-Siyāsa wa'l-lāsiyāsa fi'l-fikr al-'arabī', in: idem., *at-Turāth bayn as-sulṭān wa't-tārīkh*, Beirut and Casablanca 1987, 41–50.
al-Azmeh, Aziz. *Ibn Khaldūn in Modern Scholarship*, London, 1981.
——*Ibn Khaldūn: An Essay in Reinterpretation*, London 1982.
——*Arabic Thought and Islamic Societies*, London 1986.
—— 'Muslim Legal Theory and the Appropriation of Reality' in: al Azmeh (ed.) *Islamic Law: Social and Historical Contexts*, London, 1988, pp. 250–65.
—— 'Orthodoxy and Hanbalite Fideism' in: *Arabica*, 35 (1988), pp. 253–66.
—— 'Utopia and Islamic Political Thought' in: idem., *Islams and Modernities*, London 1992.
—— 'Mortal Enemies, Invisible Neighbours', in: *The Legacy of Muslim Spain*, ed. S. K. Jayyusi, Leiden, 1992, pp. 259–272.
—— 'Chronophagous Discourse: A Study in the Clerico-Legal Appropriation of the World in a Muslim Tradition', in: *Religion and Practical Reason*, ed. F. Reynolds and D. Tracy, Albany, 1994, pp. 163–212.
—— 'Rhetoric for the Senses: A Consideration of Muslim Paradise Narratives', in *Journal of Arabic Literature*, XXVI(1995), pp. 215–31.
—— 'The Muslim Canon: Typology, Utility and History' in *Canonization and Decanonization* , supplement to *Numen*, 1998.
al-Bāshā, H. *al-Alqāb al-islāmiyya fi't-tārīkh wa'l-wathā'iq wa'l-āthār*, Cairo 1957.
al-Bashir, S. *Muqaddima fi't-tārīkh al-ākhar. Fī naqd ar-riwāya al-islāmiyya*, Jerusalem 1984.
as-Sammān, M. H. *Khiṭāb al-junūn fi'th-thaqāfa al-'arabiyya* , London 1993.
as-Sayyid, R. 'al-Khilāf al-fiqhī bayna tamāyuzāt al-manāhij wa'l-fikr as-siyāsī min khilāl 'Tuḥfat at-Turk' li'l-Ṭarsūsī', *Dirāsāt Arabiyya* 29/5–6 (1993), 41–55.
ash-Shībī, M. K. *al-Ṣila bayn at-taṣawwuf wa't-Tashayyu'*, Cairo 1969.
Alexander, Paul J. *The Byzantine Apocalyptic Tradition.* Berkeley & Los Angeles 1975.
Allen, Terry. 'The Arabesque, the Beveled Style, and the Mirage of an Early Islamic Art', in: Clover, F. M. and Humphreys, R. S. (eds), *Tradition and Innovation in Late Antiquity*, Madison, 1989, 209–44.
'Arif, M. 'A. *Fī maṣādir at-turāth as-siyāsī al-islāmī*, Washington, 1994.
Arjomand, Said Amir. *The Shadow of God and the Hidden Imam: Religion, Political Order, and Societal Change in Shi'ite Iran from the Beginning to 1890*, Chicago, 1984.
Arnold, Sir Thomas W. *The Caliphate*, (1924) London, 1965.
Asín Palacios, M. *The Mystical Philosophy of Ibn Masarra & His Followers*, (tr. E. H. Douglas & H. W. Yoder), Leiden 1978.
Auboyer, J. 'Symbols of Sovereignty in India according to Iconography',

Indian Arts and Letters 12 (1938).
Auerbach, E. 'Figura', in: idem. *Scenes from the Drama of European Literature*, Manchester, 1984, 11–76.
Aung-Thwin, Michael. *Pagan: The Origins of Modern Burma*, Honolulu, 1985.
Ayalon, D. 'Studies in the Transfer of the Abbasid Caliphate from Baghdad to Cairo', *Arabica* VII (1960), 41–59.
Baines, H. N. *Byzantine Studies and Other Essays*, London 1955.
Bardwell-Smith, L. (ed.). *The Two Wheels of Dhamma*, Chambersburg 1972.
Bartold, V. V. *Turkistān min al-fatḥ al-ʿarabī ilā al-ghazū al-maghūlī*, tr. S. ʿU. Hāshim, Kuwait, 1981.
Becker, Carl, *Islamstudien*, 2 vols, Leipzig, 1924.
Belting, Hans. *Likeness and Presence: A History of the Image before the Era of Art*, (tr. Edmund Jephcott). Chicago, 1994.
Bin ʿAbd al-ʿĀlī, ʿA. *al-Falsafa as-siyāsiyya ʿind al-Fārābī*, Beirut, 1979.
Blachère et al. *Dictionnaire Arabe-Français-Anglais*, Paris, 1970.
Bloch, Marc. *Les rois thaumaturgues*, Intro. J. Le Goff, Paris 1983.
Bosworth, C. E. 'The Titulature of the early Ghaznavids,' *Oriens*, XV (1962), 210–33.
Boureau, Alain and Ingerflom, Caudio-Sergio (eds), *La royauté sacrée dans le monde chrétien*, Paris, 1992.
Boureau, Alain, ' Un obstacle a la sacralité royale en Occident. Le principe hiérarchique', in *La royauté sacrée dans le monde chrétien*, ed. Boureau amd Ingerflom, pp. 29–37.
Bréhier, Louis. 'Hiereus Kai Basileus', in: *Mémorial Louis Petit: Mélanges d'histoire et d'archéologie Byzantines*, (*Archives de l'orient chretien*. 1), Bucharest, 1948, 41–5.
Bremond, Claude, Le Goff, Jacques, and Schmitt, Jean-Claude, *L'«Exemplum»*, Turnhout (Belgium), 1982 (*Typologie des Sources de Moyen Age Occidental*, Fasc. 40).
Brett, C. 'The Priest-Emperor Concept in Japanese Political Thought', *Indian Journal of Pol. Science*, 23 (1962), 17–28.
Brockelmann, C. *Geschichte der arabischen Literatur*, 2 vols, Weimar 1898ff.; *Supplementbände*, 3 vols, Leiden 1937ff.
Burghart, Richard. 'Gifts to the Gods: Power, Property and Ceremonial in Nepal', in: Cannadine & Price (1988), 237–70.
Burns, J. M. (ed.), *The Cambridge History of Medieval Political Thought*, Cambridge 1988.
Busse, Heribert. *Chalif und Grosskönig: Die Buyiden in Iraq (945–1055)*, (Beiruter Beiträge, Texte u. Studien, Bd. 6), Wiesbaden, 1969.
Cahen, C. 'Notes sur les débuts de la futuwwa d'Al-Nāsir', *Oriens* 6 (1953), 18–23.
Calder, N. 'Friday Prayer and the Juristic Theory of Government: Sarakhsī, Shīrāzī, Māwardī', in *Bulletin of the School of Oriental and African Studies*, XLIX/1(1986), pp. 35–47.
Cameron, Averil. 'Eusebius of Caesarea and the Rethinking of History',

in: E. Gabba (ed.), *Tria Corda. Scritti in onore di Arnaldo Momigliano*, (*Biblioteca di Athenaeum*, I), Como (1983), 71–88.

Cameron, Averil. 'The Construction of Court Ritual: The Byzantine *Book of Ceremonies*' in Cannadine & Price (1987), 106–36.

Canard, M. 'Le cérémonial fatimide et le cérémonial byzantin. Essai de comparaison', *Byzantion*, 21 (1951), 355–420.

Cannadine, David and Price, Simon (eds), *Rituals of Royalty. Power and Ceremony in Traditional Societies*, Cambridge, 1987.

Christensen, Arthur, *Les gestes des rois dans les traditions de l'Iran antique*, Paris, 1936.

Chwolsohn, D. *Die Ssabier und der Ssabismus*, St. Petersburg, Kaiserliche Akademie der Wissenschaften, 1856, 2 vols.

Coedès, G. 'Le culte de la royauté divinisée, source d'inspiration des grands monuments du Cambodge ancien', in: *Istituto Italiano per il Medio ad Estremo Oriente: Conferenze-Serie Orientale*, No. 5 (1952), 1–23 (Rome).

Coedès, G. *The Indianized States of Southeast Asia*, ed. Walter, F. Vella (tr. Susan Brown Cowing), Honolulu, 1968.

Cohn, Norman, *Cosmos, Chaos and the World to Come. The Ancient Roots of Apolcalyptic Faith*, New Haven, 1994.

Creswell, K. A. C. *A Short Account of Early Muslim Architecture* (1958), revised & supplemented by James W. Allan, Cairo, 1989.

Croissant, Jeanne. 'Un nouveau Discours de Thémistius', *Serta Leondiensa* (Bibliothèque de la Faculté de Philosophie et des Lettres, Université de Liège, XLIV, 1930), 7–30.

Crone, Patricia & Hinds, Martin, *God's Caliph. Religious Authority in the First Centuries of Islam*, Cambridge, 1986.

Crone, P., 'Did al-Ghazāli write a Mirror for Princes? On the Authorship of Naṣīḥar al-Mulūk', in *Jerusalem Studies in Arabic and Islam*, 10(1987), pp. 167–191.

Curtius, E. R. *European Literature and the Latin Middle Ages*, tr. W. R. Trask, London, 1953.

Daftary, Farhad, *The Ismāʿīlīs. Their History and Doctrines*, Cambridge, 1990.

Dagron, Gilbert, *La romanité chrétienne en Orient*, London, 1984.

Daiber, Hans, 'The Ismāʿīlī Background of Fārābī's Political Philosophy. Abū Ḥātim ar-Rāzī as a Forerunner of Fārābī', in *Gottes ist Orient, Gottes ist Okzident. Festschrift für Abdoljavad Falaturi*, ed. Udo Tworuschka, Köln and Wien, 1991, pp. 143–50.

Dawood, Abdel Hakim Hasan Osman Mohammed, 'A Comparative Study of Arabic and Persian Mirrors of Princes from the Second to the Sixth Century AH', Unpub. PhD Thesis, University of London, 1965.

Dietrich-Heidelberg, Albert, 'Das politische Testament des zweiten ʿAbbasidenkalifen al-Manṣūr', *Der Islam* XXX (1952), 133–65.

Djaït, Hichem, *al-Kūfa. Naissance de la ville islamique*, Paris, 1986.

Dodds, Jerrilynn. *Architecture and Ideology in Early Medieval Spain*, University Park & London, The Pennsylvania State University Press, 1990.

Dumézil, G. *L'Héritage Indo-Européen à Rome*, Paris, 1949.
Dvornik, Francis. *Early Christian and Byzantine Political Philosophy. Origins and Background*, 2 vols Washington DC., 1966.
Encyclopedia of Islam, new edition ed. C. E. Bosworth et al., Leiden 1960ff.
Erdmann, Kurt. 'Die Entwicklung der Sāsānidischen Krone', *Ars Islamica* (1951), 87–93.
Ettinghausen, Richard, *From Byzantium to Sasanian Iran and the Islamic World: Three Modes of Artistic Influence*, Leiden, 1972, (The L. A. Mayer Memorial Studies in Islamic Art and Archaeology, III).
Fakhry, Majid, *A History of Islamic Philosophy*, New York, 1970.
Fawzī, I. *Tadwīn as-sunna*, London 1994.
Festugière, A.-J. 'Les inscriptions d'Ašoka et l'idéal du roi hellénistique', *Mélanges Jules Lebreton (Recherches de Science Religieuse)* XXXIX / 2–4 (1951), 31–46.
Flood, F. Barry, 'The Iconography of Light in the Monument of Mamluk Cairo', in: Emily Lyle (ed.), *Sacred Architecture in the Traditions of China, India, Judaism and Islam*, Edinburgh, 1992, *(Cosmos,* vol.8), 169–94.
Fowden, Garth, *Empire to Commonwealth. Consequences of Monotheism in Late Antiquity*, Princeton, 1993.
Fox, Robin Lane, *Alexander the Great*, Harmondsworth, 1986.
Frankfort, Henri, *Kingship and the Gods. A Study of Ancient Near Eastern Religion as the Integration of Society and Nature,* Chicago, 1948.
Frazer, James G. *The Golden Bough*, 2nd ed., London, 1898, vol. 1.
Fujairāt, A. 'Jadhīma al-Abrash al-Azdī fi'l-maṣādir al-'arabiyya', *Dirāsāt Tārīkhīya*, 47–8 (1993), 23–36.
Galston, Miriam, 'Realism & Idealism in Avicenna's Political Philosophy', *Rev. of Politics* 41 (1979), 561–77.
—— *Politics and Excellence: The Political Philosophy of Alfarabi*, Princeton, 1990.
Gardet, L. *La cité musulmane*, Paris, 1967.
Geertz, Clifford, *Negara: The Theatre State in Nineteenth-Century Bali*, Princeton, 1980.
Ghazoul, Ferial, 'Poetic Logic in the *Panchatantra* and the *Arabian Nights*', *Arab Studies Quarterly* 5 (1983), 13–21.
Gibb, H. A. R. 'al-Māwardī's Theory of the Khilafah', in: *Islamic Culture*, XI (1937), 291–302, reproduced in idem., *Studies in the Civilization of Islam*, Boston 1962, 151–65.
Gokhale, B. G. 'Dhammikō Dhammarājā. A Study in Bhuddist Constitutional Concepts', in: *Indica. The Indian Historical Research Institute Silver Jubilee Commemoration Volume*, Bombay: St Xavier's College, 1953, 161–5.
—— 'The Early Bhuddist View of the State', *Journal of the American Oriental Society* 89 (1969), 731–8.
Gombrich, Richard, *Theravada Bhuddism. A Social History from Ancient Benares to Modern Colombo*, London, 1988.
Goodenough, Erwin R. 'The Political Philosophy of Hellenistic Kingship',

Yale Classical Studies 1 (1928), 55–102.

Grabar, André, *L'Empereur dans l'art byzantin*, Paris, 1936 (Publications de la Faculté des Lettres de l'Université de Strasbourg, Fsc. 75), [London: Variorum Reprints, 1971].

Grabar, Oleg, 'Note sur les Cérémonies Umayyades', in: Myriam Rosen-Ayalon, *Studies in Memory of Gaston Wiet*, Jerusalem, 1979, pp. 51–60.

—— 'The Painting of the Six Kings at Qusayr 'Amrah', *Ars Orientalis* , 1 (1954) 185–7.

Grierson, Philip, 'The Monetary Reforms of 'Abd al-Malik', *Journal of the Economic & Social History of the Orient* 3 (1960) 241–64.

Gutas, D. *Avicenna and the Aristotelian Tradition*, Leiden, 1988.

Halm, Heinz, *Das Reich des Mahdī: Der Aufstieg der Fatimiden (875–973)*, München, 1991.

—— *Kosmologie und Heileslehre der frühen Ismāʿīliyya . Eine Studie zur islamischen Gnosis*, Wiesbaden, 1978, (Abhandlungen für die Kunde des Morgenlandes, Bd. XLIV,I).

—— *Shiism*, (Islamic Surveys, 18), Edinburgh, 1991.

Hartmann, A. *an-Nāṣir li-Dīn Allāh (1180–1225): Politik, Religion, und Kultur der späten Abbasidenzeit*, (Studien zur Sprache, Geschichte und Kultur des islamischen Orients, N. F. 8), Berlin & New York, 1975.

Hartmann, Richard, 'Eine islamische Apokalypse aus der Kreuzzugszeit', *Schriften der Königsberger Gelehrten Gesellschaft, Geisteswissenschaftliche Klasse*, 3 (1924), 89–116.

Heath, P., *Allegory and Philosophy in Avicenna*, Philadelphia, 1992.

Heidemann, S. *Das Aleppiner Kalifat (AD 1261). Von Ende des Kalifats in Bagdad über Aleppo zu den Restaurationen in Cairo*, Leiden, 1994.

Heine-Geldern, Robert, 'Conceptions of State and Kingship in Southeast Asia', *Far Eastern Quarterly* 1,1 (1942), 15–30.

Hellholm, David (ed.), *Apocalypticism in the Mediterranean World and in the Near East*, Tübingen, 1983.

Herzfeld, Ernst E. *Iran in the Ancient Near East*, London & New York, 1941.

Hillenbrand, Robert, 'The Symbolism of the Rayed Nimbus in Early Islamic Art', in: Emily Lyle (ed.) *Kingship*, (Cosmos 2), Edinburgh: Traditional Cosmology Society, 1986, 1–52.

Hussain, Jassim M. *The Occultation of the Twelfth Imam: A Historical Background*, London, 1982.

Jadʿān, F. *al-Miḥna. Baḥth fī jadaliyyat ad-dīnī wa's-siyāsī fi'l-Islām*, Amman 1989.

Johns, J. 'The Norman Kings of Sicily and the Fatimid Caliphate', In: *Anglo-Norman Studies, XV. Proceedings of the 1992 Battle Conference on Anglo–Norman Studies*, Palermo 1992.

Jacob, Robert, *Images de la justice. Essai sur l'iconographie judiciaire du Moyen Age à l'age classique*, Paris, 1994.

Jolivet, Jean, 'L'idée de la sagesse et sa fonction dans la philosophie des 4e et 5e siècles', *Arab Sciences and Philosophy*, 1/1 (1991), 31–65.

Kangle, R. P. *The Kauṭilīya Arthaśāstra, Part II: A Study*, Delhi, 1992.
Kantorowicz, E. H. *The King's Two Bodies: A Study in Medieval Political Theology*, Princeton 1957.
Kelly, I. N. D. *Early Christian Doctrines,* 5th ed., London, 1977.
Kohlberg, Etan. 'From Imāmiyya to Ithnā 'Āshariyya', *BSOAS* 39 (1976), 521–34.
Kuhrt, Amélie, 'Usurpation Conquest and Ceremonial: From Babylon to Persia', in: Cannadine & Price (1987), 20–55.
L'Orange, H. P. *Studies in the Iconography of Cosmic Kingship in the Ancient World*, Oslo, 1953.
Lambton, A. K. S. *State and Government in Medieval Islam: An Introduction to the Study of Islamic Political Theory: The Jurists.* Oxford, 1981.
Laoust, Henri, *Essai sur les doctrines morales et politiques de Takī-d-Dīn Aḥmad B. Taimīya,* Cairo, 1939.
—— 'La pensée et l'action politiques d'al-Māwardī (364/450–974/1058)', in idem. *Pluralismes dans l'Islam.* Paris, Geuthner, 1983, pp. 177–258 (*REI*, XXXVI/I (1968), 11–92).
—— *La politique de Ǧazālī*, Paris, 1970.
Laroui, A. *Islam et modernité.* Paris, 1987.
Lassner, Jacob, *The Topography of Baghdad in the Early Middle Ages.* Detroit, 1970.
Le Goff, Jacques, ' Aspects religieux et sacrés de la monarchie française du xe au xiiie siècle', in Boureau and Ingerflom, *La royauté sacrée dans le monde chrétien*, pp. 19–28.
Lewis, Bernard, *The Political Language of Islam*, London & Chicago, 1988.
Lewy, H. *Chaldean Oracles and Theurgy: Mysticism, Magic, and Platonism in the Late Roman Empire*, (ed. M. Tardieu) Paris, 1978.
Little, Donald P. 'A New Look to the *al-Aḥkām al-Sulṭāniyya*', *The Muslim World*, 64 (1974), 1–18.
Lombard, M. *The Golden Age of Islam*, (tr. I. Spencer), Amsterdam, Oxford, New York, 1975.
Loth, Otto, 'al-Kindī als Astrolog', in: *Morgenländische Forschungen. Festschrift Heinrich L. Fleischer,* Leipzig 1875 [repr. Amsterdam, APA Philo Press, 1981], 263–309 [Arabic text: 273–9].
Lotman, Y. M., and Uspenskij, B. A. 'Echoes of the Notion of 'Moscow as the Third Rome' in Peter the Great's Ideology', in: *Semiotics of Russian Culture,* ed. Ann Shukmann, Ann Arbor, 1984, 53–67.
Madelung, Wilferd. 'Authority in Twelver Shiism in the Absence of the Imam', in: *La notion d'autorité au Moyen-âge*, 163–73.
—— 'New Documents concerning al-Ma'mūn, al-Faḍl b. Sahl and 'Alī ar-Riḍā', in: *Studia Arabica et Islamica. Festschrift for Iḥsan 'Abbas*, ed. Wadād al-Qāḍī, Beirut, 1981, 333–46.
—— 'The Assumption of the Title of Shahānshāh by the Buyids and 'The Reign of the Daylam (Dawlat al-Daylam)', *Journal of Near Eastern Studies* XXVIII (1969), 84–108, 168–83.

Makdisi, G. 'Aš'arī and the Aš'arītes in Islamic Religious History, ' *Studia Islamica* XVII (1962) 37–8, XVIII (1963) 19–39.

——*Ibn 'Aqīl et la résurgence de l'Islam traditionaliste au XIe siècle,* Damascus, 1963.

——— *The Rise of the Colleges*, Edinburgh, 1981.

Mamour, P. H. *Polemics on the Origin of the Fatimid Caliphs*, London 1934.

Mann, M. *The Sources of Social Power*, Cambridge 1986.

Manzalaoui, Mahmoud, 'The Pseudo-Aristotelian *Kitāb Sirr al-Asrār*. Facts and Problems', in *Oriens*, 1974, pp. 147–257.

Mār Ighnāṭiyūs Ifrām Barṣūm, 'al-Alfāẓ as-suryāniyya fi'l-ma'ājim al-'arabiyya', in *Majallat al-Majma' al-'Ilmī al-'Arabī* (Damascus) 23 (1948), 161–81, 321–46, 481–506; 24 (1949), 3–21, 161–81, 321–24, 481–99; 25 (1950), 2–22, 161–78, 364–98.

Marquet, Y. 'Les cycles de la souveraineté selon les épitres des Iḫwān al-Ṣafā', in *Studia Islamica* XXXVI (1972), 47–69.

Marmon, S. *Eunuchs and Sacred Boundaries in Islamic Society*, New York, 1995.

Mason, Herbert, *Two Statesmen of Medieval Islam: The Vizir Ibn Hubayra and Caliph an-Nāṣir l-Dīn Allāh* , Paris/The Hague, 1972.

Mayer, L. A. *Saracenic Heraldry: A Survey.* Oxford, 1933.

McCormick, Michael, 'Analyzing Imperial Ceremonies', *Jahrbuch der österreichischen Byzantinistik* 35 (1985), 1–20.

Meier, F. 'Die Welt der Urbilder bei Ali Hamadani (+ 1385)', *Eranos-Jahrbuch* 18 (1950), 115–72.

Menocal, Maria Rosa, *The Arabic Role in Medieval Literary History*, Philadelphia, 1987.

Mikhail, Hanna, *Politics and Revelation. Māwardī and After*, Edinburgh, 1995.

Millar, Fergus, *The Roman Near East, 31 BC–AD 337,* Cambridge, Mass., 1993.

Morony, Michael, *Iraq after the Muslim Conquest.* Princeton, 1984.

Nagel, T. *Staat und Glaubensgemeinschaft im Islam*, 2 vols, Zürich and München, 1981.

Nassar, N. 'Le maître d'Ibn Khaldūn: Al-Ābilī', *Studia Islamica* 70 (1964), 103–14.

Necipoğlu, Gürlu, *Architecture, Ceremonial, and Power: The Topkapi Palace in the Fifteenth and Sixteenth Centuries.* New York & Cambridge, Mass., 1991.

Nelson, Janet L. 'The Lord's Anointed and the People's Choice: Carolingian Royal Ritual'; in: Cannadine & Price (1987), 137–80.

—— 'Symbols in Context: Rulers' Inauguration Rituals in Byzantinum and the West in the Early Middle Ages.' *Studies in Church History*, 13, (1976), 97–119.

Nicol, Donald M. *The Immortal Emperor: The Life and Legend of Constantine Palaiologos, Last Emperor of the Romans.* Cambridge, 1994.

Noth, A. *Quellenkritische Studien zu Themen, Formen und Tendenzen frühislamischer Geschichtsüberlieferung.* (Bonner Orientalische Studien, 25), Bonn, 1973.

Nwyia, P. 'Note sur quelques fragments inédits et de la correspondance

d'Ibn al-ʿArīf avec Ibn Barrajān', in *Hespéris* 43 (1956).
Oizerman, T. I. & Bogomolov, A. S. *Principles of the Theory of the Historical Process in Philosophy.* Moscow, 1986.
Ostrogorsky, George, 'The Byzantine Emperor and the Hierarchical World Order.' *The Slavonic and East-European Review* 35 (1956–57), 1–14.
Pellat, Ch. 'Le culte de Muʿāwiya au IIIe siècle de l'Hégire.' *Studia Islamica* 6 (1956), 53–66.
Peterson, Erik, *Der Monotheismus als politisches Problem: Ein Beitrag zur Geschichte der politischen Theologie im Imperium Romanum.* Leipzig, 1935.
Price, S. R. F. *Rituals and Power: The Roman Imperial Cult in Asia Minor.* Cambridge, 1984.
Ray, N. R., *Maurya and Sungha Art*, Calcutta, 1945.
Reynolds, F. 'The Two Wheels of Dhamma: A Study of Early Buddhism' in: Bardwell-Smith (1972), 6–30.
Richter, G. *Studien zur Geschichte der älteren arabischen Fürstenspiegel.* Leipzig, 1932. (repr. Leipzig (1968), Leipziger Semitische Studien, N. F., Bd. III.).
Ringgren, Helmer, 'Some Religious Aspects of the Caliphate'. In: *Sacral Kingship* (1959), 737–48.
Rodinson, M. 'Histoire économique et histoire des classes sociales dans le monde musulman'. in: Cook (1970), 139–155.
—— *The Arabs.* London: Croom Helm, 1981.
Rosenthal, E. I. J. *Political Thougth in Medieval Islam.* Cambridge, 1958.
Rosenthal, F. *A History of Muslim Historiography.* 2nd ed. Leiden, 1968.
Runciman, S. *The Byzantine Theocracy.* Cambridge, 1977.
—— *The Fall of Constantinople, 1453.* [1965] Cambridge, 1990.
Rypka, J. et al. *History of Iranian Literature*, ed. K. Jahn, Dordrecht, 1968.
Sacral Kingship (Supplement to *Numen*, IV), Leiden, 1959.
Sadan, J. 'A propos de *Martaba*: Remarques sur l'étiquette dans le monde musulman mediéval' *Revue d'Etudes Islamiques* 41 (1973), 51–69.
Sanders, P. *The Court Ceremonial of the Fatimid Caliphate in Egypt.* Ph.D. dissertation, Princeton, 1984.
Sarkisyanz, E. *Buddhist Background of the Burmese Revolution*, The Hague, 1965.
Scholem, G. *Sabbatai Sevi, the Mystical Messiah 1626–1676*, London 1973 (The Littman Library of Jewish Civilization).
Schraeder, H. *Moskau, das dritte Rom. Studien zur Geschichte der politischen Theorien in der slavischen Welt*, (1929), Darmstadt, 1957.
Schramm, P. E. et al., *Herrschaftszeichen und Staatssymbolik*, 3 vols Stuttgart, 1954–56 (Schriften der Monumenta Germaniae Historica (Deutsches Institut für Erfassung des Mittelalters), 13/I, II, III).
Setton, K., *Christian Attitudes Towards the Emperor in the Fourth Century*, New York 1941.
Seznec, Jean, *The Survival of the Pagan Gods. The Mythological Tradition and its Place in Renaissance Humanism and Art*, tr. Barbara F. Sessions, Princeton, 1992 (*The Bollingen Series*, xxxviii).

Sharāra, W. 'al-Malik/al-'āmma, aṭ-ṭabī'a, al-mawt', *Dirāsāt Arabiyya* 16/12 (1980), 19–46.
—— 'al-Muqadimma, at-tārīkh, wa jasad as-sulṭān al-mumtali', in: idem. *Ḥawla ba'ḍ mushkilāt ad-dawla fi'l-fikr wa'l-mujtama' al-'arabīyyayn*, Beirut 1980, 11–60.
Shorto, H. L. 'The Mon Genealogy of Kings: Observations in *The Nidana Arambhakatha*', in: *Historians of South East Asia*, ed. D. G. E. Hall, London, 1967, 63–72.
Smith, Bardwell L. 'The Ideal Social Order as Portrayed in the Chronicles of Ceylon', in *Smith* (1972), 31–57.
—— (ed.). *The Two Wheels of Dhamma*, Chambersburg, American Academy of Religion, 1972. (AAR Studies in Religion, No. 3).
Sourdel, D., 'La politique religieuse du Calife 'abbaside al-Ma'mūn', *Revue d'Etudes Islamiques* 30 (1962), 27–48.
—— 'Questions de Cérémonial 'Abbaside', in: *Revue d'Etudes Islamiques*; 28 (1960), 121–48.
—— *Le vizirat 'Abbāsīde de 749 à 936*, 2 vols, Damascus, 1960.
Sourdel-Thomisne, J. 'L'expression symbolique de l'autorité dans l'art islamique, in: *La notion de l'autorité au Moyen-âge-Islam, Byzance, Occident*, Paris, 1982, 273–86.
Sperl, Stefan, 'Islamic Kingship and Arabic Panegyric Poetry in the Early 9th Century', in *Journal of Arabic Literature*, 8(1977), pp. 20–35.
Stargardt, Janice, 'Social and Religious Aspects of Royal Power in Medieval Burma (From the Inscriptions of Kyansittha's Reign, 1084–12)', in *Journal of Economic & Social History of the Orient* 13 (1970), 289–308.
Stern, Samuel M. 'al-Mahdī's reign according to the *'Uyūn al-akhbār*' in: idem., *Studies in Early Ismailism*, Jerusalem & Leiden, 1983, 96–145.
Tambiah, Stanley J. *World Conqueror and World Renouncer. A Study of Buddhism and Polity in Thailand against a Historical Backround,* Cambridge, 1976.
—— 'The Galactic Polity in Southeast Asia', in idem, *Culture, Thought, and Social Action.* Cambridge, Mass. 1985, pp. 252–86.
Tardieu, Michel, 'Théorie de la mémoire et fonction prophétique', in *La mémoire des religions*, ed. Philippe Borgaud, Geneva, 1988, pp. 105–14.
Toynbee, Arnold, *A Study of History*, vol. 1, 2nd ed., London, 1951.
Treitinger, Otto. *Die oströmische Kaiser- und Reichsidee nach ihre Gestaltung im höfischen Zeremoniell.* [Jena, 1938]; 2nd ed., Darmstadt, 1956.
Tyan, Emile. *Institutions du droit public musulman. Tome premier: Le Califat*, Paris, 1954.
Urvoy, D. 'La pensée d'Ibn Tūmart', *Bulletin d'Etudes Orientales* 27 (1974), 19–44.
—— *Ibn Rushd (Averroes)*, London, 1991.
Uspenskij, B. A. 'Tsar and Pretender: *Samozvacestvo* or Royal Imposture in Russia as a Cultural–Historical Phenomenon', in: *The Semiotics of Russian Culture,* ed. Ann Shukman, Ann Arbor, Michigan Slavic Contributions No. 11, 1984, 259–92.

Vernant, J.-P. *The Origins of Greek Thought*, London, 1982.

Von Moos, P. *Geschichte als Topik Darhetorische Exemplum von der Antique zur Neuzeit und die historiae im 'Policraticus' Johanns von Salisbury*, Hildsheim, Zürich, New York, 1996.

Walker, P. *Early Philosophical Shiism: Ismaili Neoplatonism of Abū Ya'qūb al-Sijistānī*, Cambridge 1993.

Watt, W. Montgomery, 'God's Caliph: Qur'anic Interpretations and Umayyad Claims', in: C. E. Bosworth (ed.), *Iran and Islam. In Memory the Late Vladimir Minorsky*, Edinburgh, 1971, 565–74.

Wechsler, Howard J. *Offerings of Jade and Silk: Ritual and Symbol in the Legitimation of the T'ang Dynasty*, New Haven, 1985.

Weinstock, Stefan, *Divus Julius*, Oxford, 1971.

Wendell, C. 'Baghdad: Imago Mundi, and other Foundation-Lone', *International Journal of Middle East Studies* 2 (1971) 99–128.

Widengren, G. *The Ascension of the Apostle and the Heavenly Book*, Uppsala & Wiesbaden, 1950.

Wolfson, H. A. *Philo. Foundations of Religious Philosophy in Judaism, Christianity and Islam*. 2 vols 4th rev. printing. Cambridge, Mass. 1968.

Zaehner, R. C. *The Dawn and Twilight of Zoroastrianism*, London 1961.

Ziai, Hossein, 'The Source and Nature of Authority: A Study of al-Suhrawardī's Illuminationist Political Doctrine', in *The Political Aspects of Islamic Philosophy*, ed. Charles E. Butterworth, Cambridge, Mass., 1992, pp. 304–44.

Ziegler, A. W. 'Die byzantinische Religionspolitik und der sogenannte Cäsaropapismus', in: *Festgabe für Paul Diels*, ed. E. Koschmieder, München 1953.

Index